Mandarin Primer

An Intensive Course in SPOKEN CHINESE

Yuen Ren Chao

Published By
HARVARD UNIVERSITY PRESS · CAMBRIDGE
LONDON: OXFORD UNIVERSITY PRESS
1967

Copyright, 1948
by the President and Fellows of Harvard College

Fifth Printing

Printed in the United States of America

Mandarin
Primer

Preface

THIS IS an intensive course in the sense that it is designed for learning Chinese the hard and fast way — hard because the first few lessons call for very hard, concentrated work and fast because, if hard enough work is done at the start, the student will be able, at the end of one year on a double-course basis, to feel fully at ease in the use of spoken Chinese.

The contents of this book originated from a twelve-week intensive course in Cantonese given at Harvard University in the summer of 1942, which has since been published under the title of *Cantonese Primer* (1947). The text of the lessons was translated into Mandarin and used in the Army Specialized Training Program at the Harvard School for Overseas Administration in 1943–44 and subsequently in civilian courses. The present course differs from that of the *Cantonese Primer* in the following respects. The chapter on pronunciation has had to be rewritten, of course. The chapter on grammar has been reorganized and greatly expanded. Lessons 19–21 on "Renting a House," "The Walrus and the Carpenter," and "Listening and Listening In" are entirely new. On the suggestion of readers of the Cantonese book, citations in the introductory chapters have been included in the Index and in the *Character Text*.

The book may be used as a textbook for the classroom or for self-teaching with the help of a Mandarin-speaking guide or informant or of phonograph records. For the few unusual minds which can learn how to differentiate and integrate by reading the article on the calculus in an encyclopedia, it may be possible to learn to pronounce Chinese from the description of it in the chapter on pronunciation. But even the conversational lessons should be heard as spoken, with proper expression, by a Chinese. For one of the features of spoken Chinese to which this course is specially devoted is the use of various stylistic elements of the language, such as interjections of agreement and dissent, sentence intonation, and other lubricants of conversational give and take, and these things should better be learned by ear than from description.

The companion volume, *Character Text*, can be used as the text for the Chinese teacher to read from, and as a text for learning the characters. The answers to the exercises appear in cursive writing and are meant to be legible only to the teacher. However, any American student able to read Chinese cursive writing should be entitled to make use of the answers.

The author wishes to thank The Commercial Press, Ltd. of Shanghai for permission to use the Chinese version of Lesson 20 from his *Tzoou Daw Jinqtzlii* and the stories contained in Lesson 4, 6, 7, and 12 from his *Phonograph Course in the National Language* (1928). He is also indebted to Macmillan and Company of London for the use of material from *Through the Looking-Glass and What Alice Found There*, by Lewis Carroll. He is particularly grateful to Professor Serge Elisséeff for permission to use the major part of the *Cantonese Primer* as a basis for the present course.

The author's indebtedness to Leonard Bloomfield on grammatical theory is obvious and it will not be possible to make acknowledgments on all specific points. He is also indebted to Fang Kuei Li for delaying the completion of the book far beyond the deadline by suggesting the rewriting of the chapter on grammar.

Thanks are also due to all who have helped in seeing through the preparation of the book: to Anlin Wang Ku and the author's daughters Lensey and Bella for the preparation and checking of the manuscript, to his daughter Rulan for doing the exercises, and to Kao Liang Chow who wrote the whole *Character Text*. The author alone, however, should be responsible for such errors and inconsistencies as a book of this kind is likely to have and would welcome with appreciation corrections and criticisms from the reader.

YUEN REN CHAO

Cambridge, Massachusetts
March 31, 1947

For recordings to accompany the lessons,
see Folkways Records, Album FP 8002.

Contents

PART ONE: INTRODUCTION

I.	THE CHINESE LANGUAGE	3
II.	PRONUNCIATION AND ROMANIZATION	19
III.	GRAMMAR	33

A. Words, 33. B. Sentences, 34. C. Syntax, 37. D. Morphology, 39. E. Compounds, 41. F. Parts of speech, etc., 45. G. Translation of English Grammatical Categories, 50.

IV.	THE CHARACTERS	60
V.	METHOD OF STUDY	72

PART TWO: FOUNDATION WORK

A.	THE TONES	85
B.	DIFFICULT SOUNDS	92
C.	THE SYSTEM OF SOUNDS	97
D.	SYSTEM OF TONE SANDHI	107

PART THREE: THE LESSONS

1.	YOU, I, AND HE 'FOUR MEN'	120
2.	THINGS	126
3.	SPEAKING CHINESE	134
4.	TELEPHONING	140
5.	UP, DOWN, LEFT, RIGHT, FRONT, BACK, AND MIDDLE	148
6.	A SMOKE RING	158
7.	MR. CAN'T STOP TALKING	164
8.	ANTONYMS	172
9.	A GOOD MAN	180
10.	THE TAILLESS RAT	188
11.	WATCHING THE YEAR OUT	194
12.	A RESCUE AT SEA	204
13.	INQUIRING AFTER A SICK MAN	210
14.	CONVERSATION WITH THE DOCTOR	216
15.	WORLD GEOGRAPHY	224
16.	CHINESE GEOGRAPHY	230
17.	TALKING ABOUT INDUSCO	236
18.	TO THE MINSHENG WORKS	242

CONTENTS

19. RENTING A HOUSE	250
20. THE WALRUS AND THE CARPENTER	256
21. LISTENING AND LISTENING IN	266
22. STUDYING	272
23. THE VERNACULAR LITERATURE MOVEMENT	282
24. AN AMERICAN MAKES A SPEECH	290
APPENDIX: SUPPLEMENT TO LESSON 20	298
VOCABULARY AND INDEX	301
ABBREVIATIONS AND SYMBOLS	336
SYNOPSIS OF TONAL SPELLING	336

Mandarin
Primer

PART ONE: INTRODUCTION

CHAPTER I THE CHINESE LANGUAGE

1. Old and New Chinese. — Chinese is usually regarded as one of the oldest languages of the world. Chinese students entering American colleges are often allowed to offer Chinese for entrance Latin or Greek rather than for French or German. Now, the Chinese as spoken today by a radio announcer from Station XGOA, Nanking, must be as new and as unlike the Chinese of Confucius, as, say, the English heard over an American radio is new and unlike the English of Chaucer. On the other hand, whether in Europe or in China, people must have talked for thousands of years before any of their talk began to be recorded. Thus, all languages, so far as we can tell, are equally old in their origin and equally new in their present form.

How is it then that Chinese has a reputation for antiquity? There are several reasons for this. One is that the Chinese literary idiom, which is widely used for all purposes though in modern pronunciation, is largely based on the language of the ancient classics. More students in a Chinese college know their Mencius (4th century B.C.), whose style seems to them quite modern, than students in an American college know Chaucer (14th century A.D.).

Another reason is the relative social and cultural homogeneity and stability in China during more millenniums than has been the case with most other peoples of the world. Of upheavals China had plenty. But even the conquering Mongols and Manchus made no impression on the language. There was no large-scale borrowing of words such as followed the Norman invasion of Britain.

Finally, the Chinese language seems old because, instead of spreading by subdivision into various national languages, which would then seem new, as do the Romance languages descended from Latin, it spread by diffusion into culturally less advanced neighbors in the form of borrowed words and borrowed characters. These borrowed words and characters are still used in the forms known as Sino-Japanese, Sino-Korean, and Sino-Annamese and stand as testimonies to the antiquity of the Chinese language, a language which gave more than it took and maintained its identity and comparative homogeneity within the four seas. The practice of giving entrance credit for Chinese as an ancient language is therefore no mere matter of courtesy.

2. Our Knowledge of Old Chinese. — The ancient Chinese language is known to every literate Chinese, but only in the sense that the text in characters and the idiom of the composition are understood. When read aloud, it is always in the pronunciation of a modern dialect. Few Chinese scholars know what the ancient language actually sounded like. Not that the Chinese have been unconcerned with the sounds of language. The Chinese have throughout the ages been keen students of the sounds of language. But because of the relatively non-phonetic nature of the characters, they have had to deal chiefly in the abstract classification and relationship of sounds rather than with the phonetic values of the sounds themselves. Their conception of the language is accurate, but not concrete. Much of the work of Chinese scholars had to wait for Western linguists like Bernhard Karlgren or Western-trained Chinese linguists like Li Fang-kuei before it could be interpreted in phonetic terms. To use Karlgren's own figure, traditional Chinese phonology may be compared with a book of algebra. It contains great truths, but one must substitute numerical values into the formulas before the truths can be applied.

The numerical values are the modern dialects of China. By studying the sounds of modern dialects (including the present pronunciation in Japan, Korea, and Indo-China of anciently borrowed words) and comparing them with the systematizations of traditional Chinese phonology, Karlgren has made a reconstruction in all detail (except the actual melodic values of the tones) of the ancient Chinese pronunciation of about 600 A.D., which, after some revisions, has gained wide acceptance among most Occidental and the majority of Chinese scholars. This he has named Ancient Chinese. Making use of the studies by Chinese philologists in a different direction — the structure of characters and the riming patterns in *Shih Ching* — he reconstructed the pronunciation of the period roughly one millennium earlier than that of Ancient Chinese, which he calls Archaic Chinese.[1] Though he is less sure of the details of this reconstruction and has won less wide acceptance for it, there is nevertheless general agreement as to its main features.

3. Archaic and Ancient Chinese. — Broadly speaking, Archaic Chinese had a very rich system of consonants and vowels, and probably only three tones. It had four grades of initial consonants, as in t, t', d, d', i.e. voiceless unaspirated, voiceless aspirated, voiced unaspirated, and voiced aspirated.[2] It had the final consonants $-m, -n, -ng, -p, -t, -k, -b, -d, -g, -r$, but no final

---

[1] Both Ancient and Archaic Chinese are summarized in Karlgren's 471-page "article," Grammata Serica, *Bulletin of the Museum of Far Eastern Antiquities*, No. 12, Stockholm, 1940. A more popular exposition of this and related topics is found in his *Philology and Ancient China*, Oslo, 1926.

[2] In Mandarin, Cantonese, and most other modern dialects, there are only two grades of initials, e.g., (unaspirated) t and (aspirated) t', which we write as d and t in the present course. There is no real [d]-sound in Mandarin. See pp. 21, 92.

semi-vowel; in other words, it had no descending diphthong of the *au, ei* type. There were some initial consonant-clusters like *gl-, kl-, bl-, pl-*, but these were relatively infrequent.

From Archaic to Ancient Chinese, the most important change was that the pure voiced initials and endings *b, d, g* had become semi-vowels, e.g., Archaic *diog* > Ancient *iäu* (> Mandarin *yau* 'shake'). There were four tones in Ancient Chinese, Even, Rising, Going, and Entering, the last comprising words ending in *–p, –t, –k*. A large part of the Going Tone came from Archaic forms ending in *–b, –d, –g*.

4. Growth of Modern Dialects. — All modern dialects are not descendants of one line of ancestors, Archaic Chinese and Ancient Chinese. However, the majority of modern dialects are close enough descendants of them to allow statements of phonetic laws to be made with reference to one line of ancestors without leaving too unwieldy a body of exceptions. There are two reasons for this. One is that the languages reconstructed by Karlgren, in the opinion of the majority of Chinese scholars, are eclectic systems from various old dialects. By thus admitting your great-uncle's tablets into your ancestral hall, your second cousins look like first cousins and first cousins like sisters and brothers. The other reason is that today's dialects, like today's people, are descendants of relatively few ancestors, while the other old branches of the language have died off without leaving any descendants.

Now there is no Modern Chinese with a capital *M*, except *M* as in Mandarin, which, important as it is practically, is linguistically one of the least informative of the modern dialects, since it has evolved farthest away from ancient pronunciation. But we can note certain broad changes since 600 A.D. which have affected most modern dialects, including Mandarin. The Ancient voiced (sonant) initials *b', d', g', dz', z*, etc. have lost their voicing in all dialects except those of Chekiang, parts of Kiangsu, and parts of Hunan. Some of the Ancient bilabials have, under certain conditions, become dentilabials in all China except in the South and the Southeast. Ancient final consonants *–m, –p, –t, –k* are either lost or changed except in the extreme South. The four tones of Ancient Chinese have been subdivided into an upper and a lower series, according as the initials were originally voiceless or voiced. The extent of subdivision varies with the dialect, but the Even Tone is subdivided into two classes almost everywhere. In most of northern China, the Entering Tone has not only lost its consonantal endings but also its class identity, inasmuch as it has been redistributed into the other tones. Thus, the four tones of Mandarin are not the four tones of Ancient Chinese, but correspond only to its first three tones, of which the first has been split in two. On the whole, the southern dialects have preserved ancient endings and tone-classes best, the central and eastern dialects the ancient initials best, while the other dialects have departed farthest from Ancient Chinese.

5. Classification of Dialects. — The dialects of China are distributed over three zones. The zone of the greatest variety is in the southeastern coastal provinces including Kwangtung, Fukien, most of Hunan, Kiangsi, and Chekiang, and parts of Kwangsi, Anhwei, and Kiangsu. The second zone is the great Mandarin-speaking region comprising most of the rest of China proper and the greater part of Manchuria. In the third zone, in the territories and the borderlands of the southwestern provinces and the province of Sinkiang, non-Chinese languages are spoken side by side with Chinese in some form of Mandarin. While the last zone includes more than half the area of all China, it includes less than one-tenth of the population.

There are nine main groups of dialects in China, six in the first zone and three in the second zone. The first six groups are Cantonese, Kan-Hakka, Amoy-Swatow, Foochow, Wu, and Hsiang. The Cantonese group, the Kan-Hakka group (to which most of Kiangsi belongs), and the Amoy-Swatow group (to which the Chinese-speaking part of Hainan Island belongs), are characterized by their preservation of ancient consonantal endings $-m$, $-p$, $-t$, $-k$. The Foochow dialect forms a group apart, though it is near the Amoy-Swatow group in many respects and often classed together with it under the term Min group, Min being the literary name of Fukien. The Wu dialects (including those of Shanghai and Wenchow) and the Hsiang group, Hsiang being the literary name of Hunan (though Changsha, the capital of the province, is not typical of the group) are characterized by their retaining the voicing in ancient initials like b', d', g', dz', etc. In addition to the usual two Even Tones and one or two Rising Tones, these six groups have for the most part two Going Tones and two Entering Tones.

The second dialect zone, including roughly two-thirds of the population and three-fourths of the area of China proper, is the zone of the Mandarin dialects, which can be divided into a northern group, a southern group, and a southwestern group. The northern group includes the Yellow River basin and Manchuria. To this group belongs the dialect of Peiping. The southern Mandarin group covers a rather small area between Hankow and Nanking. The southwestern group covers the region of the greatest dialectal uniformity — including Szechwan, Yunnan, Kweichow, part of Kwangsi, and part of Hupeh up to and including Hankow. All Mandarin dialects agree in having relatively simple sound-systems. They have four or five tones. They have a common vocabulary for the most frequent words such as personal pronouns, demonstratives, interrogatives, and particles.[3]

[3] For further details on dialects, see Ting Wên-chiang (V. K. Ting), Wêng Wên-hao (W. H. Wong), and Tsêng Shih-ying, *Chung-kuo fen-sheng hsin-t'u* 中國分省新圖

The mutual intelligibility of different dialects depends, as in the case of other languages, both upon the dialects themselves and upon the educational background of the speakers. The three groups of Mandarin dialects may be compared with the English dialects of the British Isles, North America, and Australia. Then, if abstraction is made of the fact, with all its implications, that all China writes one common idiom in one common system of characters, we can say that the other groups of dialects are about as far from Mandarin and from each other as, say, Dutch or Low German is from English, or Spanish from French. On the whole, the differences among different groups of Chinese dialects are less radical than the difference between English and German. Speakers of different groups of Mandarin, say a native of Harbin or Mukden, a native of Urumchi in Sinkiang, a native of Chungking or Kweilin, and a native of Nanking — these representatives from the four corners of China can converse freely, each in his own dialect, without attempting too much mutual adjustment.

Among speakers of non-Mandarin dialects, ignorance of Mandarin is not so much felt as a personal shortcoming as a practical inconvenience for travelers and people in educational or public work. Most educated persons acquire a Mandarin of sorts either by "picking it up" from people who speak — or have learned to speak — Mandarin, or merely by adopting the vocabulary of Mandarin novels like the *Dream of the Red Chamber* without attempting any readjustment in pronunciation.

Among people in public life, linguistic difficulties arising from dialect differences have been relatively negligible. For the common people, with their limited base of vocabulary and limited contact with other habits of diction and articulation, it would of course be impossible to communicate orally across the boundaries of dialect groups, or even of subgroups.

6. Dialects, Mandarin, and Wenli. — Dialects differ from one another in three respects. The most important difference is that of pronunciation. Thus, the same root which means 'woods' is pronounced *lin* in Peiping, *ling* in Shanghai, and *lam* in Cantonese. Secondly, dialects differ in the choice of words for common use. Thus, the word for 'he, she,' etc. is *ta* in Mandarin, *yi* in the Shanghai dialect, and *ghöe* in Cantonese. Out of these three distinct words from the common stock of the Chinese language, some dialects choose one and other dialects choose another as the favorite form for ordinary use, leaving the others as obsolete or literary words. Thirdly, dialects differ in grammar. Thus, in Peiping, one uses the word-order 'give me some water,' while in Canton and Shanghai one says something like 'give some water me.' This third aspect is the least important, as there is comparatively great uniformity of grammar among the dialects.

(60th anniversary publication of *Shun Pao*), 2nd edition, Shanghai, 1934, Map 12; and F. K. Li, Languages and Dialects, in *The Chinese Year Book*, 1938–1939 issue, Shanghai, 1939, pp. 43–51.

Mandarin, in the narrow sense, is simply the dialect of Peiping and, like other dialects, has its phonetic system, its common vocabulary for ordinary speech, and its grammatical structure. The thing that is peculiar about Mandarin is that it is less peculiar than the other dialects. For, as we have seen, it belongs to a type of dialect which varies the least from place to place and is spoken and understood by the greatest number of people in China.

Over and above the dialects, or rather, included as a part of each dialect — there is a literary language or *wenyan*,[4] now often called "Classical Chinese" by Western scholars. *Wenyan* is not an additional dialect, for it has no pronunciation of its own. The same sentence in *wenyan* has as many ways of pronunciation as there are dialects. To be sure, a direct quotation in the *Analects* of Confucius must have been pronounced in one particular way in a dialect of *Lu* in the sixth century B.C. But what concerns us is the fact that the *Analects* as a currently read book of a still living, if not spoken, idiom exists in the collection of meaningful sounds in the mouths of literate persons of all dialects. The fact that there is one and the same system of characters throughout China has certainly played a major part in the preservation of *wenyan*, but the nature of existence of *wenyan* is not in the writing as such, but in the understanding, reading aloud, learning by rote, quoting, and free use of this common idiom, though its actual linguistic embodiment in audible form varies from dialect to dialect. In the terminology of class logic, *wenyan* is a class of certain cognate portions of dialects, and every word in *wenyan* is a class of cognate words in the dialects, usually written with the same character.

From this we can draw two corollaries. One is that it is possible to reach the whole of Chinese literature through the medium of any one of the major dialects. The other is that a thorough schooling in one dialect is an introduction to the whole Chinese language.

7. Vernacular Literature and the Literary Revolution. — The vast body of Chinese literature is in *wenyan*. Much writing of today, especially for business and official purposes, is in the same form. Writing in the colloquial style, whether in the standard Mandarin or in any other dialect, has never been done on nearly so large a scale as in *wenyan*. The amount of existing colloquial literature in the dialects is negligible. Mandarin colloquial texts exist in the form of Buddhist lectures of the 9th century, some philosophical works of the Sung dynasty (960–1278), and a comparatively small number of plays and novels from the Yuan dynasty on (since 1277). An even more insignificant amount of literature exists for other dialects such as Cantonese and the Soochow dialect.

[4] *Wenyan* used to be called *wenli* by Occidental writers on Chinese. Actually *wenlii* in Chinese means the literary quality or structure of an essay. With advanced knowledge of Chinese terminology, this non-Chinese usage of a Chinese term has been discarded in favor of *wenyan* or "Classical Chinese" for the literary language.

Since the Literary Revolution or the Vernacular Literature Movement of 1917 led by Hu Shih, the use of the Mandarin colloquial in writing has spread greatly. But, in the characteristic manner of revolutionary movements, the first articles advocating the use of the colloquial were written in the literary language, and the leaders continued, and many of them continue, to correspond in the literary language long after they had begun to write articles in the colloquial.[5] As things stand now, the movement has penetrated most deeply in the field of literature. Novels and plays, which formerly had to be read furtively from inside half-open drawers, are now placed on the top of classroom desks as part of courses in literature. (See Lesson 23.) New novels and plays, and to a less extent poetry, are written in the colloquial idiom. More than half of the publications on scientific subjects and translations of foreign books are in the colloquial. In the schools, the colloquial is taught through the sixth grade, and *wenyan* is taught only from the seventh grade, or junior middle school, on. It is in the government, in business, and in the non-academic professions that the change has been slowest, due in part no doubt to the difficulty of disturbing well-established phraseology and familiar conventional forms. A paradoxical result of this is that while news despatches, official notices, and even advertisements are in the literary idiom, the so-called literary section and frequently the editorial section of newspapers are in the colloquial. In increasing degrees, however, the written colloquial has come to stay.

8. Unification of the National Language. — Parallel with the Vernacular Literature Movement, there has been a movement towards the unification of the National Language. We have seen that there is already a great degree of underlying unity in the whole language and a still greater degree of practical unity in the second dialect-zone. Since the Revolution of 1911, when China became a republic, there has been a conscious movement to unify the spoken language of the nation. A Society for the Unification of Pronunciation was formed under the auspices of the Ministry of Education, later reorganized under the Ministry as the Committee on the Unification of the National Language. A system of 39 National Phonetic Letters, or *juh'in tzyhmuu* [6] 注音字母 was devised, a standard of pronunciation based mainly on the Peiping dialect was fixed in 1919 (revised in 1932 in the

---

[5] Hu Shih fired the first shot with his letter to the editor of *Hsin ch'ing-nien*, Vol. 2, No. 2, October 1, 1916. The letter was later expanded to an article 文學改良芻議 (A Program for Literary Reform) in the same periodical, Vol. 2, No. 5, January 1, 1917. Both the letter and the article were written in respectable *wenli* and proposed modestly among other things "not to avoid vernacular characters or vernacular words." It was not until Vol. 4, No. 1, January 15, 1918, that articles in the colloquial began to appear in this revolutionary periodical. The case was quite like that of Dante writing his *De Vulgari Eloquentia* in Latin while trying to establish Italian as a literary medium.

[6] Later changed to 40, then to 37, and called *juh'in fwuhaw* 注音符號 'phonetic symbols.'

direction of still closer approach to the pure dialect of Peiping), and machinery was set up to train teachers to teach the National Language — or *Gwoyeu*, as Mandarin is now called — in the schools. In 1937, shortly before the war, the government subsidized the four largest publishers in the country in the manufacture of type matrices in which each character is cast in one block with the pronunciation indicated on the right-hand side, and ordered all textbooks through the sixth grade henceforth to be printed in such type, so that all reading matter could be self-pronouncing.

While originally chief emphasis was laid on the unification of pronunciation, two other developments have assumed increasing importance as time goes on.

9. Learning-to-Read Movement. — One recent development is a learning-to-read movement, making use of the National Phonetic Letters now available on the side of the characters. Theoretically, the combination should help the spread of standard pronunciation, which it does to a certain extent. But in general, the result is not exactly what the promoters expected. Since it is difficult to teach and learn Mandarin with a perfect pronunciation, the National Phonetic Letters themselves are pronounced with a high degree of local accent. Instead of being harmful, however, this natural practice actually helps the reader to understand the meaning of a character, since it is nearer, in the shade of sound, if not in classification, to the dialect of the learner. It is as if in learning the Chinese word *fey* 'expense,' an English-speaking student were permitted to pronounce it something like 'fee,' thus reminding one of the English word of similar meaning — the only difference being that, in the case of Chinese, the words written with identical characters are real cognates. The phonetically unsatisfactory result is therefore educationally highly useful.

10. Romanization Movement. — The other development is the movement for adopting an alphabetic form of writing. Systems of simplified writing and stenography based on sound had been devised long before the appearance of the National Phonetic Letters. Missionaries have used various romanized texts in various dialects. A curious circumstance about the adoption of the National Phonetic Letters throws some light on how people looked at the problem at that time. When the Committee on Unification submitted its final report to the Minister of Education Fu Tsêng-hsiang, he hesitated about giving official sanction to those curious characters that looked like Japanese *katakana*. Then one day a member of the Committee arranged to have an otherwise illiterate maid read before the minister a newspaper printed in the National Phonetic Letters. He was so impressed with the performance that he straightway ordered the adoption of the system. However, as it turned out, his interest proved to be only transitory and the system of the National Phonetic Letters was relegated to the secondary function of indicating the pronunciation of characters rather than serving as an alphabet. There were and still are many technical difficulties as well as social and political hurdles to be surmounted before any form of alphabet can be used as a general means of writing.

11. Systems of Romanization: National Romanization. — The transcription of Chinese sounds in the Latin alphabet is as old as the meeting of the East and West. The earliest known systematic form of spelling was that of Matteo Ricci (1552–1610),[7] which represented the Mandarin of around 1600. Extensive use of romanized texts did not come until comparatively recently, when the Christian Bible, translated into various dialects in romanized form, began to be taught by missionaries.

In 1928, the system of *Gwoyeu Romatzyh* (G. R.), or National Romanization [8] was adopted by the government and incorporated in the revised standard of pronunciation, side by side with the National Phonetic Letters, in the official dictionary *Gwoin Charngyonq Tzyhhuey* of 1932. This is theoretically a system of transcription to be used only when Chinese names or words are mentioned in a foreign text or in public signs for foreigners (though in practice most government departments themselves follow the usage of foreigners in China by using the Wade system of romanization for most purposes). Actually, it has been regarded and used as a system of writing by promoters of the Romanization Movement.

The distinctive feature of National Romanization is that it spells syllables in different tones with different letters, instead of with diacritical marks or figures,[9] as *mai* (high rising tone) 'to bury': *mae* (low rising tone) 'to buy': *may* (falling tone) 'to sell'; or *shau* 'to burn': *shao* 'few, little': *shaw* 'youthful'. This makes the spelling more complicated, but gives an individuality to the physiognomy of words, with which it is possible to associate meaning in a way not possible in the case of forms with tone-signs added as an afterthought. It is not necessary for a foreigner or a Chinese who wishes to learn the standard dialect to decide on the possibility or desirability of writing Chinese in the Latin alphabet instead of in characters. But as an instrument of teaching, tonal spelling has proved in practice to be a most powerful aid in enabling the student to grasp the material with precision and clearness. It is for this reason that National Romanization has been adopted in this course.

12. Dragunov's System of Latinization: Latinxua. — A system of romanization devised by A. Dragunov for teaching the Chinese in Russia

[7] See Lo Ch'ang-p'ei, Contributions by the Jesuits to Chinese Phonology (in Chinese), *Bulletin of the Institute of History and Philology of Academia Sinica*, 1.3.269 (1930).

[8] See W. Simon, *The New Official Chinese Latin Script, Gwoyeu Romatzyh*, London, 1942.

[9] Without disclaiming responsibility, as a very active member of the Committee on Unification, for the merits and defects of the system, I must give credit to my colleague Lin Yutang for the idea of varying the spelling to indicate difference in tone.

to read has been popular among the Chinese Communists under the name of *Latinxua* or Latinization. The system does not distinguish tones except *ad hoc* for a few words. There has been considerable controversy between advocates of National Romanization and those of Latinxua, sometimes with quite irrelevant arguments. The former call Latinxua a communistic system, as if a system of transcription were capable of having an ideology. Advocates of Latinxua, on the other hand, have called National Romanization a tool of the bourgeoisie because it differentiates tones and the use of tonal patterns is a feature of bourgeois poetry. By the same reasoning, since bourgeois poets also make use of alliteration and assonance, a proletarian system of spelling would also have to do without consonants and vowels!

The value of either system obviously cannot be established on the basis of such arguments. The greatest difficulty with a toneless orthography like Latinxua is that it does not write the language. Given a set of certain word-forming elements in a language — consonants, vowels, and tones — the natural style of a person's speech is the result of an equilibrium between conciseness and verbosity automatically arrived at under the opposing demands of economy and auditory intelligibility. An orthography that writes less than all the word-forming elements disturbs this equilibrium and creates a dilemma for both writer and reader. If a writer uses his normal style, he will leave the reader to uncertain guessing; if he tries to compensate for the loss in distinctiveness by the use of a padded, wordy style, the result will be a kind of language that no one normally speaks or writes. To be sure, given enough context or the situation, much may be guessed from an under-differentiated orthography without padding, just as mumbled speech or even a grunt can often be understood. A sentence like: 'Aw want aw glawss awf called wataw' is quite intelligible whether heard or read, although it dispenses with distinctions of vowel quality. But if all English vowels were like 'aw' in 'awl,' many things said in a normal way would not be intelligible. 'This is called water' would then not be distinguishable from: 'This is cold water.' What the advocates of Latinxua do and advise others to do is to "blow up" their style to greater verbosity and make it a habit to write things like: 'This-here is-being ice-called water,' where the reader would then not depend upon vowel-distinction for intelligibility.

Another difficulty with any under-differentiated orthography is that the native speaker of a language cannot be dissuaded or prohibited from making use of all the word-forming elements which are already in the language. No Chinese can feel that he is talking Chinese unless he talks with tones. He may be trained to write in a very wordy style, or to write without tones, but he cannot be educated out of speaking or reading with tones. Consequently, he will be able to read words written in a toneless romanization only when they remind him of words he already knows, with tone and all. When confronted with words outside his vocabulary, he will be quite unable to say them in a Chinese way. Using again an analogy with English vowels, let us suppose that 'cold,' 'called,' and 'culled' were all written 'c'ld.' Then a person will readily supply the suitable vowel in 'c'ld' when he reads: 'It's very c'ld outside,' or: 'Mrs. Jones just c'ld up.' But if his vocabulary does not already contain the word 'culled,' he would not be able to say the word 'c'ld' at all in a sentence like: 'These flowers were c'ld from his garden,' even though he may guess its meaning correctly. In other words, it would be impossible to learn new words from reading, which would be a fatal defect for a system of alphabetic writing, especially for educational purposes. The upshot of all this is that the toneless system of romanization known as Latinxua, popular as it is in many quarters, is very artificial in style and limited in functions. No good communist, or monarchist for that matter, would want a form of writing which makes reading a guessing game. Any patriot would want a system that gives *all* the constituents of words. It should be made clear, however, that the majority of Chinese, whatever their ideologies are, are not much concerned with latinization or romanization and carry on their daily life of reading and writing in the good old characters, which 'everybody,' — alas, not everybody! — knows.

13. Romanization of Wenyan. — The average style of speech, as we have seen, is the result of an equilibrium between economy and intelligibility relative to the sounds (including tones) of the language. Now some dialects have more sounds to a syllable and a greater variety of syllables than others. Does it then take fewer syllables for some dialects than for others to say the same thing? On this point, S. W. Williams [10] has given a very suggestive answer in a comparative table of the translations of a literary text into nine dialects. There is a decided trend toward greater verbosity in the northern dialects, which are poorer in sounds, than in the southern dialects. In other words, the smaller the variety of syllables, the greater the number of syllables it takes to say the same thing. This is no surprise, since it is a case of the general symbolic principle that the size of complex symbols increases with the decrease in the variety of elements. For example, it takes two figures '16' to write the number sixteen on the usual base of ten, but five figures '10000' on the base of two; or, again, it takes longer to send a message in the Morse code than by teletype, as the code has only the three elements of dots, dashes, and pauses.

Now what about *wenyan* or the literary style, which as we said is pronounced in as many ways as there are dialects? What is *its* state of equilibrium? The answer is that since *wenyan* is not usually spoken except in the form of clichés, it has no equilibrium of auditory intelligibility. Since *wenyan*

---

[10] S. W. Williams' *Syllabic Dictionary*, 2nd ed., 1909, XXXVI–XLVII.

was very close to, if not quite identical with, the speech of ancient times, it attained its equilibrium on the basis of a system of pronunciation much richer in sounds, and therefore much more economical of syllables, than any of the modern dialects. To be sure, there are many styles of *wenyan* typical of different ages, and so all are not alike in conciseness or diffuseness. But they are all more concise than the colloquial style of any modern dialect. While Mandarin has about 1,300 different syllables (counting tones), Cantonese has about 1,800. That is why it is usually easier for speakers of Cantonese to identify by sound a literary word than for speakers of Mandarin. But even Cantonese contains too few varieties of sounds for it to come to an equilibrium of auditory intelligibility at the level of conciseness of *wenyan;* for the Ancient Chinese of 600 A.D., as represented in the dictionary *Kuang-yün*, 1007 A.D., had as many as 3,877 syllables. Here, then, is the chief objection to any all-purpose alphabetic writing for Chinese, namely, the fact that one cannot write *wenyan* in it, and any abolition of the characters would mean the drastic cutting off of China's cultural heritage, most of which is in *wenyan*. It is all very well to say that the literature of the future will be in the colloquial and therefore intelligible in romanized writing. But as for existing literature, it would be a superhuman job, if at all possible, to translate all of it into the colloquial in order to make it legible in alphabetic form.

14. Interdialectal Romanization. — To answer this objection, two Jesuit priests of Szepingkai, Liaoning, Fathers Henri Lamasse and Ernest Jasmin, devised a system of interdialectal romanization,[11] which, representing the Ancient Chinese of about 600 A.D., as reconstructed by Bernhard Karlgren, is intended to be an orthography in which both *wenyan* and the colloquial can be written. In addition, the same romanization can be pronounced in any dialect by a set of rules of pronunciation for each dialect. It is as if the one orthography 'light' were to be used to cover both English and German, with a rule stating that 'igh' is to be pronounced [ai] in English and [iç] in German, so that the form 'light' is [lait] in English and [liçt] in German. The idea is certainly very attractive, though the actual orthography could be made to look less forbidding and the system made more practical if it followed less mechanically Karlgren's reconstruction of Ancient Chinese and took as its basis a later stage of the language (which it does to a slight extent). The forms could still be distinguished and yet approximate much more closely those of the modern dialects.

15. Basic Chinese. — Another trend in the movement toward the simplification of Chinese writing is the attempt to reduce the number of characters. The leader of the Mass Education Movement, Yen Yang-ch'u (James Y. C. Yen) selected, on the basis of frequency, about 1200 charac-

---

[11] *La romanisation interdialectique, écriture alphabétique naturelle et pratique de la langue chinoise*, Peiping, 1934.

ters and had texts on elementary subjects composed to teach the illiterate. Somewhat different lists were drawn up for city dwellers and farmers, since the things they would have most frequent occasion to read or write about would be different. Since it is economically advantageous for the illiterate to know as many characters as possible, the plan calls for the teaching of more characters after the first thousand are mastered. The reform is therefore not so much of the writing as of teaching methods.

A more reformist attitude was taken by the dramatist Hung Shên when he proposed a list of 1,100 Basic Characters.[12] Like the word list of Basic English, it is not based on frequency as such, though rare words are in general not likely to be useful or necessary, but is designed with a view to flexibility in combination and sufficiency for general use. Since, however, a character represents a monosyllable and a monosyllable is rather less than a syntactical word (see p. 33), the list of 1,100 units allows much greater freedom of combination than the word list in Basic English. The result is that the language written within the limits of this list is much nearer normal Chinese and gives much less impression of a special style than is the case with Basic English. Hung Shên can write, as he does in his explanatory book, much more natural Chinese than C. K. Ogden can write English with his list of 850 words, or, from another point of view, Hung could afford to use a somewhat shorter list and still have as much freedom of style as Basic English.

Besides the pedagogical and the reformist approach, there is a linguistic sense in which the idea of Basic Chinese characters can be conceived. In the dictionary *Kuang-yün* of 1007 A.D. mentioned above, there are 3,877 different syllables under which are listed 26,194 different characters, or about 7 characters to each syllable. In the *K'ang-hsi Dictionary* of 1716, which continues to be widely used today, and in which the pronunciation is still based on that of 600 A.D., there are 40,545 characters, or more than 10 characters to each syllable. How then can Lamasse and Jasmin claim that their system of Interdialectal Romanization based on Ancient Chinese is distinctive enough for writing literary Chinese and transcribing all Chinese literature, if each romanized syllable stands ambiguously for any one of the 10 different characters? The answer is that there are not really 40,545 different *words* in the language; there were not nearly as many words, even in the language of 600 A.D., as represented in the 3,877-syllable *Kuang-yün*. Homonyms of the 'can ('able')-can ('tin')' type there were, but not anywhere near ten different words to a syllable. The multiplication of characters was a development in the direction of purely graphic differentiation. In the time of the great classics, say the 4th or 3rd century B.C. (see Lesson 22), there was much use of characters in their simple primary forms and

[12] 洪深, 一千一百個基本漢字教學使用法 (Method of Teaching and Using 1,100 Basic Characters), Shanghai, 1st ed., 1935, 2nd ed., 1936.

free interchange of characters of the same pronunciation. But the characters developed more and more in the direction of semantic differentiation. If, let us say, the English word pronounced [mæn] were written *man* 'human being,' *mann* 'a male human being,' *gman* 'to operate (a gun),' *kman* 'mankind,' *hman* 'husband,' etc., all pronounced like 'man,' then the situation would be more like the Chinese practice of writing the same spoken word by a variety of characters. (See p. 61 on enlarged characters.) If, on the other hand, the Chinese system of writing were such that each spoken word were written by one and the same character, instead of a set of characters according to *extensions* of meaning, then it would be more like the English practice of always writing 'man' for the same spoken word 'man,' irrespective of differences in meaning. The list of characters synthesized and differentiated on this principle would then form a set of Basic Chinese Characters in the linguistic sense.

It is true that divergences of ancient dialects, semantic changes and irregularity of phonetic correspondences among modern dialects arising from mutual borrowing and other factors of time and place will complicate the picture. Of the 3,877 syllables of *Kuang-yün*, many are probably obsolete; others, however, stand for homonyms or different words (not only different characters) with the same pronunciation. On the other hand, new differentiations of meaning associated with new differentiations of pronunciation will have to be reckoned as new words. As a subjective estimate, I should say that some 3,500 Basic Characters, representing as many words, pronounced with some 3,000 syllables of Ancient Chinese (as of 600 A.D.) would probably be a fair representation of the content of the Chinese language. Such a list would be of importance from the pedagogical and the reformer's point of view, precisely because it would be based on a representation of the language as a whole without limitation of style, and not on criteria of easy versus difficult characters, necessary versus unnecessary words, standard versus substandard pronunciation, or colloquial versus literary idiom. Basic writing will then be writing based on the language.

16. Recommendations to the Occidental Student. — While the various divergent and confluent currents described above are the chief concern of forward-looking Chinese, they are naturally of only passing interest to foreigners watching from the shores. The problem which an Occidental student of Chinese has to face first is to learn what the language and writing are and not what they might better be. He has no business to ask the Chinese to use fewer characters, but should try to learn as many characters as possible. If a character has a printed form and a different written form and both are commonly met with, he will just have to learn both. If he learns the pure Peiping dialect and his interlocutor has a Chungking accent, he will have to learn to attune his ears accordingly (see Lesson 18). Here, again, the most practical point of view is the scientific, empirical one of learning about what is.

In the matter of romanization, it would be well if one system could be used for all purposes. But unfortunately it will not be possible unless and until any national system is not only adopted, but actually widely used in China. As things stand, it is quite impossible to make any one system answer all purposes. In a pamphlet on *The Romanization of Chinese*, London, 1928, Bernhard Karlgren says that at least three different systems are needed: A. a philological system for scientific language study; B. a Sinological system for writers in English on Chinese subjects; and C. a popular system to be used only by the Chinese themselves in creating a new colloquial literature.

There is little difficulty in connection with Type A, since every phonetician has, and usually asserts, the right to his own system.

Type B is the system needed by the great number of people who hav occasion to cite Chinese words and names when writing in English, but do not plan to learn the language practically or study it scientifically. They would want to have some procedure to follow in writing Chinese words "in English." For this purpose, the Wade system [13] is at present the most widely used among writers in English. Certain exceptions, however, are usually made. In the first place, there are the numerous irregular forms which have already been too well-established to be changed, such as *kowtow, kumquat, Confucius, Chiang Kai-shek*, etc., and which could not be recognized if regularized in the Wade system as $k'ou^4$-$t'ou^2$, $chin^1$-$chü^2$, $K'ung^3$-fu^1-$tzŭ^3$, $Chiang^3$ $Chieh^4$-$shih^2$, etc. Another important group of exceptions is found in place names. For example, the 1936 edition of the *Postal Atlas*, published by the Directorate General of Posts of the Ministry of Communications, follows the Wade system for most names of small places, but a different system for the names of the provinces (see Lesson 16) and some of the larger cities, and still other systems in some of the names of places in the coastal provinces. The only practical procedure, then, for those who write in English on Chinese subjects is to follow the Wade system [14] in general, the *Postal Atlas* for place names, and common usage for the well-established irregular forms.

Under Type B, Karlgren includes also the romanization to be used in

---

[13] First used by Sir Thomas Francis Wade in *Hsin ching lu, or, Book of Experiments; being the First of a Series of Contributions to the Study of Chinese*, Hongkong, 1859, later revised and incorporated in his *Yü-yen tzŭ-êrh chi*, London, 1867, 3rd ed., 1903. The form now currently used is really the Wade-Giles system, as represented in Herbert Giles, *Chinese-English Dictionary*, 2nd ed., London & Shanghai, 1912.

[14] Many publications, for example *The Far Eastern Quarterly*, omit the circumflex over *e* and the breve over *u*. This results in no syllabic ambiguity. The newspaper practice of omitting all diacritical marks, however, is not recommended.

textbooks. As we shall see later (Chapter V), it is essential for a foreigner to use some form of extended romanized text in order to acquire and retain precision in the first stages of his study. For this purpose, the Wade system could, theoretically, be used. But in practice, the constant addition of the necessary diacritical marks and tonal figures makes words and sentences so confusing to the eye that it is not only extremely wasteful of effort, but usually results in the student's inability to gain any clear idea of the sounds of words or to make sure connections between sound and meaning.

There are any number of possible systems of romanization which would answer the purpose of a running text without the pedagogically fatal features of the Wade system. For teaching Mandarin, Walter Simon has chosen National Romanization for his *Chinese Sentence Series*, London, 1942, not because it was planned as a Type C romanization by the Chinese (the government has never sanctioned it as a system of alphabetic writing), but because it does something which has to be done but cannot be done by the Wade system.

Whether this form of romanization is of Type B or of Type C does not matter. We are using it here because some such orthography is necessary for getting a firm grasp of the language. With this understanding, we are now ready to take up the sounds of *Gwoyeu* and *Gwoyeu Romatzyh*.

CHAPTER II
PRONUNCIATION AND ROMANIZATION

This is a descriptive chapter, of which the contents are to be practiced in Lessons A, B, C, D in Part II. The student is not expected to gain a working knowledge of the sounds until he comes to those lessons, but should memorize the tables in this chapter which are marked "*Memorize!*"

1. Initials. — A syllable in Chinese is made of three constituents: the initial, the final, and the tone. For example, in *liang* 'cool,' *l*– is the initial, *–iang* the final, and a high-rising pitch pattern over the whole syllable [1] is the tone. The initials of Mandarin are given in Table 1,[2] which should be committed to memory *in the arrangement given*. Before going further, it is absolutely essential for the student not only to memorize what initials there are, but also be able to reproduce them in writing, with every initial in the right row and column. The encouraging fact about these sound tables is that they are quite exhaustive. If one sees no *gr–* or *zbl–* in the table of initials, then one can be sure that syllables like *gru* and *zbla* cannot be Chinese.

TABLE 1. INITIALS (*Memorize!*)

Place \ Manner	Unaspirated stops	Aspirated stops	Nasals	Fricatives	Voiced Continuants
Labials	b	p	m	f	
Dental stops, nasal, and lateral	d	t	n		l
Dental sibilants	tz	ts		s	
Retroflexes ("j_r")	j	ch		sh	r
Palatals ("j_i")	j	ch		sh	
Gutturals	g	k		h	○

2. Place of Articulation. — The rows in the table represent groups with approximately the same places of articulation, and the columns approximately the same manners of articulation.

---

[1] Or over the final, if the initial is voiceless and therefore incapable of having any pitch. For example, the high-rising tone of *chwan* 'ship' is spread over the final *–wan*.

[2] For theoretical analyses of Peiping phonemes, see Lawton M. Hartman 3rd, "The Segmental Phonemes of the Peiping Dialect," *Language* 20.1.28–42 (1944) and Charles F. Hockett, "Peiping Phonology," *Journal of American Oriental Society* 67.4.253–267 (1947). An important point in which the present system, for purely practical reasons, differs from those of Hartman and Hockett is in the treatment of the palatal initials.

The first row presents no difficulty. Apart from *b*, to be described below, the other labials have the same values as in English. The second row: *d, t, n, l*, has a tongue position slightly more advanced than English dentals, but the difference in shade is negligible. The third row: *tz, ts, s* has a decidedly forward articulation; the Chinese *s*, for example, is much nearer French or German *s* in place of articulation than the average position of English *s*. The very retracted *s* of some speakers of English, exaggerated as in 'Thish izh my shishter' is to be avoided. In pronouncing Chinese *s*, think of *th* in 'think,' but do not quite make it a real 'lithp.'

The next two rows, the retroflexes and the palatals, are very difficult for English-speaking students to distinguish, because the usual English articulation for this type of consonants lies between the two places in the Chinese consonants. The letters *j, ch, sh*, when not followed by the vowel sounds *i* or *iu* (i.e. *ü*), as well as the letter *r*, represent sounds made with the tip of the tongue curled back against the roof of the mouth, very near the place of articulation of English consonantal *r*. On the other hand, when the letters *j, ch, sh* are followed by the vowel sounds of *i* or *iu*, they represent sounds made with the flat part of the tongue — the tip being free — against the palate. It has been found very convenient in class instruction to speak of these two rows of initials as "j_r" ("jay-are") and "j_i" ("jay-eye") as reminders of their places of articulation.

The student should be warned of a disturbing feature of English habits of articulation in that English *j, ch, sh, r* are always pronounced with the lips slightly protruded or rounded. In Chinese, whether it is a case of j_r or j_i, these consonants have no lip action — unless, of course, the vowel following happens to be a rounded vowel, such as *u*. Practice in front of a mirror and say 'she,' 'cheat,' 'sharp,' then say the same words by keeping the lips back and open, and the result will be near the Chinese sounds of *shi, chi, shia*. Similarly, say English 'ran' with retracted lips and the result will be like Chinese *ran*.

The last row of initials, the gutturals, present no difficulty. It should be noted, however, that the Mandarin *h* is not the English glottal *h*, but a velar, or uvular *h*. It is like the German *ch* in *ach*, but articulated further back and with less friction. The circle at the end of this row represents words beginning with vowels. Only interjections and particles begin with true vowels. Ordinarily, words which we spell with *an, en, ou*, etc. have three kinds of beginning sound according to the individual. The majority of natives of Peiping pronounce these words with a slight squeeze in the back of the tongue, producing a sound like the rubbing sound used by many Germans in pronouncing the *g* in *lage*. A minority of speakers use a glottal stop, and a very small minority a nasal beginning *ng-*. It will create no misunderstanding or even any impression of a foreign accent if the student pronounces words like *an* 'peace,' *enn* 'press upon,' *oou* 'lotus stem' with a pure vowel beginning. But in doing so he should guard against his habit of linking a preceding word ending in –*n* with such words. Such linking should be studiously avoided. A squeeze at the back of the tongue before the vowel, as in the majority type of pronunciation, will automatically prevent such linking. (See p. 95(h).)

3. Manner of Articulation. — Looking at Table 1 again, now column by column, we shall note that the most important and difficult distinction is that between the first two columns to the left, that between unaspirated and aspirated initials. The unaspirated initials are like those in French '*ca*p*i*tal' [3] or English '*s*pool,' '*s*tool,' '*s*chool'; the aspirated stops are like those in strongly stressed '*p*ool,' '*t*ool,' '*c*ool.' For getting the aspirated sounds one device is to catch the junction sounds in 'loo*p*hole,' 'ho*t*house,' 'i*t's h*ot,' 'su*ch h*eat,' 'thin*k h*ard.' If, after persistent practice, the student still cannot get the distinction, then he can fall back, as a last resort, upon the following expedient. Let him pronounce the unaspirated column with English (voiced) consonants as in '*b*ig,' '*d*og,' '*a*dze,' '*d*ry,' '*j*eep,' '*g*ay' and pronounce the aspirated column with English voiceless consonants as in '*p*ool,' '*t*ool,' etc., paying special attention, however, on the aspiration of *ts*, which most beginners do not aspirate enough. The use of voiced consonants for the first column is not absolutely correct and will give a strong foreign accent. But foreign accent or no foreign accent, the distinction between the aspirated and the unaspirated initials must be maintained at all costs. It affects thousands of words.

Of the other three columns, only the initial *r*– needs comment. The Chinese *r* differs from English *r* in two respects. We have already noted that the j_r initials are pronounced with no lip action, unless followed by a rounded vowel. The other difference is that it is shorter and has more friction. That is why the Wade system uses the letter *j* (as in French *je*) for this sound. However, since the speakers of many Chinese dialects pronounce this sound with no friction, the English pronunciation will result in no "foreign accent" in this respect. But, it should be repeated, special practice must be made with unrounding of the lips, as it involves important word distinctions, such as between *raan* (no rounding) 'to dye,' and *roan* (with rounding before rounded vowel) 'soft.'

4. Finals. — Like the initials, all the finals of Mandarin can be exhaustively [4] enumerated in a short list and should be memorized in the regular arrangement of the tables.

---

[3] As spoken by a Frenchman, not as pronounced by most English-speaking teachers of French.

[4] Apart from a series of derived words, to be dealt with in section 13 below, and a very few words ending in –*m*, which we shall take up as we come to them in the lessons.

TABLE 2. FINALS: BASIC FORM (*Memorize!*)

Medial	Row	Ending					
		zero	–i	–u	–n	–ng	–l
None	Row-a	y a e	ai ei	au ou	an en	ang eng ong	el
i	Row-i	i ia ie	iai	iau iou	ian in	iang ing iong	
u	Row-u	u ua uo	uai uei		uan uen	uang ueng	
iu	Row-iu	iu iue			iuan iun		
Total 37		11	5	4	8	8	1

5. Row-a Finals. — Before we describe the phonetic values of the finals, it should be noted that it is much harder to get an idea of vowel qualities from description than in the case of consonants, and listening to a model is therefore even more important here.

The first final, which we represent by the letter *y*, is a vocal prolongation of the preceding consonant. It has two qualities. (1) After the dental sibilants: *tz, ts, s*, it has a buzzing quality, like a prolonged *z* in bu*zz*. Thus, the syllable *sy* sounds like *s* + vocalized *z*. After the consonant has been pronounced, the vocalic part — the buzzing part — need not, and usually does not, have much friction, but the tip of the tongue remains behind and near the teeth to give the *z*-quality. The lips are open. (2) After the retroflexes: j_r, ch_r, sh_r, r, this final is pronounced as a vocalized *r*. Thus, the syllable *shy* is pronounced like the *shr* in *shr*ill. It is more important here than in the case of *tzy, tsy, sy* to remember that there is no lip action in *y* because the English sounds of *j, ch, sh, r* do involve a protruding or rounding of the lips. (See p. 92.) In Chinese, neither *jy, chy, shy, ry*, nor *tzy, tsy, sy* have any lip action. These seven initials are the only ones which combine with the final *y*.

The final *a* is as in 'father,' with a medium quality.

The final *e* needs special practice. It is an unrounded back vowel, somewhat like *u* in '*u*p' of the so-called "southern accent." It is usually slightly diphthongized in that it starts close and opens out to end up with the more common variety of *u* in '*u*p.' (The vowels in the interjections *Ềh, Oh*, etc. are not included here, as interjections in any language often contain sounds not occurring, or not occurring in usual combinations, in the regular scheme of sounds.)

The final *ai* is as in *ai*sle, with a front *a*, that is, with a clear, rather than a "broad," quality.

The final *ei* is as in *ei*ght, distinctly diphthongized. It is more open in the 3rd and 4th Tones than in the 1st and 2nd Tones.

The final *au* is as in 's*au*erkraut.' The *a* has a back, that is, a "broad" quality. Avoid the type of pronunciation which gives an "*a*-as-in-*at*" quality for the first element.

The final *ou* is as in 's*ou*l,' also more open in the 3rd and 4th Tones.

The final *an* has a front *a*, that is, a clear quality, like the so-called "compromise *a*" in 'dem*a*nd.' It is between *an* as in '*cannon*' and *ahn* as in the name 'H*ahn*,' but nearer the former than the latter. It is, however, not necessarily short.

The final *en* is that of *en* in 'om*en*,' with a neutral quality in the vowel. Special practice should be given to keep the same neutral quality when stressed, since an English-speaking person tends naturally to change it, when stressed, to a different quality — that of *e* in 'am*en*.'

The final *eng* is like *ung* as in s*ung*, but not the very open British variety, which would make the final sound too much like *ang*.

The final *ong* is pronounced with a very close *o* or open *u*, as in German 'h*u*nger.'

The final *el* is like General American '*err*' in the first two tones and between '*err*' and '*are*' in the other tones.

6. Row-i, Row-u, Row-iu Finals. — The other finals are formed by adding the various medials to the Row-a finals. We shall pass over those which have the same sound except for the addition of the medial and only mention points of special importance.

In Row-i, the final *i* is as in 'pol*i*ce.'

The final *ie* is as in '*ye*t.' Therefore *e* in *ie* has a different quality from that of the final *e* alone.

In the final *iou*, the *o* is very short and weakly articulated in the first two tones. But that it does not quite drop out comes out from the fact that *liou* and *mu* do not rhyme, as *few* and *true* do in English.

In the final *ian*, *a* has a quality between 'man' and 'men,' whence the spelling *ien* in some other systems of transcription.

In *in* and *ing*, the vowel is nearer that of *i* in 'mach*i*ne' than in '*i*t.'

In all the Row-i finals, if *i* is followed by another vowel, it has a very open quality (like *i* in '*i*t') after the initials *b*, *p*, *m*, *d*, *t*, *n*, *l*. For example, *lian* should not be pronounced like French *lienne*, with a very tightly pronounced *i* after an almost palatal *l*, but with a clearly dental *l* followed by *i* as in '*i*t' or *é*.

In Row-u, the most difficult final is *u* itself. Unlike English *oo* as in '*oo*dles,' which has a relatively forward articulation (that is, for a back vowel), Chinese *u* has a very far back articulation, but with the tongue retracted rather than raised. It is more like the tongue position of *aw* as in '*aw*ful.' The *oo*-like quality comes from the very small opening of the lips. To get this quality of the Chinese *u*, try to whistle the lowest note possible, then vocalize instead of actually whistling. Another device is to imagine holding as much water as possible without either swallowing it or spilling any of it out of the lips. An ordinary *oo* in 'oodles' will pass with a foreign accent, but a "Southern" *oo*, which is pronounced with the central part of the tongue raised, cannot be used intelligibly here.

The final *uo* is like *wa* as in 'water,' but the lips are opened before the sound ends, so that an *uh*-sound like *ah* in 'Noah' is heard. After the labials: *b, p, m, f*, this final is written *o*, but there is still a trace of *u* before and also an unrounding at the end.

The final *uei* is like *iou* in that the *e* is weakened in the first two tones, but not so weak as to make the final rhyme with *i* itself.

Similarly, the final *uen* has a weaker *e* in the first two tones.

In Row-iu, the digraph *iu* represents the vowel sound of *u* in French 'usine,' or *ü* in German '*ü*ber.' The Chinese variety has more of an *i*-quality than an *u*-quality. While it is described as a simultaneous pronunciation of *i* and *u*, it is easier to produce by saying *u* first and thrusting the tongue forward for saying *i* without moving the lips, than the other way around.

The final *iue* rhymes with *ie*.

Of the nasal endings, those occurring after *a* are more weakly articulated than after other vowels. But in no case is a nasal ending articulated strongly enough to link with a vowel or semi-vowel at the beginning of the next word except particles. Thus in *ren'ay* 'benevolent,' the tongue avoids touching the front part of the mouth so that no sound like the syllable *nay* is heard.

7. Tone. — A Chinese word is what it is, not only in having its constituent consonants and vowels, but also in having its constituent tone. The word *gai* 'ought,' with a high level tone, and the word *gay* 'to cover,' with identical consonant and vowel, but with a high falling tone, are as different for Chinese speakers as *bad* and *bed* for English speakers. Hence the absolute necessity of learning the tone as a part of the word and not as an afterthought. A word pronounced in a wrong tone or inaccurate tone sounds as puzzling as if one said *bud* in English, meaning 'not good' or 'the thing one sleeps in.'

In Mandarin there are four tones for stressed syllables. If the average range of the speaker's voice is divided into four equal intervals separated by five points: 1 low, 2 half-low, 3 middle, 4 half-high, and 5 high, any tone can be fairly well represented by giving its starting and ending pitch, and, in the case of circumflex tones, the turning point. Moreover, if we use a short vertical line as a reference line for ordinates and plot a simplified graph to its left, with time as abscissa and pitch as ordinate, we get a letter-like symbol [5] to represent the tone, as in the last column of the following table:

[5] Y. R. Chao, A System of Tone-letters, *Le Maître Phonétique*, 1930, p. 24.

Tone	Chinese name	Description	Pitch	Graph
1st Tone	Inpyng-sheng	high-level	55:	˥
2nd Tone	Yangpyng-sheng	high-rising	35:	˧˥
3rd Tone	Shaangsheng	low-dipping	214:	˨˩˦
4th Tone	Chiuhsheng	high-falling	51:	˥˩

It should be understood that the actual height and interval of these tones are relative to the sex and voice of the individual, and to the mood of the moment. In general, each of the four steps in the preceding scheme varies between a tone and a tone and a half, so that the total range is somewhere between an augmented fifth and an octave. Needless to say, the pitch of the speaking voice in Chinese, as in a non-tonal language, moves *portamento* instead of jumping discontinuously from one pitch to another, as in music. Consequently, only on instruments with sliding pitch, such as the cello, can one give a fair imitation of Chinese tones, while a keyed instrument cannot remotely approximate any except the 1st Tone of Mandarin.

8. Tone Sandhi. — Tone sandhi is the change in the actual value of tones when syllables are spoken in succession. Next to Cantonese and Southwestern Mandarin, Peiping has the simplest tone sandhi among the major dialects. The following rules cover most ordinary cases:

(1) A 3rd-Tone word closely followed by any word except another 3rd-Tone word is pronounced without its final rise in pitch, resulting in a pure fall from half-low to low, or 21: ˨˩. This is the Half 3rd Tone. It does not represent a new class of words, but is the tone in which any 3rd-Tone word will be pronounced under the conditions described. Examples are:

3rd + 1st	˨˩˦ + ˥ → ˨˩ ˥	hao-shu	'good book'
3rd + 2nd	˨˩˦ + ˧˥ → ˨˩ ˧˥	hao-ren	'good man'
3rd + 4th	˨˩˦ + ˥˩ → ˨˩ ˥˩	hao-huah	'good word'
3rd + neutral	˨˩˦ + · → ˨˩ ·	Hao .ba!	'All right!'

In each case, the tone of *hao*, which has the pitch pattern of ˨˩˦ when spoken alone, or at the end of a phrase, now has the pitch ˨˩; in other words, it stays low instead of rising. It should be understood that a native speaker who does not happen to be a phonetician cannot give this tone in isolation. It has to be caught on the wing.

(2) A 3rd-Tone word followed by another 3rd-Tone word is pronounced in the 2nd Tone. Thus,

3rd + 3rd ˨˩˦ + ˨˩˦ → ˧˥ ˨˩˦ *hao leeng* 'how cold!'

In the romanized text of the first eight lessons we shall mark such a changed 3rd Tone by italicizing the syllable in question.

(3) If in a three-syllable word or phrase the first syllable is a 1st or 2nd Tone, the second is a 2nd Tone, and the third syllable is any except the neutral tone (to be described below), then the second syllable (which is in the 2nd Tone) is pronounced in the 1st Tone. An example of this change is *dongnan-feng* 'southeast wind,' which is 1st-2nd-1st, changing to 1st-1st-1st. For a complete list of possible applications of this rule, including its application in a chain, see Lesson D, pp. 110–113.

It should be noted that rule (3) applies only to speech at conversational speed. In very deliberate speech or slow reading, the 2nd Tone is unchanged.

(4) When a 4th Tone is followed by a 4th Tone, the first does not fall quite to the bottom, but only to the middle, as:

      4th + 4th   ╲ + ╲   →   ╲ ╲   *Tzayjiann* 'Good bye!'

9. Stress. — Most Chinese dialects have a rhythm similar to that of French, in which syllables succeed one another in a flat-footed fashion, except for enclitic particles. Mandarin, on the other hand, is one of the few Chinese dialects which is a mixture of French rhythm and English rhythm. The majority of syntactic words (p. 33) — the majority from a lexical point of view — have the French rhythm, that is, each syllable of a word is moderately stressed, with the last syllable slightly more stressed than the rest, as ˌ*shiann*ˈ*tzay* 'now,' ˌ*ji*ˈ*tzeel* ' (hen's) egg,' where the lower bar indicates secondary stress and the upper bar primary stress. When a group has three or four syllables, the last has the loudest stress, the first the next and the inside syllable or syllables have the least stress, as ˌ*hua*ˌˌ*sheng*ˈ*tarng* 'peanut candy,' ˌ*shia*ˌˌ*shuo*ˌˌ*ba*ˈ*daw* 'stuff and nonsense,' where the double bars indicate tertiary stress.

A minority of syntactic words — but a majority in frequency of occurrence — have a tonic accent on the first syllable, followed by one or more completely unstressed syllables, as ˈ*mian.hua* 'cotton,' ˈ*yii.ba* 'tail,' where the dot indicates that the following syllable is completely unstressed. Thus, while *mian.hua* literally means 'cotton-flower,' the word has the rhythm of the word "cotton.'

There are of course variations in stress and rhythm between syntactic words in the sentence. But these do not differ in principle from similar variations in English and need not be described here except for two points. One is that stress for prominence or contrast results in a widening of the pitch range, that is, the high points become higher and the low points lower, so that a 3rd-Tone word, which normally dips down almost to the lower limit of one's voice, tend to be squeezed to a grunting quality of the voice.

The other point is that the 4th Tone, which has the widest range of all (from top to bottom), is normally associated with very strong stress in English, as in '*Yes*, I *do!*' It may do for a start to acquire this wide pitch range by giving 4th-Tone words an extra stress, but it is better to learn the tone without this aid, as the extra stress will have to be unlearned later and the 4th Tone should be given a wide range even without special stress.

10. The Neutral Tone. — When a syllable is completely unstressed, its tone disappears and is said to be atonic or in the neutral tone. We mark it by placing a dot before the syllable so pronounced. Interjections, however, form a special class in that they are usually atonic but usually stressed. They are usually pronounced with the same pitch as that of an ordinary stressed syllable of a non-tonal language such as English, namely, middle falling or 42: ╲ for most cases, and rising for expressing doubt, etc.

A correct understanding of the neutral tone presupposes a clear distinction between the two following problems. The first problem is, how is a neutral tone actually pronounced when we do have a neutral tone? This is a problem of tone sandhi and can be adequately covered in two or three paragraphs or tables. The pitch of the neutral tone is:

ˌ		Half-low	after 1st Tone	*ta.de*	'his'
ˈ		Middle	after 2nd Tone	*sheir.de*	'whose?'
ˈ‖	Half-high	after 3rd Tone	*nii.de*	'your(s)'
ˌ‖	Low	after 4th Tone	*dah .de*	'big one(s)'

In the relatively infrequent cases where the neutral tone begins a phrase, its pitch is usually about middle.

For the pitch of the neutral tone in three-syllable groups, see Lesson D, pp. 110–113.

The second of the two problems of the neutral tone is, when does a word have a neutral tone and when does it not? On the whole, words having neutral tones may be divided into grammatical cases and lexical cases, though the two often shade into each other. Interjections, suffixes, pronouns after verbs, reduplicated verbs, and the not-A in A-not-A questions (p. 59) always have the neutral tone. A two-syllable group consisting of verb and noun-object (*he-char* 'drink tea') has no neutral tone, except when the whole thing is used as something other than a verb-object construction, as *huh.shu* 'protect-document,' old term for 'brief case.' As a rule, literary expressions, new terms, and scientific terms do not contain the neutral tone. There remain then the colloquial expressions of old standing, of which some contain the neutral tone and some do not. In our romanized text, all neutral tones are marked with a dot through Lesson 8, after which only lexical neutral tones are marked in the lesson in which a new case is introduced. Some neutral tones are optional, as ʼ*Jeh.jiang* or ˌ*Jehʼjiang* 'Chekiang.' Only one pronunciation is given in a given place in the running text. In the Vocabulary and Index, optional neutral tone is indicated by a circle before the syllable in question, as *Jeh₀jiang*.

28   INTRODUCTION

11. Neutral Tone and Sound Quality. — Syllables in the neutral tone have certain phonetic features not found in stressed syllables with full tones.

An unaspirated initial becomes a true voiced sound. Thus, in ₁ba'bae 'eight hundred,' the b in both syllables has the difficult unaspirated *voiceless b*, but in *'li.ba* 'fence,' the b is pronounced like an English b, so that 'li.ba approximately rhymes with 'Reba.' Similarly, in *hei .de* 'a black one,' *penq.jaur* 'meet with,' *kann.jiann* 'see,' *wuug* 'five,' the d, j_r, j_i, and g are voiced. The initial *tz*, however, is not so regularly voiced in neutral-tone syllables.

The difficult final *e*, with an unrounded back diphthongized articulation, becomes a simple neutral vowel [ə] in the neutral tone, somewhat like *a* in 'America.' Thus, *sou .de* (the d becoming voiced) 'something turned sour,' sounds very much like English 'soda.' The vowel *a* also tends to be pronounced with the neutral quality of *a* in 'America,' as *daa .ta* 'strike him,' where *.ta* sounds like *.te*, *mian.hua* 'cotton,' where *.hua* sounds like *.hue* or *.huo*.

After a 4th Tone, a neutral tone tends to become voiceless, or whispered, in the following type of syllables: *.fu*, *.tsy*, *.sy*, *.chy*, *.shy*, *.chu*, *.chi*, *.shi*, *.chiu*, *.shiu*. For example, *dow.fu* 'bean curd' sounds like *dowf; yih.sy* 'meaning' like *yihs; yaw.shyr* 'key' like *yawsh; keh.chih* 'polite' like *kehch$_i$; jinn.chiuh* 'go in' like *jinnch(iu)*, with the *iu* is formed but not vocalized.

Our special orthography of *sh* for the sound of *shyh* 'be, is' and *–tz* for *.tzy*, noun suffix, *–j* for *–.jy* or *.je* '–ing,' and *g* for *–.geh* 'individual, piece,' are, however, only for graphical convenience and have nothing to do with the phenomenon described above.

12. Tonal Spelling.[6] — The system of tonal spelling in National Romanization may be presented in two ways. One is to give the rules of orthography. The other is to give the result of the application of the rules in the form of a complete table of all finals in all tones. As it is sometimes easier to remember two sides of the same thing than only one side of it, we shall give the system in both forms.

Rules of Tonal Spelling[7]

1st Tone:
 (1) Use basic form: *ta, shuo, uan, ia.*
2nd Tone:
 (2) Add *r* after the vowel for Row-a finals: *char, her, hair, pern.*

---

[6] Before proceeding, make sure to have memorized Table 2 in order to read this Section more profitably.
[7] See also Synopsis at the back of the book.

PRONUNCIATION AND ROMANIZATION 29

(3) In Row-i, Row-u, and Row-iu, change *i, u, iu*, into *y, w, yu* respectively: *shyang, hwa, chyng,* **yuan**. Note, however, that *i* and *u* as complete finals are changed into *yi* and *wu*: *chyi, hwu,* **yi, wu**.

3rd Tone:
(4) Single vowel letters as well as the *e* in *ei* and *ie*, and the *o* in *ou* and *uo* are doubled: *jyy, baa, chiing, geei, huoo.*
(5) Change the medial or the ending *i, u* and *iu* into *e, o*, and *eu* respectively: *jeang, goai, bae, hao, jeuan.*

4th Tone:
(6) Change endings zero, *-i, -u, -n, -ng, -l*, into *-h, -y, -w, -nn, -nq, -ll* respectively: *duh, pay, low, mann, shanq, ell.*

Supplementary rules:
△ (7) Insert *h* after *m, n, l, r* for the 1st Tone, as **mha, nhie, lha, rheng**, but use basic form for the 2nd Tone, as **ma, niang, lai, ren**.
(8) When finals of Row-i, Row-u, and Row-iu occur as words without any initial, write an *additional* letter *y-* or *w-*, as the case may be, for 3rd-Tone words, *yeou* (as against *jeou*), *woan* (as against *goan*),

TABLE 3. FINALS IN ALL TONES (*Memorize!*)

Row	Tone	Ending										
		zero			-i		-u		-n		-ng			-l
a	1	y	a	e	ai	ei	au	ou	an	en	ang	eng	ong	el
	2	yr	ar	er	air	eir	aur	our	arn	ern	arng	erng	orng	erl
	3	yy	aa	ee	ae	eei	ao	oou	aan	een	aang	eeng	oong	eel
	4	yh	ah	eh	ay	ey	aw	ow	ann	enn	anq	enq	onq	ell
i	1	i	ia	ie			iau	iou	ian	in	iang	ing	iong	
	2	yi	ya	ye	yai		yau	you	yan	yn	yang	yng	yong	
	-3	ii	ea	iee			eau	eou	ean	iin	eang	iing	eong	
	-4	ih	iah	ieh			iaw	iow	iann	inn	ianq	inq	ionq	
	3	yii	yea	yee			yeau	yeou	yean	yiin	yeang	yiing	yeong	
	4	yih	yah	yeh			yaw	yow	yann	yinn	yanq	yinq	yonq	
u	1	u	ua	uo⁹	uai	uei			uan	uen	uang	ueng		
	2	wu	wa	wo	wai	wei			wan	wen	wang			
	-3	uu	oa	uoo	oai	oei			oan	oen	oang			
	-4	uh	uah	uoh	uay	uey			uann	uenn	uanq			
	3	wuu	woa	woo	woai	woei			woan	woen	woang	woeng		
	4	wuh	wah	woh	way	wey			wann	wenn	wanq	wenq		
iu	1	iu		iue					iuan	iun				
	2	yu		yue					yuan	yun				
	-3	eu		eue					euan	eun				
	-4	iuh		iueh					iuann	iunn				
	3	yeu		yeue					yeuan	yeun				
	4	yuh		yueh					yuann	yunn				

[8] Rows headed by "-3" and "-4" contain forms to be used in combination with initials only. See Rules (8) and (9).

[9] Since the sound of *uo* after *b, p, m, f* is spelt *o* (p. 24), the tonal forms will be *bo, bor, boo, boh,* etc.

except that the finals *–iee* and *–uoo* are changed into *yee* and *woo* (instead of *adding y* and *w*).

(9) The same finals will have their *i–*, *u–*, or *iu– changed* into *y–* or *w–* or *yu–* for 4th-Tone words, as *yaw* (as against *jiaw*), *wey* (as against *guey*), except that *y–* or *w–* is added to *–ih*, *–uh*, *–inn*, *–inq* to form *yih*, *wuh*, *yinn*, *yinq*.

In memorizing Table 3, note that the four lines for the 1st Tone are the same as the basic finals of Table 2.

13. The Retroflex Finals and the Diminutive Suffix. — There are two kinds of words with retroflex endings.[10] One is a very small number of primary words, of which the only common words are *erl* 'child,' *erl* 'while, moreover,' *eel* 'ear,' *eel* 'thou' L, *eel* 'near' L, *ell* 'two.' The other class consists of a vast number of monosyllabic words which are morphologically complex in that each is derived from a primary word plus a diminutive suffix (derived, in most cases, from the word *erl* 'child'). This suffix forms no additional syllable, but gives an *r*-coloring to the preceding vowel. The exact manners in which the preceding sounds are affected are as follows:

(1) When the final of the primary word has the ending *–i* or *–n* (in any tone), the ending is replaced by *–l* or *–el* (like the vowel in General American 'berth').

(2) When the primary word ends in *–u* or *–ng*, we add *–l* in the spelling, but the actual pronunciation consists of a retroflexion of *au* or *ou* throughout the diphthong, or, in the case of *–ng*, of a simultaneously retroflexed and nasalized vowel, so that what we write as *fengl*, for example, is actually pronounced [fə̃$_r$]. Note that *ing* + *–l* → *iengl*, i.e. [iə̃$_r$].

(3) The finals *y*, *i*, and *iu* take the ending *–el*, thus *sy* + *–l* → *sel*; *ji* + *–l* → *jiel*; *yu* + *–l* → *yuel*. This applies also to the case when *–n* drops under (1), e.g. *jin* + *–l* → *ji* + *–l* → *jiel*.

(4) The vowel *u* as a complete final takes *–l* without an additional vowel, as *hwu* + *–l* → *hwul* 'fruit stone' (as against *hwen* + *–l* → *hwel* 'soul, ghost').

(5) The vowels *a* and *o* take the ending *–l* and are pronounced like General American 'art,' 'ordinary.'

(6) In the finals *e*, *ie*, *uo*, *iue* the vowel is rather prolonged before a retroflex ending, so that *ge'l* 'song' is not homonymous with *gen* + *–l* → *gel* 'root,' nor is *luol* 'small mule' homonymous with *luen* + *–l* → *luel* 'wheel.' In the 3rd and 4th Tones, however, the *ie*, *iue* derivatives are not distinguished from the *i*, *iu*, *in*, *iun* derivatives, as can be seen from the blank spaces in the last column of Table 4. This table need not be memorized, as the tonal spelling is based on the same principles as for ordinary syllables.

---

[10] The retroflex ending, which consists of an *r*-coloring of the preceding vowel is indicated by a final *–l* (the letter *r* at the end of a syllable being a sign for the 2nd Tone).

TABLE 4. RETROFLEX FINALS IN ALL TONES

Row	Tone	Ending zero + l				−u + l		−ng + l		
a	1	el*	al	e'l*		aul	oul	angl	engl	ongl
	2	erl	arl	er'l		aurl	ourl	arngl	erngl	orngl
	3	eel	aal	ee'l		aol	ooul	aangl	eengl	oongl
	4	ell	all	ehl		awl	owl	anql	enql	onql
i	1	iel[12]	ial	ie'l[12]		iaul	ioul	iangl	iengl	iongl
	2	yel	yal	ye'l		yaul	youl	yangl	yengl	yongl
	−3	ieel	eal			eaul	eoul	eangl	ieengl	eongl
	−4	iell	iall			iawl	iowl	ianql	ienql	ionql
	3	yeel	yeal			yeaul	yeoul	yeangl	yeengl	yeongl
	4	yell	yall			yawl	yowl	yanql	yenql	yonql
u	1	ul	ual	uol	uel			uangl	uengl	
	2	wul	wal	wol	wel			wangl		
	−3	uul	oal	uool	oel			oangl		
	−4	ull	uall	uoll	uell			uanql		
	3	wuul	woal	wool	woel			woangl	woengl	
	4	wull	wall	woll	well			wanql	wenql	
iu	1	iuel*	iual	iue'l*						
	2	yuel	yual	yue'l						
	−3	euel	eual							
	−4	iuell	iuall							
	3	yeuel	yeual							
	4	yuell	yuall							

The meaning of the diminutive suffix is much wider and more varied than the original idea of 'child' or 'smallness,' as can be seen from the various occurrences of this suffix in the lessons. A misunderstanding should be corrected as to the social standing of these derivative forms. The forms given in the lessons represent the normal usage of an educated person from Peiping in an informal conversation. When one is being very formal (as in Lessons 15 and 18) or feels that the listener may be a speaker of some other dialect, he will use a much more bookish style and drop a great many retroflex endings. For getting an accurate knowledge of how

* In the finals e'l, er'l, ee'l, ehl, the vowel is longer and farther back in quality than in el, erl, eel, ell; in the finals ie'l, ye'l and iue'l, yue'l, the vowel is longer and farther front in quality than in iel, yel and iuel, yuel.

the language is spoken, therefore, it is much more important to listen to the forms people do use than to ask them what they think they use. In this connection, note also the characteristic fact that the free use of the diminutive ending seems to be a feature of the speech of capitals — Nanking, Hangchow, Chungking, as well as Peiping.

CHAPTER III GRAMMAR

Since this is a conversational course, grammar is to be learned inductively and the various points will be practiced as they come up in the lessons. In this chapter we shall give a general outline of Chinese grammar for purposes of reference and review.

A. WORDS

1. Morphemes and Syntactic Words. — Chinese scholars recognize two kinds of word-like subunits in speech. The commonest small change of everyday speech is the monosyllable or *tzyh*. Examples are *ren* 'man,' *yeou* 'have,' *meei–* 'each,' *jin–* 'this, the present,' *–.de*, subordinative suffix. It is the kind of thing which a child learns to say, which a teacher teaches children to read and write in school, which a clerk in a telegraph office counts and charges you for, the kind of thing you make slips of the tongue on, and for the right or wrong use of which you are praised or criticized. In short, a *tzyh* plays the same social part in Chinese life as a word plays in English. For this reason Western Sinologists have called *tzyh* a "word."

But if we analyze the structure of Chinese sentences, we shall find that the syntactic subunits which are capable of being uttered independently or combined with a high degree of freedom are not always monosyllables, but often combinations of two or more syllables. Such syntactic units, whether of one or more syllables, are more like the words in other languages. There is, however, no common Chinese name for them. Chinese grammarians call them *tsyr*, which is a learned term and not an everyday word. Examples of *tsyr* are *ren* 'man,' *yeou* 'have,' *meei-hwei* 'each time,' *jin.tian* 'today,' *jy.daw* 'know,' *idinq* 'sure.' On the whole, polysyllabic units of this kind are not quite such close-knit words as 'particular,' 'random,' 'patter,' but more like words of the 'cranberry,' 'teacher,' or 'windmill' type.

In the present course we shall speak of either *tzyh* or *tsyr* as a *word* if the reference is obvious, or where it would make no difference; otherwise we shall call *tzyh* a *morpheme* [1] and *tsyr* a *syntactic word*.

2. Free and Bound Words. — A morpheme is a *free word* when it is also a syntactic word, as *hao* 'good,' *wuh* 'fog.' It is a *bound word* [2] if it must

---

[1] But see Section 11. Note also that we are using the term "word" in a wider sense than it is usually understood in linguistic usage.

[2] Note that a 'bound word' is always bound, but that a 'free word' means only sometimes free. Practically all free words except interjections can be bound to form longer words, as *che* 'vehicle,' *tour* 'head,' from which *chetour* 'locomotive.'

combine with one or more words (whether bound or free) to form a syntactic word, as *jin–* 'this,' *–nian* 'year,' from which the syntactic word *jin.nian* 'this year' can be formed.

In general, a syntactic word corresponds in translation to a word in English, and is usually written as "one word" in our romanized text. But this is only a rough correspondence, as the same Chinese form may have different English translations and vice versa. For example, *haokann* may be variously translated as 'good to look at' or 'good-looking' or 'beautiful,' depending upon the actual sentence in which *haokann* is used.

A free word, when spoken alone, is more likely to be understood than a bound word, when pronounced [3] alone. But whether bound or free, words are rarely used out of context. The understanding of words depends on a number of factors: (1) frequency of the word, (2) absence of homonyms, (3) relative frequency among homonymous words, (4) linguistic context, (5) situational context. Thus, (1) the free word *chuay* 'to trample' may not be easy to understand out of context because of its infrequency. (2) The bound word *way* 'outside' (as in *way.tou* 'outside') is easily understood because there is no other homonymous word. (3) If one hears *yaw*, it is likely to be understood as the word *yaw* 'to want,' which is by far the most frequent one among homonymous words pronounced *yaw*. (4) But in a context such as *chy-yaw* 'take medicine,' *yaw* will be easily understood as the noun for 'medicine,' while (5) if a nurse holding a bottle says to a patient *Yaw*, the situational context will also be sufficient to identify it as the word for 'medicine.'

B. SENTENCES

3. Full Sentences and Minor Sentences. — Most Chinese sentences are *full sentences*, that is, sentences with a subject and a predicate, as *Woo bu shinn-goei* 'I do not believe in ghosts.' Occurring less frequently, but not so infrequently as in English, are *minor sentences:* some with predicates only, as *Bugaushinq chiuh* '(I) don't care to go'; *Kee.yii char.char tzyhdean* '(One) can look it up in a dictionary'; *Shiah-yeu le* '(It) is raining.' (See also Note 14, p. 192.) As in English, answers to questions and commands or requests form predicate sentences, as *Wey sherm buyaw? Inwey buhao* 'Why don't you (doesn't he, etc.) want it? Because it's not good'; *Chiing tzuoh .ia!* 'Please sit down!' Interjections are also minor sentences.

In a full sentence, the subject and predicate are separated or separable by a pause, or a particle of pause *.a*, *.ne*, or *.me*, between them. For example, *Nii tay show* 'You are too thin,' or *Nii .a, tay show* '(As for) you, (you) are too thin.' When a subject is long, it is usually followed by a pause or a particle of pause. It is, in fact, a practice in Chinese punctuation

---

[3] Since, by definition, a bound word is never *spoken* alone.

to mark off a long subject with the sign which is equivalent to a comma. (For omission of pause, as in *Nah.sh* 'That's,' see Lesson 2, Note 2, p. 129.)

4. The Meaning of Predication. — The phonetically loose connection between subject and predicate is paralleled by a semantic looseness. In a Chinese sentence, the subject is literally the subject matter and the predicate is just something said about the subject matter. The predicate does not necessarily denote an action or a characteristic of what is denoted by the subject.[4] For example, *Jeh dih.fangl kee.yii fuh-shoei* 'This place can swim, — at this place one can swim'; *Woo sh leang-mau chyan* 'I am twenty cents, — as for me, the thing I bought was twenty cents.'

An important corollary to this is that the direction of action in verbs is to be inferred from the context. Thus, in talking about feeding poultry, *Ji bu chy .le* means 'The chickens are not eating any more,' but as a reply to a host offering more chicken, the same sentence would mean '(As for) chicken, (I) am not going to eat any more.' Again, *Leangg ren tzuoh i-baa yiitz* 'Two people sit on one chair': *I-baa yiitz tzuoh leangg ren* 'One chair seats two people.' In short, there is no distinction of voice in Chinese verbs. On the methods of specifying direction of action, see p. 54.

5. Types of Predicates —

(a) *Verbal Predicates:* The commonest type of predicate is, as in English, one which contains a verb, as *Ta yaw .deal jeou.chyan* 'He wants some tips'; *Jehyanql shyng* 'This way goes, — this way will do.'

(b) *Substantive Predicates: Woo shaatz?* 'I a fool?'; *Woo tay.tay An.hueiren* 'My wife (is) a native of Anhwei'; *Jiel jieel? Jiel chusan* 'What day (is) today? Today (is) the third'; *Ta wuu-chyy-bann* 'He (is) five feet and a half'; *Woo ba-dean daw .de* 'I (am) one who arrived at eight o'clock, — it was at eight o'clock that I arrived.'

While the substantive predicate is much more frequent in Chinese than similar forms in English, the commonest way of predicating a substantive expression is to use the verb *sh* 'be, is,' thus making the whole predicate a verbal one, as *Jang San sh ren* 'Jang San is a man.' (See, however, preceding section on 'I am twenty cents.')

(c) *S–P Predicates:* A subject-predicate construction can serve as predicate to another subject, as *Jeyg ren shin hao* 'This man (is such that his) heart is good.' The sentence is synonymous with *Jeyg ren .de shin hao* 'This man's heart is good,' which is a simple sentence, with one subject, but it is not the same sentence. Other examples are: *Woo daw.luh sheng* 'I, the roads are unfamiliar, — I don't know my way here'; *Woo sheir jy.daw?* 'I, who knows?, — how should I know?' (See also Note 50, p. 186.)

---

[4] Much of Chinese poetry should be interpreted in this light. See, for example, the poem 'Mooring by Maple Bridge at Night,' p. 275, but do not follow the English translation too closely.

There are some predicates which are S–P in origin, but actually used as inseparable syntactic words, as *Nin heen miannshann* 'You very face-kindly, — your face looks familiar'; *Ta tay shinqjyi* 'He is too nature-hurry, — he is too quick-tempered,' where the predicate can be preceded by adverbs like *bu* 'not,' *heen* 'very,' *tay* 'too.' In a true S–P predicate, such adverbs must be placed inside, as *Ta jih.shinq heen hao* 'He, memory very good, — he has a very good memory.' To negate a true S–P predicate either place *bu* inside or *bu.sh* 'it is not a case of, not that' outside, as *Ta bu.sh jih.shinq huay* 'He is not memory bad, — not that his memory is bad.' A few S–P predicates take both forms, as *Woo tour bu terng .le* 'I, head does not ache any more,' or *Woo bu tour-terng .le* 'I don't head-ache any more.'

6. Types of Subjects. —

(a) *Substantive Subjects:* Substantive expressions form by far the majority type of subjects. *Fann hao .le* 'Dinner is ready'; *Nii shanq naal .chiuh?* 'Where are you going?'; *Jell leeng* 'This place is cold.'

A special, frequent type of substantive subject is one ending in *.de* followed by an adjective as predicate, as *Ta shiee .de hao* 'He writes well'; *Jeyg hao .de duo* 'This is much better.' Apparently the combinations *.de hao* and *.de duo* are adverbs 'well' and 'much.' They cannot be, since modifiers in Chinese must precede the modified (Section 8, p. 37). The correct analysis of the sentences is *Ta shiee .de (dong.shi, yanqtz,* etc.) *hao* '(The stuff, the manner, etc.) he writes is good'; *Jeyg hao .de (dih.fangl, cherng.duh,* etc.) *duo* '(The respect in which, extent to which, etc.) this is good is much.' (See Lesson 5, Note 20, pp. 153–154.)

(b) *Verbal Subjects:* [5] Examples of verbal subjects are: *Tzoou shyng, bu tzoou yee shyng* 'To go is all right, not to go is also all right'; *Daa sh terng, mah sh ay* 'To spank is to be fond of, to scold is to love.'

(c) *S–P Subjects:* Examples of full sentences as subjects are: *Bing bii shoei ching sh jen.de* 'That ice is lighter than water is true'; *Ta bu lai heen hao* 'That he is not coming is very good.' [6]

(d) *Object-Subject:* A substantive expression may be the object of a preceding verb and the subject of a following predicate, thus serving as the overlapping part of two telescoped sentences. For example, *Woo jiaw .ta lai* 'I tell him to come'; *Guei sheir fuh-chyan?* 'It's up to whom to pay?' The most common case of the object-subject is after the verb *yeou* 'have,' as *Woo yeou g perng.yeou huey chanq-shih* 'I have a friend who can sing (musical) plays.' The object-subject is also called a *pivot.*

[5] A verbal subject with a substantive predicate must be very rare if it exists at all. A possible case is *Taur tsann.tou* 'To run away is coward.' However, since it is possible to say *jen tsann.tou,* where *jen* 'really, very' is an adverb, *tsann.tou* may be regarded as a predicative adjective '*cowardly*' here.

[6] An actual example of a student's translation of 'I cannot speak Chinese very well' was *Woo buneng shuo Jong.gwo-huah heen hao,* which would mean 'That I cannot speak Chinese is very good.'

C. SYNTAX

Syntax is the study of constructions in terms of syntactic words. *Morphology* is the study of syntactic words in terms of their constituent morphemes. Morphemes enter into syntactic relations only in so far as they are free words.

Since a free word is defined as a word which *can* be uttered alone, the question may be raised as to how we can tell whether a word is actually free when used in a sentence. We have already seen that between subject and predicate, a pause or a particle of pause may be inserted. Within a subject or a predicate, syntactic words are capable of being separated by sound of hesitation such as *.e* — or *.eng* [ŋ:] 'uh —, er —,' *.jeyg* — *.jeyg* 'the — the —,' or, more frequently, by a prolongation of the last vowel (at low pitch after a 3rd Tone and at the ending pitch after other tones). On the other hand, a speaker does not hesitate in the middle of a complex syntactic word in these ways. If a hesitant speaker or a stutterer is put off in the middle of a syntactic word, he begins from the beginning on resumption, as *Woo yaw lii–, lii–, lii-fah* 'I want a hair–, hair–, haircut.'

Besides the relation of subject and predicate, which we have already described, we shall consider the following syntactic constructions:

7. Coordination. — *Coordination* in Chinese is expressed by mere juxtaposition, as *Nii woo ta dou lai .le* 'You, I, and he have all come'; *Jang San Lii Syh sh leangg ren* 'Jang San and Lii Syh are two men.' Coordinated items may be separated by pauses or particles for pause, as *Jurow, yangrow, niourow, sherm dou mae.bu-jaur* 'Pork, mutton, beef — nothing is available.' In the last example, the particle *.a* or *.le* can be inserted after each item. In constructions like *Nii gen woo dou chiuh* 'You and I both go,' the word *gen* 'follow, with, and' is not a true coordinate conjunction. It is really a case of verbal expressions in series: 'You, following me, all go.' In *yow benn yow shaa* 'both stupid and foolish,' *yow* is an adverb: 'moreover stupid moreover foolish.' It is therefore also a case of coordination by juxtaposition. The A-not-A and disjunctive questions (p. 59) are also coordinate constructions.

8. Subordination. — The simplest rule about *subordination* (qualification, or modification) is that the modifier precedes the modified, as *farngtz .de dieengl* 'house's roof, — the roof of the house,' *bao-shean .de gongsy* 'insure-kind of company, — a company which does insurance business.' (More examples in Note 38, p. 132.) In direct subordination without the interposition of the particle *.de*, the construction is usually so close as to form one syntactic word, as *farngdieengl* 'roof,' *bair-jyy* 'white paper,' *buhao* 'not good,' *baoshean-gongsy* 'insurance company.' Such constructions are intermediate between syntactic and morphological. In so far as the elements can be free in other constructions, the student should learn them as independent units.

9. Verb-object Constructions. — Like subordinate constructions, *verb-object constructions* are also usually close-knit units intermediate between a syntactic word and a phrase. In a true verb-object construction, the object is always stressed except when it is a pronoun, which is in the neutral tone unless specially stressed for contrast. When a verb takes a suffix or the object has a modifier, then the result is a phrase. For example, *he-shoei* 'drink water': *Ta he.le i-woan liang-shoei* 'He drank a bowl of cold water.'

Some verb-object constructions consist of otherwise bound words, except that either the verb or the object may be free when the other word is in a nearby context. For example, in *lii-fah* 'dress-hair, — to have (or give) a haircut,' *lii* in the sense of 'dress (as hair)' and *fah* 'hair' are not free words elsewhere. But one can ask *Nii jiel chiuh lii-fah .bu .lii?* 'Are you going to have a haircut today?' and the answer can be *Lii* 'Yes, I am.' Contrast this with *Woo shianntzay leu .woo.de tour.fah* 'I am now fixing (patting, combing, etc.) my hair,' where *leu* 'put in order' and *tour.fah* 'hair' are syntactic words which can be used in any context. Other examples of separation of bound words are *fey-shern* 'expend-energy, — to trouble (someone with a request)': *Woo fey.le Nın sheuduo shern* 'I have expended much of your energy, — I am much obliged to you,' where *shern*, in this sense, is not otherwise a free word. From analogy with ions in electrolytes, we shall call such words "ionized words."

10. Verbal Expressions in Series. — A very important syntactic construction which has no parallel in English is that of *verbal expressions in series*. We have already seen that coordination consists of juxtaposition, as *Ta tiantial shiee-shinn huey-keh* 'He writes letters and receives callers every day.' In a coordinate syntactic construction, the order is usually reversible, as *Ta tiantial huey-keh shiee-shinn*. But under the term verbal expressions in series, we shall understand verbal expressions in a fixed order. Taking the point of view of the *first* verbal expression, it has the following principal meanings:

(a) *First in time: Deeng .i.hoel chiuh* 'wait a while (before) going'; *chiuh deeng .i.hoel* 'go wait a while'; *Woo chii.lai kann.le i-fell baw* 'I got up and read a newspaper': *Woo kann.le i-fell baw chiilai* 'I read a newspaper and got up'; *Na-dau .geei .ta* 'Take a knife and give to him.'

(b) *Condition: Bu nanshow bu ku* '(If one) does not feel bad, (one) does not cry': *Bu ku bu nanshow* '(If one) does not cry, (one) does not feel bad.'

(c) *Place: Daa jell tzoou* 'from here go'; *li ta tay yeuan* 'from him too far'; *tzay shoei.lii rheng chyou* 'in the water throw a ball (as in playing water polo)'; *wann-dong tzoou* 'go east go, — go toward the east'; *duey .ta fanq-chiang* 'facing him fire gun, — fire at him.'

(d) *Manner: Na shoou chy dong.shi* 'take hand eat things, — eat with the hand'; *yonq-shin tzuoh* 'use mind do, — do it carefully.'

(e) *Interest: Tih woo shuo-huah* 'substitute me speak, — speak for me'; *geei .ta na dau* 'give him take knife, — take a knife for him'; *Geei .woo goen!* 'Give me roll (away), — get out of here!' *duey .ta daw-chean* 'facing him say apology, — apologize to him.'

(f) *Comparison: Nii bii ta ae* 'You compare him short, — you are shorter than he'; *Woo yueh shuey yueh kuenn* 'I the more sleep the more sleepy, — the more I sleep the sleepier I am.'

(g) *Pretransitives: Bae woan tzar.le* 'take bowl smashed, — smashed the bowl.' On the uses of this form, see Note 49, p. 162.

D. MORPHOLOGY

11. Morphological Processes. — Practically all morphemes are monosyllabic, as *ren* 'person,' *keen* 'to be willing,' *duey* 'correct.' A very small number of morphemes of obscure etymology or of foreign origin have more than one syllable, as *luo.bo* 'radish,' *ji.gu* 'to grumble,' *pwu.sah* 'bodhisat,' *luojih* 'logic.' Although these are written with two characters (and called two *tzyh*), and often morphologically complex in origin, they are not analyzed, in the spoken language, into further meaningful parts.

Morphological processes in Chinese can be considered at the following three levels: *reduplication* and *phonetic modification* of one morpheme; *affixation*;[7] and *compounding*.

12. Reduplication and Phonetic Modification. — Reduplication has a number of functions. The beginning student should only learn two of the most important ones and leave the rest to individual cases as they come up. (1) Any verb of action can be reduplicated, with neutral tone on the repeated verb, with meaning of 'just, once,' German 'einmal, mal,' as *tzoou.tzoou* 'just walk, — take a walk,' *kann.kann* 'just look, take a look,' *hwa.suann.hwa.suann* 'think it over.' Most auxiliary nouns (p. 45 and Note 4, p. 122) and a few nouns can be reduplicated (with no loss of tone), with the meaning of 'every,' as *jang-jang* 'every sheet,' *renren* 'every man.' A reduplicated verb *occasionally* takes the suffix –*l*, as *deeng.deengl* 'wait a little'; a reduplicated AN *usually* takes the suffix –*l*, as *jang-jangl* 'every sheet,' *gehgehl* 'everyone.'

(2) A morpheme adjective or adverb may be reduplicated (the repeated word changing into 1st Tone, if not already in the 1st Tone), usually with addition of the suffix –*l* and optional addition of .*de*, the meaning is that of 'liveliness' or 'good and . . . ,' as *kuaykual(.de)* 'good and fast.'

---

[7] Words with affixes are often called "compounds" by Sinologists because they are written with two or more characters. Some linguists regard reduplication as a form of affixation.

Each syllable of a two-syllable adjective or adverb may be duplicated, with addition of .*de* and recovery of stress and tone on the original second syllable, if it was in the neutral tone, the meaning being that of 'intensification,' as *huang.jang* 'flustered': *huang₀huangjangjang.de* 'helter-skelter.'

Terms of direct address as *bah.bah* 'papa,' *mha.mha* 'mamma,' and special words, like *chiu.chiuel* 'cricket,' *wa.wa* 'doll,' should be learned individually. Thus, from the bound word *shing* 'star,' we have the syntactic word *shing.shing* 'star,' but from the bound word *yueh* 'moon,' there is no *yueh.yueh*, except in child language.

Examples of phonetic modification (including change in tone) are: *charng* 'long': *jaang* 'grow'; *liang* 'cool': *lianq* 'to sun, to dry'; *chwan* 'to hand on, pass on': *juann* 'record, biography'; *jiann* 'to see': *shiann* 'appear,' etc. Although these are pairs of cognate words (and often written with the same characters), they should, for practical purposes, be learned as separate words.

13. Affixes. — Chinese has few *prefixes*. The only common ones are *dih–*, prefix for ordinal numbers, as *dih'i* 'first,' *chu–* prefix for the first ten days of the month, as *chusan* 'the third of the month,' and *lao–*, prefix before monosyllabic surnames expressing medium familiarity, and for the names of a few animals.

Chinese has only a small number of *suffixes*, but they occur with great frequency. The most important suffixes are:

The diminutive suffix *–l*[8] (p. 31), which is more often used as a noun suffix than as a suffix expressing smallness, as *hwang* 'yellow': *hwangl* 'yolk.' The only verbs with the suffix *–l* are *wal* 'to play,' and the very colloquial forms *huool .le* 'to get mad' and *dial .le* 'to go, beat it.'

Noun suffix *–tz* (pron. *–.tzy*), as *yiitz* 'chair,' *wahtz* 'sock, stocking.'

Noun suffix *–.tou*, as *shyr.tou* 'stone,' *way.tou* 'outside.'

Noun suffix *–.ba*, limited to a small number of words for physical objects, as *yii.ba* 'tail,' *li.ba* 'fence.'

Modal suffix *–m* (or *–.me* before a pause), as *sherm* 'what?' *tzemm* 'so, this way,' *nemm* 'so, that way,' *tzeem* 'how?' *neem* (rare) 'which way?' *dwom* 'how, to what extent?'

Plural ending for pronouns and collective nouns for persons *–.men* or *–m*, as *ta.men* 'they,' *hairtz.men* 'children (collectively).'

Word suffix *–.le* for completed action, etc., as *daa-poh.le* 'strike-broken, — smashed.'

Phrase suffix *.le*[9] for new situation (Note 36, p. 132), as *Fann hao .le*

---

[8] This suffix, as well as the *–m* form of the suffixes *–.me* and *–.men* given below, form no additional syllable, although in a character text they are, like other affixes, written with separate characters just like ordinary words.

[9] In the dialects and in *wenli*, the two suffixes are often not homonymous, as they are in Mandarin. Thus, *Nii shang.le feng .le* 'You have caught a cold' is *Nee sheung-cox jong thoh* in Cantonese and *Nong sang-zy fong zé* in Shanghai. In *wenyan* the phrase suffix *.le* is *yii* and there is no corresponding word suffix.

'Dinner is ready'; for progress in narration, as *Dih'ell-tian ta howhoei .le* 'The next day, he regretted it,' etc., etc. Note that when the two suffixes come into juxtaposition, they are telescoped into one, as *Nii bae beitz daa-poh.le* 'You have broken the cup.' [10]

Suffix for progressive action *-j* (pron. *-.jy* or *-.je*), as *Woo deengj .nii .ne* 'I am waiting for you'; *Shuoj huah .ne* '(They) are talking, — the line is busy.'

Suffix for possibility or ability *-.de*, as *jih.de* '(can) remember,' *renn.de* 'can recognize, — acquainted with,' *yaw.de* 'can be desired, — desirable.'

Suffix of subordination *-.de*, as *woo.de mawtz* 'my hat,' *kuaykual.de pao* 'run good and fast.'

Infixes are very rare in Chinese. The only common ones occur in conjunction with partial reduplication. They are of the types (1) *dingdang* 'ding dong': *dinglhing-danglhang* 'jingling-jangling,' consisting of adding the initial *lh-* followed by a reduplication of the two finals *-ing* and *-ang*, and (2) *hwu.twu* 'muddled': *hwu.lihwutwu* 'fuzzy-wuzzy,' consisting of adding the syllable *-.li* after the first syllable of a two-syllable word and then repeating the whole word, with recovered stress and tone on the second syllable, if unstressed.

E. COMPOUNDS

14. Classification of Compounds. — The morphological process of compounding (proper) is so important in Chinese that it deserves a separate main heading. A compound is a syntactic word consisting of two words. Compounds can be classified in a number of ways:

(a) A compound may or may not have one of its components in the neutral tone, as *lawbiing* 'bake-cake, — a large, coarse hot-cake,' but *shau.biing* 'burn-cake, — a hot biscuit with sesame seeds.'

(b) Either one of the components in a compound may be bound or (otherwise) free. Thus *law* 'bake,' *shau* 'burn,' and *biing* 'cake,' are free words, but in *shyhbiing* 'dried persimmon,' *shyh* is the bound root morpheme in *shyhtz* 'persimmon'; in *Jonghwa Mingwo* 'The Chinese Republic,' *Jonghwa* is always bound and *Mingwo* can be free.

(c) The components of a compound may or may not be in syntactic relation. Thus, in *mae.may* 'trade,' *mae* 'buy' and *may* 'sell' are in coordinate relation (cf. *Mae may dou iyanql jiah.chyan* 'Buy or sell same price'); but in *daa.shoou* 'beat-hand, — a hand hired to beat, — rioter,' *daa* a transitive verb cannot be used as a modifier without a modifying particle *.de*.

(d) A compound may or may not have the same grammatical function

---

[10] In Cantonese both *-cox* and *lhoh* are kept: *Nee tzeung ceak pui° taa-laann-cox lhoh*.

of one or both of its constituent words. For example, *shau.biing* is a kind of *biing*, but *mae.may* is a noun, while *mae* and *may* are verbs.

(e) Either one of the words in a compound may be a morpheme, a derived word, or itself a compound. Thus, in *gua-tzeel* 'melon-seeds,' *tzeel* is derived from *tzyy* + *-l*, and in *shan.ja-gau* 'hawthorn-jelly,' *shan.ja* 'mountain-*ja*, — hawthorn' is itself a compound.

(f) The components of a compound may be a very active word or only used in one or very few compounds. For example, in *yeouyih* 'intentionally,' both the free word *yeou* 'have' and the bound word *yih* 'idea, intention' are very active words, while in *ee.shin* 'nausea-heart, — nauseated,' *ee* is rarely used outside of this compound.

(g) Finally, some bound words are so active that an unlimited number of *transient* words can be formed by even a beginning student, others are *synthesizable* in the sense that a student knowing the meaning of the components can guess correctly at the meaning of the compound, while still others are *lexical* in nature and have to be learned as a new word even though its components are already known. Thus, *ney-shuang* 'that pair,' *utz.lii* 'in the room' are transient words; *feichwan* 'flying boat,' *haokann* 'good-looking' are synthesizable compounds; and *bairshuu* 'white-potatoes, — sweet* potatoes,' *yueh.lianq* 'moon-bright, — the moon' are lexical compounds.

It would of course lead to endless details of cross-classification if we tried to apply all these seven principles together. For our purposes, we shall consider chiefly the syntactic relations, if any, between the components of compounds and note other important features in passing.

15. S–P Compounds. — In connection with types of predicates (p. 35), we have noted that a true S–P predicate admits insertion of words, while an S–P compound is a frozen unit. Besides serving as predicate, an S–P compound may have other functions. For example, *shin.terng* 'heart-hurt, — to grudge' in *Ta binq bu shin.terng ta.de chyan* 'He does not really grudge his money.'

16. Coordinate Compounds (including synonyms and antonyms). — *lihhay* 'profit-harm, — consideration of advantages and disadvantages,' *lih.hay* 'fierce,' *chyr.tsuenn* 'size' (< *chyy* 'foot' + *tsuenn* 'inch'), *shichyi* 'rare-strange, — strange, to find strange,' *tsair.ferng* 'cut-sew, — tailor.'

Note that syntactic coordination is reversible, though usually one order is more idiomatic than the other, while morphological coordination is fixed in order. In the relatively few cases where both orders are possible, the meanings are usually different, as *yawjiin*, lit. 'important-urgent' means only 'important,' while *jiinyaw*, a somewhat more literary word, means 'urgent and important.'

17. Subordinate Compounds. — *shinlii* 'mind-principle, — psychology,' *shin.lii* 'mind's inside, — in the mind,' *shiaw.huah* 'laugh-word, — a joke, to laugh at,' *sanbae* 'three hundred,' *nanshow* 'hard to take, — can't take it, — uncomfortable, miserable,' *masherngl* 'hemp-cord.'

Localizer compounds form a very important class of subordinate compounds consisting of a noun (or pronoun) followed by a localizer, or a place word, usually in the neutral tone. Thus, *juotz .de shanq.tou* 'table's upper part,' is a phrase, where *shanq.tou* is a noun, but *juo.shanq* 'table-top, — on the table' is a substantive compound with a localizer. In translation, localizers are usually rendered by English prepositions (p. 53 and Lesson 5).

Subordinate verb-noun compounds are nouns and not verbs. Examples are: *byejel* 'pinning-needle, — pin,' *jiachyan* 'pinch-forceps, — pliers,' *fwu.shoou* 'support-hand, — bannister, doorknob,' *pin.faa* 'spell-method, — spelling, orthography,' *shoutyaul* 'receive-slip, — receipt,' *tswenkoan* 'deposit-funds, — bank deposit' (cf. § 18 below).

Since we are regarding an adjective as a kind of verb, adjective-noun compounds also fall under this heading. Examples are: *shiangjiau* 'fragrant-banana, — banana,' *chow.chorng* 'stinking-insect, — bedbug,' *hao-ren* 'good man,' *dahshyy* 'great-envoy, — ambassador.'

D–AN compounds are subordinate compounds of determinatives and auxiliary nouns, as *i-tian* 'one day,' *jey-kuay* 'this piece.' For details, see pp. 45–46.

18. Verb-object Compounds. — Verb-object constructions, as we have seen, are intermediate between syntactic and morphological in nature. The student would do well to treat those cases as compounds when the components have special lexical meanings or when not actually used as verb-object. If the object has full tone, the construction may or may not be a true verb-object construction. For example, *tswen-koan* means either 'to deposit money' or 'bank deposit.' But if the object is in the neutral tone, then the compound always has a different function. Examples are: *huh.shu* 'protect-document, — (old style) brief case,' *doong.shyh* 'supervise-affairs, — member of a board, trustee,' *dean.shin* 'dot the heart, — refreshment, breakfast,' *jeen.tour* 'pillow the head, — a pillow.'

19. Verb-complement Compounds. — The morphological analogue of verbal expressions in series is the *verb-complement compound*, as *Woo chy-bao.le* 'I have eaten full, — I have had enough.' While in verbal expressions in series the first verb usually has an object, the first verb in a verb-complement compound never has an object. For example, in *Feng gua-dao.le i-suoo farngtz* 'The wind blow-toppled a house, — blew down a house,' the object follows the second verb or complement, not after the main verb, as in English 'blow it down.' The meaning of a verb-complement compound is usually that of result, and not so varied as in verbal expressions in series: *gua-dao.le* 'blow, (with the result) toppled.'

The minimum complement is the word suffix –*.le*, as *bae shoei he.le* 'take water drink (it) up, drink up the water,' the first *.le* in *sha.le ren .le* 'have killed (off) somebody.'

Directional complements form a very important class of complements, consisting of verbs of motion indicating the direction of action of the preceding verb, as *fei.lai* 'fly-come, — fly (to) here,' *sonq.chiuh* 'send-go, — send away.'

A verb with a directional complement, such as *jinn.lai* 'enter-come, — come in,' may itself be used as a directional complement, as *sonq.jinn.lai* 'send enter-come, — send in (toward the speaker).' A compound complement with *-.lai* (and less frequently *-.chiuh*) is often split by an inserted object, as *na.chu i-beel shu .lai* 'take out a book.' For further details see Lesson 6, especially Note 28, p. 161.

Potential complements form another important special class. We have seen that the suffix *-.de* as in *jih.de* 'can remember, — remember,' *renn.de* 'can recognize, — to be acquainted with,' etc. (not the subordinative suffix *-.de* as in *woo.de* 'my') expresses possibility, ability. While this suffix is not very active and verbs ending in it must be learned individually, almost any verb may take this suffix if followed by a complement, which will then be called a potential complement. Thus, although one does not say **na.de* for 'can take,' one can say *na.de-shiahlai* 'can take down,' with *shiahlai* 'come down' as potential complement. (See also Note 39, p. 145.)

20. Decompounds and Particles. — A suffix is not only attached to root words but also to compounds or phrases [11] as a whole. For example, *weiborl* 'muffler' has a different construction from *guatzeel* 'melon seeds,' for, while *tzeel* (< *tzyy* + *-l*) is a derived word meaning 'seeds,' there is no such word as *borl. The word *weiborl* is to be analyzed as *wei* 'surround' + *bor-* 'neck' (as in *bortz* 'neck'), with a noun suffix *-l* for the whole thing: 'something around the neck, — muffler.' Being apparently a compound but no longer a compound because of the suffix for the whole, it is called a *decompound*.

A *particle* is a suffix attached to a phrase (or sentence) as a whole. For example, in *woo juh .de leugoan* 'I live, .de hotel, — the hotel I stay at,' the addition of the subordinative suffix *.de* to the phrase *woo juh* makes it a syntactic word. For practical purposes, we shall write such forms, including the suffix, as separate words, just as 'That umbrella is the young lady I go with's' [12] is written without hyphens. This applies also to localizers for phrases, as *baw.shanq* 'in the newspaper,' but *woo jiel mae .de baw .shanq* 'I today bought .de newspaper therein, — in the paper I bought today,' with a space before *.shanq*, which is bound with the preceding phrase as a whole.

[11] In the wider sense, also including sentences.
[12] H. L. Mencken, *The American Language*, 4th ed., p. 461.

F. PARTS OF SPEECH, ETC.

21. Parts of Speech and Form Classes. — It has often been said that Chinese has no parts of speech, but only functional position in the sentence, and stock examples from the literary style such as *jiun jiun* 'the king is a king,' *chern chern* 'the minister acts as a minister,' *fuh fuh* 'the father is fatherly,' *tzyy tzyy* 'the son is filial' are familiar features of the grammatical section of writings on Chinese. While there is a greater range of functional variation for Chinese words than those of most Indo-European languages, if not more than in English, there is still the element of selection which limits the range of variation. Thus, *jeou* 'wine' is never followed by the suffix for completed action *.le; genq* 'still more' is never combined with a numeral, nor is *taangj* 'to be lying down' ever followed by an object. On the other hand, *daa* 'to beat' is usually followed by a substantive. In other words, we can mark in a dictionary that normally *jeou* is a noun, *genq* is an adverb, *taangj* is an intransitive verb, *daa* is a transitive verb, etc., etc. For, as a rule, every form does have a limited range of functions, which have to be learned in connection with it.

A *form class* is a class of forms which have the same grammatical function, such as noun suffixes, transitive verbs, and substantive expressions. A *part of speech* is a form class whose members are syntactic words. In the present section, we shall consider the parts of speech, together with such form classes of bound forms as will be profitable for the student to learn as separable units.

22. Determinatives and Auxiliary Nouns. — *Determinatives* consist of numerals and demonstratives, interrogatives, and a few other bound words. They are: numerals from one to ten, *jeh–* 'this,' *nah–* 'that,' *naa–* 'which?' *tzeem–* 'how?' *sherm–* 'what?' *neem–* 'which way?' *meei–* 'each,' *geh–* 'the various' (unrelated homonym of the AN *–geh*), *shiah–* 'next,' *shanq–* 'last,' *bye–* 'other,' *jii–* 'how many?' *bann–* 'half a.'

Except numerals, determinatives can form syntactic words with suffixes, often with phonetic modification, as *naal* 'where?' *neyg* ($<$ *nah* $+$ *i* $+$ *.geh*) 'that (one),' *tzeem.me* 'how?' *tzemm.me* ($<$ *jeh* $+$ *.me*), *bye.de* 'other, something else.'

The most important type of words containing determinatives is one formed by the addition of an auxiliary noun or AN.

An *auxiliary noun* or AN is a bound word forming, when preceded by numerals or certain other determinatives, a substantive compound, which we have called a D–AN compound. There are five classes of AN:

(a) *AN proper*, also called "classifiers," or "numerary adjuncts" (NA). Every word for an individual person or thing has its specific AN, which should be learned in connection with the word. Other examples are *i-baa yiitz* 'one-handle chair, — a chair,' *leang-jaan deng* 'two-dish lamps,

— two lamps.' There is no corresponding feature in English except such infrequent instances as 'two head of cattle,' 'a copy of the Bible.' The AN *-geh* (written *-g* when unstressed) is the commonest AN for individual things and persons. In case of doubt about the specific AN for a noun, it is usually safe to use the general AN *-geh*, as *ig yiitz* 'a chair,' *leangg deng* 'two lamps.'

(b) *Measure words*, like *-wann* '10,000,' *-lii* 'li,' *doou* 'peck,' *-chyy* 'foot,' *-jin* 'catty,' as *san-doou mii*, 'three pecks of rice.' Some writers use the term "measure word" for all classes of AN.

(c) *Temporary measure words.* These are ordinary nouns which are used temporarily as measure words. For example, in *i-jian utz* 'a room,' *utz* is a noun, with its own AN *-jian* 'partition.' But in *i-utz ren* 'a roomful of people,' *utz* is used as a temporary measure word, since *utz* is not a regular unit of measure. Similarly, in *i-juotz tsay* 'a tableful of dishes,' *juotz* is a temporary measure word, but in *i-juo tsay* 'a regular set of dishes forming a dinner for one table,' *-juo* is a regular measure word. Between a temporary measure word (less frequently, also a regular measure word) and a noun, the subordinative suffix *.de* is often inserted, as *i-dih .de jyy* 'a floorful of paper.'

(d) *AN for verbs*, that is, objects of verbs which, together with a preceding numeral, specifies the number of times the action is performed, as *shuey i-jiaw* 'sleep a sleep, — have a nap,' *wenn i-sheng* 'ask a voice, — make an inquiry,' *chy jii-koou* 'eat several mouthfuls, — have a few bites.'

(e) *Quasi-AN*, consisting of a small number of nouns which can follow determinatives directly but are not associated with ordinary nouns and not themselves regular units of measure, as *i-keh* 'one lesson,' *san-sheeng* 'three provinces,' *leang-jih* 'two seasons.'

A D–AN compound can be used either in apposition with a noun, as *ig ren*, or independently, as *Leangg leangg syhg* 'Two and two are four.'

23. Nouns, Time and Place Words, and Localizers. — A *noun* is a syntactic word which can be placed in apposition with a D–AN compound, as *ren* in *jeyg ren* 'this man,' *shoei* in *i-bei shoei* 'a cup of water,' *yan* in *leang-jin yan* (or *yan leang-jin* in bookkeeping style) 'two catties of salt.'

Time and place words are like nouns in being used as subjects or objects, but they do not occur after D–AN compounds.[13] For example, *Shianntzay jenqhaol* 'Now is just right,' *Jell sh naal?* 'Where is here?' When there are two or three subjects including time and place words, the whole sentence can be regarded as layers of S–P predicates — Chinese-box fashion. The order is free to a certain extent, with preference for the order of actor:

[13] In this respect proper names are formally more like time and place words than nouns. From the point of formal logic, pronouns, time and place words, and descriptive phrases of the form "the so-and-so" all have reference to a particular and therefore cannot be further specified by a D–AN compound.

time: place. For example, *Woo jin.tian cherng.lii yeou-shyh* 'As for me, as for today, in-town has business, — I have business in town today.' Note that *shyr.howl* 'time,' *dih.fangl* 'place,' and similar words are nouns and not time and place words, as *ig dih.fangl* 'a place.'

A *localizer* is a bound word forming the second component of a subordinate compound, resulting in a time or place word. For details see Note 2, p. 152.

24. Substitutes. — The most important class of substitutes are the personal pronouns *nii* 'you (sing.),' *woo* 'I, me,' *ta* 'he, him, she, her, it,' *nii.men* 'you (pl.),' *woo.men* 'we, us,' *tzar.men* 'we, us,' *ta.men* 'they, them,' *sheir* 'who, whom?' (Lesson 1). The suffix *–.men* is abbreviated to *–m* before labials, often also before *–.de*. *Woom* is often further abbreviated to *mm* (a syllabic *m* on the 3rd Tone).

Of the two forms of 'we,' *woo.men* is the *exclusive* 'we' and *tzar.men* is the *inclusive* 'we.' For example, *Nii.men sh neu.ren, woo.men sh nan.ren; tzar.men dou.sh ren* 'You are women, we are men; we are all people.' (See Notes 17, p. 123 and 29, p. 134, and Figs. 1 and 2, p. 125.)

When *ta* refers to inanimate things, it is usually limited to the object position. *Ta.men* is not used for inanimate things in any position. Thus, *Jey.shie jyutz huay .le, bae .ta rheng.le .ba* 'These tangerines have spoiled, better throw it (i.e. them) away.'

Possessives of personal pronouns are formed by adding the subordinative suffix *.de*. Possessive pronouns are not used, as they are in English, when the possessor is obvious, as *Woo day.le mawtz jiow tzoou .le* 'I put on (my) hat and went away,' since it is presumably my own hat that I put on. On the other hand, there is a special use of the possessive pronoun not paralleled by English usage. Certain verb-object compounds take an inserted possessive where there would normally be a pronoun object in English, as *bang-mang* 'help-busy, — to help': *bang ta.de mang* 'help his being busy, — help him'; *daa-chah* 'strike digression, — to interrupt': *daa ta.de chah* 'strike his digression, — to interrupt him.' We shall speak of such verb-object compounds as taking a *possessive object*.

D–AN compounds form another large class of substitutes. For example, in *Jell yeou leangg cherntz, geei nii ig* 'There are two oranges here, I give you one,' the D–AN compound *ig* is a substitute.

The verb *lai* 'come' may be regarded as a substitute, or *pro-verb*, as in *Nii buhuey pu-chwang, ranq woo lai* 'You don't know how to make the bed, let me do it.' Compounds with *–yang* or *–yanql* 'manner' can also be used as pro-verbs, as *Bye nemm.yanql!* 'Don't do that!'

25. Verbs, Adjectives, and Prepositions. — A *verb* is a syntactic word which can be modified by the adverb *bu* (except that the verb *yeou* takes *mei*) and can be followed by the phrase suffix *.le*. These two characteristics are common to all verbs. From other characteristics we can distinguish seven types of verbs. We shall first describe the meanings of various types of verbs and then state their formal features in the form of a table.

Under *intransitive verbs (v.i.)*, we have (a) *action v.i.*, as *lai* 'come,' *tzuoh* 'sit,' *ku* 'cry, weep'; (b) *quality v.i.*, or *adjectives*, as *dah* 'big,' *shaa* 'foolish,' *shyng* 'all right, will do'; (c) *status v.i.*, as *binq* 'sick,' *terng* 'to ache,' *naw* 'to be noisy.' Under *transitive verbs (v.t.)* we have (d) *action v.t.*: the verbs in *kann-shih* 'see a play,' *chu-hann* 'issue sweat, — to sweat,' *sha-ren* 'kill people'; (e) *quality v.t.*: the verbs in *ay-tsair* 'love wealth, — avaricious,' *fey-shyh* 'cost work, — troublesome,' *shinn-for* 'believe in Buddha'; (f) *classificatory v.t.*, the verbs in *tzay-jia* 'is at home,' *shinq Wu* 'to have the surname of Wu,' *sh iatz* 'is a duck'; (g) *Auxiliary verbs*: the first verbs in *huey fei* 'can fly,' *keen shuo-huah* 'willing to talk,' *sheang chiuh* 'desire to go.'

As formal differentia of these types of verbs, we shall, besides the common points about *bu* and the phrase *.le*, consider the possibility of combination with the following:

Before the word suffix *–.le* (p. 40), before the progressive suffix *–j* (pronounced *–.jy* or *–.je*), after adverbs of degree like *heen* 'very' *genq* 'still more,' etc., and after and in series with the pretransitive *bae* (with object). In the following table, a " + " sign indicates that the form in question combines with the verb and a " – " sign that it does not.

	bu	*.le*	*–.le*	*–j*	*heen–*	*bae*
Action v.i. *lai* 'come'	+	+	(+) [14]	+	–	
Quality v.i. *dah* 'big'	+	+	(+)	– [15]	+	
Status v.i. *binq* 'sick'	+	+	(+)	+	+	
Action v.t. *kann-shih* 'see a play'	+	+	+	+	–	+
Quality v.t. *ay-tsair* 'love wealth'	+	+	+	–	+	–
Classif. v.t. *tzay-jia* 'is at home'	+	+	(+) [16]	–	–	–
Aux. v.(t.) *huey fei* 'can fly'	+	+	–	–	+	–

For bound verbs as complements, see verb-complement compounds, p. 43.

Prepositions are verbs which are usually in the first position in verbal expressions in series. For example, in *Woo sheir yee bu wey* 'I am not for

---

[14] Intransitive verbs take the word suffix *–.le* only before cognate objects or quantified objects, as in *binq.le san-tian* 'sick for three days.'

[15] Quality verbs take the suffix *–j* only in the special idiom *–j .ne* as in *dahj .ne!* 'bigger than you think!' Note that while *–j* is normally a suffix to the verb, it is placed, in this idiom, after the verb-object as a whole, as *Fey-shyh j .ne!* 'It takes an awful lot of trouble!'

[16] Classificatory verbs, especially the verb *sh* 'is,' rarely take the word suffix *–.le*.

anybody (in particular),' *wey* 'to be for' is the main verb, but the principal use of *wey* is in constructions like *Woo wey* (or *weyj* or *wey.le*) *nii show-tzuey* 'I suffer on your account.' Again, *Ta tzay-jia .ne* 'He is at home,' but *Ta tzay jia chiing-keh .ne* 'He is having company at home.' Other examples of prepositions are *tsorng* 'follow, from,' *daa* 'strike, from,' *jiee* 'from' (< *chii* 'rise'), *bii* 'compare, than.' Pretransitives (p. 162) *bae* (alternating with *bay* and *baa*) 'take,' *geei* 'give, for,' *ranq* 'yield, let,' *bey* 'covered,' 'by (agent),' *goan* 'control,' used as pretransitive to go with *jiaw* 'call,' *na* 'take, with,' — all these are prepositions in the sense defined here. The two words *yii* 'take, with' and *yu* '(to be) at' and compounds with *yu* as *guanyu* 'concerning' and *jyhyu* [17] 'as for' are always used in verbal expressions in series and not used as main verbs in the colloquial. The current usage of writing *Yu Beeipyng* 'at Peiping' at the end of prefaces still seems queer to many readers.

26. Adverbs and Conjunctions. — Monosyllabic adverbs are bound words in Chinese,[18] as *jiow lai* 'coming right away,' *buneng* 'cannot,' *dahshiaw* 'laugh loudly,' *shian tzoou* 'go first.' Adverbs of two or more syllables are free words, as they can be separated by pause, as *Nii yiijinq shu .le*, or *Nii .a, yiijinq .a, shu .le* 'You have already lost (the bet, etc.)'; *Ta meijoel yng .le* 'He, there is no telling, has won, — he possibly has won.' Other examples of free adverbs are: *idinq* 'certainly,' *tzyhran* 'of course,' *swo.shinq* 'might as well,' *shinq.kuei* 'fortunately,' *yeuan'iual* 'at a good distance.'

There are probably no true *conjunctions* in Chinese. Some words like coordinate conjunctions are really verbs. Thus, *Jeyg gen neyg iyanq* 'This and that are alike' is to be analyzed as 'This following that is same,' so that *gen neyg* is really the first member of verbal expressions in series. Similarly, *Jang San gen Lii Syh sh ren* 'Jang San following Lii Syh is human being, — Jang San and Lii Syh are men.' The word ₒ*hann* (alternating with ₒ*hay* and reading pronunciation *her*) is used in the same way as *gen*.

Other words which are like conjunctions are free adverbs, which can be set off like miniature sentences. For example, *Kee.sh ta bu doong* 'It's however (like this): he doesn't understand,' or, again, *Ta kee.sh bu doong* 'He, however, doesn't understand.' In fact, practically all conjunctions can be inserted between the subject and the verb and are thus like interpolated comments of 'it-seems-to-me' type. Other examples are *yaw.sh* 'if' (from 'being like that'), *jearu* 'if' (from 'granting as'), *jihran* 'since' (from 'already so'), *binqchiee* 'moreover' (from 'together also'), *suooₒyii* 'therefore' (from 'there with'). *Jiow* 'then' and *kee* 'however,' being monosyllabic adverbs, are always bound with the following verb and must

---

[17] But *bujyhyu* 'not as bad as' (Lesson 21, Exercise 1, p. 273.) is always a main verb.
[18] For pedagogical reasons, we spell them separately in most cases.

therefore follow the subject, as *Bu shiah-yeu woo jiow lai* '(If) it doesn't rain, then I will go.' *Woo kee gow .le* 'I, however, have had enough.'

27. Interjections and Vocatives. — *Interjections* are the only words which are always free. Another formal feature of an interjection is that it has no tone, but only an intonation, usually of the pitch pattern of 42: ↘. We shall spell interjections in the basic form of the finals, but if the same syllable serves either as a phrase suffix (which is always bound) or as an interjection (which is always free), we spell the former in the basic form and the latter in the 4th Tone. For example, *Lai .a!* 'Do come!' but *Lai, .ah!* 'Come, please do!' Some interjections have special intonations which are even more important in carrying the meaning than the sounds. For example, *Ae! Mm!* or *Eeng!* (i.e. [ə̄:] or [ŋ:]), with a long 3rd Tone, often with a fall after the rise, all mean 'Oh, no indeed!'

Other parts of speech used as interjections lose most or all of their tones. For example, in *Hao-jia.huoo!* 'My goodness!' *Hao* (3rd Tone) is only a shade lower than *jia* (1st Tone), as compared with the phrase *hao jia.huoo* 'a good tool,' in which *hao* is distinctly low and *jia* is distinctly high in pitch.

Terms of direct address also lose most or all of their tones. Thus, in the word *jiee.jiee* 'elder sister' in a sentence has the tone pattern of ⌐ ˈ|, but in calling *Jiee.jiee!* the first syllable is only slightly lower than the second, ending with a lengthening of the vowel and a drop in pitch. We can therefore say that Chinese nouns have a vocative case, characterized by narrowing or loss of tone and a suffix consisting of a drop in pitch.

G. TRANSLATION OF ENGLISH GRAMMATICAL CATEGORIES

While Chinese grammar proper should deal only with the grammatical features which are actually found in the Chinese language, an English-speaking student of Chinese cannot help being concerned about how English grammatical categories will be translated into Chinese. This is a perfectly healthy state of mind, provided that the student remembers the general fact that every grammatical feature of one language does not necessarily correspond to some similar feature, or even any grammatical feature, of another language. Any utterance in an actual context can be translated fairly accurately, to be sure, but not necessarily by the same means of expression. Thus, the English phrase 'No, thank you!' can be translated more "idiomatically" by a smile and a polite gesture than by the recent translation borrowing *Duoshieh, buyaw .le!* 'Many thanks, I don't want any more.' Keeping in mind the fact that grammatical features do not correspond, we shall now try to see how in general various forms in English grammar can be translated into Chinese.

28. Article and Number of Nouns. — No articles are required before Chinese nouns; nor has Chinese distinction of number. Nouns taken in the generic sense also take the simple form. We do not say, '*The lion* is a noble animal,' or '*A fool* and his money are soon parted,' or '*Houses* are scarce,' but simply say, '*Man* is a rational animal.' In first mentioning a particular individual, as in telling a story, *i* 'one' plus some AN will play the part of the indefinite article, as *Tsorngchyan yeou ig hwu.li* 'Formerly there was a fox.' After a verb, *i* is often omitted, as *Na .beel shu .lai* 'Bring a book here,' where *beel* is the AN in *i-beel* 'a volume.'

Definite and indefinite reference is often determined by word order. A noun in subject position usually refers to something definite,[19] while a noun in object position usually refers to something indefinite. For example, *Shu tzay naal?* 'Where is the book?' but, *Naal yeou shu?* 'Where is a book (or are some books)? (lit. 'What place has book?') If an object has a definite reference, the fact is indicated by a demonstrative or some other suitable modifier, as *Woo kann-wan.le jey-beel shu .le* 'I have finished reading this book.' But the preferred construction is *Jey-beel shu woo kann-wan.le*, or, with the pretransitive (Note 49, p. 162), *Woo bae jey-beel shu kann-wan.le*. (See also Note 1, p. 206.)

Nouns in apposition have two rather different types of translational equivalents, a loose kind and a close kind. For example, *woo.de jerl Wenlan* 'my nephew Wenlan' or *Wenlan, woo.de ig jerl* 'Wenlan, a nephew of mine,' are cases of loose apposition, which are coordinate phrases. On the other hand, in a close apposition, with the specific word before the generic, the whole construction is one subordinate compound and the order is not reversible, as '*dah'-tzyh* 'the word "dah",' '*a'-in* 'the sound "a",' *Wang .Shian.sheng* 'Mr. Wang.'

29. Each, Every, All, Some, Any, etc. — 'Each' is translated by the determinative *meei-* plus an AN, as *meei-yanql ig* 'one of each kind.' The determinative *geh-* (not the AN *-geh*) is often translated as 'each' in Chinese-English dictionaries, but actually it is more accurate to equate it to 'the various,' as *geh-sheeng* 'the various provinces.' *Geh-ren* (but more commonly *meeig ren*) is the only common word in which *geh-* is to be translated as 'each.'

'Every,' as we have seen is translated by reduplication of the AN plus an optional *-l*, as *hweihwei* or *hweihwel* 'every time.'

'All' is translated by the adverb *dou* 'in all cases, without exception,' as *Keh.ren dou daw .le* 'The guests have all arrived'; or by *suoo yeou .de . . . dou* 'whatever there is . . . in all cases,' as *Suoo yeou .de tzarjyh woo dou yaw dinq* 'I want to order all the magazines.'

---

[19] See Joseph Mullie, *The Structural Principles of the Chinese Language*, English translation by A. C. Versichel, Peiping, 1932, vol. 1, pp. 160 ff. The point was brought out still more explicitly by Lien Sheng Yang in discussions with the author

'Some' is expressed by *yeou .de* 'there are those which,' [20] as *Yeou .de ren bu chy suann* 'There are people who don't eat garlic, — some people don't eat garlic.' 'Some' in the sense of 'a little' is *-.deal* or *-.i.deal* and 'a few' is *jiig* 'several' or *yeou jiig* 'there are a few.'

Compounds with 'some' are expressed by *sherm.me* 'what' or *naal* 'where,' as *Woo sheang chy .deal .sherm.me* 'I want to eat something'; *Tzar.men sheang g sherm fartz .lai shuo-shinn .ta* 'Let's think of some way to convince him'; *Tzar.men deei shanq naal wal.wal* 'We must go somewhere and have a good time.'

'Any' and forms with 'any' are expressed by *sherm.me, tzeem.me, naal, neei–*, etc. plus *dou*, as *Ta sherm dou chy* 'He eats anything'; *Jeyg sheir dou neng gaw.sonq .nii* 'Anybody can tell you that'; *Tzeem gae dou shyng* 'It will be all right to alter it any old way.' 'Not any' or 'no–' compounds are translated by ... *dou bu* (or *mei*) or ... *yee bu* (or *mei*), as *Ta sherm dou bu doong* 'He doesn't understand anything'; *Naal yee jao.bu-jaur farngtz* 'Can't find a house anywhere'; *Ta tzeem yee bucherng* 'There is no pleasing him'; *Neeig dou bu hershyh* 'None is suitable.'

'Either' and 'neither' are translated like 'any' and 'not any,' as *Neeig dou shyng* 'Either one will do'; *Neei-baa yaw.shyr dou bu pey jey-baa suoo* 'Neither key fits this lock.'

'Another' in the sense of 'a different one' is *bye.de*, as *Geei .woo i-baa bye.de gaanjuei* 'Give me another screwdriver' (the one you gave me was too small). 'Another' in the sense of 'an additional one' is rendered by placing the adverb *hair* 'still' or *tzay* 'again' before the verb, as *Tzay geei .woo i-baa gaanjuei* 'Give me another screwdriver' (one is not enough). 'The other' (of two) is expressed by *ney–* plus AN, as *Mei ren kann.jiann.guoh yueh.lianq .de ney.miall* 'Nobody has seen the other side of the moon.'

30. Adjectives. — Since Chinese adjectives are verbs, they form predicates without requiring a verb 'to be,' as *Ta chyong* 'He is poor.' The verb *sh* is used before an adjective only under the following conditions: (1) when there is a *.de* at the end, which makes the expression following *sh* a substantive, as *Jeyg shoeiguoo sh sheng .de* 'This fruit is unripe,' where *sheng .de* stands for *sheng .de shoeiguoo* 'unripe fruit' or *sheng .de dong.shi* 'something unripe'; (2) for contrast, as *Ta sh deryih, bu.sh jiau.aw* 'He is proud, not conceited'; (3) for emphatic assertion, as *Ta* **sh** *chyong* 'He *is* poor'; (4) in the concessive form V–.sh–V (Note 12, p. 184), which is really a variety of the preceding, as *Hao .sh hao, (kee.sh ...)* '(As for being) good, it *is* good, — it's good, to be sure, (but ...)'

All such uses of *sh* are also possible before other verbs as well as adjectives, as (1) *Ta sh lai bay.wanq .nii .de* 'He came to call on you,' where *.de* has the force of 'He is one who ...' or 'His is a case of ...'; (2) *Woo sh*

---

[20] This fits in with the principle in formal logic that particular propositions imply existence.

chiuh song .ta, bu.sh jie .ta 'I went to see him off, not to meet him'; (3) *Ta sh shinn Jidujiaw* 'He does believe in Christianity'; (4) *Ta jieh .sh jieh, kee.sh bu geei* 'He does lend, it's true, but he doesn't give.'

For adjectives which admit of degrees, the comparative is expressed by *-.deal* 'some' or *-.i.deal* 'a little,' as *Ta jiel hao.deal .le* 'He is better today.' Sometimes, the simple form is used if the comparison is obvious, as *Hair.sh jeyg hao* 'After all this is good, — this is better.' In explicit comparison, 'than' is translated by *bii* 'compare' in the first member of verbal expressions in series, as *Ta bii ta sheau* 'He is smaller (or younger) than he.' When *bii* is used, *-.deal* or *-.i.deal* is optional.

Equality is expressed by *yeou* 'have,' as *Woo yeou nii (nemm) gau* 'I have you (that) tall, — I am as tall as you.' Another form of expressing equality is *gen . . . iyanq* 'with . . . same,' as *Shoei gen huoo iyanq weishean* 'Water with fire same dangerous, — water is as dangerous as fire.' Inferior degree is expressed by *mei* or *mei.yeou*, as *Jeyg mei neyg (nemm) hao* 'This has not that (that) good, — this is not so good as that.'

Superlative degree is expressed by *diing* or *tzuey* 'most, -est,' as *diing hao* 'best.' Note that 'had better' is rendered by the superlative form, as *Tzar.men diing hao tzoou .ba* 'We had better go.' For further examples see Lesson 7, esp. Note 21, p. 169.

Intensives are expressed by *heen* 'very,' *tiing* 'pretty, rather,' *-.jyi.le* 'awfully,' as *hao-jyi.le* 'awfully good,' *. . . .de heen* 'extremely,' as *kuoh .de heen* 'extremely wealthy,' and by many other forms. Because *heen* is frequently used only to round out a monosyllabic predicative adjective, its intensive force is somewhat weaker than English 'very.'

31. Prepositions. — English prepositions may be translated in four different ways. (1) A verb 'to be' followed by a preposition can be translated by the transitive verb *tzay* 'to be at,' as *Ta tzay Hannkoou* 'He is at Hankow.' If the preposition expresses a more specific locality than 'at,' a localizer is added to the object in Chinese. Thus, *Chwan tzay hae.shanq*, lit. 'The ship is at sea-top,' where *tzay* translates 'is on' so far as 'being there' is concerned, but it takes a localizer *-.shanq* 'upper part' to give the 'on' part, as distinguished from 'in,' 'under,' etc. (Lesson 5). (2) When a prepositional phrase modifies a noun in English, it must precede the noun in Chinese, usually with the modifying particle *.de*, as *tzay hae.shanq .de chwan* 'being on sea-top kind of ship, — the ship on the sea.' *Tzay* can usually be omitted, as *shu.lii .de tzyh* 'book-inside's word, — the words in the book.' (3) If a prepositional phrase follows a verb in English and expresses a modifying circumstance or manner, it is translated as the first member of verbal expressions in series, as *Ta tzay Meei.gwo niann-shu* 'He being in America studies, — he studies in America.' (See also pp. 48–49.) (4) When an English prepositional phrase following a verb expresses a result or an important point in the predication, it is translated by a complement, that is, a phrase after the verb. For example, *Ta juh .tzay Beeipyng* 'He lives in Peiping,' emphasizing the idea that his home is Peiping, whereas *Ta tzay Beeipyng juh* 'He lives in Peiping' emphasizes the idea of his maintaining an abode and the locality is only an accompanying circumstance (Note 28, p.154). In a similar way, an adverbial phrase expressing an important point of a sentence is often placed in a predicate position, as *Ta chy .de mann* 'The way he eats (is) slow, — he eats slowly,' since the point is not that he eats — for he eats anyway — but that he eats slowly.

32. Voice of verbs. — There is no distinction of voice in Chinese, the direction of action depending upon the context (p. 35). Thus, *Woo yaw shii lean* 'I want to wash my face': *Lean hair mei shii .ne* 'My face has not yet been washed.' An agent expression similar to the 'by'-form in English passive construction is translated into the first part of a verbal expression in series with *geei* 'give' or *bey* 'suffer' as the verb. For example, *Liingtz geei .ta sy-poh.le* 'The collar give him tore-broken, — the collar has been torn by him.' (See also Note 45, p. 193.) A more frequent way of translating an agent expression for past action is to make it into a substantive-predicate construction. Thus, *I.fwu sh woo mae .de* 'The clothes are I-bought ones, — the clothes were bought by me'; *Jey-tyau kuhtz sh ta tanq .de* 'This trouser is he-ironed one, — this pair of trousers was ironed by him.'

33. Tense and Aspect of Verbs. — Chinese verbs have no tense. Thus, the same form *sh* is used both in *Woo sh Jong.gworen* 'I am a Chinese,' and *Koong Tzyy sh Luu.gworen* 'Confucius was a native of the State of Lu.' In *Jiel guoh-nian* 'Today (we) celebrate the New Year,' the same verb will also do for *tzwol* 'yesterday' or *miengl* 'tomorrow.' When it is desired to state explicitly that a thing has already happened or did happen on a previous occasion, the verb may be followed by the suffix *–.guoh*, the word suffix *–.le* or the phrase suffix *.le.* That these are not Chinese tense forms can be seen from the fact that they are not constant features of verbs determined automatically by the time of the event, but may or may not be used according to whether the speaker wishes to bring out explicitly the time element. Note that action verbs (p. 48) are more likely to have these suffixes than the other types of verbs.

When the object expresses a specified quantity or number (including 'one') and the verb refers to a past event, the verb always takes the suffix *.le*, as *shuey.le i-jiaw* 'slept a nap, — had a nap,' *kann.jiann.le shyrg ren* 'saw ten people.' The difference between the English simple past form for an isolated event and the perfect form for an event regarded as now having been completed often corresponds, respectively, to the use of the word suffix *–.le* and the use of both the word suffix and the phrase suffix *.le*. For example, *Woo jaw.le i-jang shianq* 'I took a photograph' (and the incident is considered closed): *Woo jaw.le i-jang shianq .le* 'I have taken a photograph' (and may take another or do something else). If the object is not in quantified form, it is possible to say, for example, *Woo jaw.le shianq .le* or *Woo jaw-shianq .le* 'I have taken (a) photograph,' but a form like *Woo jaw.le shianq* does not usually stand alone as a complete utterance. (See also Note 48, p. 193.)

Past time is often implied by the use of the phrase suffix *.de* in the predicate, especially when there is a specific point about the event. For example, *Ta tzwol lai .de* or *Ta sh tzwol lai .de* 'He is one who came yesterday, — it was yesterday that he came, — he came yesterday,' where the use of *.de* implies that his coming can already be classified and is therefore presumably a past event.

If there is an object, the preferred form (not used in central or southern dialects) is to put *.de* before the object. For example, *Woo sh gangtsair gua .de lean*, lit. 'I am a face which was scraped just a while ago, — I had a shave just a while ago.' A sentence of this form could be really ambiguous if taken out of context. Thus, *Ta sh chiuh.nian sheng .de sheauharl* could mean either 'He (or she) is a child who was born last year' or 'It was last year that she gave birth to a child.' A sentence like *Ta sh i-jeou-syh-ba nian sheuanjeu .de tzoongtoong* may mean (1) 'He was the president who was elected in 1948,' or (2) 'It was in 1948 that he was elected President,' or (3) 'It was in 1948 that he voted for a president,' the last being the construction under discussion. In an actual context there is, of course, little chance for ambiguity.

Progressive action or event is expressed by the adverbs ₀*tzay.nall*, ₀*day.nall*, *tzay* 'right there,' *jenq* 'just,' the word suffix *-j* '-ing,' or the phrase suffix *.ne*, or combination of these, as *Ta jenq tzay.nall kannj baw .ne* 'He right there reading newspaper, — he is reading a newspaper.'

Chinese is like English in having no future form of the verb, as *Miengl fanq-jiah* 'Tomorrow is holiday.' When necessary, the idea of future events is expressed by auxiliary verbs like *yaw* 'will,' *huey* 'will likely,' or by adverbs like *jiow* 'then, soon,' *kuay* 'fast, on the point of.' Note that an intransitive verb of action without any adverb or suffix is usually understood to apply to future time, as *Woo chiuh* 'I am going,' or 'I plan to go.'

34. Infinitives. — Since infinitives are used for a variety of purposes, there is no one way of translating them. Infinitives as subjects are translated as verbal subjects (p. 36). Infinitives after verbs are translated as the second verb in verbal expressions in series, as *jiaw .ta lai* 'tell him to come.' Infinitives of purpose are usually expressed by ₀*chiuh* before the verb in question, *.chiuh* 'go' after it, or both ₀*chiuh* before and *.chiuh* after, or, less frequently, by *lai* in a similar way. For example:

56   INTRODUCTION

$$day\ chyan \begin{cases} .chiuh\ mae\text{-}tsay \\ mae\text{-}tsay\ .chiuh \\ .chiuh\ mae\text{-}tsay\ .chiuh \end{cases} \begin{matrix} \text{'bring money go} \\ \text{buy provisions'} \end{matrix}$$

$$pay\ ren \begin{cases} .lai\ kann\ .woo \\ kann\ .woo\ .lai\ ^{21} \\ .lai\ kann\ .woo\ .lai\ ^{21} \end{cases} \begin{matrix} \text{'send someone} \\ \text{to see me'} \end{matrix}$$

$$sheang.chu\ .deal\ wanyell\ .lai\ ^{22} \begin{cases} .chiuh\ piann\text{-}ren \\ piann\text{-}ren\ .chiuh \\ .chiuh\ piann\text{-}ren\ .chiuh \\ .lai\ piann\text{-}ren \\ piann\text{-}ren\ .lai \\ .lai\ piann\text{-}ren\ .lai \end{cases}$$

All the six forms mean 'think of some trick to fool people.'
Instead of *lai* or *chiuh* before the verb, it is also possible to use *hao* '(in order) the better to,' which may or may not be followed by *.chiuh* after the main verb, but rarely followed by *.lai*. For examples of *hao* in this sense, see Exercise 2, p. 249.

35. Coordinate Conjunctions. — We have seen that coordination in Chinese takes no conjunction and that Chinese conjunctions and adverbs are hard to distinguish. English 'and' between clauses is usually not translated, as *Jiel tial hao, woo deei haohaul lih.yonq .ta* 'It's a fine day, and I must make good use of it.' For special emphasis, adverbs like *erlchiee* or *binqchiee* 'moreover' and *yow* 'again' (the last always after the subject) can be used, as *Ta tzoou .le, erlchiee ta tzoou .de heen jyi* 'He has left, and he left in a hurry.'

'Both ... and' is rendered by the adverbs *yow ... yow*, or *yee ... yee*, as *Ta yow cheau yow tsong.ming* 'He is both skillful and clever'; *Muu.dan yee kai-hual.le, meiguey yee kai-hual .le* 'Both the peonies and the roses have opened their flowers' (note repetition of the predicate).

'Either ... or' can be rendered by $_o$*huoh.jee* (alternating with $_o$*huoh.sh*, *.he.je*, *.he.sh*) ... $_o$*huoh.jee*, as *Huoh.sh nii shanq woo.jell lai, huoh.sh woo shanq nii.nall chiuh* 'Either you come to my place, or I go to your place.' A much commoner way of saying that, however, is to put the alternatives in the form of a condition. Thus, *Bu.sh nii shanq woo.jell lai, jiow.sh woo shanq nii.nall chiuh* 'If it isn't a case of your coming to my place, then it's a case of my going to your place.' [23] (See Note 32, p. 161.)

---

[21] *Lai* with full tone here would mean 'see me come.'
[22] This *.lai* is the second part of the split complement *-.chu.lai* and has nothing to do with the indication of purpose.
[23] This fits in with the principle in formal logic that 'p or q' is equivalent to 'if not p, then q.'

36. Relatives and Dependent Clauses. — Non-restrictive relatives are translated by a pivotal object-subject construction or by using a resuming *ta* if it is a person, as *Woo yeou ig perng.yeou (ta) tzuey ay shuo-huah* 'I have a friend, who is most fond of talking.' Restrictive relatives are translated by using the subordinative suffix *.de*, as *tzuey ay shuo-huah .de ren* 'the man who is most fond of talking' (Note 38, p. 132). If the relative is an object in the relative clause (often omitted in English), it can be translated by the emphatic adverb *suoo*, as *Jyakeh (suoo) tzaw de farngtz* 'the house (that) Jack built' (Note 20, p. 184). If the relative is in a possessive form or follows a preposition, it can be disregarded in the translation, as *tzyh tay sheau .de shu* 'a book whose (or in which the) print is too small,' *woo lai .de dih.fangl* 'the place I come from.' If necessary for clearness, a preposition *with an object* is used in the *.de* construction, as *Woo tsorng nall lai .de dih.fangl* 'the place I come from (there)' (Note 34, p. 201).

'When' can be translated as *.de ₒshyr.howl*, as *Ta shuey-jaur.le .de .shyr.howl hair shuo-huah* 'He fall asleep's time still talks, — he still talks when he is asleep.' But when 'when' means 'after' or 'as soon as,' then the suffix *-.le* is added to the verb and no *.de ₒshyr.howl* is necessary, as *Ta shuo-wan.le huah jiow tzoou .le* 'When he finished talking, he went away'; *Ta kann.jiann.le woo shiah.le i-tiaw* 'When he saw me, he was startled.'

The translation of a conditional or concessive clause precedes that of the main clause to which it is subordinated, as *Yaw.sh shiah-yeu woo jiow bu chiuh* 'If it rains, (then) I won't go.' A conditional or concessive clause never follows the main clause except as an afterthought after a dash, in which case the words *.de .huah* '(if it is) a matter of,' are added, as *Woo bu chiuh — yaw.sh tial bu chyng .de .huah* 'I am not going — unless it clears up.' A premeditated dependent clause placed without pause after the main clause (found in some contemporary writing) is definitely a Europeanism and is appreciated as such.

'Because' or 'since' is mostly translated by *inₒwey*, and 'so' or 'therefore' by *suooₒyii* as *Ta in.wey shang.le feng, suoo.yii bu lai .le* 'He has caught cold, so is not coming, — as he has caught cold, he is not coming.' A clause with *inₒwey* can be placed last if *.de ₒyuan.guh* 'the reason of' is placed at the end, thus making it substantive predicate. *Yeou .de meei.gworen buhuey shuo Jong.gwo-huah, (sh) in.wey ta.men tsornglai mei haohaul shyue.guoh .de .yuan.guh* 'Some Americans cannot speak Chinese, (that's) because they have never studied it properly.'

37. Negation and Interrogation. — Simple negation is expressed by using *bu* 'not' before the word negated, as *keen lai* 'willing to come,' *bukeen lai* 'not willing to come,' *keen bu lai* 'willing not to come,' *bukeen bu lai* 'unwilling not to come.' The negative of *yeou* 'have' is *mei*, or *meiₒyeou*.

The negative of an imperative verb is *bye* or *buyaw* 'don't . . . !' or *berng* (< *buyonq*) 'no use, — need not.'

The negative of a verb ending in *–.guoh*, *–.le*, or *.le* expressing completion or past time, takes the form of *mei* or *mei.yeou* before, as *lai.le*, *lai.guoh* 'have come, did come,' *mei lai*, *mei.yeou lai* 'have not come, did not come'; *–.guoh* can also be retained when *mei* or *mei.yeou* is used, but *.le* (in this sense) always drops out in the negative.

The negative of a verb with a potential complement of the form V.*de*–C takes the form V.*bu*–C, as *tsa.bu-gan* 'cannot wipe dry.' (See Note 39, p. 145.)

The negative of a verb with the progressive suffix *–j* takes *mei(.yeou)* or *bu.sh* according as the denial is applied to the fact or to the content. Thus, *Woo mei denqj yeal* 'I was *not* staring': *Wo bu.sh denqj yeal* 'I was not *staring*' (but doing something else).

When negation is applied to a phrase or a whole sentence, *bu.sh* 'it is not that . . .' is used instead of the simple *bu*, as *Woo bu.sh idinq bukeen* 'Not that I insist on refusing.'

Questions in Chinese can be divided into four types: (a) questions with interrogative words, (b) disjunctive questions, (c) A-not-A questions, (d) yes-or-no questions.

(a) *Questions with interrogative words* are the easiest to ask and answer. The rule is: Ask as you would be answered. Thus, *Nii sh sheir?* 'You are who, — who are you?' because the answer is not in the order 'Wang am I,' but, as in English, 'I am Wang.' *Nii yaw kann liibayjii .de baw?* 'You want to read what-day-of-the-week's newspaper?' *Woo yaw kann liibay'ell .de* 'I want to read Tuesday's.' (This question, which is a perfectly natural one in Chinese, cannot even be asked in the same specific way in English.)

(b) *Disjunctive questions*, or questions requesting a choice of alternatives, are asked by putting the alternatives in coordination by juxtaposition, as *Nii chy-fann chy miann?* 'Will you eat rice or noodles?' A much more frequent form, however, consists in adding a verb *sh* 'it is a case of,' or ₀*hair.sh*, 'it is after all a case of' (both usually in the neutral tone), before both terms or before the second term only. Thus,

(1) *Nii .sh   chy-fann .sh   chy-miann?*
(2) *Nii   chy-fann .sh   chy-miann?*
(3) *Nii .hair.sh chy-fann .hair.sh chy-miann?*
(4) *Nii   chy-fann .hair.sh chy-miann?*

Of these, the last is the commonest form.

Note that the English question written as 'Will you eat rice or noodles?' is ambiguous if the intonation is not known. If the intonation rises on 'rice' and falls on 'noodles,' it is a disjunctive question and the translation will be: *Nii chy-fann .hair.sh chy-miann .a?* to which the answer may be

Chy-fann or *Chy-miann*. With a generally rising intonation (or, in southern British intonation, with a dip before the final rise), it is a yes-or-no question and the Chinese will be: *Nii chy .bu .chy fann .huoh.jee miann .a?* to which the expected answer will be *Chy* 'Yes, I will eat (either of the two)' or *Bu chy* 'No (I am not hungry).' In the first case, 'or' is translated by ₀*hair.sh;* in the second case, by ₀*huoh.jee*. For further examples see Note 47, p. 145.

(c) *A-not-A questions* are disjunctive questions in which the choice is between something and its negative. In such cases, the word ₀*hair.sh* or *.sh* is almost always omitted. The English equivalent of such a question is the common yes-or-no question. *Nii chou-ian .bu .chou .a?* 'You smoke (or) don't smoke, — do you smoke?' *Nii daw.guoh Beeipyng .mei.yeou* 'You have been to Peiping or have not, — have you ever been to Peiping?' Since these are disjunctive questions, they cannot be answered by words expressing agreement or disagreement, like *Duey .le, Sh .de* or *Bu.sh*, but must have the terms in the disjunction repeated, as *Woo chou* 'I do (smoke)' or *Bu chou* 'I don't'; *Daw.guoh* 'I have been there' or *Mei.yeou* 'I have not.' Of course if *sh* happens to be the main verb in the original question, then the answer will be *Sh .de* or *Bu.sh*, on a par with *Chy* or *Bu chy*.

Note that when the verb is *yeou*, the 'not-A' part of the A-not-A form of question becomes *.mei.yeou*, as *Jell yeou deng .mei.yeou?* 'Has this place a light?' Since, also, the negation of a verb with *.le* is *mei.yeou*, a question with *.le* in the A-not-A form take the following form: *Ta daw le .mei.yeou?* 'He has arrived (or) has not, — has he arrived?'

(d) True *yes-or-no questions* are less frequent than in English, since most yes-or-no questions are put in the disjunctive A-not-A form, as described above. Yes-or-no questions are in the form of posed statements with the addition of one of the particles *.ma, .a, .ba* (< *bu .a*) (cf. Ex. 3, p. 139), or of a miniature disjunctive question *.sh .bu.sh*, like the French *'n'est-ce pas?'* For assent to such questions one can use *Sh .de* 'It is so,' *Duey .le* 'That's right,' *.Ềh* 'Uh-huh' or a syllabic *.M* or *.Eng* 'M-hm!' 'Yeah;' and for dissent *Bu* 'No,' *Bu.jie* 'No,' *Bu.sh* 'Not so,' or *Buduey* 'wrong!'

Note that while yes-or-no questions in English call for affirmation or negation, questions under (d) call for agreement or disagreement, which is not the same thing unless the question is in the positive form. If the question is in the negative, then the answer in Chinese will seem to be the opposite to that of the English. For example, if the question is: *Nii bu shii.huan leushyng .ma?* 'You don't like to travel?' and if the answer is one of dissent, it will be: *Bu, woo shii.huan leushyng* 'Not so, I do like to travel.' On the other hand, if the question is: *Niim mei.yeou shiangjiau .ma?* 'Have you no bananas?' and if the answer is one of agreement (and therefore in the negative), it will be: *Sh .de, woom mei.yeou shiangjiau* 'Yes, we have no bananas.'

CHAPTER IV THE CHARACTERS

This course is so designed that the student can either start learning the characters with the first lesson, or, as a better alternative, go through all the twenty-four lessons in romanization to acquire a speaking knowledge of the language and then begin again from Lesson 1 to study the same text in characters. For certain purposes, one can go on studying the spoken language without learning the characters. But if one wishes to gain access to written or printed material, or to any part of the vast body of Chinese literature, the difficult task of learning to read characters will have to be faced sooner or later. In starting with characters, however, one should never allow them to be merely associated with English words, thus short-circuiting the Chinese pronunciation and losing the feeling of the Chinese constructions. This practice would vitiate not only the learning of the language, but also the proper learning of the writing. You cannot read a living language by regarding it as dead.

1. Pictographs and Ideographs. — Ancient Chinese writing is usually described as being pictorial or ideographic. Thus, a circle with a dot inside it is the character for 'sun' and three horizontal strokes represent the number 'three.' In Chinese tradition, six categories of characters called *liowshu* [1] are recognized. (1) *Shianqshyng* 'pictographs' are the easiest to understand. (2) *Jyyshyh* 'simple ideographs' are characters consisting of simple diagrammatic indications of ideas, as ⊥ for 'up' and ⊤ for 'down' or 一, 二, 三 for the numbers 'one, two, three.' (3) *Hueyyih* 'compound ideographs' are characters whose meaning is the combination of the meanings of their parts. Stock examples of these are 止 'stop' + 戈 'arms' = 武 'military'; 亻 'man' + 言 'word' = 信 'honest'; 日 'sun' + 月 'moon' = 明 'bright.' Characters under the preceding three categories form only a small minority of all characters. They are comparatively independent of the words in the language they represent. For example, three strokes would form as good a sign for the English word 'three' as for the Chinese word *san*. Conceivably the Chinese system of writing could have developed along its own line into a complete system of symbols, independently of the Chinese language. Actually, however, from very ancient times, the written characters have become so intimately associated with the words of the language that they have lost their functions as pictographs or ideographs in their own right and become conventionalized visual representations of spoken words, or "logographs." They are no longer direct symbols

---

[1] First used systematically by Hsü Shên (d. circa 120 A.D.) in his 9353-word dictionary *Shuo-wên*.

of ideas, but only symbols of ideas in so far as the spoken words they represent are symbols of ideas.[2] One should not, therefore, be misled by the popular conception that an analysis of the formation of characters will lead to a correct understanding of the Chinese words written with them. To be sure, characters often contain stories and histories which are helpful to the memory, but the actual meaning of each word has to be learned as such. Thus, the word *wuu* 'military,' is written with the character 武, made up of 止 'stop' and 戈 'weapons, arms,' i.e. '(the power to) stop armed force.' Likewise, the word *shinn*, written 信, means 'honest.' The traditional analysis of the character is 'a man's word,' but it requires a further act of memory to know that it is the proverbial "Chinaman's word" that is meant.

2. **Loan Characters, Phonetic Compounds, and Derivative Characters.** — The vast majority of characters belong to three other categories, which have to do with phases of the development of characters functioning as logographs. In devising characters for words, obviously the meaning of many words could not be pictured. A common practice was to borrow a character whose word had the same sound as the word for which a character was sought. Thus, in Archaic Chinese, there was a word *ləg* for a kind of wheat, which was written with a picture of the plant. (See Table 2A, p. 67.) Now there was a homonymous word *ləg* 'come.' Rather than invent another character for this word with a meaning that was hard to picture or indicate diagrammatically, the ancient writers simply borrowed the character for the plant and wrote the word for 'come' with it. Such characters are known as (4) *jeajieh* 'loan characters' or 'borrowed characters.'

In the example cited, the original word happens to have become obsolete long ago. In some cases, both the original word and the word for which the character was borrowed exist side by side, as *ran* 然 'to burn,' the character also used for the word *ran* 'thus, so.' To differentiate the two, an extra part 火 'fire' was added to the character (which, as an ideographic compound, already contains a part meaning 'fire' in the form of four dots at the bottom), thus making an 'enlarged character' 燃 for *ran* 'to burn,'

[2] This point was brought out clearly by Peter S. Du Ponceau in his book *A Dissertation on the Nature and Character of the Chinese System of Writing*, Philadelphia, 1838, esp. pp. xi and xxii. William F. Edgerton, in his note on Ideograms in English Writing, *Language*, 17.2. 148–50 (1941), cited some interesting cases, such as the symbol *2* standing for an idea represented by various words or parts of words like *two*, *sec-* (in *2nd*), etc. Though similar cases exist in Chinese writing, they are not much more frequent than in English. For practically all Chinese characters have long since become logographs. Thus, both 二 and 兩 seem to represent the idea of 'two,' but one represents the word *ell* (or, strictly, the class of words in all dialects cognate with Mandarin *ell*) and the other the word *leang* (and its cognates). These words and the characters representing them are not interchangeable, and their occurrence is governed by purely grammatical, and not by mathematical, conditions. See also Peter A. Boodberg, "Some Proleptical Remarks on the Evolution of Archaic Chinese," *Harvard Journal of Asiatic Studies*, 2.344.331.

allowing the original character to be used only for the word *ran* 'thus, so.' Characters so enlarged belong to a group called (5) *shyngsheng* or *shyesheng* 'phonetic compounds.' The original character 然 *ran* is called the 'phonetic' and the added part is called the 'signific,' which in the majority of cases is also the radical. (See § 3 below.) Similarly, *woang* 'a net,' 罔, is now written 網, enlarged by 糸, a signific associated with threads or strings, while the original character 罔 is borrowed exclusively to write the homonymous word *woang* 'have not.'

Besides the enlargement of a loan character, there is a second source of phonetic compounds. Words in every language acquire extended meanings. Thus, the word *wen* 'line, streak' is written with the ideograph 文. By extension (not by loan), the same word also has the figurative meanings of 'writing, literature, culture.' To distinguish in writing between the literal and the figurative meanings of the same word *wen*, a signific 糸 is added to form the character 紋, to be used in the literal meaning, leaving the original character 文 for the figurative meanings only. Sometimes it is the other way around: the derived meaning has the enlarged character. Thus, the word *fang* means 'square' in the general sense and 'a square' as a place in a city. To differentiate between the two, the word is written 方 for 'square' in general and 坊, with an additional graph 土 which has to do with places, for 'square, market place.' It is as if one were to write *Harvard Squerre*, with a suggestion of *terre* in the second word.

Thirdly, there is the group of pure phonetic compounds in which the signific is added to a phonetic which was never a loan or a semantic extension in the first place, but was expressly used for its sound to combine with the signific, as *tarng* 'sugar,' written 糖, consisting of 米 the signific relating to cereal foods and the phonetic 唐 *tarng*; or *yu* 'elm,' written 榆, consisting of 木 the signific for 'tree' and the phonetic 俞 *yu*. Pure phonetic compounds are of relatively recent origin. Many characters of the preceding categories *seem* to be pure phonetic compounds because most people are not aware that the unenlarged character or 'phonetic' was used as a loan character or used in a related meaning in old texts for centuries before the enlarged form came into use. (Cf. pp. 15–16.)

Phonetic compounds form by far the majority of all characters. When they were formed, whether through loan from unrelated homonymous words or by extension of meaning of the same word, the sound of the original character and that of the compounded character were identical or very similar. However, differences in sound between a compound and its phonetic, usually caused by interdialectal borrowing [3] of words, developed and increased, and it is now no longer practical to infer the present sound of a compound character from the present sound of its phonetic or the other

---

[3] Borrowing in the linguistic sense.

way around. But *after* the sounds of both the compound and its phonetic are learned, it will be of help to note the phonetic similarity.

Finally, the traditional classification of characters recognizes a category called (6) *joanjuh* which we can translate as 'derivative characters.' Scholars differ widely as to what this class should include. Some regard it as the derivation of characters by graphic inversion. Others regard it as a change in the word itself when a modification of the sound is associated with a modification of meaning and a modification in the graph, as 亨 *heng* 'propitious': 享 *sheang* 'enjoy.' The membership of this class is both small and uncertain.

3. Radicals. — For purposes of reference, Chinese characters have been arranged according to their component parts. Various systems have been used through the ages. The system most widely used by the Chinese and by Western scholars of Chinese is that of the 214 radicals.[4] In most cases, a radical is the signific or the character minus its phonetic, since the majority of characters are phonetic compounds. Thus, in the character 坊, 土 is the radical and 方 is the phonetic. In the relatively small number of cases where the character is not phonetically formed, the analysis of the radical and the residual part is a matter of arbitrary convention, which is often at variance with the actual history of the character. Because of this, we should never make any scientific conclusion on the basis of the present scheme of radicals.

The chief use of the radicals is for looking up unknown characters in a dictionary. Many foreign students of Chinese learn the numbers of the 214 radicals by heart. They can tell you that 75 is 木, 149 is 言, 187 is 馬, etc., a feat which never fails to impress the Chinese. No Chinese can even tell what the number of the radical 人 is, just as few English-speaking people can say offhand what the 17th letter of the alphabet is, though they have not the slightest trouble in locating words in a dictionary. It is, however, helpful to memorize the numbers of the most important radicals, since one-fourth of these will cover three fourths of all characters.

Referring to the table of radicals on p. 71, we see that the order of the radicals is arranged by the number of strokes, beginning with 1 stroke for No. 1 一 and ending with 17 strokes for No. 214 龠. Within each group having the same number of strokes, the order is purely conventional. Note that many of the radicals have one or more variant forms. With certain radicals, such as 9 or 85, the variants are more frequent than the main form. Radicals 140 and 162 always occur in their variant forms. The main

---

[4] Variously called 'classifiers, significs, determinatives, and keys.' We are simply following the usage of the majority. There is no danger, in the use of the term 'radical,' of any etymological connotation, since we are not using the term in any linguistic sense. In the present form, the list of 214 radicals was first used by Mei Ting-tso in his dictionary *Tzŭ-hui*, 1615 A.D.

forms are kept, however, in their conventional positions in the list, since the variant forms do not have the same number of strokes as the main forms.

In a dictionary arranged by radicals, the characters under each radical are arranged in the order of the number of strokes. For example, under radical 75 木 *muh* 'tree, wood,' there is first the radical itself as character, then come characters with one residual stroke, as 未 *wey* 'have not (yet),' 本 *been* 'root,' next, characters with two residual strokes, as 朱 *Ju*, a surname, down to characters with as many as twenty-four residual strokes, as 欞 *ling* 'sill.' For different characters under the same radical with the same number of residual strokes, dictionaries differ in their order of arrangement.

The problem of finding a character is thus resolved to (1) classifying it under the right radical, and (2) counting the number of the residual strokes. For finding the radical, the following hints may be helpful:

Learn by heart the twenty most frequent radicals, namely, 9, 30, 32, 38, 61, 64, 72, 75, 85, 86, 104, 118, 120, 130, 140, 142, 149, 157, 162, 167. More than 50% of all characters belong to one of these.

Find out whether the character in question is a radical, for certain apparently compounded characters are themselves radicals. Thus, 攴 比 父 爻 穴 老 而 耒 至 舌 舛 色 行 見 谷 豆 赤 走 辛 面 音 頁 風 飛 香 高 髟 鹿 麻 黃 黍 黑 鼓 are radicals.

Try to divide the character into parts. A majority of characters can be broken down into a left-hand side and a right-hand side, in which case the left-hand side is most likely to be the radical, as in 你 好 徐 輪 點. Important exceptions are radicals 18 variant, 59, 62, 66 variant, 69, 76, 163 variant, 172, 181, 196, which, when occurring laterally, occupy the right-hand side, as 收 到 部 難 鴨. Other characters can be divided into an upper and a lower part. While there is a greater variety of radicals which can occupy the lower half of the character, as in 光 無 當 盆 買, the radicals 土 宀 穴 爫 罒 竹 艹 雨, which occur at the top, have a greater number of characters under them. Finally, certain radicals enclose, or partially enclose, or are otherwise mixed up with, the residual strokes, as 困 開 展 道 裏 年 奉, whose radicals are respectively 囗 門 尸 辵 衣 干 大.

While these rules will cover most of the cases, many irregular cases will have to be learned individually. For example, 相 is under 目 and not 木, 穀 under 禾 and not 殳, 歸 under 止, etc. Most dictionaries have a list of difficult characters arranged under the total number of strokes. Some dictionaries, especially those prepared by foreigners, give characters under several apparently possible radicals with cross references to the right radical, e.g. 相 under 木, with the notation "see under Radical 109 目." Table 1 gives examples of positions which radicals may occupy.

TABLE 1. EXAMPLES OF POSITIONS OF RADICALS

No.	Rad.	L.	R.	Up	Down	Others	No.	Rad.	L.	R.	Up	Down	Others
1	一			不	並	世	108	皿			盍		眞
4	丿			乖	之	五	109	目	眼	相	眾	省	
7	二	況		云	些		112	石	硬		磨		
8	亠			亦			113	示	福		禁	禀	
9	人	你	以	企		來	115	禾	種	穌	禿		穀
15	冫	凍					116	穴			空		
18	刀		到	分		勝	118	竹			等		
19	力	加	助	勞	古		119	米	粉		粟	緊	粥 縣
30	口	叫	和	吊	同	因	120	糸	紅		肯	舊	腐 與
31	囗				坐	夾	130	肉	肚	胡			蜀
32	土	地		堯	奇		134	臼			舅		舊
37	大				天	委	140	艸			花		
38	女	好			學		142	虫	蝦	融	蠹	蜜	街 裏
39	子	孫					144	行					裔
40	宀			定	屋		145	衣	衫		裝	警	賴 與
44	尸						149	言	記		貴	蕢	
46	山	岐		岳	布		154	貝	賊		路		
50	巾	帖	帥		度		157	足	路			轟	輿
53	广					弟	159	車	輕				
57	弓	強		彎			162	辵	送			邑	
60	彳	得				必	163	邑		都		醫	鬱
61	心	忙		忘 恭	才		164	酉	醋	酒		鑒	衛
64	手	打		掌	整		167	金	鋪				開
66	攴	收	旭	是	畫		169	門					
72	日	時		李	春	東	170	阜	陳				
75	木	板		柴	永	灰	172	隹	雖	隻	雁	雀	題
85	水	法		蠡	然		173	雨	雲				
86	火	燈		營			181	頁	頭			餐	騰
94	犬	狗	獸		壁	畫	184	食	飯	馮		驚	
96	玉	理		琴	當		187	馬	騎	鮮		鯊	鷹
102	田	略			男		195	魚	鴨	魯			
104	疒				病		196	鳥					

4. Order and Number of Strokes. — In teaching children to write, Chinese teachers lay great stress on the order of strokes in which a character is written. There are both esthetic and practical reasons for this. When made with the brush-pen, characters will not have the right shape unless the order of the strokes is right. Moreover, since most everyday writing is in a running hand in which separate strokes become connected, a wrong order may result in unrecognizable forms. For example, in writing the character 土, the order is: upper horizontal stroke, vertical stroke, lower horizontal stroke. In rapid writing, the right end of the upper horizontal is joined to the top of the vertical by a short line. The resulting form 土, however, is so familiar to the Chinese reader that he hardly notices any difference between this and the printed form 土. But if the order is wrong and the two horizontal strokes are made in succession, so as to make a form like 土, then the result will be quite illegible.

The general principle of making the strokes is from left to right and from top to bottom. In strokes which thin down to a sharp point, the direction is from the thick to the thin end, which in some cases involves making strokes from below upwards or from right to left, as 丿 in 氵 and 一 in 千.

When a horizontal stroke and another stroke intersect, the former is usually made first. In a character containing a vertical stroke with two symmetrical parts on both sides, as in 水, the vertical stroke is made first, followed by the left-hand side, then the right-hand side. In complete enclosures, the left-hand wall is made, then the top and the right-hand side are made in one stroke, the content filled in, and the bottom stroke finally added. For examples, see characters 四 and 個 in the writing exercises for Lesson 1 in the *Character Text*, p. 136.

In counting strokes, a horizontal line and a vertical line joining it from the right end down are counted as one stroke. Similarly an L-shaped combination of lines is usually counted as one stroke. These operations are sometimes combined, as in the last stroke of 弓. See 張 in the writing exercises for Lesson 1; also 亞 for Lesson 15 in the *Character Text*, p. 142.

A time-saving device is to memorize the number of strokes in frequently recurring parts of characters, e.g. 舟 6 strokes, 殳 4 strokes, so that one can analyze 般 quickly as 6 + 4 = 10 strokes, without counting every single stroke.

There are many special cases involving the order and number of strokes which are illustrated in the writing exercises in the *Character Text*. The student should turn to those pages while reading the preceding descriptions for a second time.

5. Styles of Script. — The earliest known Chinese writing consisted of inscriptions on ox bones and tortoise shells, recording oracles of divination under the rulers of the Shang dynasty (ca. 1766 – ca. 1122 B.C.). Next in antiquity we find existing inscriptions, mostly on bronzes, of the Chou

THE CHARACTERS 67

dynasty (ca. 1122 – 246 B.C.). Characters written for the same word differed widely from age to age until finally, under the Ch'in dynasty (246–206 B.C.), a system of characters known as 'seal characters' (or 'small seal,' as contrasted with the 'great seal' of Chou), was established. From the time of this system to the present day, there has been much less change in the main structure of the majority of characters, though the type and finish of the strokes have changed considerably as a result of the change from the stylus to the brush as a writing instrument.

Current styles of writing consist of *juanntzyh* 'seal characters,' now used only in actual seals, *lihshu* or *lihtzyh* 'scribe's writing,' now occasionally used for ornamental purposes, *kaeshu* 'model or regular writing,' *kebaantzyh* 'printed characters,' [5] which are the same as the regular characters except for certain details to be noted below, *shyngshu* 'running hand' (literally 'walking style of writing') a more flowing and slightly abbreviated form of ordinary characters, and *tsaoshu* or *tsaotzyh* 'cursive characters' (literally 'grass characters') consisting of extremely abbreviated forms of characters for quick scribbling and for ornamental use. The accompanying cut in Table 2 gives some examples of the various types of characters.

TABLE 2. STYLES OF CHARACTERS

A	B	C	D	E	F		
來	爲	彳	囗	夅	舞		Shang dyn. inscript.
來	爲	彳	囗	夅	舞		Chou dyn. inscript.
來	爲	彳	其	降	舞	*juann*	seal
來	爲	行	其	降	無	*lih*	scribe
來	為	行	其	降	無	*kae*	regular
來	爲	行	其	降	無	*kebaan*	printed
来	为	彳	其	降	無	*shyng*	running
术	为	丿	玊	降	无	*tsao*	cursive

A is the word *lai* 'come' (< Archaic *lǝg*), borrowed from a homonym meaning a kind of wheat. B is the word *wei* 'to do, to be,' originally a picture of a hand leading an elephant. C is the word *shyng* 'walk,' originally a picture of crossroads, later interpreted (wrongly) as a picture of

[5] This category has no place in the traditional way of reckoning the styles of characters.

steps. D is the word *chyi* 'his,' originally a picture of a dustpan. The present character for dustpan 箕, pronounced *ji*, is an enlarged form. E *jianq* 'descend' started with a picture of feet going down a flight of stairs. F *wu* started with a character meaning 'dancing' which was at an early age borrowed for a homonym meaning 'have not.' The seal form is enlarged by a signific, which was dropped later. The modern character for *wuu* 'dance' is in an enlarged form 舞, in which the phonetic 無 occurs in the abbreviated form 无.

For the purposes of this course, the student would do well to concentrate on the regular style. This agrees in the main with the printed style except that the latter has small flourishes and exaggerated shadings like the serifs and shadings in the printed types of the Latin alphabet. In a relatively small number of cases, differences of structure exist. It is essential to know both the printed and the written styles, since radical indexes are based on the printed style and yet nobody writes in the printed style if the written style is very different. For example, the character 爲 has the radical 爪 (in variant form) on the top, but in the written form, as shown in the fifth character under B, Table 2, the radical cannot even be seen. Where the number of residual strokes differs in the two styles, the printed style is followed in counting. Thus, in 都 the number of residual strokes in 者 is 9 (counting the central dot) though the dot is rarely made when the character is written.

Table 3 gives some common differences between the printed and written styles of characters and parts of characters. These differences are looked

TABLE 3. COMMON DIFFERENCES BETWEEN PRINTED AND WRITTEN FORMS

Printed	Written	Printed	Written	Printed	Written	Printed	Written
丶	丶	又	又	直	直	礻	礻
人	人	忄	忄	眞	真	訁	訁
令	令	戶	户	礻	礻	辶	辶
入	入	文	文	糹	糹	雨	雨
八	八	爲	為	者	者	青	青
兌	兌	畱	畱	艹	艹	飠	飠

upon as geometrical and non-significant and the characters are treated, not as variant characters for identical words, but as "identical" characters. (See § 6 below.)

6. Variant Forms of Characters. — Aside from the differences between the printed and written forms, many characters have important variations in structure which occur both in the printed and in the written style, as shown in Table 4. A variant form of a character may belong to one of the following categories: (1) restylized seal forms, in which the general pattern of seal characters is kept although the actual strokes are modernized; (2) normal variations, which are equally acceptable with the main form; (3) inscriptional forms, which are considered informal but in good taste; (4) popular characters, usually in the form of abbreviations; (5) popular differentiations not recognized by the old-school scholars; (6) simplified forms originally in good standing, but later regarded as popular abbreviations after their origins have generally been forgotten; (7) restylized cursive forms, that is, characters which follow the pattern of cursive characters but have regularized strokes; (8) dialect characters.

The frequent use of archaic forms is considered a mannerism. Normal variations and inscriptional forms are both respectable usage. The forms from (3) to (7) are shunned by educated people of the older generation, but are accepted more and more by the younger generation.

Dialect forms are rarely used, since dialects are seldom written in any case. They are included here under variants, since many of them can be identified with normal characters, as shown in the examples in the accompanying table.

For a list of common variants of common characters, see *Character Text*, p. 10.

TABLE 4. EXAMPLES OF VARIANT CHARACTERS

Normal   *Variant*

(1) 旁   㫄 (< 㫄)   *parng* 'side, lateral' B
    草   艸 (< 艸)   *tsao* 'grass'

(2) 侯   矦   *hour* 'marquis' B
    筍   笋   *soen* 'bamboo shoots'

(3) 於   扵   *yu* 'at'
    處   䖏   *chuh* 'place' B

(4) 過   过   *guoh* 'to pass'
    亂   乿   *luann* 'confused'

(5) 乾   {乾 / 乾}   *chyan* 'positive principle' B
                gan 'dry'
    鋪   {鋪 / 鋪}   *pu* 'to spread'
                puh 'shop' B

(6) 處   处   *chuh* 'place' B
    號   号   *haw* 'number' B

(7) 盡   尽 (< 㞡)   *jinn* 'to exhaust' B
    時   时 (< 旹)   *shyr* 'time' B

(8) 瞓   瞓   Cantonese *fann* 'to sleep'
    會   噲   Cantonese *wue* 'know how to'

TABLE 5. LIST OF RADICALS

	1	2	3	4	5	6	7	8	9	
0	一	丨	丶	丿	乙	亅	二	亠	人亻	0
10	儿	入	八	冂	冖	冫	几	凵	刀刂	10
20	力	勹	匕	匚	匸	卜	卩㔾	厂	厶	又	20
30	口	囗	土	士	夂	夊	夕	大	女	子	30
40	宀	寸	小	尢	尸	屮	山	巛川	工	己	40
50	巾	干	幺	广	廴	廾	弋	弓	彐彑	彡	50
60	彳忄	心忄	戈	戶	手扌	支	攴攵	文	斗	斤	60
70	方	无旡	日	曰	月	木	欠	止	歹	殳	70
80	母	比	毛	氏	气	水氵	火灬	爪爫	父	爻	80
90	爿	片	牙	牛牜	犬犭	玄	玉王	瓜	瓦	甘	90
100	生	用	田	疋	疒	癶	白	皮	皿	目罒	100
110	矛	矢	石	示礻	禸	禾	穴	立	竹⺮	米	110
120	糸	缶	网罒	羊	羽	老	而	耒	耳	聿	120
130	肉月	臣	自	至	臼	舌	舛	舟	艮	色	130
140	艸艹	虍	虫	血	行	衣衤	襾西	見	角	言	140
150	谷	豆	豕	豸	貝	赤	走	足⻊	身	車	150
160	辛	辰	辵辶	邑阝	酉	釆	里	金	長镸	門	160
170	阜阝	隶	隹	雨	青	非	面	革	韋	韭	170
180	音	頁	風	飛	食飠	首	香	馬	骨	高	180
190	髟	鬥	鬯	鬲	鬼	魚	鳥	鹵	鹿	麥	190
200	麻	黃	黍	黑	黹	黽	鼎	鼓	鼠	鼻	200
210	齊	齒	龍	龜	龠						210
	1	2	3	4	5	6	7	8	9	

CHAPTER V METHOD OF STUDY

1. Phonetic Foundation. — In language study, there is a great difference between foundation work and development work. It will save much time and energy if both teacher and student make sure at each moment to which of the two kinds the task in hand belongs. Foundation work in language study consists in acquiring the ability to recognize by ear and reproduce intelligibly all the distinctive phonetic elements, or phonemes, of the language under study. It is not necessary to aim at a perfect accent. It is not even desirable at the initial stage to divert attention from the main task of auditory recognition and intelligible reproduction of the phonemes. The only necessary and sufficient rule for the foundation work is: Sounds which are different should not be heard or pronounced alike. If the consonants in *jow* 'wrinkled' and *jiow* 'old' can be learned exactly, well and good. If not, it will be better to pronounce *jow* as in English '*dro*ve' and *jiow* as in English '*Joe*' than to pronounce them alike, even though the result sounds exactly like *one* of the Chinese words. The main thing is to distinguish them somehow, and this applies to vowel and tone, as well as to consonant.

2. Meaning and Sound. — The reason for insisting that different sounds be heard and pronounced differently is that sounds form the stuff of words and carry distinctions of meaning. Hazy sounds cannot be the vehicle of clear ideas. It is true that the same syllable often has different meanings, as in cases of homonyms. But a language can always afford a certain proportion of homonyms, and its speaker is not troubled by them, since he has grown up with an average style of speech which has attained such a degree of equilibrium between economy and explicitness that it does not depend for its clearness upon the difference of meaning in homonyms.[1] When, however, a foreigner confuses *jow* 'wrinkled' and *jiow* 'old' for which the native speaker is totally unprepared since he often does depend on the distinction in sound between *jow* and *jiow* for clearness, he is disturbing that equilibrium and the result is either misinterpretation or unintelligibility. (Cf. p. 12.)

In many cases, the student of Chinese probably does not expect to go to China or to have much occasion to converse in Chinese, but wishes to acquire a reading knowledge of the language. For him, it is not only unnecessary to acquire a perfect accent, but it would theoretically answer the purpose even if he pronounced *ideal* 'a little' like English 'ideal' or *par* 'crawl'

---

[1] Excluding, of course, cases of the clumsy speaker who gets into ambiguities unwittingly and the punster who does the same thing wittily.

(where the final r is merely the sign of the 2nd Tone) like American 'par' instead of [pʻɑː]. But it will not do if he works with fewer word-distinguishing elements than there are, or there would not be enough of them to carry the semantic burden of the language in the style in which it exists. If the language does make use of such a given set of word-distinguishing elements, he cannot afford to work with fewer. Since, however, there is no point in inventing an artificial pronunciation, he might as well try to approximate the real one.

3. Amount of Time for Foundation Work. — Because of the essential nature of the foundation work and its all-pervading effect on subsequent work, no time spent on it is too long and no energy given to it too strenuous. It has been found to be fully worth while to devote to it the first 100 hours. The consequent ease and precision with which the students grasp the formation of new words will fully justify the cost in time. The objectives to be aimed at in the foundation work should be in the following order: (1) ability to reproduce in writing (without pronouncing) the basic sound-tables, namely Tables 1, 2, and 3 in Chapter II, (2) ability to write down any initial, final, or tones from dictation, (3) ability to pronounce any initial, final, or tone from the romanization without confusing any two elements (4) ability to romanize any syllable from dictation, (5) ability to pronounce any syllable from the romanization without confusing any two syllables. When, after these objectives have been attained, the student goes on to the learning of words and sentences, the words and sentences will stick and the meanings will have something definite to be attached to.

4. Development Work. — We may call development work the acquisition of the vocabulary, grammar, and idioms of the language in the extended lessons. While the foundation work is a strenuous but short piece of work, demanding the fullest alertness of all faculties for a period of from one week to a month, depending upon the program and individual capacity, development work is a comparatively smooth-going (if the foundation has been properly laid) but a most time-consuming process. For it will take the student months of actual practice and memorizing before he attains readiness in conversation, and years of study before he can read comfortably. It must always be remembered, however, that precision in the foundation work will influence the development work, not by saving a few hours here and a few days there, but by multiplying the efficiency by integral factors, so that a student who works twice as hard for the first two weeks will cut down the number of years of study to one half, while, if the foundation is sufficiently bad, as it often is, he may never learn the language.

5. Focusing and Exposure in Language Study. — Development work is largely a matter of focusing and exposure. A good foundation will make it possible to bring the details into focus. Then it takes adequate exposure to make a deep enough impression to develop. In taking up a new lesson, study of the vocabulary, analysis of the grammatical constructions and idioms in the text, and the translation of the text in the student's own language — these constitute the act of focusing. If, as is the common practice in many language classes, the lesson at this stage is considered learned and the class goes on to the next assignment, it would be as if a photographer, after setting the right frame and focus, were to turn the roll, to repeat the same procedure on the next film. The resulting film, when developed after such treatment, will, of course, be as blank as the impression of the foreign language in the student's mind after such a lesson. In fairness to most teachers, it should be added that they usually do make some exposure by reading the text once or twice and having the class read it after them. But the picture is so underexposed that the procedure helps little toward the development.

6. Aids to Focusing: The Echo Method. — The first necessary condition of clear focusing is of course the first weeks of foundation work. This can be compared with the proper grinding of the photographic lens. In this phase of the work the teacher may well use the native language of the student, at least for the first few lessons. For the later lessons, it may be advantageous to use the foreign language under study if it does not take too long to get a point across,[2] but it should be understood that the advantage of doing so lies in the opportunity for increased exposure, and not in better focus, since the teacher can always explain phonetic and grammatical points more efficiently in the student's own language. The "direct method" should be suspended the moment it interferes with the direct understanding of a focal point.

For the clear focusing as well as initial exposure of an extended text, the method of "echoing" will be found very helpful. After the student reads aloud a phrase or sentence, he should immediately repeat it as an echo without looking at the book. Then he may check the echo by the text, and finally repeat the corrected echo. This may be tried with short phrases first, then with larger units up to complete sentences extending over two or three lines. There is no point, so far as the echo method is concerned, in trying to span whole long paragraphs, as that would constitute memorization work, which, though useful, need not be applied to all the material one learns. But all the texts in these elementary lessons should be "echoed" by the student as part of his homework.

The greatest virtue of this echo method is that it automatically strengthens any point on which the student is weak, while the parts already learned will be echoed correctly and so passed by comparatively unnoticed. Whether he has omitted a word, inverted a word order, substituted a wrong word in

[2] When this course was first given in the Army Specialized Training Program at Harvard, all instruction was given in Chinese from the ninth lesson on.

the echo, or simply has difficulty in spanning a certain construction, the relevant parts of the text against which he checks his work will stand out vividly, so that they will be focused clearly in his mind. It is therefore absolutely essential for the student, in order to gain full advantage from the echo method, not to let any sentence pass until he can do it perfectly from beginning to end. Moreover, while the echo method is intended for focusing the sentence with all its contents, it proves in actual practice to be a very powerful aid in learning grammar. Frequently, rules about word order, use of particles, etc., are driven home only after they have been broken and the error corrected in the echo.

7. Aids to Exposure: The Use of Phonograph Records. — "Learn Chinese while you shave" is a method which works only in the exposure stage. If listening to a language could of itself teach it, there would not be so many people who live in a foreign country for years without ever learning the language. A phonograph record begins to be useful only after a sufficiently clear focus is attained, so that its contents can be followed understandingly, at first with the accompanying text before one, and later "while you shave."

Phonograph records are not absolutely necessary if enough exposure can be had from reading aloud, doing the exercises, and practicing conversation, whether on the part of the students themselves or with the aid of the teacher. In the early stages, however, when the students are not sure of their focus, exposure will have to come from perfect models, and unless teachers can afford more time than is usually available in class schedules, supplementary listening to phonograph records is practically a necessity.

8. Language Lessons and Music Lessons. — Music gives a still closer analogy to language than photography. When a music student is assigned a piece to learn, he looks over the printed notes, finds out what sounds they stand for (if he is really musical-minded), where the fingers should go, what the tempo and dynamics should be, and tries out various vertical or horizontal parts of the music on the instrument. This corresponds to the focusing; only after doing this does he really begin to practice. He must make no slips, he must not hesitate. Every hesitation counts as a mistake and the passage must be repeated. In repeating, he does not begin exactly where he went wrong, or he would surely make the same mistake when he came to it again, but starts a little further back. He must work up to the right tempo and yet must not sacrifice accuracy. Not every piece needs to be learned by heart, but no piece is considered learned until it can be played through at tempo, with the right expression, and without more than an occasional mistake. The application to language study is obvious. A language lesson is not only to be looked over, but actually practiced and learned. The usual difficulty is in persuading the teacher and the student to see that, just as a music lesson is not the same thing as a class in theoretical harmony, so no amount of classroom discussion of the language material, important as it is, can take the place of practice in the language.

9. Optimum speed. — The speed of reading or speaking by the drillmaster should be such that the maximum amount of utterances can be heard and apperceived by the majority of the drill group in a given time. If he speaks so slowly that every member in the group can catch every word of some new material from the start, then he is evidently speaking too slowly,[3] and the disadvantage of that is that he will not be able to go over so much material or make so many repetitions of a given text in a given drill hour. On the other hand, if he starts at normal conversational speed to a group of beginning students, so little will be clearly perceived, that the repetitions cannot really count. It is up to the drillmaster to judge what is the optimum speed to use according to the nature of the material and the degree of advancement of the group. As for the speed of recordings, it should be timed a little too fast to follow for the first few hearings, so that it will be just right to listen to after careful study and practice.

10. Vocabulary and Text. — The material of language study is not words but text or connected speech. Vocabularies are aids to focusing, but exposure should be made mainly on the text. The meaning of words is not only to be learned in context, but *is* the context, whether of words or of the situation in which the speech is being used. Once, a student in my class imagined he was learning Chinese by trying to memorize English words in one-to-one correspondence with Chinese characters. He was told to pay more attention to the connected text. After a while he complained that he could not remember the meaning of words except in the sentences in which they occurred, and was worried for fear he would have to learn a million possible sentences instead of a few thousand words. He did not realize that he was worrying over having succeeded in doing the right thing. If a student familiarizes himself with a few thousand sentences in good representative texts, the millions will take care of themselves.

11. Syntax and Morphology. — It will save the student much time if he remembers all the time whether he is analyzing a given material at a syntactic level or a morphological level. Every student should aim at learning the meanings of all the syntactic words and acquiring an active mastery of all the syntactic constructions taught. But he should be satisfied, until he is much farther along, with a passive understanding of most of the morphological constructions. Apart from certain very active morphological processes for which special exercises are provided, he should not try to learn to make up syntactic words from bound words. For example he should use the notation 'ground-board, — floor' only as a help to remember the meaning of the word *dihbaan* as a whole and not be expected to

---

[3] We are now talking about the "exposure" stage, of course.

make up a word like *tianbaan* 'sky-board' for 'ceiling.' As a matter of fact, there is a central-dialect word *tianhua-baan* 'sky-flower board' for 'ceiling,' which will have to be regarded as a separate item.

One of the disadvantages of using a character text for beginning students is in fact the obscuring of the distinction between syntax and morphology. Because a character, with its root meaning, has been taught, both teacher and student usually assume unconsciously that henceforward it can be used in all combinations. This results in two very common types of error in method. On the one hand, the teacher may use a character in a new (syntactic) word, without explanation, in exercises and in new text where the student has no way of knowing the meaning of the new word. On the other hand, the student may put bound forms together and make nonexistent forms on the pattern of his own language. To be sure, even at the syntactic level, there are often special idiomatic meanings in phrases and limitation in combinations of words. But that is all the more reason why the student should not attempt to do a kind of work only suitable for a very advanced stage of study. Even a freshman in a Chinese university cannot always be trusted with the making up of compounds which he has not heard or seen before.

12. The Exercises: Active and Passive Knowledge. — At the syntactic level, and for certain very regular and simple morphological constructions (for which specific exercises are given), the student should be required to gain an active knowledge of the material taught. For this purpose, the exercises at the end of each lesson form an essential part of the lesson. All the exercises of the lessons should be done, and done both orally and in writing (in romanization), as far as both apply. They are designed to increase the amount of exposure without adding to the monotony of identical repetitions of the text. When done orally, both the questions and the answers may be given by students, and the answers should be made without looking at the book, except of course where the exercises consist of filling in blanks. An exercise is not done until the correct answer is given *without hesitation*. Generally speaking, the main text is the material for a passive knowledge (i.e., ability to listen and read intelligently) and the exercises are materials for an active knowledge of the language (i.e., ability to speak and write intelligibly). But even students whose aim is only to have a passive knowledge must also do the exercises. Unless one acquires a minimum amount of active command of the language, it is impossible to have a passive knowledge with any precision. All reading is partly composing. The theoretical possibilities of meaning and construction in any succession of words are so numerous that reading degenerates into hit-or-miss guessing unless the reader is ready at all times with the few likely choices of meaning and construction for the whole sentence before his eyes are halfway through. In other words the reader must be able to anticipate in a general way what is coming next. He may be surprised [4] if he has anticipated the wrong thing, but he should not be totally unprepared and have to guess at each thing as it comes. The value of an active knowledge for the purpose of reading lies not only in increased speed and comfort, but also in greater precision in interpretation.

13. The Romanized Text. — Every student of this course should work with the romanized text, either exclusively or in addition to the character text. He should have a sure and accurate picture of the romanized orthography of every word he learns. Only in this way can he keep the material of the language in sharp focus. An important feature of the romanization used here is the spelling of tones with letters. In this orthography, not only are the tones better remembered, but words acquire more individuality of physiognomy and are more easily associated with their meanings. It is possible to learn to speak Chinese without the use of characters, but it is not possible to learn it without some form of transcribed text unless one grew up among the Chinese, and even then, some form of transcription helps to establish the linguistic forms more clearly in one's mind.

14. Romanization Not an Aid to the Learning of the Sounds. — A word of caution. Important as the use of romanization is, the student should understand that romanization is of no use for the initial learning of the sounds. All phonetic transcription, whether in the ordinary letters of National Romanization, or in the modified letters of a phonetic alphabet, serve only as fixed and easily identifiable reminders of Chinese sounds which the student is supposed to have learned after hard practice in his foundation work. There is no such thing as a self-pronouncing system of transcription. Marks on paper do not of themselves pronounce. Only the teacher or the phonograph record pronounces, and they are the *sole sources* from which the student learns the sounds. Only after having first learned to recognize and reproduce the sounds distinguishably can he begin to profit from the use of any form of transcription.

15. The Learning of the Characters. — Any student who wishes to learn the literary idiom, as used in most printed matter, including newspapers and periodicals, must learn to read in character texts. Whether he studies characters from the beginning or starts later, the task of learning the characters should be undertaken seriously as a study in itself and should not be confused with the study of the language. After familiarizing himself with the general principles of Chinese writing as explained in Chapter IV, the student should do the exercises at the end of the *Character Text*.

Since the chief object of learning the characters is to read connected text, all the lessons should be gone over in characters until the text can be read without hesitation and until any phrase in it, without being previously memorized, can be written out from dictation. In other words, study of

---

[4] If so, he is ready to appreciate humor in the foreign language.

the lessons in characters should consist in reading aloud understandingly at tempo, and in taking down dictation in characters. The exercises as provided for in the character version should be done in characters.

Now it might seem a duplication of work and waste of effort to do the same thing twice in two systems of writing, one in romanization and the other in characters. As a matter of fact, both are necessary. Exclusive use of characters will not do the job. We have already seen that the use of the romanized text is really necessary for the proper learning of the language. Once the student has learned the *language* of a lesson, then he is in a doubly favorable position for learning the characters; for he will then have worked up an appetite for the characters, since he will feel the need of knowing how to write in Chinese what he already knows, and in addition he will now be able to concentrate on a hard task of a totally different nature. If the study of characters is undertaken from the very beginning of the course, the work, at least in its first stages, should be kept separate from the study of the language. By giving special attention to each as a different kind of task, one gets better and surer results in both.

16. Translation into English. — Those who are used to the translation method commonly used in language courses may feel disconcerted when they encounter no exercises of translation, since the text has already been translated for them. There will, of course, be plenty of work to do in class if the suggestions given above are followed. Even when the student takes up the study of an untranslated text, translation should be used only as an aid to, and test for, the understanding of the text. It should not take so much time as to exceed its function as an aid to focusing and thus usurp the function of exposure. For one does not learn Chinese by being constantly exposed to English.

Translation as an objective is an entirely different matter. One of the chief purposes of knowing a foreign language is, in fact, to be able to translate it into one's own language. But the work of translation presupposes a knowledge of the foreign language, which can best be acquired by means other than translation. A condition for good translating is to consider what one would naturally say or write in one's own language in the same context or under the same circumstances, and the result will usually be very different from the kind of translation done in our elementary language classes. There are many turns and tricks that may be learned about translation, but they are useful in the advanced practice of translation as an art rather than for the elementary learning of a foreign language. Too much concern with translation as a formal task at an early stage usually results in creating a strange kind of "translatese" in one's own language rather than in learning the foreign language.

17. Suggestions to the Chinese Student. — The problem of a Chinese who speaks a dialect other than Mandarin and wishes to learn the standard language is quite different from that of one who does not know any Chinese. While an English-speaking student has to learn everything anew, a Chinese student is already familiar with all the Chinese roots in cognate forms in his own dialect, uses about the same grammar, has learned the same literary and scientific terms in school, and writes the same characters. His chief problems are three: (1) what sounds there are in Mandarin, (2) when to use what sounds in what words, and (3) what words to use.

The first part is the foundation work, in which the task for the Chinese student is identical with that of the English-speaking student. The only things in which the Chinese student will have an advantage will probably be his ability to distinguish between unaspirated and aspirated sounds and his being psychologically prepared for the fact that words are distinguished by tone — although the tones themselves will be as hard or as easy for him to make as for any non-Chinese. The Chinese student should therefore expect to do just as strenuous and exacting work at this initial stage as the Occidental student. He will be making a false start if he is under the impression that he has an advantage over foreigners because he knows some form of Chinese. No, he has not, not at this stage. He must do the same memorizing of tables and go through the same phonetic drills as an American student.

In the matter of choosing the right sounds for words, the Chinese student has both advantages and disadvantages. To the English-speaking student there is no problem, as everything is new and must be learned as such. With the Chinese student, practically everything reminds him of something in his own dialect. If Cantonese *low* 'road' is Mandarin *luh*, Cantonese *dow* 'degree' is Mandarin *duh*, why isn't Cantonese *how* 'number' *huh in Mandarin? To be sure, it is much easier for a speaker of Cantonese to remember that 'number' is *haw* in Mandarin — merely noting that it is not exactly *huh after the analogy of *luh* and *duh* — than for a foreigner to learn an entirely new root *haw*. Consequently, the time it takes him to learn the whole vocabulary of the language will be only a small fraction of what it takes his American fellow student to cover the same ground. But the trouble with the Chinese who tries to learn another dialect is that he does not take it seriously enough, but assumes that he can "pick it up" by discovering the trick from a few key words and typical idioms. What he should do is to make a mental note of the form of every new word as he comes across it; he should never feel safe in any guess by analogy until the new word has been properly checked. His motto should be: Exceptions are the rule and the rule is the exception.

To avoid such dangers, the Chinese student should stay away entirely from characters, not only for the foundation work, but also for the first few lessons, where the proportion of irregular relation between cognate words is the greatest. He should work exclusively with the romanization until he is sure of his foundation and until he has acquired the habit of suspicion against analogies. If he starts with characters, his own dialect will perpetually stand in the way to prevent direct access to the standard dialect.

The matter of learning what words to use is easy. The 24 lessons cover practically all the features that the speaker of a different dialect needs to know in order to speak Mandarin naturally. From then on, it is a matter of further practice in conversation and of learning the pronunciation of all the important characters. For the Chinese student, the more advanced he gets the fewer differences he will find between Mandarin and his own dialect, while the American student will still have before him all the work of acquiring the learned words and the literary style. For the Chinese student, the completion of this course will be his graduation. For the American student, it will be his commencement.

PART II FOUNDATION WORK

TO THE STUDENT

These preparatory lessons, Lessons A, B, C, and D, form the foundation of all your subsequent study. The period of the first three or four weeks to be devoted to this is the most critical of the whole course. This part of the work will be very strenuous and will demand the fullest alertness of all your faculties at all times. Conscientious work at this phonetic stage will result in great ease in subsequent command of the language material in grammar, vocabulary, and idiom, while poor work now will result in a crippled equipment affecting all your work later, or in your total failure to learn the language.

LESSON A   THE TONES

Figure 1 is a design for a wall chart to be hung in the classroom. For the first few exercises, and later as needed, the student should be required frequently to trace the tones with his finger on the chart and later in the air.

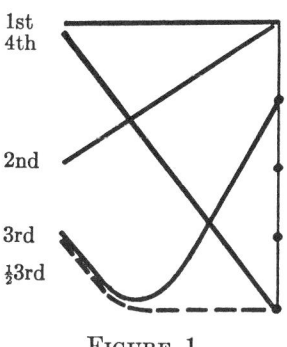

FIGURE 1

For class instruction, a convenient key to pitch the tones is about as in Figure 2. Better err in pitching tones too low than too high. For women's voices, make the tones an octave higher than in Figure 2.

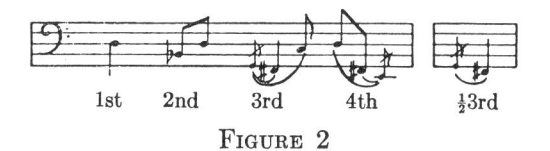

FIGURE 2

1. Single Tones. — The teacher will say the tones from the character text, and the class will repeat them after him. The lines indicate whether the order of reading is to be vertical or horizontal. Phonograph recordings should provide space for the repetitions. For an informant who is not phonetically sophisticated, the Half 3rd Tone in isolation will have to be omitted, as this tone is the very tone that is normally followed by another syllable.

Teacher:	a, 1st Tone, a.	ar, 2nd Tone, ar.	aa, 3rd Tone, aa.	ah, 4th Tone, ah.	$\frac{1}{2}$aa– $\frac{1}{2}$3rd Tone $\frac{1}{2}$aa–
CLASS:	A.	AR.	AA.	AH.	$\frac{1}{2}$AA–

FOUNDATION WORK

T:	a.	ar.	aa.	ah.	‖ $\frac{1}{2}$aa–
CL:	A.	AR.	AA.	AH.	‖ $\frac{1}{2}$AA–

T:	a.	ar.	aa.	ah.	‖ $\frac{1}{2}$aa–
CL:	A.	AR.	AA.	AH.	‖ $\frac{1}{2}$AA–

T:	Mha, 'mother,' Mha.	Ma, 'hemp,' Ma.	Maa, 'horse,' Maa.	Mah, 'to scold,' Mah.
CL:	MHA.	MA.	MAA.	MAH.

T:	Mha.	Ma.	Maa.	Mah.
CL:	MHA.	MA.	MAA.	MAH.

T:	Mha.	Ma.	Maa.[1]	Mah.
CL:	MHA.	MA.	MAA.	MAH.

T:	I, 'one,' I.	Yi, 'soap' B,[2] Yi.	Yii, 'chair' B, Yii.	Yih, 'meaning' B, Yih.
CL:	I.	YI.	YII.	YIH.

T:	I.	Yi.	Yii.	Yih.
CL:	I.	YI.	YII.	YIH.

T:	I.	Yi.	Yii.	Yih.
CL:	I.	YI.	YII.	YIH.

T:	Fei, 'to fly,' Fei.	Feir, 'fat,' Feir.	Feei, 'bandit,' Feei.	Fey, 'to waste,' Fey.
CL:	FEI.	FEIR.	FEEI.	FEY.

T:	Fei.	Feir.	Feei.	Fey.
CL:	FEI.	FEIR.	FEEI.	FEY.

[1] The teacher must be careful to make *a full stop* here, for if he pronounced *maa mah* too closely together, he would naturally give *maa* a $\frac{1}{2}$3rd Tone, which is not a part of the present exercise.

[2] "B" indicates that the word is bound, i.e., not used independently.

THE TONES

T:	Fei.	Feir.	Feei.	Fey.
CL:	FEI.	FEIR.	FEEI.	FEY.

T:	Tang, 'soup,' Tang.	Tarng, 'sugar,' Tarng.	Taang, 'lie down,' Taang.	Tanq, 'hot,' Tanq.
CL:	TANG.	TARNG.	TAANG.	TANQ.

T:	Tang.	Tarng.	Taang.	Tanq.
CL:	TANG.	TARNG.	TAANG.	TANQ.

T:	Tang.	Tarng.	Taang.	Tanq.
CL:	TANG.	TARNG.	TAANG.	TANQ.

T:	Mha.	I.	Fei.	Tang.
CL:	MHA.	I.	FEI.	TANG.

T:	Ma.	Yi.	Feir.	Tarng.
CL:	MA.	YI.	FEIR.	TARNG.

T:	Maa.	Yii.	Feei.	Taang.
CL:	MAA.	YII.	FEEI.	TAANG.

T:	Mah.	Yih.	Fey.	Tanq.
CL:	MAH.	YIH.	FEY.	TANQ.

T:	Mha.	Ma.	Maa.	Mah.
CL:	MHA.	MA.	MAA.	MAH.

T:	(sol) [3]	What?!	Well?	Now!
CL:	(HUM)	WHAT?!	WELL?	NOW!

After practicing the tones while looking at the text, have individual members of the class trace the tone signs on the blackboard or the tone charts as they hear or say the tones.

[3] As in *do, re, mi, fa, sol.*

EXERCISES

(a) Read the following aloud:
(1) aa. (2) a. (3) a. (4) ah. (5) ar.
(6) ½aa– (7) aa. (8) ah. (9) ½aa– (10) aa.
(11) ar. (12) ar. (13) ½aa– (14) a. (15) ah.
(16) ½aa– (17) ar. (18) a. (19) ah. (20) aa.

(b) Without looking at the above, indicate tones on paper or on the wall chart by the signs ˥, ˧, ˩, ˨, or ˩ as heard from the record. Repeat the exercise as dictated by the teacher, who will vary the order of the sounds.

(c) Repeat the same, writing *a, ar, aa, ah,* and *½aa–* instead of tone-signs.

(d) Read the following aloud:
(1) Fei. (2) Mah. (3) ½Feei– (4) Yi. (5) ½Taang–
(6) Feei. (7) I. (8) Feir. (9) Maa. (10) Ma.
(11) Yih. (12) Yii. (13) Yii. (14) Mha. (15) Fey.
(16) ½Maa– (17) Tang. (18) Taang. (19) ½Feei– (20) Tarng.
(21) Yi. (22) Maa. (23) Taang. (24) Tang. (25) Mah.

(e) Without looking at the above, indicate by tone signs (on paper or on the wall chart) the tones of the words as heard from a record or as dictated by the teacher.

(f) Repeat the same, writing out the words instead of tone-signs.

2. Tones in Combinations. —

T: Ta.	Ting.	Ta ting,	'he listens,'	ta ting.
CL: TA.	TING.	TA TING,	˥ ˥[*]	TA TING.
T: Ta.	Lai.	Ta lai,	'he comes,'	ta lai.
CL: TA.	LAI.	TA LAI,	˥ ˧	TA LAI.
T: Ta.	Mae.	Ta mae	'he buys,'	ta mae.
CL: TA.	MAE.	TA MAE,	˥ ˩	TA MAE.
T: Ta.	May.	Ta may,	'he sells,'	ta may.
CL: TA.	MAY.	TA MAY,	˥ ˨	TA MAY.

[*] The class will hum the tones here.

(b)	*T:*	Mei.	Ting.	Mei ting,	'did not listen,'	mei ting.
	CL:	MEI.	TING.	MEI TING,	˧˥ ˥	MEI TING.
	T:	Mei.	Lai.	Mei lai,	'did not come,'	mei lai.
	CL:	MEI.	LAI.	MEI LAI,	˧˥ ˧˥	MEI LAI.
	T:	Mei.	Mae.	Mei mae,	'did not buy,'	mei mae.
	CL:	MEI.	MAE.	MEI MAE,	˧˥ ˨˩˦	MEI MAE.
	T:	Mei.	May.	Mei may,	'did not sell,'	mei may.
	CL:	MEI.	MAY.	MEI MAY,	˧˥ ˥˩	MEI MAY.
(c)	*T:*	$\frac{1}{2}$Nii — ting.		$\frac{1}{2}$Nii ting,	'you listen,'	$\frac{1}{2}$nii ting.
	CL:	$\frac{1}{2}$NII — TING.		$\frac{1}{2}$NII TING,	˨˩ ˥	$\frac{1}{2}$NII TING.
	T:	$\frac{1}{2}$Nii — lai.		$\frac{1}{2}$Nii lai,	'you come,'	$\frac{1}{2}$Nii lai.
	CL:	$\frac{1}{2}$NII — LAI.		$\frac{1}{2}$NII LAI,	˨˩ ˧˥	$\frac{1}{2}$NII LAI.
	T:	*Nii* — mae.[5]		*Nii* mae,	'you buy,'	*nii* mae.
	CL:	*NII* — MAE.		*NII* MAE,	˧˥ ˨˩˦	*NII* MAE.
	T:	$\frac{1}{2}$Nii — may.		$\frac{1}{2}$Nii may,	'you sell,'	$\frac{1}{2}$nii may.
	CL:	$\frac{1}{2}$NII — MAY.		$\frac{1}{2}$NII MAY,	˨˩ ˥˩	$\frac{1}{2}$NII MAY.
(d)	*T:*	Yaw.	Ting.	Yaw ting,	'want to listen,'	yaw ting.
	CL:	YAW.	TING.	YAW TING,	˥˩ ˥	YAW TING.
	T:	Yaw.	Lai.	Yaw lai,	'want to come,'	yaw lai.
	CL:	YAW.	LAI.	YAW LAI,	˥˩ ˧˥	YAW LAI.
	T:	Yaw.	Mae.	Yaw mae,	'want to buy,'	yaw mae.
	CL:	YAW.	MAE	YAW MAE,	˥˩ ˨˩˦	YAW MAE.

[5] See p. 25.

T:	Yaw.	May.	Yaw may, 'want to sell,' yaw may.
CL:	YAW.	MAY	YAW MAY, ˥⁶ ˩ YAW MAY.

(e)

	˥ ting	˧˥ lai	˨˩˦ mae	˩ may
˥ Ta	Ta ting.	Ta lai.	Ta mae.	Ta may.
˧˥ Mei	Mei ting.	Mei lai.	Mei mae.	Mei may.
˨˩˦ Nii	½Nii ting.	½Nii lai.	*Nii* mae.	½Nii may.
˩ Yaw	Yaw ting.	Yaw lai.	Yaw mae.	Yaw may.

(f) Difficult combinations:

1st + 2nd	T:	Ta lai.	a ar.	Ta lai.
˥ ˧˥	CL:	TA LAI.	A AR.	TA LAI.

2nd + 1st	T:	Mei ting.	ar a.	mei ting
˧˥ ˥	CL:	MEI TING.	AR A.	MEI TING.

2nd + 2nd	T:	Mei lai.	ar ar.	Mei lai.
˧˥ ˧˥	CL:	MEI LAI.	AR AR.	MEI LAI.

3. The Neutral Tone. —

Half-low	Middle	Half-high	Low
after 1st	after 2nd	after 3rd	after 4th

Teacher: *CLASS:*

(1)
˥ ˌ	Ting .le[7]	'has heard,'	ting .le.	TING .LE.
˧˥ ˌ	Lai .le	'has come,'	lai .le.	LAI .LE.
˨˩˦ ˈ	½Mae .le	'has bought,'	½mae .le.	½MAE .LE.
˩ ˌ	May .le	'has sold,'	may .le.	MAY .LE.

(2)
˥ ˌ	San'g	'three,'	san'g.	SAN'G.
˧˥ ˌ	*Ig*	'one, a,'	*ig.*	*IG.*
˨˩˦ ˈ	½Wuug	'five,'	½wuug.	½WUUG.
˩ ˌ	Liowg	'six,'	liowg.	LIOWG.

(3)
˥ ˌ	Fei .de	'that which flies,'	fei .de.	FEI .DE.
˧˥ ˌ	Par .de	'that which crawls,'	par .de.	PAR .DE.
˨˩˦ ˈ	½Pao .de	'that which runs,'	½pao .de.	½PAO .DE.
˩ ˌ	Tiaw .de	'that which jumps,'	tiaw .de.	TIAW .DE.

---

[6] See p. 26.

[7] Some speakers pronounce a 1st Tone before a neutral tone with a slight fall in pitch, approaching 53: or ˥˧.

THE TONES

(4) ⌐ ·| Ting .le   san'g   fei .de.   (*CL* repeat)
    ⌐ ·| Lai .le   *ig*   par .de.   (*CL* repeat)
    ⌐ ·| Mae .le   wuug   pao .de.   (*CL* repeat)
    ⌐ ·| May .le   liowg   tiaw .de.   (*CL* repeat)

EXERCISES

(a) Read aloud:
   (1) Mei tarng.   (2) Ta pao.   (3) ½Nii yaw.   (4) Fei .le.
   (5) May tarng.   (6) Mha ting.   (7) ½Mae ma.   (8) ½Nii ting.
   (9) Ta tiaw.   (10) Tiaw .le   (11) *Mae* maa.   (12) Yaw fei.
   (13) Lai may.   (14) Yaw mah.   (15) ½Pao .le.   (16) May maa.
   (17) Lai ting.   (18) *Ig*.   (19) Ta lai.   (20) Lai mae.

(b) From listening to a similar list of phrases as given by the teacher or a record, indicate the tones by tone-signs.

(c) Spell out the words.

Remember that when you hear a 2nd Tone before a 3rd Tone, it may be an original 2nd Tone or a 3rd Tone changed into a 2nd, depending on which makes better sense.

LESSON B DIFFICULT SOUNDS

1. **Difficult Consonants.** —
   (a) Unaspirated and Aspirated Voiceless Initials:

   English consonant: *by* [1] as contrasted with —
   Chinese consonants: s*p*y   (spelt *b*)
                         *p*ie   (spelt *p*)

*b*enq	⌐ ⇘ ⌐ ⇘ lao benq vx	'hopping all the time'
*p*enq	⌐ ⇘ ⌐ ⇘ lao penq vx	'colliding all the time'

   English consonant: *d*eem   as contrasted with —
   Chinese consonants: s*t*eam   (spelt *d*)
                         *t*eam   (spelt *t*)

*d*uey	⇘ ∙l ⇘ ∙l	Duey .le vx.	'That's right, that's right.'
*t*uey	⇘ ∙l ⇘ ∙l	Tuey .le vx.	'Have retreated, have retreated.'

   English consonant: *g*ate   as contrasted with —
   Chinese consonants: s*k*ate   (spelt *g*)
                         *K*ate   (spelt *k*)

*g*ann	⇘ ⌐ ∙l	gann-wan.le	'finished doing (it)'
*k*ann	⇘ ⌐ ∙l	kann-wan.le	'finished looking at (it)'

*tz*uey	⇘ ∙l ∙l	Tzuey .le .ba?	'Drunk, I suppose?'
*ts*uey	⇘ ∙l ∙l	Tsuey .le .ba?	'Become brittle, I suppose?'

   (b) The j_r-initials (retroflexes), j_r, ch_r, sh_r, represent sounds with the tip of the tongue retracted and turned up in the position of English (untrilled) *r*. When pronouncing Chinese *juh*, *chuh*, *shuh*, *ruh*, think of English '*drew*,' '*true*,' '*shrew*,' '*rue*.' The lips must however be spread out if the vowel does not have the sound *u*. The *r*-element contained in j_r, ch_r, sh_r, and *r* is shorter than in English *dr*, *tr*, *shr*, and *r*.

   (1) Without spreading of lips.

j_ru	(dr–) ⌐ ⇘ ⌐	Ju bu lai.	'The pig does not come.'
ch_ru	(tr–) ⌐ ∙l ⌐	chu.bu-lai	'cannot come out'
sh_ru	(shr–) ⌐ ⇘ ⌐	Shu bu lai.	'The book does not come.'

   (2) With spreading of lips.

$j_r$anq	(dr–) ⇘ ∙l	$j_r$anq .le	'have swollen'
ch_ranq	(tr–) ⇘ ∙l	ch_ranq .le	'have sung'
sh_ranq	(shr–) ⇘ ∙l	sh_ranq .le	'have taken up'

[1] A Chinese teacher whose dialect has no true voiced stops had better not try to pronounce these English words.

$j_r$ao	(dr–) ⩗ ⩘ yaw $j_r$ao	'want to look for'
ch_rao	(tr–) ⩗ ⩘ yaw ch_rao	'want to fry'
sh_rao	(shr–) ⩗ ⩘ yaw sh_rao	'want it to be scarce'

(c) The retroflex initial *r* is not trilled and is shorter than English *r*. As in the other j_r-initials, the lips are spread out unless the vowel itself calls for lip rounding.

(1) Without spreading of lips.

*r*uh	$r$uh	⩗ ⩘ *r*uhkoou	'entrance (door)'

(2) With spreading of lips.

*r*en	$r$en	⩘ ⊦ ⩘ *ig* *r*en	'a person'
*r*ow	$r$ow	⌐ ⩗ mae *r*ow	'buy meat'

(d) In pronouncing the j_i-initials, think, for j_i, ch_i, sh_i, of English 'jeep,' 'cheese,' 'she' (or better, German 'ich'), but spread your lips, except before the sound represented by *iu* (French *u*).

$j_i$iang	⌐ ⩘ ⌐ Woo mei $j_i$iang.	'I have no ginger.'
ch_iiang	⌐ ⩘ ⌐ Woo mei ch_iiang.	'I have no rifle.'
sh_iiang	⌐ ⩘ ⌐ Woo mei sh_iiang.	'I have no incense.'

(e) Practice distinguishing between j_r– and j_i– initials.

$j_r$ow	⌐ ⊦ ⩗ ⊦ I.fwu $j_r$ow .le.	'The clothes have become wrinkled.'
$j_i$iow	⌐ ⊦ ⩗ ⊦ I.fwu $j_i$iow .le.	'The clothes have become old.'
ch_ranq	⌐ ⩗ ⊦ Ta ch_ranq .le.	'He has sung.'
ch_iianq	⌐ ⩗ ⊦ Ta ch_iianq .le.	'He has got something in his windpipe.'
sh_rao	⩗ ⌐ ⊦ Tay sh_rao .le.	'Too few, too little.'
sh_ieau	⩗ ⌐ ⊦ Tay sh_ieau .le.	'Too small.'

(f) Write out the following words from dictation and indicate subscripts *r* or *i* under *j*, *ch*, or *sh*.

(1) shao. (2) shanq. (3) sheau. (4) shiang. (5) janq.
(6) chu.   (7) ju.   (8) jao.   (9) chanq.   (10) chiang.
(11) jiow. (12) chao. (13) shu.   (14) jow.   (15) chianq.

(g) Chinese *h* has a rougher sound than English *h* and approaches that of *ch* in German 'rau*ch*en.' As this is easy to learn, no special exercise need be given.

2. **Difficult Vowels, etc.** —

(a) The final *y:*

(1) After *tz*, *ts*, *s*, the vowel *y* has the quality of a vocalized *z*.

94   FOUNDATION WORK

    tzyh tsyh syh   'word' 'prickle' 'four' B
    tsy   tsyr   tsyy   tsyh
    'deviation' L[2] 'porcelain' 'this' L 'prickle'

After having learned to make the buzzing sound in all the tones, the student should practice releasing the pressure at the tip of the tongue so as to make less frictional sound during the vowel part.

(2) After j_r, ch_r, sh_r, r, the final y has the quality of a prolonged r, with spread lips. (This final does not occur after j_i, ch_i, sh_i.)

    jyh chyh shyh ryh   'heal' 'wing' B 'affair' 'day' B
    chy chyr chyy chyh   'eat' 'late' 'a foot' 'wing' B

(b) The High-Back Vowel u, as in *oo*dles, gives no trouble to English-speaking persons except those from the southern states of the United States. One or more of the following methods may be tried until the desired dark, hollow, back quality is produced.

(1) Get ready to whistle the lowest note you can and vocalize the sound instead of actually whistling.

(2) Hold (or imagine holding) a mouthful of water and try not to swallow it or to let it flow out by rounding your lips. The sound emitted will be the Chinese u.

(3) Pinch your cheek from the sides to force the tongue back.

(4) Round your lips to a small opening while saying *awe*, *all*, *tall*, *law*, etc.

(5) Use a resonant singing voice, with loosened jaw and throat, as in singing "Lullaby and g*oo*d night."

(6) Use the Swedish *o* as in *god* 'good.'

    tu twu tuu tuh   'bald' 'diagram' 'soil' 'vomit'
    u   wu   wuu wuh   'crow' L 'have not' L 'five' B 'fog'

(c) The high front vowel iu (French u or German $ü$) can be formed by saying u (as in 'r*u*le') and simultaneously thrusting the tongue forward to say i (as in 'pol*i*ce'). Another way is to get ready to whistle the highest note possible and vocalizing instead of actually whistling.[3] Be sure to keep the tongue tightly in the front position for i (as in 'pol*i*ce') during the *whole* time of the vowel. Note that although spelt iu, it is one homogeneous vowel, with no change of quality in time.

[2] "L" stands for 'literary' or *wenli*.
[3] The highest whistling position corresponds to Chinese iu; the lowest whistling position corresponds to Chinese u; the position for whistling a medium pitch, when vocalized, will give the sound used in "the South" in words like 'o*o*dles,' 'tr*u*e,' etc., which is not a Chinese vowel.

DIFFICULT SOUNDS

u	iu	u	iu	i iu i iu
iu	yu	yeu	yuh	'literal-minded' 'fish' 'rain' 'jade'
iuan	yuan	yeuan	yuann	'wronged' 'round' 'far' 'willing' B
iun	yun	yeun	yunn	'dizzy' 'cloud' B 'promise' B 'rhyme'

(d) The Back Vowels *e* and *uo:* The Chinese vowel *e* should best be learned from a model than from description (p. 22). In pronouncing the final *uo*, open the lips toward the end.

e	Ta	eh.		'He's hungry.'	Eh.gwo	'Russia'
ke	ker	kee	keh	'carve' 'cough' B 'thirsty' 'guest'		
uo	duo	shuo		'talk much'	Woo shuo.	'I say.'
guo	gwo	guoo	guoh	'pot' 'country' 'fruit' B 'pass'		

(e) The vowel *e* has a front quality, as in '*e*dge,' in the finals *ie* and *iue*. Remember that *iue* consists of two, not three, sounds.

ie	shie.x	'rest a little'	Shieh.x!	'Thank you!'
iue	dahiue	'approximately'	dahshyue	'university'

(f) The obscure vowel [ə] in *en, uen*. The vowel here is not like *e* in 'am*e*n,' but like *e* in 'om*e*n.' The thing to practice on is to keep this obscure vowel quality in all tones, whether stressed or not.

en	gen	'with, and'	wenn ren	'ask people'

(g) Nasalized Retroflex Vowels:

miengl 'tomorrow' dahshengl 'loudly' yanql 'form' chorngl 'bug'

(h) Final *-n* must not be linked to a following vowel or semi-vowel, as in Enlgish 'an iceman,' 'when you.' Learn to slur the *-n* by not letting the tongue touch the front part of the mouth.

sa^n-ell	we^{n}yan	je^n hao
'three-two'	'literary language'	'how nice!'

3. Easy Sounds Difficult to Remember from the Orthography. —

(a) Front or "clear" *a:*

ai	uai	Kuay lai mae.	'Hurry up and come to buy.'
an	ian [4]	uan iuan	san-tian	wanchyuan
			'three days.'	'completely'

(b) Medium *a:*

a ia ua   Ta shia jua.   'He grabs at random.'

[4] See p. 23.

(c) Back or "broad" *a:*

au	iau	lao tiaw		yaw pao	
		'keep jumping.'		'want to run.'	
ang	iang [5]	uang	lang	liang	hwang
			'wolf'	'cool'	'yellow'

(d) Special values of vowels: *ou* as in 'd*ou*gh,' *in* as in 'mach*in*e,' *eng* as in '*un*cle,' *ong* as in German 'j*ung*.'

ou	j_rou	in	j_iin	eng	j_reng	ong	j_rong
	'congee'		'now' B		'to steam'		'middle' B

(e) Change of vowel values with tones (pp. 23–24):

huei   hwei   hoei   huey   'dust' 'return' B 'destroy' 'meet'
iou   you   yeou   yow   'quiet' B 'oil' 'have' 'again'
jiel   erl   eel   ell   'today' 'child' B 'ear' B 'two' B

EXERCISES

(a) Write down tone signs and orthography of words as dictated. Examples:

(1) liowg   (2) Ta mae.   (3) yaw lai
(4) *Nii* mae.   (5) mei tiaw   (6) pao .le
(7) Nii yaw fei.   (8) *Nii mae* maa. (9) Ta mae tarng.
(10) Tang lai .le.

(b) Write tone signs and orthography of phrases as dictated and give meanings. Examples:

(1) lao penq vx   lao bcnq vx   (2) Duey .le vx.   Tuey .le vx.
(3) kann-wan.le   gann-wan.le   (4) Tsuey .le .ba? tzuey .le .ba?

(c) Write down tone signs and orthography of words as dictated. Examples:

(1) tuu	(2) jiang	(3) syh	(4) chiang	(5) chianq
(6) shiang	(7) chanq	(8) jow	(9) shuo	(10) shieh
(11) sheau	(12) jao	(13) shu	(14) shia	(15) jua
(16) shanq	(17) ju	(18) chao	(19) ryh	(20) jin
(21) shao	(22) chu	(23) jiow	(24) jeng	(25) jong
(26) yuan	(27) eh	(28) ker	(29) wenn	(30) penq

[5] The *a* in *iang* is not quite so far back and approaches a medium value.

LESSON C THE SYSTEM OF SOUNDS

After learning the sounds and tones which need special attention, the student is ready to learn the complete system of sounds of Mandarin.

1. The Initials. — The initials should be memorized both by rows and by columns. The teacher should read each row and the class repeat after him after each row. Then the whole table is read again column by column. Since some of the consonants cannot be sounded, — *b*, for example, consisting of merely closing the lips — each of the initials should be sounded by giving it a final. The finals used here are the ones used in the names of the National Phonetic Letters.

(a) Read the initials by rows (toward the right):

Row-*b*	*T:*	bo	po	`mho	fo		(*CL*)
Row-*d*	*T:*	de	te	nhe		lhe	(*CL*)
Row-*tz*	*T:*	tzy	tsy		sy		(*CL*)
Row-*j*$_r$	*T:*	j$_r$y	ch$_r$y		sh$_r$y	rhy	(*CL*)
Row-*j*$_i$	*T:*	j$_i$i	ch$_i$i		sh$_i$i		(*CL*)
Row-*g*	*T:*	ge	ke		he		(*CL*)

(b) Read the initials by columns (downwards):

Col. *b*	Col. *p*	Col. *m*	Col. *f*	Col. *l*
T:	*T:*	*T:*	*T:*	*T:*
bo	po	mho	fo	
de	te	nhe		lhe
tzy	tsy		sy	
j$_r$y	ch$_r$y		sh$_r$y	rhy
j$_i$i	ch$_i$i		sh$_i$i	
ge	ke		he	
(*CL*)	(*CL*)	(*CL*)	(*CL*)	(*CL*)

(c) Copy the table of initials, cut the paper into small bits with one initial on each, mix them up, and try to rearrange the bits in the original order.

2. Finals in Basic Form. — The finals can be pronounced alone, except that *y* is to be named as "*sy, shy.*" Finals in the first three tones are to be read horizontally only, the class interrupting with its repeating three times in each row, as indicated. The 4th-Tone finals are to be read vertically only. For simplicity, we have omitted the finals *iai*, *ueng*, and *el*. The present table is sufficient for the purposes of this lesson.

(a) Read the finals by rows (to the right):

98 FOUNDATION WORK

	T(Class repeat)	T(Cl)	T(Cl)
Row-a	sy, shy[1] a e;	ai ei au ou;	an en ang eng ong
Row-i	i ia ie;	iau iou;	ian in iang ing iong
Row-u	u ua uo[2];	uai uei ;	uan uen uang
Row-iu	iu[3] iue;		iuan iun

(b) Cut up and rearrange the table of finals, as with the initials.

EXERCISE

Read the following words; then write them from dictation in a different order:

(1) uan   (2) shiun   (3) shin   (4) j$_i$ia   (5) huen
(6) j$_r$uai (7) biau   (8) sy   (9) iue   (10) die
(11) sh$_r$eng (12) ch$_r$an (13) ch$_r$y   (14) iuan   (15) tza
(16) e   (17) tian   (18) iong   (19) j$_r$ong   (20) sh$_r$uo
(21) duei (22) sou   (23) ch$_i$iou (24) sh$_i$iang (25) ch$_r$u

3. Finals in 2nd Tone. — Referring to Rule 2, p. 28, we form the 2nd-Tone finals in Row-a by adding r after the vowel in Row-a. For Row-i, Row-u, and Row-iu, apply Rule 3 by changing i–, u–, iu– into y–, w–, and yu– respectively, but note that i and u as complete finals are written yi and wu.

(a) Read the 2nd-Tone finals by rows:

Row-a syr, shyr ar er; air eir aur our; arn ern arng erng orng.
Row-i   yi   ya ye;   yau you; yan yn   yang yng yong.
Row-u   wu   wa wo; wai wei;   wan wen wang.
Row-iu yu   yue;   yuan yun.

(Class repeat after each semicolon or period.)

(b) Supplementary Rule 7: Insert h after m, n, l, r for the 1st Tone, as mha, nhie, lha, rheng, but use basic form for the 2nd Tone, as ma, nian, lai, ren.

EXERCISE

Read the following words in the 1st and 2nd Tones; then write them from dictation in a different order:

---

[1] Boldface letters represent sounds difficult to make; italics indicate sounds of letters difficult to remember.

[2] The final uo is abbreviated to o after labial initials. Thus, a syllable pronounced buo is written bo.

[3] Since the diagraph iu represents one simple vowel, the finals in this row always have one sound fewer than there are letters. Thus, iu has one sound, iue has two sounds, iuan has three sounds, and iun has two sounds.

THE SYSTEM OF SOUNDS

(1) sheir   (2) wang   (3) ren   (4) mha   (5) sh$_r$yr
(6) wen   (7) gwo   (8) iang   (9) torng   (10) wen
(11) ling   (12) tair   (13) lai   (14) tzwo   (15) ch$_i$yuan
(16) rheng   (17) her   (18) tour   (19) lhuo   (20) ch$_i$yi
(21) yau   (22) tyan   (23) sh$_i$yue (24) twu   (25) yn
(26) ian   (27) chyang (28) mei   (29) tarng   (30) nian

4. Finals in 3rd Tone. — Rule 4: To form the 3rd-Tone finals, single vowel letters are doubled, as *syy*, *maa*, *bii*ng. In *ei*, *ie*, *ou*, *uo*, the *e* or *o* is doubled, as *meei*, *suoo*. Rule 5: In the other cases, change medial or the ending *i* into *e*, and *u* into *o*, *iu* into *eu*, as *leang*, *goang*, *mae*, *hao*, *sheau*.

(a) Read the 3rd-Tone finals by rows:

Row-*a*   tzyy, jyy aa   ee;   ae   eei; ao   oou; aan   een   aang eeng oong
Row-*i* (j$_i$)   jii   jea⁴ jiee;   jeau jeou; jean jiin jeang jiing jeong
Row-*u* (j$_r$)   juu   joa   juoo; joai joei;   joan joen joang.
Row-*iu* (j$_i$) jeu⁴   jeue;   jeuan jeun.

This table should be read very slowly, with a pause after each final, since running two 3rd Tones together would make the first change into a 2nd Tone.

EXERCISE

Read the following words in the 3rd Tone; then write them from dictation in a different order:

(1) hao   (2) lea   (3) liing   (4) sh$_i$euan   (5) goa
(6) sh$_i$eue (7) jiin   (8) neu   (9) taang   (10) baan
(11) sh$_r$eeng (12) j$_i$iee (13) feen   (14) mae   (15) aa
(16) goang   (17) doong   (18) j$_i$eong (19) dean   (20) jyy
(21) meei   (22) leang   (23) tsyy   (24) sh$_r$oou   (25) sh$_r$oei

(b) Supplementary Rule 8: When finals of Rows –*i*, –*u*, –*iu* occur as words without any initial, they are spelt with the *addition* of *y* or *w*, except that in –*iee*, –*uoo* the *i* and *u* are *changed* into *y* and *w*.

Row-*i* yii yea yee;   yeau yeou; yean yiin yeang yiing yeong.
Row-*u* wuu woa woo; woai woei; ;   woan woen woang.
Row-*iu* yeu   yeue;   yeuan yeun.

EXERCISE

Read the following words in the 3rd Tone; then write them from dictation in a different order:

(1) yee   (2) tuu   (3) jeou   (4) woan   (5) leu
(6) wuu   (7) doan   (8) woo   (9) yeou   (10) yeu

⁴ Since *ea*, etc. are merely the 3rd-Tone forms of *ia* etc., the *j* still has sound of a j$_i$.

5. Finals in 4th Tone.

Rule 6: The 4th-Tone finals are formed by changing the endings zero, –*i*, –*u*, –*n*, –*ng* to –*h*, –*y*, –*w*, –*nn*, and –*nq*, respectively. Note that the finals *y*, *i*, *u*, and *iu* come under finals with zero endings.

(a) Read the 4th-Tone finals by *columns* (downwards).

(Basic) 4th Tone	(zero) –h			(–i) –y		(–u) –w		(–n) –nn		(–ng) –nq		
	T:	*T:*	*T:*	*T:*	*T:*	*T:*	*T:*	*T:*	*T:*	*T:*	*T:*	*T:*
Row-*a*	syh, shyh	ah	eh	ay	ey	aw	ow	ann	enn	anq	enq	onq
Row-*i* jᵢ	jih	jiah	jieh			jiaw	jiow	jiann	jinn	jianq	jinq	jionq
Row-*u* jᵣ	juh	juah	juoh	juay	juey			juann	juenn	juanq		
Row-*iu* jᵢ	jiuh		jiueh					jiuann	jiunn			
	(CL)	(CL)	(CL)	(CL)	(CL)	(CL)	(CL)	(CL)	(CL)	(CL)	(CL)	(CL)

EXERCISE

Read the following words in the 4th Tone; then write them from dictation in a different order:

(1) may   (2) dih   (3) huey   (4) tuh   (5) syh
(6) poh   (7) how   (8) denq   (9) shinn   (10) donq
(11) shiunn (12) shieh   (13) liueh   (14) chuanq (15) guann
(16) shiah   (17) liow   (18) kuay   (19) chiuh   (20) jiann
(21) shanq   (22) daw   (23) jiaw   (24) reh   (25) jey

(b) Supplementary Rule 9: When finals of Rows –*i*, –*u*, –*iu* occur as words without any initial, they are spelt by *changing* the medial *i* or *u* (or *i* of *iu*) into *y* and *w* respectively, except that *y* or *w* is *added* in y*ih*, w*uh*, y*inn*, y*inq*.

Row-*i*   *y*ih yah yeh ;   yaw yow; yann *y*inn yanq *y*inq yonq.
Row-*u*   *w*uh wah woh ;   way wey   ; wann wenn wanq.
Row-*iu* yuh   yueh;   yuann yunn.

EXERCISE

Read the following words in the 4th Tone; then write them from dictation in a different order:

(1) huann   (2) yeh   (3) tiaw   (4) wann   (5) wuh
(6) chih   (7) yaw   (8) yih   (9) duh   (10) jieh

6. Finals in All Tones.

If the student has not yet memorized Table 3, p. 29, he should copy it on a sheet of paper, cut it up, and try to rearrange the jumbled bits into the original order.

7. Related Syllables.

Sound and spelling are best understood and remembered when a syllable is grouped with its nearest related syllables.

THE SYSTEM OF SOUNDS

A group of related syllables consists of an initial (including zero as a special case) in one column of finals in all tones, in other words, one whole column of Table 3, p. 29. For example, starting with syllable *wann*, we get the four tones *uan, wan, woan, wann*. Moreover, to complete the column of finals, we get *ann, yann, wann, yuann*. Filling out all the 16 possibilities, we get:

	1st Tone	2nd Tone	3rd Tone	4th Tone
Row-a	an	arn	aan	ann
Row-i	ian	yan	yean	yann
Row-u	uan	wan	woan	*wann*
Row-iu	iuan	yuan	yeuan	yuann

For the purposes of these exercises, we shall put the j_i's and j_r's into one group. For example, starting with a syllable like *chern*, we get the group of related syllables as follows:

	1st Tone	2nd Tone	3rd Tone	4th Tone
Row-a	chen	*chern*	cheen	chenn
Row-i	chin	chyn	chiin	chinn
Row-u	chuen	chwen	choen	chuenn
Row-iu	chiun	chyun	cheun	chiunn

To save unnecessary spelling of non-existent types of words, leave blank rows in accordance with the following features of sound distribution in Mandarin:

(1) The initials *g, k, h; tz, ts, s* do not combine with *Row-i* or *Row-iu* finals. Thus *ki, siu*, etc., are ruled out.

(2) The final *y* (as in *sy, shy*) combines exclusively with *j, ch, sh, r; tz, ts, s* and does not combine with any other initial or stand alone.

(3) Non-existent finals should of course be left out. For example, starting from *jiang*, we get *jang, jiang, juang*, but no *jiuang*, since there is no such final as *–iuang*.

In the following examples, start from the syllable in italics and reconstruct the whole table without looking. The exercise may be varied by starting from some syllable other than the one in italics. Students weak in pronunciation or romanization should be given occasional practice in related syllables even after he has taken up the conversational lessons.

(1)					(2)				(3)			
di	dyi	dii	*dih*	*i*	yi	yii	yih		ja	jar	jaa	jah
du	dwu	duu	duh	u	wu	wuu	wuh		jia	jya	*jea*	jiah
diu	dyu	deu	diuh	iu	yu	yeu	yuh		jua	jwa	joa	juah

FOUNDATION WORK

(4)
e	er	ee	eh
ie	ye	yee	yeh
uo	wo	*woo*	woh
iue	yue	yeue	yueh

(5)
shy	*shyr*	shyy	shyh
shi	shyi	shii	shih
shu	shwu	shuu	shuh
shiu	shyu	sheu	shiuh

(6)
chen	chern	cheen	chenn
chin	chyn	chiin	chinn
chuen	chwen	choen	chuenn
chiun	*chyun*	cheun	chiunn

(7)
ai	air	ae	*ay*
uai	wai	woai	way

(8)
lheng	leng	*leeng*	lenq
lhing	ling	liing	linq

(9)
ge	ger	gee	geh
guo	*gwo*	guoo	guoh

(10)
nhi	ni	*nii*	nih
nhu	nu	nuu	nuh
nhiu	niu	neu	niuh

(11)
ang	arng	aang	anq
iang	*yang*	yeang	yanq
uang	wang	woang	wanq

(12)
a	ar	aa	ah
ia	ya	yea	*yah*
ua	wa	woa	wah

(13)
rhen	*ren*	reen	renn
rhuen	ruen	roen	ruenn

(14)
shei	*sheir*	sheei	shey
shuei	shwei	shoei	shuey

(15)
hai	hair	hae	hay
huai	hwai	hoai	*huay*

(16)
eng	erng	eeng	enq
ing	yng	yiing	yinq

(17)
san	sarn	*saan*	sann
suan	swan	soan	suann

(18)
jong	jorng	joong	jonq
jiong	jyong	*jeong*	jionq

(19)
dei	deir	*deei*	dey
duei	dwei	doei	duey

(20)
mhau	mau	mao	maw
mhiau	*miau*	meau	miaw

(21)
ou	our	oou	ow
iou	you	*yeou*	yow

(22)
lhe	le	lee	leh
lhie	lie	liee	lieh
lhuo	*luo*	luoo	luoh
lhiue	liue	leue	liueh

(23)
an	arn	aan	ann
ian	yan	yean	yann
uan	wan	*woan*	wann
iuan	yuan	yeuan	yuann

(24)
jen	jern	jeen	jenn
jin	jyn	*jiin*	jinn
juen	jwen	joen	juenn
jiun	jyun	jeun	jiunn

8. Review. —

EXERCISES

Write from dictation:

(a) First Tone

(1) i   e   uo   a   (2) sy   en   ei   shy
(3) uan iue   ia   ing   (4) ang an   ie   sy
(5) iang shy   u   ian   (6) ai   ong au   iue
(7) iou in   uen   eng   (8) iau ie   iu   uai
(9) uei ou   iuan uo   (10) iou ua   ian iun

(b) Second Tone

(1) ar   wo   yng   er   (2) shyr eir   syr   ern
(3) ya   yan   yi   yu   (4) ye   yue   syr   arn
(5) wu   erng wang shyr   (6) aur   wai   arng orng
(7) wen   ar   yang yn   (8) yu   yun   air   ye
(9) yuan you   our   wei   (10) yan yau   wa   you

THE SYSTEM OF SOUNDS 103

(c) Third Tone with initials

(1) bii   kee   goang suoo   (2) syy   feen   jaang meei
(3) beau   leang maa   lean   (4) gaan   mae   jyy   shiee
(5) tzyy   jeou   chiing tuu   (6) doong   sheau   syy   lao
(7) jiin   shoei dean   goan   (8) jiee   leou   sheue neu
(9) shoou   deeng jeuan doan   (10) goa   goai   jean   sheun

(d) Third Tone without initials

(1) yii   woang yeang yeou   (2) woei   yiin   woo   yea
(3) wuu   woen   yeuan yiing   (4) yean   yeau   yeou   yee
(5) woa   yee   yeu   yean   (6) yeun   wuu   yiin   woei

(e) Fourth Tone with initials

(1) shyh   fey   syh   benn   (2) shieh   liueh   tzyh   fann
(3) daw   kuay   fanq   sonq   (4) chiuh   jiunn   may   jieh
(5) jiann   jiaw   huah   liow   (6) pah   guoh   shinq keh
(7) guenn   panq   chianq shinn   (8) chiuann jiow   dow   duey

(f) Fourth Tone without initials

(1) yah   woh   yeh   yinn   (2) wey   yaw   yinn   yow
(3) yann   wuh   yanq   yinq   (4) yunn   wanq   yuann yann
(5) yih   wenn   yow   wey   (6) yuh   wuh   yeh   wah

(g) Mixed Tones with or without initials

(1) chiou   doong duey   yau   (2) sonq   wenn   yang   chuen
(3) lian   ya   shiann liow   (4) doou   juh   shye   benn
(5) lianq   jiu   torng shuo   (6) syh   taur   jenq   tiau
(7) iuan   dou   tzuoh chyi   (8) lha   daw   yeong yaw
(9) chiuann tour   woo   chyn   (10) par   sheir   tian   yonq
(11) tarn   ren   jiang tarng   (12) rheng   mhau   bao   mei
(13) shiah   shiong jong   shanq   (14) keh   jia   dinq   joen
(15) juei   fann   deeng ni   (16) shinn   chy   shoei kuay
(17) tang   heen   jey   ting   (18) goang   wanq   wu   syy
(19) shan   meei   yeun   in   (20) doan   wann   swo   yun
(21) hair   kee   sheue diing   (22) goai   shuang wen   shyue
(23) kai   sheau yeuan yiin   (24) goa   guan   wei   chyuan
(25) pah   leang yeu   jii   (26) shiunn guai   wang   yu
(27) mae   dean   terng dih   (28) jiun   wah   chwan shyr
(29) jaang   jea   shern shieh   (30) liuh   gua   hwai   you
(31) jaan   ge   der   yee   (32) yueh   shu   hwa   chyong

9. Check List of Points on Pronunciation. — For the convenience of teachers, the following check list on pronunciation is given for following up the students' work.

No.	Code	Weight	Point
1.	3rd	C	Use of lower limit of voice for the 3rd Tone.
2.	ton	A	Pronouncing and recognition of tones singly.
3.	asp	A	Distinguishing unaspirated and aspirated initials.
4.	bdg	C	Use of voiceless sounds (French *p, t,* etc.) for the unaspirates *b, d, tz, j_r, j_i, g,* instead of English *b, d,* etc., which are voiced.
5.	j_r	A	Placing of retroflex initials *j_r, ch_r, sh_r, r,* in the *tongue position* of English *dr, tr, shr, r*.
6.	ren	C	Avoidance of lip action usually associated with English *r* for *j_r, ch_r, sh_r, r* (except with *ju, chu,* etc.)
7.	jin	C	Avoidance of lip action usually associated with English *j, ch, sh* for *j_i, ch_i, sh_i* (except with *jiu, chiu,* etc.)
8.	h–	D	Rough pronunciation of *h,* as in German *ach.*
9.	sy	B	Tongue-tip pronunciation and spreading of lips for *y* as final, i.e., for *tz, ts, s; j, ch, sh, r.*
10.	iu	B	Use of correct value for the vowel *iu* (French *u*).
11.	uo	C	Unrounding at the end of *uo* as if it were *uo^a*.
12.	e	D	Diphthongal pronunciation of *e,* more open at the end.
13.	en	D	Central value of *e* in *en* and *uen* ('omen' vs. 'amen').
14.	el	C	General American pronunciation of 'err,' 'art,' etc.
15.	ngl	D	Nasalized retroflex vowels.
16.	–n	C	Slurring of final *–n* before vowels.
17.	u	C	Back, dark, hollow quality of *u* (avoidance of "Southern" pronunciation).
18.	I	D	Visual memory of initials.
19.	II	D	Visual memory of finals.
20.	III	B	Visual memory of finals in the 4 tones.
21.	mnl	C	1st- and 2nd-Tone forms of *m, n, l, r.*
22.	yea	C	Adding or changing of *y* or *w* for 3rd and 4th Tones.
23.	4 × x	B	Construction of square or rectangular tables of related syllables from a given syllable.
24.	ini	D	Oral recitation of initials by rows and columns.
25.	fin	D	Oral recitation of finals by rows and columns.
26.	ai	D	Front, clear, bright quality of *a* in *ai, an,* etc.
27.	au	D	Back, dark, broad quality of *a* in *au, ang,* etc.
28.	ian	D	Special value of *a* in *ian.*
29.	ie	C	Value of *e* in *ie* and *iue* (different from e in Row-a).
30.	in	D	Use of vowel in English *seen* (not as in English *in*).

THE SYSTEM OF SOUNDS   105

No. Code   Weight Point
31. eng   D   Use of vowel as in English *uncle*.
32. ong   C   Very close *o* in *ong* and *iong*, as in German *jung*.
33. uei   D   More open vowels in 3rd and 4th Tones for *iou, uei, el*.
34. ½3   B   Automatic use of half 3rd Tone in combinations when speaking, or reading from unmarked text.
35. 33   B   Automatic use of 2nd Tone when a 3rd is followed by another 3rd.
36. ibu   C   Automatic use of the right tones for *i* and *bu* (p. 107).
37. 1 + 2   C   Correct use of two-syllable phrase tones when both syllables are in the 2nd Tone or one in the first and the other in the second (p. 90).
38. 4 × 5   C   Humming of all two-tone combinations.
39. ˥   C   Tracing or writing out of tone-signs from orthography or from hearing words pronounced.
40. x   A   Writing from dictation any word or phrase.

In assigning weights to the various points, if A, B, C, and D are given the numerical values of 8, 4, 2, and 1 respectively, then the total for the 40 points will add up to 100. Following is a sample test on the 40 points of the check list.

1. Daa. Tzoou. Lii. Hao. Heen.
2. Hum the following tones: ˧, ˦, ˨, ˧, ˥, ˦, ˩, ˥, ˧, ˩.
   Identify the following tones as spoken by the teacher:
   (a) Lai.   (b) Jenn.   (c) Yeong.   (d) Pern.   (e) Sy.
   (f) Chian (g) Pah.   (h) Wey.   (i) Sheau. (j) Ru.
3. daa   ta   bu   pah   tsa   tzoei jiann chyau kai   guan
   char juol tzao chi   pia   tsuoh jao   chiual tsu   chianq
4. ba   duey tzuoh jang jia   guai
5. shuang jenq roan shoei chy   ju   chuan ren   shuh shuo
6. ren   char shoou sheir jy
7. ching jea   chyan sheang jih
8. hair how   horng huen heh
9. shyr tsy   tzyy chyh jyy   sy   ryh
10. jiu liueh chiuh yeuan yunn
11. shuo guoh duoo poh   hwo
12. er   kee   che   keh   der
13. men goen fen   duenn heen
14. jiel ell   harl dall woal
15. shengl yeengl liengl hwangl yanql
16. weⁿⁿ–an faⁿ–yinn faⁿ.yih jiⁿyn huaⁿyng
17. hwu twu   chu   ruh   shu

106   FOUNDATION WORK

18. (See p. 19.)
19. (See p. 22.)
20. (See p. 29.)
21. Give the 1st and 2nd tone spellings of the following syllables: baa maa ling dao law reeng jean nean huoh luo
22. Give the 3rd and 4th tone spellings of the following syllables: jea iang shoei wei uo liuh ye yn huan u
23. Construct tables of related syllables starting with: shan choang jieh shern chy
24. (See p. 97.)
25. (See pp. 98–100.)
26. kuay lai mae kann wan
27. mhau jiaw shang liang chwang
28. tian bian jean chyan yan
29. shyue jieh sheue iue shye
30. shin lin jinn yiin pin
31. feng deeng cherng sheng genq
32. long yonq chyong doong horng
33. jeou hwei ell liou duey
34. Yeou ren.   Nii yaw.   Tzoou .le   Lao shuo.   Daa-pair.
    Yiitz.   Faanduey. Liibay.   Huooche.   Nii.de.
35. Mae jeou. Lao Lii.   Laoshuu.   Jeang-lii. Suooyii.
    Yeou mii. Tzoou-woen.le. Naal yeou? Woo sheang. Chii-tzao.
36. Bu nan.   Ideal.   Ikuall.   Bush.   Ell.shyri.
37. Charng chy. Renmiengl. Shuo lai. Fenhorng.   Laihwei.
38. (See p. 109.)
39. Use wall chart (p. 85) and words in Ex. 40 below.
40. iue   ruoh   ji   guu   dih   yau   fanq   shiun
    chin   minq   wen   sy   an   yeun   gong   keh
    ranq   guang bey   syh   beau   ger   yu   shanq
    shiah

LESSON D SYSTEM OF TONE SANDHI

In this lesson all forms of tonal succession in two- and three-syllable groups are exemplified in words or phrases of common occurrence, including both cases where there is change of tone, or tone sandhi, and cases where the individual tones remain unchanged.

1. Special Tones for I and Bu. — The words *i* 'one, a' B, and *bu* 'not' have special tonal behavior. Because of their extremely frequent occurrence, it is important for the student to learn to make the proper changes so that he will give the right tone automatically without the aid of tonal spelling. For this and other reasons, we are writing these two words with the invariant forms *i* and *bu*.

Before 1st, 2nd, and 3rd Tones, *i* and *bu* are pronounced in the 4th Tone. Before a 4th Tone it is pronounced in 2nd Tone (marked in italics through Lesson 8). When used alone (*i* as in counting, *bu* as in answering 'No'), or at the end of a phrase, *i* is pronounced in the 1st Tone and *bu* in the 4th Tone.[1]

When *i* and *bu* are unstressed, they are treated like any other unstressed syllable and need no special exercise.

(a) Tones of *I*:

i-tian	'a day'	i-jy	'a' (pencil, etc.)	i-jang	'a sheet'
i-nian	'a year'	i-hwei	'once'	i-gwo	'a country'
i-hoel	'a moment'	i-jaan	'a' (lamp)	ideal	'a little'
*i*yanq	'alike'	*i*-dih	'a floorful'	*i*g	'a' [2]
shyri	'eleven'	chu'i	'first' (of the month)	Liibay'i	'Monday'

(b) Tones of *Bu*:

bu shuo	'not say'	bu hei	'not black'	bujydaw	'not know'
butorng	'different'	bu chyuan	'not complete'	bu *i*yanq	'not alike'
bu doong	'not understand'	bu hao	'not good'	bu sheang	'not desire'
*bu*duey	'wrong'	*bu*yaw	'not want'	*bu*.sh	'is not' [3]

Bu! 'No!'   Ta bu. 'He won't.'
Bu.jie! 'No.'   Ta bu .le. 'He no longer does.'

[1] When strongly stressed, a non-final *i* has an optional pronunciation in the 1st Tone, as *Woo shuo* 'i-*dean jong*' 'I said "*one* o'clock."' *Bu* also has an optional 1st Tone when standing alone or followed by the suffix –.*jie* in the interjection *Bu.jie* 'No.'

[2] This means that although –*g* (i.e. .*geh*) is in the neutral tone, it still affects the preceding *i* as does a 4th-Tone word. In *i*-'*geh* 'one' where *geh* retains the 4th Tone, the case is of course like that of *i-dih*.

[3] The *bu* takes the 2nd Tone whether the following *sh* (i.e. *shyh*) has a neutral tone or a full 4th Tone. Cf. Note 2.

EXERCISE

Pronounce the following examples, giving special attention to the tones of *i* and *bu*.

(1) i-wey	(2) buhuey	(3) iyanq	(4) i-baa	(5) butorng
(6) bu iyanq	(7) Ding I	(8) buhao	(9) i-been	(10) bujydaw
(11) buyawjiin	(12) i-jiann	(13) ig	(14) bu doong	(15) i-shann
(16) bush	(17) i-jang	(18) i-kuay	(19) dih'i-keh	(20) bu wanchyuan
(21) i-jian	(22) ideal	(23) buduey	(24) bu.sh	(25) i, ell, san

2. Two Syllable Groups. — Before reading the examples in the table the teacher and students should first hum the tunes as indicated by the tone signs, then read all the four examples in each box and go on to the next box to the right.

3. Three-Syllable Groups. — In the table of three-syllable groups in all possible combinations, the first column gives the numbers of the tones. The figure "*3*" in italics indicates a 3rd Tone changed to a 2nd Tone because of a following 3rd Tone.

The cases of a 2nd Tone changing into 1st Tone have already been noted in Chapter II (p. 26), and the present table gives all the types of application of the rules. The changes are as follows:

$$\downarrow \begin{matrix} 121, 122, 123, 124; & 221, 222, 223, 224 \\ 111, 112, 113, 114; & 211, 212, 213, 214 \end{matrix} \downarrow$$

Moreover, since a 3rd Tone becomes a 2nd Tone, we have the following changes:

$$\downarrow \begin{matrix} 133, 233, 333 \\ 123, 223, 223 \\ 113, 213, 213 \end{matrix} \downarrow$$

There are some changes in the pitch of the neutral tone in three-syllable groups. The neutral tone in:

104 changes from half-low to half-high or high,
204 changes from middle to half-high or high,
301 changes from half-high to half-low,
302 changes from half-high to half-low.

These are marked "(!)" in the table.

In three-syllable groups, as in two-syllable groups, an original 3rd Tone, though actually pronounced in the neutral tone, still raises the pitch of a preceding 3rd Tone, as *woo daa .nii* 'I beat you' ˧ ˧ ˧ ; *geei .woo .le* 'have given me' ˧ ˧ ˧ ; *dah-sheau.jiee* 'young lady, Miss' ˅ ˧ ˧ (cf. Note 4).

SYSTEM OF TONE SANDHI

	˥	ˊ	ˇ (or ·˩)	ˋ	·˩, ·˧, ·˥, or ·˩
˥	˥ ˥ Ding I *proper name* Jang San *proper name* gen ta 'with him' kai-deng 'turn on the light'	˥ ˊ shinwen 'news' Ing'wen 'English' Jongwen 'Chinese' kai-men 'open the door'	˥ ˇ gen woo 'with me' gen nii 'with you' chianbii 'pencil' Jong-Meei 'Sino-American'	˥ ˋ ta yaw 'he wants' i ell 'one two' san syh 'three four' shuo-huah 'talk'	˥ ·˩ ta.de 'his' san'g 'three' dong.shi 'thing' juotz 'table'
ˊ	ˊ ˥ shyr-jang 'ten sheets' shyr-jy 'ten' mei shuo 'did not say' lian ta 'including him'	ˊ ˊ wanchyuan 'entirely' Sheir lai? 'Who comes?' Mei ren. 'There is nobody.' renren 'everybody'	ˊ ˇ lian nii 'including you' meiyeou 'have not' shyrjeou 'nineteen' maubii 'writing brush'	ˊ ˋ Wang Ell *proper name* bush 'is not' i-dih 'a floorful' bu tzay 'not present'	ˊ ·˩ Sheir .a? 'Who is it?' ig 'a' tzar.men 'you and I (or we)' shyr.howl 'time'
ˇ or ˊ	ˇ ˥ woo shuo 'I say' jii-jang 'several sheets' leang-jy 'two' yeou deng 'have lamp'	ˇ ˊ leang-nian 'two years' Nii chyau! 'You look!' Meeiwen 'American language' neei-gwo 'which country?'	ˊ ˇ Woo yeou. 'I have!' jao nii 'look for *you*' jao .nii[4] 'look for you' mae .deal[4] 'buy some'	ˇ ˋ Nii kann! 'You look!' Woo sh. 'I am.' Lii Syh *proper name* wuu liow 'five six'	ˇ ·˩ nii.de 'your(s)' leangg 'two' yiitz 'chair' Tzoou .ba! 'Let's go!'
ˋ or ˦	ˋ ˥ dih'i 'first' dianndeng 'electric light' yaw ting 'want to listen' huey shuo 'can speak'	ˋ ˊ Wenn sheir? 'Ask whom?' kann ren 'call on people' butorng 'different' Kuay lai! 'Come quick!'	ˋ ˇ Wenn woo! 'Ask *me!*' yonq bii 'use pen' bawjyy 'newspaper (as paper)' shanq naal? 'where to?'	˦ ˋ[5] dih'ell 'second' shianntzay 'now' tzay jell 'is here' tzay nall 'is there'	ˋ ·˩ jeyg 'this one' neyg 'that one' tzay.jell 'is present here' tzay.nall 'is present there'

[4] Note that although the 3rd-Tone words *.nii* and *.deal* are actually pronounced in the neutral tone they still cause the pitch of the preceding syllable to be raised. In such cases, however, the preceding syllable does not quite acquire a 2nd Tone, but still retains some of the glottal stricture characteristic of the original 3rd Tone.

[5] Since in a dissyllable with no neutral tone the first syllable is usually less stressed than the second (p. 26), it will naturally have a smaller range of fall in pitch. It is therefore also possible to mark this tonal pattern simply as ˋ ˋ and let the narrowed range in the first syllable be implied by the stress pattern.

111 ˥ ˥ ˥		sanshian-tang	'three-flavor soup'
112 ˥ ˥ ˊ		shuo Ing'wen	'speak English'
113 ˥ ˥ ˇ		duo he-shoei	'drink a lot of water'
114 ˥ ˥ ˋ		Ta shuo-huah	'He talks.'
110 ˥ ˥ ˙		Kai-deng .ba!	'Turn on the light!'
121 ˥ ˊ ˥ → ˥ ˥ ˥		dongnan-feng	'southeast wind'
122 ˥ ˊ ˊ → ˥ ˥ ˊ		sannian-jyi	'third-year class'
123 ˥ ˊ ˇ → ˥ ˥ ˇ		shianren-jaang	'immortal's palm, — cactus'
124 ˥ ˊ ˋ → ˥ ˥ ˋ		shihorng-shyh	'tomato'
120 ˥ ˊ ˙		shau-mei .de	'coal burner'
131 ˥ ˇ ˥		ta yee shuo	'he also says'
132 ˥ ˇ ˊ		Ta lao lai.	'He keeps coming.'
133 ˥ ˊ ˇ → ˥ ˥ ˇ		San*yean* Jieengl	'Threehole Well' (street name)
134 ˥ ˇ ˋ		Guei woo fuh.	'It's for me to pay.'
130 ˥ ˇ ˙		jen gaan.ji	'really grateful'
141 ˥ ˋ ˥		jidanngau	'sponge cake'
142 ˥ ˋ ˊ		Ta yaw char.	'He wants tea.'
143 ˥ ˋ ˇ		Shu tay sheau	'The book is too small.'
144 ˥ ˋ ˋ		shuang-guahhaw	'register with return receipt'
140 ˥ ˋ ˙		Ta eh .le.	'He is hungry.'
101 ˥ ˙ ˥		ga.jy'uo	'armpit'
102 ˥ ˙ ˊ		shuo.de-lai	'congenial'
103 ˥ ˙ ˇ		ting.bu-doong	'cannot understand'
104 ˥ ˙ ˋ (!)		Jong.gwo-huah	'Chinese language'
100 ˥ ˙ ˙		fei.lai .le	'have flown here'

211 ˧˥ ˥ ˥		sheir shian shuo	'who talks first'
212 ˧˥ ˥ ˧˥		Lugou Chyau	'Marco Polo Bridge'
213 ˧˥ ˥ ˨˩˦		wuhua-guool	'flowerless fruit, — fig'
214 ˧˥ ˥ ˥˩		horngshau-row	'pork stewed with soy sauce'
210 ˧˥ ˥ ˙		Lai chy .ba!	'Come and eat!'
221 ˧˥ ˧˥ ˥ → ˧˥ ˥ ˥		Mei Lanfang	'Mei Lan-fang'
222 ˧˥ ˧˥ ˧˥ → ˧˥ ˥ ˧˥		hair mei lai	'have not yet come'
223 ˧˥ ˧˥ ˨˩˦ → ˧˥ ˥ ˨˩˦		wanchyuan doong	'completely understand'
224 ˧˥ ˧˥ ˥˩ → ˧˥ ˥ ˥˩		shyunyang-jiann	'cruiser'
220 ˧˥ ˧˥ ˙		yang lutz	'foreign-style stove'
231 ˧˥ ˨˩˦ ˥		yang cheudengl	'matches'
232 ˧˥ ˨˩˦ ˧˥		tsorng naal lai?	'come from where?'
233 ˧˥ ˧˥ ˨˩˦ → ˧˥ ˥ ˨˩˦		harn*shuu*-beau	'(household) thermometer'
234 ˧˥ ˨˩˦ ˥˩		Bairtaa Syh	'White Pagoda Temple'
230 ˧˥ ˨˩˦ ˙		lai-woan.le	'have come late'
241 ˧˥ ˥˩ ˥		charng-shinnfengl	'long envelope'
242 ˧˥ ˥˩ ˧˥		youjenqjyu	'post office'
243 ˧˥ ˥˩ ˨˩˦		shyr'ell-dean	'twelve o'clock'
244 ˧˥ ˥˩ ˥˩		wushiann-diann	'wireless'
240 ˧˥ ˥˩ ˙		mei kann.jiann	'have not seen'
201 ˧˥ ˙ ˥		nan .de duo	'much more difficult'
202 ˧˥ ˙ ˧˥		*ig* ren	'a person'
203 ˧˥ ˙ ˨˩˦		sheir.de bii?	'whose writing brush?'
204 ˧˥ ˙ ˥˩ (!)		shyue.bu-huey	'cannot learn'
200 ˧˥ ˙ ˙		Wang .Shian.sheng	'Mr. Wang'

FOUNDATION WORK

311	⌙ ⌐ ⌐	lao chou-ian	'keep smoking (tobacco)'
312	⌙ ⌐ ⌒	hao shinwen	'good news'
313	⌙ ⌐ ⌿	faangsha-chaang	'cotton mill'
314	⌙ ⌐ ⌵	huooche-jann	'railroad station'
310	⌙ ⌐ ⌶	mae shi.gua	'buy watermelon'
321	⌙ ⌒ ⌐	Beeimen Jie	'North Gate Street'
322	⌙ ⌒ ⌒	leang-tyau yu	'two fish'
323	⌙ ⌒ ⌿	Nii mei doong.	'You did not understand.'
324	⌙ ⌒ ⌵	Woo mei konql.	'I have no time.'
320	⌙ ⌒ ⌶	Hao-jyi.le!	'That's fine!'
331	⌒ ⌙ ⌐	*Yeou* jii-jang?	'How many sheets are there?'
332	⌒ ⌙ ⌒	*lao* sheang lai	'always wanting to come'
333	⌒ ⌒ ⌿ → ⌒ ⌐ ⌿	*Woo yee* yeou.	'I also have.'
334	⌒ ⌙ ⌵	*Nii* yee huey.	'You also can.'
330	⌒ ⌙ ⌶	*Lao* Lii .ne?	'How about Lii?'
341	⌙ ⌵ ⌐	Gaankuay shuo!	'Hurry up and say it!'
342	⌙ ⌵ ⌒	Nii wenn sheir?	'Whom are you asking?'
343	⌙ ⌵ ⌿	Bii tay roan.	'The writing brush is too soft.'
344	⌙ ⌵ ⌵	daa-diannhuah	'to telephone'
340	⌙ ⌵ ⌶	Tzoou jey.bial!	'Go this way!'
301	⌙ ⌶ ⌐ (!)	Tzoou.bu-kai	'cannot get away'
302	⌙ ⌶ ⌒ (!)	leangg ren	'two people'
303	⌙ ⌶ ⌿	sheang .de heen	'desire very much'
304	⌙ ⌶ ⌵	saangtz dah	'loud-voiced'
300	⌙ ⌶ ⌶	Yiitz .ne?	'Where's the chair?'

SYSTEM OF TONE SANDHI 113

411 ↘ ┐ ┐	Jiow Jinshan	'San Francisco'; 'California'
412 ↘ ┐ ⊣	Dahshi Yang	'Atlantic Ocean'
413 ↘ ┐ ⌟	Dihjong Hae	'Mediterranean Sea'
414 ↘ ┐ ↘	bujydaw	'don't know'
410 ↘ ┐ ˌ	dihsan'g	'third'
421 ↘ ⊣ ┐	tzyhshyng-che'l	'bicycle'
422 ↘ ⊣ ⊣	juh yangfarng	'live in a foreign-style house'
423 ↘ ⊣ ⌟	Dianntair hao.	'The radio station is good.'
424 ↘ ⊣ ↘	dowyaltsay	'beansprouts'
420 ↘ ⊣ ˌ	shinq Wang .de	'one whose surname is Wang'
431 ↘ ⌞ ┐	liow-jaan deng	'six lamps'
432 ↘ ⌞ ⊣	fuhshoei-chyr	'swimming pool'
433 ↘ ⊣ ⌟	tzyh*jyy*-looul	'waste-basket'
434 ↘ ⌞ ↘	wanqyeuan-jinq	'telescope'
430 ↘ ⌞ ˈ	Tzay naal .ne?	'Where is it?'
441 ⊢ ↘ ┐	tzuoh chihche	'ride in an automobile'
442 ⊢ ↘ ⊣	dah-wenntyi	'great problem'
443 ⊢ ↘ ⌟	kann diannyeengl	'see a movie'
444 ⊢ ⊢ ↘	dahgay huey	'probably would'
440 ⊢ ↘ ˌ	Shianntzay .ne?	'And now?'
401 ↘ ˌ ┐	daw.le jia	'reached home'
402 ↘ ˌ ⊣	Jiow.sh nan.	'Only thing is, it's hard.'
403 ↘ ˌ ⌟	dow.funaol	'soft bean curd'
404 ⊢ ˌ ↘	kann.de-jiann	'able to see'
400 ↘ ˌ ˌ	Duey .le .ba?	'That's right, isn't it?'

PART III CONVERSATIONAL LESSONS

TO THE STUDENT

1. Foundation. — Starting with Lesson 1, you are learning to talk Chinese. Everything to be learned from now on depends, in every detail, upon the fundamental elements learned in Lessons A, B, C, and D. For example, unless you have, by now, learned to hear and pronounce the difference in tone between *mae* and *may* you won't be able to distinguish between 'buy' and 'sell'; unless you give a retroflex pronunciation for *ch* in *char*, you won't get anything like tea when you think you are asking for 'tea.' Since you will be hearing or using thousands of words and phrases, running into millions of repetitions of the same few dozen sounds and tones, each sound and tone will proportionally be of such enormous importance that no one should be considered ready for Lesson 1 until he has succeeded in hearing and making every distinction in initial, final, and tone.

2. Utterances as the Stuff of Language. — With the foundation firmly laid to build the structure of the language on, you now face a new set of problems. As language learning usually goes, you will probably expect to have to (1) memorize a large number of words with their meanings in English and (2) know a whole set of rules about Chinese grammar. To be sure, both of these things are useful and important. But if you imagine, or take for granted, that these are the main things in the learning of Chinese, then you will never learn to understand or to talk Chinese. For language learning is learning of the language, and language is utterances made in actual situations. The chief material you are going to work with are actual utterances, not words. The degree of your advancement (after acquiring a firm grasp of fundamentals) is solely measured by, and directly proportional to, the amount of hearing or making of typical utterances of the kind that people in China make when they talk.

Consequently, the conduct of this course is planned on the basis of the maximum repetitions of correct utterances of all types. Each lesson represents a connected text of a situation, a story, or a discussion. As much time as possible should be given to the repetition of correct forms in class, in small drill groups, in listening to phonograph records, if available, and in doing the exercises aloud.

3. Focusing and Exposure (p. 73). — Before the repeating of the materials at normal or nearly normal conversational speed, it is of course necessary for you, with the aid of your class instructor, to get all the sounds clearly, analyze the grammatical structure, and understand the meanings of the sentences. These are the preliminary steps for the main business of listening to or talking the language. It may be compared with the focusing of the subject before taking a photograph. When the focusing is done, there must be sufficient exposure. Just as you cannot get a picture without adequate exposure, you cannot learn any language without adequate repetition. None of the lessons here need be committed to memory, but you should listen and read aloud enough number of times, say 15 or 20 times, so that you can complete any of the sentences after its first half is given.

4. **The Echo Method** (p. 74). — An intermediate stage of work between the preliminary analysis and the main work of repetition consists in echoing the text phrase by phrase. Read a sentence or short phrase aloud: close or turn away from the book and try to say it over; then look at the book and read it aloud once more. If you make any mistake by using a wrong word, missing a word, or using a wrong word order, the mistake will stare you in the face on the rechecking and the correction will be firmly remembered. Take longer and longer phrases or sentences in one breath as you progress.

5. **Vocabulary and Grammar.** — The meaning of words and grammatical points will be given in the English translation, in the notes, and in class instruction. You should, however, not get into the habit of equating every Chinese word with one or two English words in a mechanical way. That would be a sure way to talking pidgin Chinese. The meaning of complete utterances in Chinese can be equated to utterances in English and remembered, but the use of Chinese words should preferably be memorized in terms of the Chinese phrases in which it occurs and in terms of the story in which it occurs. New terms like *yuantzyy* 'atom' or translation borrowings from English like *jihhuah-jingjih* 'planned economy,' do represent one-to-one correspondence between English and Chinese, but these form a very small minority of words you will have to learn. The meanings of the vast majority of Chinese words have to be remembered in terms of their place in Chinese phrases, comparison with their opposites and correlatives in Chinese, etc. You learn more Chinese and acquire a more genuine feeling for the language by being able to know how to use a relatively small number of sentences than to be able to give the English for thousands of words, since, except the special types of words referred to above, the dictionary meanings in English are usually not safe to use.

6. **Learning Grammar by Doing the Exercises.** — You *understand* grammar by reading the Introduction and the notes, but you *learn* grammar by acquiring fluency in saying the text and by doing the exercises. Like the text itself, the exercises should be carefully analyzed for clear understanding and then repeated for fluency. By doing a sufficient number of exercises on similar grammatical patterns, you will be able to form new sentences which you have never heard before.

7. Routine for Lessons. — On the basis of the preceding considerations the routine of study for each lesson is planned as follows:

ROUTINE FOR LESSONS

(a) *Class Instruction.* —

(To be conducted in English for Lessons 1–8, in Chinese after Lesson 8.)

(1) Explanation of pronunciation, grammar, vocabulary, & idioms.
(2) Reading aloud of text.
(3) Doing some sample exercises.
(4) Supplementary material or talks in Chinese.

(b) *Listening to Records.* —

(If records are not available, the teacher should do more reading aloud of the text.)

(c) *Group Drill.* —

(Instructions regarding procedure to be conducted in English for Lessons 1–4, in Chinese after Lesson 4.)

(1) Listening to reading by teacher alone. (Tempo from 4 to 5 minutes for each lesson.)
(2) Class repeating after teacher.
(3) Individual reading aloud for accuracy.
(4) Individual reading aloud for tempo. (Passing tempo 7 minutes for each lesson.)
(5) Reading of text in Chinese from looking at or hearing the English.
(6) Correction of oral and written exercises.
(7) Oral exercises at tempo after correction.
(8) Supplementary oral exercises.
(9) Phonetic drill in the form of dictation of unfamiliar syllables and unknown words.

(d) *Homework.* —

(1) Reading aloud of text five times for accuracy.
(2) Study of meaning and study of notes.
(3) Reading aloud of text five more times for concatenation.
(4) Echoing of the text phrase by phrase.
(5) Reading aloud of text as many times as needed for attaining tempo.[1]
(6) Reading aloud of text in Chinese from looking at the English.

---

[1] The writer was required at school to read his lessons aloud sixty times; that was for reading books in his own language.

(7) Answering written exercises.
(8) Reading of corrected written exercises for tempo.

Any or all of the preceding steps can be simplified or abbreviated in proportion to your ability to master the material. The burden of proof is on you that you don't need all the prescribed steps.

LESSON I
YOU, I, AND HE 'FOUR MEN'

Ding 1: Who is it?
Wang 2: I, it is I.[7]
D 1: Who are you?
W 2: I am Wang Ell. And you? Who are *you?*
D 1: Oh me? I am Ding I. Who is he?
W 2: He is Jang San.
D 1: How about him? Who is he then?
W 2: Oh him? He is Lii Syh.
D 1: What is Jang San?
W 2: Jang San is a man.
D 1: How about Lii Syh? What is Lii Syh then?
W 2: Lii Syh is a man; Lii Syh is also a man.
D 1: Jang San is a man; Lii Syh is also a man. Well, then, how many men are Jang San and Lii Syh?
W 2: Jang San and Lii Syh are two men, they are two men.
D 1: How many men are you and I? You and I, how many men are we?
W 2: I and you, we are also two men.
D 1: That's right, we are also two men. Jang San and Lii Syh are two men; you and I are also two men. Well, then, how many men are two men and two men? Are they three men?
W 2: No, two and two are four.
D 1: One, two, three, four — 1, 2, 3, 4 — yes, four.
W 2: You and Jang San are two men; Jang San and Lii Syh are also two men. Two and two are four. Therefore you and Jang San and Lii Syh, you are four men, aren't you?
D 1: No! No! We are not four men. Hey! Jang San! Lii Syh! You two and I, are we four men?
Jang 3, Lii 4: No, we are three men, it seems.
D 1: One, two, three — yeah, that's right, we are three men. — Say, Wang Ell! We are not four men; we are three men. Only including you are we four men.

NOTES

1. *Dih–*, prefix for ordinal numbers. *Dih'i, dih'ell, dihsan, dihsyh,* ... 'first, second, third, fourth, ...' *Dih'i-keh* 'first lesson.' See also Note 4 (e).

DIH'I [1] KEH
NII [2] WOO TA [3] 'SYHG [4] REN' [5]

Ding 1: Sheir .a? [6]
Wang 2: Woo, sh [7] woo.
D 1: Nii sh sheir? [8]
W 2: Woo sh Wang Ell. Nii .ne? [9] Nii sh sheir .ne?
D 1: Woo .ia,[10] woo sh Ding I. Ta sh sheir .a?
W 2: Ta sh Jang San.
D 1: .Ne.me ta .ne? Ta sh sheir .ne?
W 2: Ta .ia, ta sh Lii Syh.
D 1: Jang San sh sherm.me? [11]
W 2: Jang San sh ren.[12]
D 1: .Ne.me Lii Syh .ne? Lii Syh sh sherm .ne?
W 2: Lii Syh sh ren .a; [13] Lii Syh yee.sh [14] ren .a.
D 1: Jang San sh *ig* ren; Lii Syh yee.sh *ig* ren. .Ne.me Jang San gen [15] Lii Syh sh jiig ren .ne?
W 2: Jang San gen Lii Syh sh leangg ren, ta.men [16] sh leangg ren.
D 1: Nii gen woo sh jiig ren? Nii gen woo, tzar.men [17] sh jiig ren?
W 2: Woo gen nii, tzar.men yee.sh leangg ren.
D 1: Duey .le,[18] tzar.men yee.sh leangg ren. Jang San Lii Syh sh leangg ren; nii gen *woo* yee.sh leangg ren. .Ne.me leangg ren gen leangg ren sh jiig ren .ne? Sh san'g ren .bu.sh? [19]
W 2: *Bu*.sh,[20] leangg leangg [21] sh syhg.
D 1: *Ig*, leangg, san'g, syhg — i, ell,[22] san, syh — duey .le, syhg.
W 2: Nii gen Jang San sh leangg ren; Jang San Lii Syh yee.sh leangg ren. Leangg leangg syhg.[23] *Suoo*.yii nii gen Jang San gen Lii Syh, nii.men sh syhg ren, sh .bu.sh? [24]
D 1: Bu! *Bu*.sh! *Bu*.sh syhg ren. .Ėh! [25] Jang San! Lii Syh! Nii.men lea [26] gen woo, tzar.men sh .bu.sh [27] syhg ren .a?
Jang 3, Lii 4: *Bu*.sh, tzar.men sh san'g ren .ba?
D 1: I, ell, san — .èh, sh .de,[28] tzar.men sh san'g ren. — Ėh, Wang Ell! Woom [29] *bu*.sh syhg ren; woo.men sh san'g ren. Lian nii tzar.men tsair sh syhg ren .ne.[30]

---

2. *Nii woo ta* 'you, I, and he.' There is no definite order in mentioning the personal pronouns. Note, too, that in mentioning a number of co-ordinate items in succession, it is not necessary to insert conjunctions, such as *gen*, or pauses between the items. (See p. 37.)

3. *Ta* is the general third-person pronoun 'he, him, she, her, it.' Used as 'it,' *ta* occurs almost always in the object position.

4. **Auxiliary Nouns (AN).** — A numeral in Chinese is not a free word and is usually bound with a following auxiliary noun (AN) before an ordinary noun can be added. Thus, *syhg ren* 'four piece man, — four men.' There are five classes of AN: (a) AN proper, which is a word specifically associated with every noun for an individual person or thing and should be learned in connection with the noun, for example, *i-baa yiitz* 'a chair,' *leang-jaan deng* 'two lamps'; (b) measure words, as *leang-chyy buh* 'two feet of cloth'; (c) temporary measure words, which are ordinary nouns temporarily used as a measure, as *i-toong shoei* 'a pail of water'; (d) AN for verbs, expressing the number of times of an action, as *tzoou i-tanq* 'go one trip, — go there once'; (e) quasi-AN, words like nouns which can follow numerals directly, as *syh-jih* 'four seasons.' For further details, see p. 45.

The syntactic word consisting of a numeral and an AN is a substantive and can be used either in conjunction with a following noun, as *ig ren*, or independently, as *Leangg leangg sh syhg* 'Two and two are four.'

5. *Ren* is the general word, and the only common word, for 'man, woman, person, human being, people.' Note that there is no distinction of number in Chinese nouns.

6. *.A*, a common particle with many functions. Here it has the meaning of 'I am asking a new question.' A question ending in *.a* has a softer tone than a question without a particle.

7. Note that in *sh woo* 'it is I' no subject ('it') is required in the Chinese.

Since *woo* is used for both 'I' and 'me,' the form *Sh woo* has neither the informality of 'It's me' nor the formal tone of 'It is I,' but is quite neutral in style.

The spelling *sh* is used as an abbreviated form of the word *shyh* 'be, is, etc.' The final *-yh* is almost always sounded and the abbreviation is purely graphic. (See p. 22.)

8. *Nii sh sheir*, lit. 'you are who?' In determining the word order of a question containing an interrogative word like *sheir* 'who,' *neeig* 'which,' *naal* 'where,' *sherm.me* 'what,' *tzeem.me* 'how,' etc., the rule is: ask as you will be answered. Since the answer to this question is *woo sh Wang Ell* 'I am Wang Ell' (and not 'Wang Ell am I'), the same order is used in the question. (See p. 58.)

9. *.Ne*, interrogative particle meaning 'and...?' 'how about...?' 'then...?' The second *.ne* here is translated by putting a stress on 'you.'

10. *.Ia*, particle before a pause. It is an alternate form of the particle

.a, used when the preceeding word ends in an open vowel (not counting the tone signs *-r* and *-h*, of course).

Because the particle *.a* begins with a true vowel (p. 20), it is often linked with a preceding consonant or semi-vowel, so that *ren .a* sounds like *ren .na*, *lai .a* sounds like *lai .ia*, *dau .a* sounds like *dau .ua*, etc., as reflected in the use of characters pronounced *.na*, *.ia*, *.ua*, etc. for *.a* in such positions in books in the colloquial. In the present course, we shall write this particle in the invariant form *.a* (and the corresponding character in the Character Text), except after open vowels, where we write *.ia*, since this is not a result of linking.

11. The form *sherm.me* is used only before a pause, otherwise the form *sherm* is used. The same is true of *tzeem(.me)* 'how?' *tzemm(.me)* 'so, this way,' and *nemm(.me)* 'so, that way.'

12. Unlike English nouns, a Chinese noun for an individual person or thing does not have to have an article. Thus the form *woo sh ren* is as frequent as, or a little more frequent than, the form *woo sh ig ren*. Contrast the relative infrequency of English sentences, like 'I am king' as compared with 'I am a man.'

13. This *.a*, with a high pitch, indicates obviousness: 'Lii Syh is a man, of course!'

14. *Yee.sh* 'also is.' Chinese adverbs always precede the words they modify. *Sh* is unstressed and joined to *yee* closely like a suffix.

15. *Gen* 'with, together with, and.' See also Note 2.

16. *–.men* (*–m* before labial initials), plural suffix for pronouns. The form *ta.men* 'they, them' is limited to persons and the higher animals. The singular form *ta* is used in referring to a number of inanimate objects (with the limitation as stated in Note 3).

17. There are two forms of 'we' in the dialect of Peiping (and certain other places): the inclusive 'we,' *tzar.men* 'you and I, you and we,' and the exclusive 'we,' *woo.men* 'he (she, it) and I, they and I.' *Tzar.men* includes the person or persons spoken to, *woo.men* does not. On formal occasions, such as in a speech, when a native of Peiping expects the presence of speakers from other places, he is likely to follow the more general usage of using *woo.men* for both *tzar.men* and *woo.men*. (See diagrams on p. 125.)

18. $_o$*Duey .le* 'Right,' here simply an interjection of agreement. (See p. 59.)

19. Lit. '(they) are three men (or) not are?' This is the normal way of asking 'Are (they) three men?' (See p. 59.)

20. *Bu* (pron. *bu* or *buh*) and *bu.sh* (pron. *bwu.shyh*) are the most common interjections of disagreement. (See p. 59.)

21. *Leangg leangg* as written may mean 'two and two' or 'twice two.' In actual speech, an even stress on both words, without necessarily a pause

in between (cf. Note 2), means 'two and two,' while with greater stress on the first *leangg* the phrase means 'twice two.'

22. Note the two forms *leang-* and *ell*, both meaning 'two.' *Leang-* is used before an AN, while *ell* is used in simple counting, in ordinal numbers, compound numbers, and other compounds, and before monosyllabic measure words of old standing.

23. Note absence of *sh*. This is often possible and the predicate is called a nominal predicate.

24. *Sh .bu.sh?* 'is (or) not-is? is used like French 'n'est-ce pas?' and may be translated variously as 'isn't it so?' 'isn't it?' 'didn't they?' etc.

25. *.Ĕh* (pron. *èh* as in English 'edge') is a common interjection for calling attention. (See also Note 28.)

26. *Lea* is a fused abbreviation of *leangg*. Although the character 倆 for *lea* has the 'man' radical, the word is applicable to both things and persons.

27. Note the slight difference in word order between this and the sentence under Note 19. When *sh* is immediately followed by *.bu.sh* (or with any other verb instead of *sh*), we call this the close form of the question. When something else is inserted between *sh* and *.bu.sh*, we call it the open form of the question.

28. *.Ĕh*, with half-low pitch, is another interjection of agreement, 'uh-huh, yeah'; *sh.de* 'that is so.'

29. Note use of *woo.men*, the exclusive 'we,' when the person addressed (Wang Ell) is not being counted as one of them, while in the last sentence *tzar.men* is used, because it means 'you as well as we three.'

30. Lit. 'Including you we begin to be four men then.' *Tsair* or *Tsair* ....*ne* 'for the first time, only then (are we ...).' Cf. Germ. '*erst.*'

EXERCISES

Do all exercises both in (romanized) writing and orally as far as both forms are applicable. Oral answers should be given without looking at the notes. As far as the forms apply, teacher and student or two students should do the questions and answers in the manner of a conversation.

1. *Practice pronouncing words with difficult sounds.* — Initials in *ren*, *sheir*, *Jang*, *sherm*, *tzar.men*, *jiig* (spreading the lips on *j-*), *tsair*. Finals in *keh*, *woo*, *syh*, *sh(yh)*, *ell*, *lian*.

2. *Mark the whole text with tone signs.* — (Students who have mastered the tones may be excused from doing this exercise.)

3. *Comment on the following statements as to truth.* — If true, say *Duey .le*, *Sh .de*, or *.Ĕh* and repeat the sentence given. If false,* say *Bu*, *Bu.sh*,

* Warning: If the teacher has occasion to make up supplementary exercises, he may make up any statement which is factually false or even absurd, but never make a sentence which is grammatically wrong!

YOU, I, AND HE 'FOUR MEN' 125

FIGURE 1. N_{II} Woo Ta

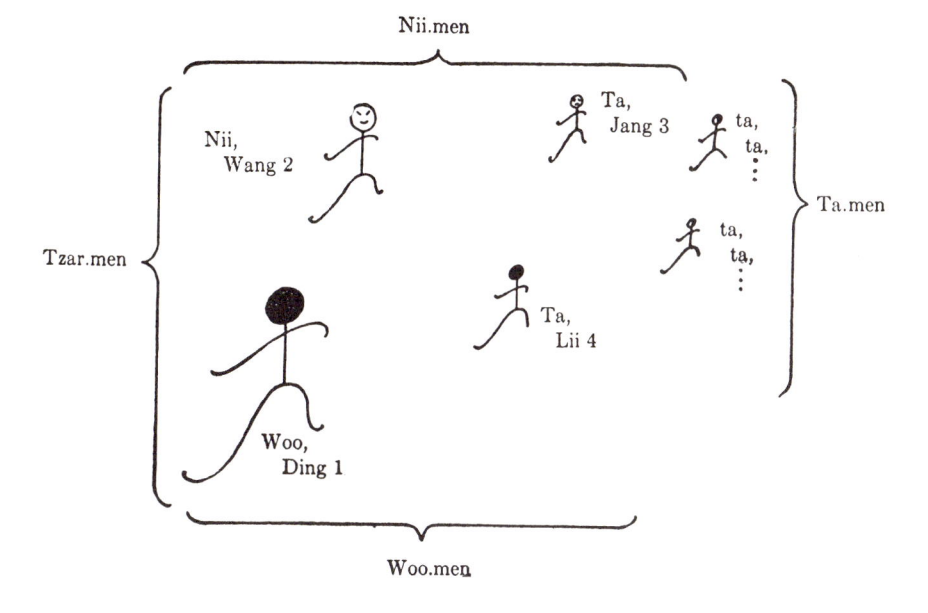

Nii.men

Nii, Wang 2

Ta, Jang 3

ta, ta, ⋮

Ta.men

Tzar.men

Ta, Lii 4

Woo, Ding 1

ta, ta, ⋮

Woo.men

FIGURE 2. THE .MEN-FORMS

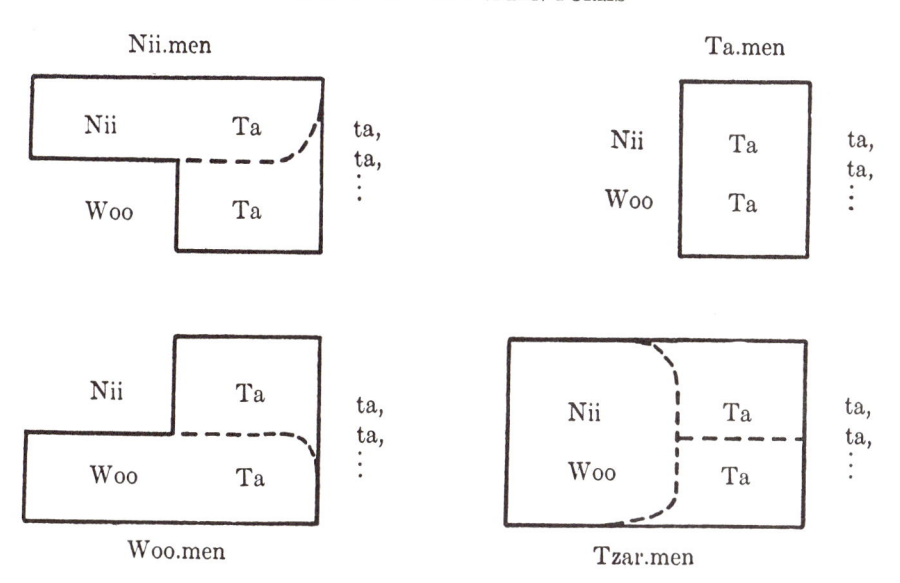

Nii.men

Nii	Ta
Woo	Ta

ta, ta, ⋮

Ta.men

Nii	Ta
Woo	Ta

ta, ta, ⋮

Nii	Ta
Woo	Ta

ta, ta, ⋮

Woo.men

Nii	Ta
Woo	Ta

ta, ta, ⋮

Tzar.men

The broken lines indicate optional scope of inclusion.

Bu.sh .de, or *Buduey* (irrespective of the false statement being in the affirmative or negative form), and give the true statement by making the necessary changes. Use the proper pronouns. Example: Nii sh ren. Duey .le, woo sh ren. Jang San sh leangg ren. *Bu*sh, ta sh *ig* ren.

(a) Woo gen ta sh leangg ren. (b) Woo gen *nii* yee.sh leangg ren. (c) Nii gen woo gen ta, tzar.men sh leangg ren. (d) Lii Syh gen ta gen woo, woo.men sh san'g ren. (e) Lii Syh gen ta, ta.men sh san'g ren. (f) Nii gen ta, nii.men sh syhg ren. (g) Dih'i Keh, Dih'ell Keh, Dihsan Keh sh san'g ren. (h) Jang San Lii Syh sh ren. (i) Woo sh Jang San, nii sh Lii Syh, *suoo*.yii woo, Jang San, nii, Lii Syh, sh syhg ren. (j) Dih'i Keh, Dih'ell Keh, Dihsan Keh, sh syh-keh. (k) Nii.men lea gen woo.men lea, tzar.men sh syhg ren. (l) Ta.men lea gen woo.men lea, woo.men yee.sh syhg ren.

4. *Answer the following:*

(a) Ta sh sheir? (b) Lii Syh sh sherm.me? (c) Nii gen woo gen ta sh jiig ren .a? (d) Dih'i, Dih'ell, Dihsyh Keh sh jii-keh? (e) Leangg gen leangg sh .bu.sh san'g? (f) Dih'*ig* ren gen dihsan'g ren, ta.men sh jiig ren?

LESSON 2
THINGS

A: What's this? What is this?
B: This, you mean?
A: Uh-huh, this.
B: This is a table. A table is a thing.
A: And what's that? What is that?
B: Which one? That one?
A: No, not that one. *That* one.
B: Oh, that one? That's the door. The door is also a thing.
A: What are these?
B: These are writing instruments. These are a few writing instruments.
A: What sort of things are those?
B: I don't know. What sort of writing instruments are these? Do you know?
A: I don't know what kind of writing instruments they are. I think they are pencils, aren't they?
B: Probably not. I think they are writing brushes. Those are pencils. The brushes are here; the pencils are not here.
A: If they are not here, where are they then?
B: The pencils are there, I suppose.

THINGS 127

(g) Dih'ellg gen dihsyhg ren .ne? (h) Jang San sh dihjii .a? (i) *Suoo*.yii Lii Syh .ne? Wang Ell .ne? (j) Wang Ell .a! Woo gen Lii Syh sh leangg ren, lian nii tzar.men jiig ren .a? (k) "*Nii* Woo Ta 'Syhg Ren'" sh dihjii-keh .ia? (l) Nii gen woo, tzar.men sh .bu.sh *ig* ren?

5. *Translate into Chinese:*

(a) What is the first lesson? (b) How about the second lesson? And (don't use *gen!*) the third? (c) Two and two are four. Therefore two people and two people are four people. (d) Which (*dih-jiig*) man is Jang San? And Lii Syh? (e) You two men with me, one man, are three men. (f) That's right, two and one are three. (g) One and three are four. One, two, three, four — you are four men, not (*bu.sh*) three. (h) Jang San, Lii Syh, and he, they are three people, aren't they? (i) How many are two and two? (j) And two and three?

6. *Supplementary statements and questions with reference to Figures 1 and 2.*

DIH'ELL KEH DONG.SHI [1]

A: Jeh.sh [2] sherm.me? Jeyg [2] sh sherm.me?
B: Jeyg .a? [3] (*Low pitch.*)
A: .Eng,[4] jeyg.
B: Jeh.sh i-jang [5] juotz. Juotz sh *i*-jiann [6] dong.shi.
A: Nah.sh sherm .ne? Neyg sh sherm.me?
B: Neeig? Neyg .a?
A: *Bu*.sh, *bu*.sh neyg, sh neyg.
B: .Oh,[7] neyg .a? Nah.sh *i*-shann [8] men. Men yee.sh *i*-jiann dong.shi.
A: Jey.shieg [9] sh sherm.me?
B: Jeh.sh bii. Jeh.sh jii-jy [10] bii.
A: Ney.shie sh sherm [11] dong.shi .ne?
B: Woo bujydaw.[12] Jeh.sh .shie sherm bii .a? Nii jy.daw .bu.jy.daw?
A: Bujydaw [13] sh sherm bii. *Woo* sheang sh chianbii [14] .ba?
B: *Bu*sh .ba? *Woo* sheang sh maubii.[15] Ney.shieg sh chianbii. Maubii [16] tzay [17] jell; [18] chianbii *bu* tzay jell.
A: *Bu* tzay jell tzay naal .ne? [19]
B: Chianbii tzay nall .ba?

A: Where is there?
B: There, where Wang is.
A: Hey, Wang! Are the pencils there with you?
Wang: Yes, I have them.
A: How many pencils have you there? How many pencils have you?
Wang: I have — one, two, three, four, five, six, seven — I have seven — no, no — 1, 2, 3, 4, 5, 6 — 1 2 3 4 5 6 — I haven't seven pencils, I have only six. These six are my pencils; these pencils are mine, not yours, nor his either.
A: Goodness, what a floorful of paper here!
B: What kind of paper?
A: I don't know. I think it's newspaper.
B: Newspaper? How many sheets of newspaper are there?
A: There are — one, two, three, four, five, six, seven, eight, nine, ten — 1, 2, 3, 4, 5, 6, 7, 8, 9, 10 — 1 2 3 4 5 6 7 8 9 10 — there are ten sheets.
B: See what news there is. What news is there in the newspaper?
A: I don't know what news there is. Has this place a lamp? Is there a light?
B: I think there is, I think there are two lamps here. Let's turn on the light and look, shall we?
A: Where are those two lamps? — My goodness, What is this?
B: This is a stool.
A: Oh, no, it's a chair. Ah, here is the lamp.
B: Turn on the light!
A: The light's on. Look! Just look at these things! This is not newspaper; this is wrapping paper!
B: Look, those are not pencils, nor brushes, nor pens, nor chalks: they are a few pairs of chopsticks!

NOTES

1. *Dong.shi* 'thing' in the sense of 'object, article,' as contrasted with *shyh, shell,* or *shyh.chyng* 'thing' in the sense of 'affair, event.'

2. **Determinatives.** — Demonstratives like *jeh–, jey–* 'this,' *nah–, ney–* 'that,' interrogatives like *naa–, neei–* 'which?' distributives like *meei–* 'each,' and a few other forms, together with all numerals *i–* 'one,' *leang–* 'two,' . . . , *jii–* 'how many,' — these are called determinatives. A determinative can be compounded with an AN to form a substantive, as *jeyg* 'this (one)' or 'this (thing),' after which a noun can be added, as *jeyg ren* 'this man.'

THINGS

A: Nall sh naal .a?
B: Ney.bial,[20] Lao [21] Wang .nall.[22]
A: .Êh, Lao Wang! Chianbii tzay nii.nall .bu .tzay?
Wang: Tzay.jell,[23] tzay woo.jell.
A: Nii.nall *yeou* [24] jii-jy chianbii .a? *Nii yeou* jii-jy chianbii .a?
Wang: Woo yeou — i-jy, leang-jy, san-jy, syh-jy, wuu-jy, liow-jy, chi-jy — *woo* yeou chi-jy — *bu*.sh, *bu*.sh — i, ell, san, syh, wuu, liow — i ell san syh wuu liow — woo mei.yeou [25] chi-jy chianbii, woo *jyy* yeou liow-jy. Jey-liow-jy sh woo.de [26] bii; jey.shie bii sh woo.de, *bu*sh nii.de, yee *bu*sh ta.de.
A: .Ai.ia, jell *i*-dih .de jyy! [27]
B: Sherm jyy .a?
A: Woo bujydaw .a. *Woo* sheang sh bawjyy [28] .ba?
B: Bawjyy .a? *Yeou* [29] jii-jang bawjyy .a?
A: Yeou — i-jang, leang-jang, san-jang, syh-jang, wuu-jang, liow-jang, chi-jang, ba-jang, jeou-jang, shyr-jang — i, ell, san, syh, wuu, liow, chi, ba, jeou, shyr — i ell san syh wuu liow chi ba jeou shyr — yeou shyr-jang.
B: Kann.x [30] yeou sherm shinwen. Baw.shanq [31] yeou sherm shinwen?
A: Woo bujydaw yeou sherm shinwen. Jell yeou .mei.yeou deng .a? Yeou deng .mei.yeou? [32]
B: Woo sheang yeou, *woo* sheang jell yeou *leang*-jaan deng. Tzar.men kai.x [33] deng kann.x .ba.
A: Ney-*leang*-jaan deng tzay naal .ne? — .Ai.ia, jeh.sh sherm.me .ia?
B: Jeh.sh i-jang denqtz.
A: .Êh, *bu*.sh, sh i-*baa* [34] yiitz. Ah, deng tzay jell.
B: Kai-deng .ba!
A: Deng kai [35] .le.[36] Chyau.x! [37] Nii chyau.x jey.shie dong.shi! Jeh *bu*.sh bawjyy; jeh.sh bau dong.shi .de jyy! [38]
B: Nii chyau, ney.shieg *bu*.sh chianbii, yee *bu*.sh maubii, yee *bu*.sh gangbii, yee *bu*.sh *feen*bii: nah.sh jii-shuang [39] kuaytz!

Like numerals, demonstratives and other determinatives are normally followed by AN's. Exceptions are *jeh* 'this' and *nah* 'that,' which are sometimes followed directly by a noun or a verb, as *jeh ren* 'this man,' *jeh.sh* 'this is.' Note that *jeh.sh* and *nah.sh* are among the very few cases where subject and verb are bound together.

The forms *jey-, ney-, neei-* are derived from the phonetic fusion of *jeh-i* 'this one,' *nah-i* 'that one,' *naa-i* 'which one?' In actual use, however, their use is not limited to cases of a single individual, thus, *jey-leang-jaan deng* 'these two lamps.'

3. When the particle .*a* (or .*ia*) is used for confirming an echo ('You mean ...?'), the pitch of the second half of the sentence is extra low.

This needs special practice, since a question like 'This one (you mean)?' would rise to extra *high* pitch in English. (Cf. Ex. 3, p. 139.)

4. *.Eng* is actually pronounced either as a nasalized vowel [ə̃] or as a nasal consonant *ng* or *m*. When expressing agreement, it has a low pitch, like a Half 3rd Tone.

5. *Jang*, AN for tables, beds, also for sheets of paper.

6. *Jiann*, AN for words meaning 'thing, affair.'

7. *.Oh* in Chinese is pronounced more like English 'awe,' although it has a meaning similar to English 'Oh (I see).'

8. *Shann*, AN for *men* 'door.'

9. *Shie* is a measure word for an indefinite number or quantity, 'some, lot, amount.' Both the form *jey.shie* and *jey.shieg* are common. Since Chinese has no distinction of number, they should not be regarded as the plural form for *jeyg*. For example, in the next two sentences 'these are' takes the form of *jeh.sh*.

10. *Jy*, AN for stick-like things.

11. Note attributive use of *sherm* 'what kind of?'

12. In the negative of *jy.daw* 'know,' *daw* recovers stress and tone.

13. While sentences without subjects like 'Don't know what they are' represent a style of some speakers of English, they are common usage with all speakers of Chinese in all situations.

14. *Chianbii* 'lead writing instrument, — pencil.'

15. *Mau* 'fur, hair (of the body)'; 'feather.' *Maubii* 'writing brush.'

16. A word in the subject position usually has a definite reference, hence the translation '*the* brushes.' (See p. 51.)

17. *Tzay* 'to be at, in, on.'

18. *Jell* (< *jeh* + –*l*) 'this place, here.' The suffix –*l* (–*.lii* in more formal style) here denotes locality. Similarly, *nall* (< *nah* + –*l*) 'that place, there'; *naal* (< *naa* + –*l*) 'which place, where?'

In *Maubii tzay jell* 'The writing brushes are here,' there is an apparent (but grammatically misleading) correspondence between *tzay* and 'are' and between *jell* and 'here.' Grammatically, the correspondence is as follows:

```
        tzay              jell
   ⎴            ⎴
   are    in      this   place
          ⎵
   are            here
```

Consequently, it is misleading to say, as students are often tempted to say, *Maubii[1] *sh jell*, which would be saying 'The brushes are this place.' Once the real structure of such sentences is understood, there is no harm

---

[1] An asterisk * before a word or expression indicates that it is non-existent in the language.

in associating in one's mind *jell* with 'here,' *nall* with 'there,' and *naal* with 'where?' provided that the rest of the sentence is correctly formed.

19. In short sentences where the implication is clear, words like *yaw.sh* 'if,' *jihran* 'since,' etc. are usually omitted in Chinese 'If they are not here,' 'since they are not here,' 'Not being here. . . .'

Note omission of subject in both clauses. If it were to be expressed, it would be necessary either to repeat *chianbii* 'pencils' (as in the next sentence) or say *ney.shieg* 'those,' since *ta.men* 'they' is not applicable to inanimate objects. (See p. 47.)

20. The suffix –.*bial* (*bian* 'side' + –*l*) also indicates locality, with more emphasis on the 'side' idea. *Ney.bial* 'that side, over there'; *jey.bial* 'over here'; *neei.bial* 'which side?'

21. *Lao* 'old' is used here as a prefix to surnames. The addition of *Lao* to a surname indicates a degree of familiarity like the dropping of 'Mr.' Hence the translation of *Lao Wang* by plain 'Wang.'

22. After nouns, locality is indicated by the suffix –.*nall* (for middle or distant objects or persons) or the suffix –.*jell* (for near ones). *Ta.nall* 'he-locality, where he is, *chez lui*'; *woo.jell* 'I-locality, where I am, *chez moi*'; *juotz.nall* 'table locality, where the table is, at the table'; *Lao Wang .nall* 'Wang's place' (at his home, where he stands, in his pocket, etc.). Here, again, it should be remembered that all forms with –.*nall* (or –.*jell*) are substantives. (See diagram under Note 18.)

23. *Tzay.jell*, *tzay.nall*, with –.*jell* or –.*nall* unstressed means simply 'present,' with no emphasis on the location. (See p. 109.)

24. *Nii.nall yeou*, lit. 'your place has . . .'

25. The negative of *yeou* 'have' is *meiyeou*, *mei.yeou*, or *mei*, the last not occurring in final position.

26. –.*de* particle of subordination or modification. *Woo.de* 'my, mine'; *nii.de* 'your(s)'; *ta.de* 'his, her(s),' less commonly 'its'; *woo.men.de*, *tzar.men.de* 'our(s)'; *nii.men.de* 'your(s)'; *ta.men.de* 'their(s).'

27. *Jyy* 'paper' is an unrelated homonym of *jyy* 'only.' The sentence is to be analyzed as 'This place has a floorful of paper.'

28. *Baw* 'newspaper' (as something to read or as paper); *bawjyy* 'newspaper' (usually as paper only).

29. When *yeou* 'have' cannot be attached to any subject, it is really the universe that is supposed to 'have' what follows. In such cases, the corresponding English is 'there is, there are,' etc.

30. The letter x stands for a repeated syllable.

The common translation of *kann.kann* as 'look-see' as if it were a compound of two synonyms is grammatically wrong. *Kann.kann* is an abbreviated form of *kann .i.kann* 'take a look' where *.i.kann* is an AN for verbs, meaning 'once,' or Germ. 'mal, einmal.' A more idiomatic translation is 'just look' or just 'look.'

31. *Baw.shanq* 'newspaper-top, on the newspaper, — in the newspaper.' *Baw.shanq yeou shinwen* 'newspaper-top has news, — there is news in the newspaper.'

32. These are examples of the close and open forms (Note 27, p. 124).

33. *Kai.x* may mean either 'just open' (Note 30) or 'open up,' the second syllable –.*kai* expressing the result of the action.

34. *Baa*, AN for things with handles (the back, in the case of a chair'.

35. There is no voice in Chinese verbs and the direction of the action is to be inferred from the context. Here, since the light cannot turn on something else, *Deng kai .le* must mean 'The lamp is turned on.' (See also p. 54.)

36. *.Le*, particle indicating a new situation (from 'off' to 'on' of the light), or the new realization of an existing situation (a person entering a room which he left in a darkened state may return to say *Ah, deng kai .le*, 'Ah, the lamp is on,' though he does not know how long it has already been on).

37. *Chyau* 'look,' a little more lively and informal than *kann*.

38. *Bau dong.shi .de jyy* 'wrap things kind of paper, — paper for wrapping things.' The modifying expression before *.de* can be one word or any number of words. Whereas a modifier in English may precede or follow the modified, in Chinese it always precedes, as:

Lii Syh .de jyy	'Lii Syh's paper'
bau dong.shi .de jyy	'wrapping paper'
bau chianbii .de jyy	'paper for wrapping pencils'
woo bau .de dong.shi	'the things I wrap'
woo bau dong.shi .de jyy	'the paper I wrap things with'
bau dong.shi .de ren	'the person who wraps things'
jell .de dong.shi	'the things here'
baw.shanq .de shinwen	'the news in the paper'
tzay jell .de dong.shi	'the things which are here'

39. *Jii-shuang* 'several pairs.' In general, an interrogative word can be used in an indefinite sense. The context will determine which meaning applies.

EXERCISES

Do the exercises both orally and in writing as far as both forms are applicable.

1. *Practice pronouncing words with difficult sounds:* Initials in *dong.shi, jeyg, juotz, i-jiann, i-shann, sheang, chianbii, tzay, chi, shinwen, chyau.x, shuang.* Finals in *juotz, men, jell, nall, naal, ney.bial, yeou, jyy, shyr.*

2. *Mark the whole text with tone signs* (for those who have not yet mastered their tones).

3. *Comment on the following statements as to truth:*

(a) I-jang juotz, *i*-shann men, leang-jang denqtz, sh syh-jiann dong.shi. (b) Nii gen woo gen ta.men lea yee.sh syh-jiann dong.shi. (c) Nii gen juotz sh leang-jiann dong.shi. (d) Lao Wang yeou chi-jy bii. (e) Jell yeou shyr-jang bawjyy. (*Answer according to the story.*) (f) Ta.men *yeou* jii-jy chianbii gen maubii. (*Not a question.*) (g) Baw.shanq yeou shinwen. (h) Bau dong.shi .de jyy .shanq mei.yeou shinwen. (i) Jell *yeou* leang-san'g ('two or three') ren. (j) Wuu-shuang kuaytz sh shyr-jiann dong.shi. (k) Chianbii *bu* tzay Lao Wang .nall. (l) Denqtz gen deng sh *i*-jiann dong.shi.

4. *Answer the following:*

(a) San'g gen leangg sh jiig? (b) I-jang juotz gen san-jaan deng sh jii-jiann dong.shi? (c) Lao Wang *yeou* jii-jy chianbii .a? (d) Jell .de *i*-dih .de jyy sh sherm jyy .a? (e) Ta.men yeou *jii*-jaan deng? (f) Nii chyau.x ney-jang bau dong.shi .de jyy .shanq yeou sherm shinwen. (g) Leang-shann men sh *i*-jiann dong.shi .bu.sh? (h) Nii tzay naal? (i) Jey-i-keh sh dihjii-keh? (j) San-jy gen wuu-jy sh jii-jy .a? (k) *Nii* yeou sherm bii .a? (l) *Nii* sheang sherm.me?

5. *Exercises according to examples.* — In these exercises a phrase or a sentence is given and some sentences based on it are to be made according to the example or examples shown. The original is to be spoken by one student and the answer by one or more students, possibly including the first one. The answers may be prepared in writing, and should be so prepared for these early lessons. But it should be borne in mind that the exercises proper consist in the student's giving the answers orally in response to the sentences without looking at the notes.

Examples:

Given:
1st Student: Woo bu.sh *Jang San.*

1st S: Ta mei.yeou *ma*ubii.

Answer:
2nd Student: Nii bu.sh Jang San sh sheir .ne?
1st Student: Woo sh Lii Syh.
2nd S: Ta mei.yeou maubii yeou sherm bii .ne?
1st S: Ta yeou chianbii.

(a) Baw bu tzay *nall.* (b) *Tam* bu kai-men. (c) Tam bu kai-*men.* (d) Lii Syh mei.yeou *shyr'ell*-jy chianbii. (e) Jell .de ren mei.yeou *ma*ubii. (f) Jang San gen Lii Syh .de denqtz bu tzay *nall.* (g) Juotz.shanq mei.yeou *denqtz.* (h) Jell mei.yeou *baw*jyy. (i) *Nii* bujydaw woo sheang sherm.me. (j) Woo mei.yeou *san*-jy gangbii. (k) *Jey*g bu.sh nii.de baw. (l) Jeyg bu.sh *nii*.de baw.

6. *Change each statement into a question, first in close form, then in open form, then give an answer.*

Example:

Given:
Woo yeou chianbii.

Answer:
Nii yeou .mei.yeou chianbii .a?
Nii yeou chianbii .mei.yeou?
Yeou, *woo* yeou chianbii.

LESSON 3
SPEAKING CHINESE

A: I am (a)² Chinese, I am a Chinese. I speak Chinese, you speak Chinese, he also speaks Chinese — everyone of us speaks Chinese. Can you (people) speak Chinese?

B: Yes, we can. You can, we also can, therefore you and we, we all can.

A: Are you a Chinese?

B: No, I am a foreigner.

A: What country are you a native of? Where do you come from?

B: As for me, I come from America, so I am an American. He comes from England, he is a man who comes from England, therefore he is an Englishman.

A: Englishmen speak English and ¹³ Americans speak American, isn't that right?

B: It's not like that, Englishmen speak English —

A: What do you mean by 'English'?

B: English is simply the English language — as I was saying, Englishmen speak English, Americans also speak English. English and 'American' are the same, you see.

A: Do (you) the people of the two countries talk exactly alike?

B: No, not exactly alike, it's not quite the same thing, there is however only a slight difference. Uh — what is meant by 'Chinese *wen*'? What kind of language is Chinese *wen*? In what way is Chinese *wen* different from Chinese language?

A: There isn't any difference, there isn't any great difference, Chinese *wen* is simply the Chinese language.

B: Well, why is it called both 'Chinese *wen*' and 'Chinese language,' then?

A: Sometimes one says 'Chinese *wen*' sometimes one says 'Chinese language.' Sometimes one speaks one way, sometimes the other way.

(a) *Woo* yeou ta.de bii. (b) *Lao* Lii tzay jell. (c) Juotz, yiitz, denqtz, deng, sh syh-jiann dong.shi. (d) Lao Jang yeou baw. (e) Nah.sh jii-shuang kuaytz. (f) Ta yeou shyr-jang bau dong.shi .de bawjyy. (g) Jey-leang-jang sh bau kuaytz .de jyy. (h) Woo kai .de men sh ney-shann men. (i) Woo kai .de deng sh jey-jaan deng. (j) Jey-jang sh ta bau dong.shi .de jyy. (k) Ney-san-jang sh Wang Ell bau chianbii .de jyy. (l) Yeou ren.

DIHSAN KEH
SHUO JONG.GWO-HUAH [1]

A: Woo sh Jong.gworen,[2] woo sh *ig* Jong.gworen. Woo shuo Jong.gwo-huah, nii shuo Jong.gwo-huah, ta yee shuo Jong.gwo-huah — woo.men gehgehl[3] dou shuo Jong.gwo-huah. Nii.men huey[4] shuo Jong.gwo-huah .bu.huey .a?

B: Huey,[5] woo.men huey. Nii.men huey, woo.men yee huey, *suoo*.yii nii.men gen woo.men, tzar.men dou huey.

A: Nii sh Jong.gworen .bu.sh?

B: Bu.sh, woo sh way.gworen.[6]

A: Nii sh neei-gwo .de ren[7] .ne? Nii sh tsorng naal lai[8] .de ren[9] .ne?

B: Woo .ia, woo sh tsorng Meei.gwo[10] lai .de,[11] *suoo*.yii woo sh Meei.gwo-ren. Ta tsorng Ing.gwo[12] lai, ta sh tsorng Ing.gwo lai .de, *suoo*.yii ta sh Ing.gworen.

A: Ing.gworen shuo Ing.gwo-huah,[13] Meei.gworen shuo Meei.gwo-huah, sh .bu.sh?

B: Bu.sh tzemm[14] shuo, Ing.gworen shuo Ing'wen —

A: Sherm jiaw[15] Ing'wen .a?

B: Ing'wen jiow.sh[16] Ing.gwo-huah — woo shuo[17] Ing.gworen shuo Ing'wen, Meei.gworen yee shuo Ing'wen. Ing'wen, 'Meeiwen,' sh *i*yanq[18] .d'è![19]

A: Nii.men leang-gwo ren shuo-huah,[20] sh wanchyuan[21] *i*yanq .de .ma?[22]

B: Bu, bu wanchyuan *i*yanq, *bu*.sh wanchyuan *i*yanq .de, *jyy* yeou ideal butorng[23] .jiow.sh.le.[24] .E[25] — sherm jiaw 'Jongwen' .a? Jongwen sh sherm-wen .ne? Jongwen gen Jong.gwo-huah yeou sherm butorng .a?

A: Mei sherm[26] butorng, meiyeou sherm dah butorng, Jongwen jiow.sh Jong.gwo-huah.

B: .Ne.me weysherm[27] yow[28] jiaw 'Jongwen,' yow jiaw 'Jong.gwo-huah' .ne?

A: Yeou shyr.howl[29] shuo 'Jongwen,' yeou shyr.howl shuo 'Jong.gwo-huah.' Yeou shyr.howl tzemm shuo; yeou shyr.howl nemm[30] shuo.

B: When does one speak one way and when the other way then?
A: That I don't know. (I have heard both kinds.) I think it's probably like this: 'Chinese language' is something one speaks, 'Chinese *wen*' is something one writes.
B: Oh, I see, now I understand, now I begin to understand!

NOTES

1. *Jong.gwo* 'middle-country, — China'; *huah* 'speech, words'; *–huah* 'language, dialect.' *Jong.gwo-huah* '(spoken) Chinese.' On the pitch of *.gwo*, see "104," pp. 108 and 110.

2. There is optional neutral tone on *–ren* in *Jong.gwo₀ren, Ing.gwo₀ren, way.gwo₀ren,* and similar words. On the omission of *ig*, see Note 12, p. 123.

3. **Reduplicated AN.** — *Geh*, the stressed form of the general AN for individuals. A reduplicated AN (*gehgeh*), often with addition of the suffix *–l* (*gehgehl*), has a distributive sense, as *gehgehl ren* 'every man,' *jangjang jyy* 'every sheet of paper.' (See also p. 51.)

Although *dou* is often translated by 'all' or 'every,' it is actually an adverb like 'in all cases, uniformly' and belongs to a following verb.

4. *Huey* 'can,' in the sense of 'know how to, have the skill to.'

5. Note that the answer (*huey* for 'yes') to question in the A-not-A form must be either 'A' or 'not-A' and not *Duey .le, Bu.sh,* etc. — unless, of course, the main predicate 'A' itself happens to be one of these words. The reason for this is that the A-not-A form of a question is essentially a disjunctive question, and since a choice (between A and not-A) has to be made, it would not make sense to agree or disagree with it. (See p. 59.)

6. *Way.gwo* 'outside-country, — foreign country'; *way.gworen* 'foreigner'; *way.gwo-huah* 'foreign language.'

7. *Neei-gwo .de ren,* lit. 'a man of which country?'

8. *Tsorng* occurs usually as the first verb in verbal expressions in series. *Tsorng naal lai* 'come from where?'

9. This is a *.de* construction (Note 38, p. 132) with a long modifier 'You are from-where-come kind of man, — you are a man who comes from where, — where do you come from?'

10. *Meei* 'beautiful,' here used to transliterate *–me–* of 'America.' *Meei.gwo* 'Meei-country, — America, the United States.'

11. In a *.de* construction, the word after *.de* is often understood. In such cases, *.de* may either be omitted in the translation or translated by a substantive such as 'one, that which, –er.' Thus, *tsorng Meei.gwo lai .de ren* 'man who comes from America'; *tsorng Meei.gwo lai .de* 'one who comes from America.'

B: Sherm .shyr.howl tzemm shuo, sherm .shyr.howl nemm shuo .ne?
A: Nah — woo bujydaw .le.[31] Woo leang-yanql [32] dou ting.jiann.guoh.[33] Woo sheang dahgay [34] sh tzemm.yanql .de: 'Jong.gwo-huah' sh shuo .de, 'Jongwen' sh shiee .de.
B: Oh, doong .le, shianntzay *woo* doong .le, shianntzay woo tsair [35] doong!

---

12. *Ing.gwo* 'Eng-country, — England'; loosely also 'Great Britain' and 'United Kingdom.'
13. Since Chinese has no distinction of number, this can be translated either as 'An Englishman speaks English' or as 'Englishmen speak English.' The question of number here does not arise in the mind of the Chinese speaker.
Note that the 'and' in the English translation corresponds to nothing in the Chinese. The word *gen* cannot be used here since it cannot join predicates or sentences.
14. *Tzemm.me* 'so' ('in this manner' or 'to this degree') alternates with the more formal *jemm.me* ($<$ *jeh* $+$ *.me*).
15. *Jiaw* 'call, is called, mean (by), is meant (by).' See Note 35, p. 132 on the absence of voice in Chinese verbs.
16. *Jiow* 'namely, simply, just.'
17. *Woo shuo* 'I say,' here used as 'I was saying (when you interrupted me).'
18. *Iyanq* 'one-sort, — same kind, same, alike, identical.'
19. *Iyanq .de* 'same sort of thing' (Note 11). The final particle .è (not the interjection .*Êh*) 'you know, you see, of course' is fused with the preceding .*de* into one syllable .*d'è*.
20. *Shuo-huah* 'speak-speech, — to talk.' Many types of action expressed by an intransitive verb in English are thus expressed by verb-object compounds. Other examples are *shuey-jiaw* 'sleep-nap, — to sleep'; *dwu-shu* 'read-book, — to study.'
The clause *Nii.men leang-gworen shuo-huah* is the subject of *sh:* '(The way) you people of the two countries talk is....'
21. *Wanchyuan* 'completely, entirely, quite.'
22. The final particle .*ma* is added to a statement to change it into a question calling for agreement or disagreement. It leans a tiny bit more towards a dissenting answer and is therefore often used in rhetorical questions.
A sentence ending in .*ma* has a generally high pitch (cf. Exercise 3.)
23. *Butorng* 'not-same, — different.'
24. .*Jiow.sh.le* is used as a compound particle, meaning 'that's the only thing, that's all that's to it.'

25. *.E* — 'er —,' 'uh —,' sound of hesitation. Being unstressed, the sound of *.e* has a neutral quality, as in 'sod*a*' (p. 28).

26. On the use of an interrogative in an indefinite sense, see Note 39, p. 132.

27. *Weysherm(.me)* 'for what, — what for, why?'

28. *Yow ... yow ...* 'again ... again ..., — both ... and ...,' limited to use before predicates only.

29. *Yeou .shyr.howl* 'there are times, — sometimes.'

30. *Nemm(.me)* 'so' ('in that manner' or 'to that degree'). It is derived from *nah* + *.me*. *.Ne.me* 'Well, in that case,' is simply a weakened form of *nemm.me*; it usually retains the final –*.me* because of the usual pause of hesitation.

Note that, although four combinations of meanings are possible with manner and degree combined with near and far reference, they are covered incompletely by English and Chinese words as follows:

Reference Manner or degree	Near	Far
Manner	*tzemm(.me)* 'so, thus'	*nemm(.me)* 'so, thus'
degree	*tzemm(.me)* 'so, this'	*nemm(.me)* 'so, that'

When it is not important to distinguish between near and far reference, *nemm(.me)* is used. (See also Note 11, p. 123.)

31. The new situation expressed by *.le* is: 'Here is a question that stumps me.'

32. *Leang-yanql* 'two kinds.' Distinguish from *leangyanq* 'different.'

33. *Ting* 'listen'; –*.jiann* complement expressing successful perception; *ting.jiann* 'listen, resulting in perceiving, — hear.' Similarly, *kann* 'look'; *kann.jiann* 'see.'

The complement –*.guoh* expresses the idea of 'did or have once before." *Ting.jiann.guoh* 'have heard once before.' It is not a sign of a past or perfect tense, since a verb expressing a past event does not always have the time indicated.

34. *Dahgay* 'great-outline, — in the main; probably.'

35. Cf. last sentence of Lesson 1.

36. (Exercise 3, Example.) A high-pitched sentence ending in *.ma* implies 'Is it true that (you understand Chinese)?' A low-pitched sentence ending in *.a* (or *.ia* when preceded by an open vowel) implies 'Did you say' or 'Am I repeating your statement correctly that (you understand Chinese)?' (Cf. Note 22.)

EXERCISES

1. *Answer the following:*

(a) Lao Syh sh neei-gwo .de ren .a? (b) Meei.gworen shuo sherm-yanql .de huah .ia? (c) 'Jongwen' gen 'Jong.gwo-huah' yeou sherm butorng? (d) *Nii* doong Jong.gwo-huah .bu.doong? (e) Nii huey shiee Jongwen .bu.huey? (f) Meei.gwo-huah gen Ing.gwo-huah sh wanchyuan *i*yanq .de .bu.sh? (g) Nii huey shuo neei-gwo .de huah? (h) Kann.x jell *yeou* jiig Jong.gworen, jiig way.gworen. (i) *Woo yeou* jii-jy chianbii, jii-jy maubii? (j) Shianntzay .ne? (k) Jell yeou *jii*-jaan deng jii-jang denqtz .a? (l) Ta sh .bu.sh *i*g huey shuo Jong.gwo-huah .de way.gworen .a?

2. *Example:*

Given:	Answer:
Woo shuo Jong.gwo-huah.	Nii sh shuo Jong.gwo-huah .de, nii sh *i*g shuo Jong.gwo-huah .de ren.

(a) Jang San huey shuo Ingwen. (b) *Nii* sheang ('want to') shuo-huah. (c) Woom bu doong Jong.gwo-huah. (d) Ta tsorng Jong.gwo lai. (e) Nii gen ta, nii.men tsorng naal lai? (f) Nii huey shuo leang-gwo .de huah. (g) Lii Syh *yeou* jyy. (h) Woo yow mei.yeou denqtz, yow mei.yeou deng. (i) Ta jiaw Wang Ell. (j) Nii shuo sherm.me? (k) *Lao* Lii dahgay *bu* kann-baw. (l) Neyg way.gworen huey shuo Jong.gwo-huah.

3. *Example:*

Given:
Woo doong Jongwen.

Answer: (only orally)

(1) *A:* *Nii* doong Jongwen .bu.doong?
 B: Doong, *woo* doong Jongwen.
 A: (*High intonation.*) *Nii* doong Jongwen .ma?
 B: Duey .le, *woo* doong.
 A: (*Low intonation.*) *Nii* doong Jongwen .a?
 B: Ếh, *woo* doong.

(2) *A:* Ta doong Jongwen .bu.doong?
 B: Bu doong, ta bu doong Jongwen.
 A: Ta bu doong Jongwen .ma?
 B: Sh .de, ta bu doong.
 A: Ta bu doong Jongwen .a?
 B: .Eng, ta bu doong.

(a) Woo huey shuo Jong.gwo-huah. (b) Woo sh Meei.gworen. (c) Woo huey shuo '*i* ell san syh.' (d) Jell yeou deng. (e) Woo jydaw nii tzay naal. (f) Tzemm shuo duey. ('Speaking this way is correct.')

(g) Tzar.men shianntzay shuo Jong.gwo-huah. (Use .ia instead of .a.)
(h) Jeyg baw .shanq yeou Jong.gwo shinwen. (Use neyg under No. (2).)
(i) Ta sheang lai. (j) Woo.men.jell yeou ren. (A. Nii.men.nall yeou ren

LESSON 4
TELEPHONING

Main 3141 ... Not 3747 — 3141, three thousand one hundred forty-one. ... That's right.

. . . . .

Listen! Listen! What's ringing? What sound is it? Is it a bell that's ringing? Is it an electric bell? It is? What electric bell? Is it the doorbell or the telephone bell?

Where is the telephone? Which way do I go?[10] How do I go? Do I go this way or that way? Which side? This side or that side? Which door do I go by? Which door?

The third door?

. . . .

Hello, hello, who is this? — Who is this, please? What is your name, please? Your name is —?

What? Your name is what? Your name is Wang? Your first name, Mr. Wang, is —?

Oh, you are just Wang Ell! I couldn't make out it was just you, I couldn't make out it was you! Why haven't you come to see me for such a long time?

You *did* come? When did you come? What day did you come? What day of the week? Sunday or Monday? Today or yesterday? Was it yesterday? What time yesterday? Yesterday morning or yesterday afternoon?

Two o'clock in the afternoon? Uh — how did you come? Did you walk here, take a car, or come by boat?

Oh, you came by plane. What plane was it? When did it (*or* you) arrive here?

It arrived at twelve o'clock? How is it that I did not see the plane? How is it that I did not hear the noise from the plane?

Huh? What? What did you say? I cannot understand you. Please speak a little more slowly. Please speak a little more slowly.

The plane — what? I cannot hear you clearly. Will you say it once more, please?

DIHSYH KEH
DAA [1] DIANNHUAH [2]

Tzoongjyu,[3] 3-1-4-1, . . . *Bu*.sh 3-7-4-7 — 3-1-4-1, sanchian ibae syh.shyri-haw.[4] . . . Duey.le.

. . . . .

Ting! Nii [5] ting! Sherm sheang? Sherm sheng.in sheang? [6] Sh liengl [7] sheang .bu.sh? (*High:*) Sh diannliengl .ma? (*Low:*) Sh diannliengl .a? Naal .de diannliengl? [8] Sh menliengl .hair.sh [9] diannhuah .ia? Diannhuah tzay naal? Tsorng *naal* tzoou? [10] *Tzeem* tzoou? Tzemm tzoou .hair.sh nemm tzoou .a? *Tzoou* neei.bial? Tzoou jey.bial .hair.sh tzoou ney.bial .a? *Tzoou* neeig men [11] .a? Dihjiig [12] men?
(*Low:*) Dihsan'g men .a?

. . . . .

.Uai,[13] .uai, Nin naal? [14] — Nin sh neei-i-wey? [15] Gueyshinq [16] .a? Nin Gueyshinq .sh —
Ar? Shinq [17] sherm.me? Shinq Wang .a? [18] Wang .Shian.sheng [19] Tairfuu [20] .sh —?
.Oh, nii jiow.sh Wang Ell! [21] Woo mei [22] ting.chu.lai [23] jiow.sh nii, woo mei ting.chu sh nii .lai! [24] *Nii* tzeem [25] tzemm.shie [26] shyr.howl yee [27] mei lai kann [28] .woo [29] .ia?
Nii lai.guoh .ma? Nii sherm .shyr.howl lai .de? Neei-tian lai .de? Liibayjii? [30] Liibayryh .hair.sh Liibay'i .a? Jiel .hair.sh tzwol .a? Sh tzwol .ma? Tzwol sherm shyr.howl? Tzwol shanq.wuu [31] .hair.sh shiah.wuu .a?
Shiah.wuu *leang*-dean jong [32] .a? .E — *nii* tzeem lai .de? [33] Sh tzooudawl [34] lai .de, sh tzuoh-che [35] lai .de, .hair.sh tzuoh-chwan lai .de?
.Oh, nii sh tzuoh feiji lai .de! *Jii*-dean jong .de feiji? [36] Sherm .shyr.howl daw .de? [37]
Shyr'ell-dean daw .d'a? *Woo* tzeem mei kann.jiann feiji .ne? *Woo* tzeem mei ting.jiann ney-jiah [38] feiji .de sheng.in .ne?
Ar? Sherm.me? Nii shuo sherm.me? Woo ting.bu-doong.[39] *Chiing* .nii mànn.i.deal [40] shuo. *Chiing* .nii shuo-mann.i.deal.[41]
Feiji — sherm.me? Woo ting.bu-ching.chuu. *Chiing* .nii [42] tzay [43] shuo .i.biann.[44]
Fei — feiji 'wuh-dean'? Sherm jiaw 'wuh-dean' .a? 'Wuh-dean' sh sherm yih.sy? [45]

The pl — the plane 'missed the hour'? What do you mean by 'missed the hour'? What does 'missed the hour' mean?

I see, 'to have missed the hour' is simply 'to have come late'? 'Missed the hour' simply means 'came late'? Oh, I see. Er — How about Lii? Has he come too?

He says he wants me to do what? He wants me to go and do what?

Do I understand that he wants me to go and see him today or tomorrow? Well, shall I go see him right away today, or wait until tomorrow to go, or until when?

I think I shall be busy the next few days; I have business here and can't get away. You two gentlemen had better come to me, will that be all right?

Oh, no, that's all right!
Oh, no, it doesn't matter, that's all right! You better come to me.
Good, that would be best!

Yuh, yup, that'll be fine! Well, we'll see each other tomorrow. See you tomorrow! Goodbye!

NOTES

1. *Daa*, with a basic meaning of 'strike, beat,' has many uses. Cf. Germ. *schlagen*.

2. *Diannhuah* 'electric-speech, — telephone'; *Daa ig diannhuah* 'to make a telephone call.'

3. *Tzoongjyu* 'main-bureau, — main exchange.'

4. **Numbers.** — Numbers from 1 to 100 are counted as follows:

1 i	11 shyri	21 ell.shyri	. . .	91 jeou.shyri
2 ell	12 shyr'ell	22 ell.shyr'ell	. . .	92 jeou.shyr'ell
3 san	13 shyrsan	23 ell.shyrsan	. . .	93 jeou.shyrsan
4 syh	14 shyrsyh	24 ell.shyrsyh	. . .	94 jeou.shyrsyh
5 wuu	15 shyrwuu	25 ell.shyrwuu	. . .	95 jeou.shyrwuu
6 liow	16 shyrliow	26 ell.shyrliow	. . .	96 jeou.shyrliow
7 chi	17 shyrchi	27 ell.shyrchi	. . .	97 jeou.shyrchi
8 ba	18 shyrba	28 ell.shyrba	. . .	98 jeou.shyrba
9 jeou	19 shyrjeou	29 ell.shyrjeou	. . .	99 jeou.shyrjeou
10 shyr	20 ellshyr	30 sanshyr	. . .	100 ibae

When followed by an AN, 2 is usually *leang-* instead of *ell*, but 12, 22, . . . , 92 are still *shyr'ell, ell.shyr'ell, . . . , jeou.shyr'ell*, even when followed by an AN. The use of *ell* before an AN is limited to measure words of old standing.

When *ellshyr, sanshyr*, etc. are followed by an AN, *shyr* has the neutral tone, thus *ell.shyrg ren*, 'twenty people,' *san.shyr-jang jyy*, 'thirty sheets of paper.'

TELEPHONING 143

.Oh, 'wuh-dean' jiow.sh 'lai-woan.l(e)' .a? 'Wuh-dean' jiow.sh 'lai-woan.le' .de yih.sy .a? .Oh, *woo* doong .le. .E — *Lao* Lii .ne? Ta yee lai .le .ma?
Ta shuo ta yaw *woo* tzeem.me? [46] Ta shuo ta yaw woo chiuh tzuoh sherm.me?
(*Low:*) Yaw woo jiel .huoh.jee miengl chiuh kann.x .ta .ia? [47] .Ne.me woo jiel jiow [48] chiuh kann .ta .ne, .hair.sh miengl tzay [49] chiuh .ne, hair.sh jii.shyr chiuh .ne?
Woo sheang woo jey-leang-tian [50] mei konql; [51] woo jell yeou shyh tzoou.bu-kai.　　Nii.men　leang-wey [52] shanq [53] woo.jell lai .ba, .hao .bu.hao? [54]
Mm, [55] *bu*yawjiin! [56]
Ae! [57] *Bu*yawjiin, *bu*yawjiin!　Hair.sh [58] nii.men shanq woo.jell lai .hao.
.Hao, tzemmyanql .hao.
.Ėh, .èh, tzemmyanql hao-jyi.le!　.Ne.me — Tzarm miengl tzay jiann .le.[59] Miengl jiann, .ah! [60] .Tzay.jiann vx! [61]

Ordinal numbers are formed by adding the prefix *dih–* (as we have seen) and/or the AN *–haw*, as *dihsan, san-haw,* or *dihsan-haw. Haw* cannot be used if there is already another AN, as *dihsan'g men* 'the third door.'

5. While *nii* or *nii.men* is usually not expressed in commands and requests, their use is much less rare than the use of 'you' before the imperative form of English verbs.
6. *Sherm sheng.in sheang,* lit. 'What sound sounds?'
7. *Liengl* (< *ling* + *l*) '(small) bell.' Be careful to pronounce the vowel with simultaneous nasality and curling of the tongue: [liə̃ᵣ].
8. *Naal .de diannliengl,* lit. 'electric bell of what place?'
9. On *.hair.sh,* see Note 47.
10. *Tsorng naal tzoou,* lit. 'by way of where go?'
11. *I-shann men* means 'a door' as a physical object; *ig men* means 'a door' either as a physical object or in the sense of 'a doorway.'
12. *Dihjiig men,* lit. 'number-what door, which-eth door?'
13. *Uai* 'Hello' in telephoning or in hailing someone, 'Hey, you there!' Not used for the greeting 'Hello!'
14. *Nin* 'you,' polite form, used only in the Peiping region. *Nin naal* 'you (are) where?' Since telephone subscribers in China are regarded as residences or organizations, the usual first question to ask is 'What place are you?' rather than 'Who are you?' or 'Who is this?'
15. The polite form for *–g* is *–wey,* rendered by 'please' in the translation of the sentence.
16. *Guey* 'noble'; 'expensive'; 'your' (honorific form). *Shinq* 'surname'; 'to have the surname of.'

144   LESSON 4

17. *Shinq*, here used as a transitive verb.
18. Warning! After *Wang*, the particle *.ba* 'I suppose?' should be avoided as *Wang .ba* would be homonymous with *wang.ba* 'cuckold,' a term of abuse. The same particle should be avoided after the syllable *ji*, because of homophony with the word for 'male organ.'
19. *Shian.sheng*, lit. 'first born,' — 'teacher'; 'gentleman'; 'sir'; *.Shian.sheng* (with neutral tone both in *shian* and in *sheng*) 'Mr.,' also applied to professional women.
20. **Chinese Names.** — Every Chinese has a *shinq* 'surname,' inherited from his father. (Most surnames are monosyllabic and are bound words.) Then he has a *ming.tzyh* '(formal) name' (of one or two syllables), his individual name, used in school, in business, and at law. Finally, he has a *haw*, variously translated as 'style' or 'courtesy name,' used in social intercourse. To ask somebody's *haw*, however, the honorific form *tairfuu* should be used.
21. The other man turns out to be one whom the first speaker knows well enough to call him familiarly *Wang Ell* 'Wang Number Two (among his brothers).'
22. *Mei, mei.yeou*, 'have not, did not.'
23. *Ting.chu.lai* 'listen with the result of "out," — make out (by listening).'
24. The complement *-.chu.lai* 'out' is often separated by an inserted object, in this case the clause *sh nii* '(that it) was you.'
25. *Tzeem* 'how? how is it that?' Note that it can either follow or precede the subject.
26. *Tzemm₀shie* 'such a lot of, so much.'
27. *Yee* 'too, even (for such a long time).'
28. *Kann* 'see' in the sense of 'call on, look up.'
29. A pronoun after a verb is in the neutral tone, unless it is emphasized for a contrast.
30. *Liibay* 'week.' The Chinese week, which begins with Monday, is as follows:

Liibay'i   Liibay'ell   Liibaysan   Liibaysyh   Liibaywuu   Liibayliow   Liibayryh
'Monday' 'Tuesday' 'Wednesday' 'Thursday' 'Friday'   'Saturday'   'Sunday'

Sunday is also called Liibay or Liibaytian

31. *Shanq.wuu* 'morning, forenoon.'
32. *Jong* '(large) bell'; 'clock'; *–dean jong* 'point (of) clock, — o'clock,' *–dean* being a measure word.
33. *Nii (sh) tzeem lai .de*, lit. 'You (are) one who came how?'
34. *Tzoou-dawl* 'walk-road, — to walk' (Cf. *shuo-huah*, Note 20, p. 137.)
35. *Tzuoh* 'sit'; 'ride'; *che* 'vehicle.' The word *che* is always used when it is not necessary to specify what kind of a vehicle is meant.

36. *Jii-dean .de feiji*, lit. 'plane of what o'clock?'

37. The last few sentences all refer to past events about which some specific points were involved. In such cases, the *.de* form is the favorite form used. *Nii .sh leang-dean jong daw .de* 'You are one who arrived at two o'clock' similar to, but a little less emphatic than 'It was at two o'clock that you arrived.'

38. *Jiah*, AN for airplanes and machines.

39. Potential Complements. — The usual way of expressing 'can' or 'cannot' when there is a compound verb consisting of a main verb and a complement is to insert *-.de-* for 'can' and *-.bu-* for 'cannot.' Thus, *kann.de-jiann* 'can see'; *kann.bu-jiann* 'cannot see.' *Ting.de-doong* 'can understand (from listening)'; *ting.bu-doong* 'cannot understand.' (See also p. 44.)

40. *Mann* 'slow, slowly,' *mann.i.deal* 'slow by a little, a little more slowly.'

41. *Mann.i.deal* is in an adverbial position in the first sentence and in a complement position in the second sentence. The former emphasizes the manner or appearance and the latter the result. The difference is, however, rather slight in this case.

42. *Chiing nii* '(I) request you.' *Nii* can be omitted, in which case *chiing* corresponds in use to the word 'please.'

43. *Tzay* 'again,' homonymous with *tzay*, 'to be at.'

44. *Biann* 'number of times,' AN for verbs. (See 4(d), p. 46.)

45. *X sh sherm yih.sy*, lit. '*X* is (of) what meaning?' is the normal way of asking the meaning of a word, and the answer to that, as exemplified in the next sentence, is *X sh* (insert meaning here) *.de ₒyih.sy*. Since this is an unusual use of *.de*, it would be advisable for the student to learn the formula just as it is. It is really like the use of 'of' in 'the continent of Asia.'

46. *Tzeem.me* here is an interrogative verb 'do what?'

47. Disjunctive and Non-disjunctive ' Or.' — The written sentence 'Are you going today or tomorrow?' is ambiguous. (a) Spoken with a rising intonation on 'today' (with or without a pause) and with a falling intonation on 'tomorrow,' it is a disjunctive question and the person answering is expected to make a choice between 'today' and 'tomorrow.' (b) If the same words are spoken with a gradually rising intonation with no pause, then it is a yes-or-no question and the person answering is expected to say 'Yes (I am going today or tomorrow)' or 'No (I am not going either today or tomorrow).' (See also p. 58.)

In Chinese, different words are used for the two kinds of 'or's.' *ₒHair.sh* (or simply *.sh*) is used in the first case, while *ₒhuoh.jee* (alternating with *ₒhuoh.sh*, *.he.je*, and *.he.sh*) is used in the second. Thus, *Nii yaw chianbii .hair.sh gangbii?* 'Do you want a pencil or a pen? (which do you want?)'

Nii yaw chianbii .huoh.jee gangbii .bu.yaw? 'Do you (or do you not) want a pencil or a pen?'

Note that in a statement — unless it contains an indirect disjunctive question — 'or' will always be translated by *.huoh.jee* (or one of its variants).

48. *Jiow* 'immediately, right away.'

49. *Tzay* 'again,' here used like *tsair* (last sentence of Lesson 1). *.Hair.sh miengl tzay chiuh* 'or, again, go tomorrow, — not go till tomorrow.'

50. *Jey-leang-tian,* lit. 'these two days.' Like 'a couple' in English, the numeral *leang-* plus AN can also be taken in the general sense of 'a few.'

51. *Mei konql* 'have no leisure.' *Kong* 'empty,' *konq* 'unoccupied,' *konql* 'unoccupied space or time.'

52. *Leang-wey* is simply the polite form for *leangg*, here translated as 'two gentlemen' (though also applicable to two ladies or one lady and one gentleman).

53. *Shanq* 'up'; 'go up'; 'go to.' *Shanq woo.jell lai* 'to my place come.'

54. *Hao* 'good'; 'all right.' In the latter sense, especially when used interjectionally, it has a Half 3rd Tone or neutral tone. (See p. 50.)

55. *Mm,* a nasal labial sound in a long 3rd Tone (often with a falling ending after the rise), interjection for emphatic disagreement.

56. *Buyawjiin* 'not important, — it doesn't matter.'

57. *Ae!* (often with a fall after the 3rd Tone), interjection of disagreement or disapproval.

58. *Hair.sh* 'after all it is (a case for) —.' *Hair sh X .hao* 'After all, X is better.'

59. This *.le* indicates that 'we have come to the new situation of stopping our conversation till tomorrow.'

60. This interjection *.ah,* separated from the sentence by a pause (sometimes with a glottal stop), softens a command, request, or greeting.

61. The greeting *Tzay-jiann vx* is often extremely underarticulated so as to sound like *tzeyanzeyan.* (The abbreviation *vx* stands for two syllables repeated.) The greeting *Tzay-jiann* is rarely used alone. It is either repeated (without pause) or followed, after a pause, by the interjection *.ah!*

62. *Exercise 1(h).* Here is a case of the S–P predicate (p. 35): 'As for you, the telephone is what number, — what is your telephone number?' Insertion of *.de* after *nii* would make the sentence more like the English.

EXERCISES

1. *Answer the Following:*

(a) Nii ting, sh menliengl .hair.sh diannhuah .ia? (b) Wang Ell shinq sherm.me? (c) .Ne.me Lii Syh .ne? (d) Tzwol Liibayliow, jiel

TELEPHONING

Liibayjii .ne? (e) Miengl .ne? (f) Jong.gwo *yee* yeou feiji .mei.yeou? (g) Ing.gwo feiji hao hair.sh Meei.gwo feiji hao .a? (h) Nii diannhuah [62] sh jii-haw? (i) Tsorng Liibaysan daw Liibayliow *yeou* jii-tian? (j) Jiel Liibaysan. *Lao* Lii shuo, 'Lao Jang, woo jiel mei konql shanq nii.jell lai, woo miengl tzay lai .ba.' .Ne.me *nii* sheang *Lao Lii* neei-tian shanq Lao Jang.nall .chiuh .ne? (k) Ta yaw woo jiel .he.je miengl lai .a? (l) Nii shuo .de sh Meei.gwo-huah .hair.sh Ing.gwo-huah .ia?

2. *Practice in counting numbers:*

(a) *Count orally from one to one hundred.* (Passing tempo 80 seconds.)

(b) *Count orally by fives:* i-wuu, i-shyr, shyrwuu, ellshyr, ell.shyrwuu, sanshyr, . . . jeou.shyrwuu, ibae. (20 seconds.)

(c) *Count from one to forty, using the* AN -g: ig, leangg, san'g, . . . shyrg, shyrig, shyr'ellg, . . . ell.shyrg, ell.shyrig, ell.shyr'ellg, . . . (50 seconds.)

(d) *Write out and count orally from one to forty using the* AN -baa. *Be careful to make the usual changes in the 3rd Tone. Make a full pause after each* baa. (60 seconds.)

(e) *Count* dih'i, dih'ell, dihsan, . . . dihsyh.shyr. (60 sec.)

(f) *Count the hours:* I-dean jong, *leang*-dean jong, . . . shyr'ell-dean jong. *Repeat without* jong. (20 seconds.)

3. (a) *Example* — Tzwol Liibayryh, jiel Liibay'i, miengl Liibay'ell. *Complete same form starting from each of the other six days of the week.*

(b) *Example* — Tzwol sh *i*-haw, jiel sh ell-haw, miengl sh san-haw. *Complete same form starting from the fourth, seventh, tenth, . . . twenty-fifth, twenty-eighth, and twenty-ninth.*

4. *Fill out the blanks:*

(a) Woo ting.jiann _____ sheang, *suoo*.yii woo shanq _____ .nall .chiuh kai _____. (b) *Bu*.sh diannhuah sheang, *suoo*.yii woo *bu* shanq diannhuah _____. (c) Liibay'i sh *i*-haw, Liibay'ell sh _____ haw, *suoo*.yii Liibayryh sh _____ haw. (d) Tsorng Jong.gwo lai de baw .shanq yeou Jong.gwo .de _____, tsorng Ing.gwo lai .de baw .shanq yeou _____. (e) Nii sh tzuoh-chwan lai .de _____ tzuoh feiji _____? (f) Deng tzay jell. Denqtz *bu* tzay jell, denqtz tzay _____. (g) Jiel chiuh _____ miengl chiuh dou hao. (h) Jiel bu kai-men, miengl _____ kai-men .ne. (i) Nii jy.daw .bu.jy.daw ta shianntzay jiow lai _____ miengl tzay [49] lai .a? (j) Woo _____ ta jiel jiow _____. (k) Nii yaw _____ che .lai .ne, _____ yaw tzuoh _____ .lai .ne? (l) _____ .lai _____ tzuoh _____ .lai mei sherm bu-torng.

5. *Example:*

Given:
Wuh-dean = lai-woan.le'

Answer:
Sherm jiaw wuh-dean .a?
Wuh-dean sh sherm yih.sy .a?
Wuh-dean jiow.sh 'lai-woan.le' .de yih.sy.

(a) Sheir? = sherm ren? (b) Tzar.men = nii gen woo, .huoh.jee nii.men gen woo.men. (c) Woo.men = woo gen ta, .huoh.jee woo gen ta.men. (d) Sh .bu.sh = sh, hair.sh *bu*sh. (e) Yeou .mei.yeou = yeou, hair.sh mei.yeou. (f) Chyau.x = kann.x. (g) I-shuang = leangg. (h) Woo.men gehgehl = woo.men renren. (i) Huey shuo = jy.daw tzeem shuo. (j) Ing'wen = Ing.gwo-huah. (k) Butorng = bu *i*yanq. (1) Doong = jy.daw sh sherm yih.sy.

LESSON 5

UP, DOWN, LEFT, RIGHT, FRONT, BACK, AND MIDDLE

A: 'On the desk' means 'on top of the desk.' 'On the chair' means 'on top of the chair.' There are books on the desk, there are one, two, three, ... there are ten-odd books; therefore the books are on the desk. There are no books on the chair; therefore the books are not on the chair. There is a door in (lit. 'on') the wall; therefore the door is in the wall.

B: Is the door above the wall?

A: No, *men tzay chyang.shanq* simply means that it is where the wall is, it does not mean that it is above the wall.

B: I see.

A: Well — the opposite of 'above' is 'below.' Under this book are several sheets of paper, under the paper is the desk, and under the desk is the floor. There are newspapers under this chair. There is writing on the newspapers. Look, there is writing on the newspapers.

B: Yeah, there's writing on the newspapers.

A: There is no writing on the white paper. Now I write a few characters on the paper, I write a few words. Now there is writing on the paper, do you see it?

B: Yes, I see it, I see that there is writing there now.

A: There is a blackboard on the wall here; there is no writing on the blackboard. See, I write some characters on the blackboard, I write a couple of characters on the blackboard. Now there is writing on the blackboard, too.

UP, DOWN, LEFT, RIGHT, FRONT, BACK, AND MIDDLE   149

6. *Translate into Chinese:*

East (*Dongjyu*) 5199. That's right. Hello! Is this Mr. Wang? Which Mr. Wang is this? Mr. Wang Two or Mr. Wang Three? What? I can't hear clearly what you say. Will you talk more slowly, please? What? Aren't you Mr. Wang? (Use .*ma*) You are not Mr. Wang? (Use .*a*, low pitch.) Oh, it's (just) Jang San! I didn't know 'twas (just) you. Why didn't you come and see me yesterday? Huh? What? You did? When did you come? Did you come today? (.*de .ma*) You came today? (.*d'a*) What did you ride when you came? ('You ride what come .*de?*') Did you come in the morning or in the afternoon? How about Lii Syh? Didn't (*mei*) he come with you? He said he was too busy these days? (.*a*, low pitch.) Oh, I see, now I begin to see what you mean. Well, see you tomorrow. Goodbye!

DIHWUU KEH
SHANQ SHIAH TZUOO YOW CHYAN HOW [1] JONGJIALL

A: Juol.shanq [2] jiow.sh juotz .de shanq.tou.[3] Yiitz.shanq [4] jiow.sh yiitz .de shanq.tou. Juol.shanq yeou shu,[5] yeou i-been, *leang*-been, san-been, . . . yeou shyr*jii*-been shu; *suoo*.yii shu tzay juol.shanq.[6] Yiitz.shanq mei shu; *suoo*.yii shu *bu* tzay yiitz.shanq. Chyang.shanq yeou men; *suoo*.yii men tzay chyang.shanq.

B: Men tzay chyang .de shanq.tou .ma?

A: *Bu*.sh, 'men tzay chyang.shanq' jiow.sh 'tzay chyang.nall' .de .yih.sy, *bu*.sh 'tzay chyang .de shanq.tou' .de .yih.sy.

B: .Oh.

A: .Ne.me — shanq.tou .de dueymiall [7] jiow jiaw dii.shiah.[8] Jeyg shu .de dii.shiah *yeou* jii-jang jyy, *jyy* dii.shiah sh [9] juotz, juotz dii.shiah sh dih. Jey-*baa* yiitz dii.shiah yeou baw. Baw.shanq yeou tzyh.[10] Nii kann, baw.shanq yeou tzyh.

B: .Èh, baw.(s)hanq [11] yeou tzyh.

A: Bair-jyy .shanq mei tzyh. Shianntzay woo tzay jyy.shanq shiee-tzyh, *shiee* jiig tzyh. Shianntzay jyy.shanq yeou tzyh .le, nii kann.jiann .le .ma?

B: Èè,[12] woo kann.jiann .le, woo kann.jiann yeou tzyh .le.

A: Jell chyang.shanq yeou *i*-kuay [13] heibaan; heibaan.shanq mei.yeou tzyh. Nii kann, woo tzay heibaan.shanq shiee-tzyh, tzay heibaan.shanq *shiee* .leangg [14] tzyh. Shianntzay heibaan.shanq *yee* yeou tzyh .le.

B: Which hand do you write with? Do you write with your right hand or with your left hand? Which hand is it that you write with?
A: I write with my right hand, I cannot write with my left hand.
B: Say, *I* can. Look, *I* can write with my left hand.
A: But you don't write well (with it), you see. You look at you!
B: (*Laughs.*) I don't write well.
A: Well, you know, in writing Chinese you write from top right-hand side down. When you write foreign words, however, then it is different.
B: How are foreign words written then?
A: Foreign words are written from the top left-hand side toward the right.
B: I see.
A: Now the desk is in front of me, in front of me there is a desk. The chair is back of me, in back of me there is a chair. As for me, I am between these two things. Between the desk and the chair is me. Now I walk to the back of the chair, then the chair is in front of me. Again, I walk to the front of the desk, now the desk is between me and the chair.
B: Is this book black or white? Is it a black book or a white book?
A: As for this book, the outside is black, but the inside is not black, the inside is not all black.
B: How is that?
A: Because the paper of the book is white paper, you see! It's only the writing on the paper that's black; that's why the outside and the inside of the book are not the same.
B: That's right, they are not the same. Uh — are we now outside or inside?
A: We are inside, of course.
B: Inside of what?
A: Inside the building, inside a building, also inside a room, inside a classroom.
B: I see. When people talk outside the classroom, can those inside the classroom hear them?
A: I don't think they can.
Outside: Iu, yu, yeu, yuh!
A: But sometimes perhaps you hear a little too.
Outside: Tu, twu, tuu, tuh!
A: Listen, there are people shouting outside, there are people shouting loudly.
Outside: Mha, ma, maa, mah!
B: I don't think so, they are having a class in another classroom, I guess.

UP, DOWN, LEFT, RIGHT, FRONT, BACK, AND MIDDLE 151

B: Nii na neei-jy *shoou* shiee-tzyh [15] .a? Nii na yowshoou [16] .hair.sh na tzuoò.shoou [17] shiee-tzyh .a? Nii sh na neeig *shoou* shiee-tzyh .d'a?
A: Woo .ia, woo sh yonq yow.shoou shiee-tzyh .de, woo *bu*huey yonq *tzuoo*.shoou shiee-tzyh.
B: È,[18] **woo** huey. Nii kann, **woo** neng [19] na *tzuoo*.shoou shiee-tzyh.
A: Kee.sh *nii* shiee .de buhao [20] .è.[21] Nii chyau .nii!
B: .He.he,[22] shiee .de buhao.
A: .E — nii jy.daw shiee Jong.gwo-tzyh sh tsorng shanq.tou yow.bial wanq [23] dii.shiah shiee .de. Shiee way.gwo-tzyh .de .shyr.howl .ne, nah jiow butorng .le.
B: Way.gwo-tzyh sh [24] *tzeem* shiee .de .ne?
A: Way.gwo-tzyh sh tsorng shanq.tou tzuoo.bial wanq yow shiee .de.
B: .Oh.
A: Shianntzay juotz tzay woo.de chyan.tou, woo chyan.tou yeou .jang [25] juotz. Yiitz tzay woo.de how.tou, woo [26] how.tou *yeou baa* yiitz. Woo .ne, woo jiow tzay jey-leang-jiann dong.shi .de jongjiall.[27] Juotz gen yiitz .de jongjiall sh woo. Shianntzay *woo* tzoou .daw yiitz how.tou,[28] .ne.me yiitz jiow tzay woo chyan.tou .le. Woo yow tzoou .daw juotz .de chyan.tou, shianntzay juotz tzay woo gen [29] yiitz .de jongjiall .le.
B: Jey-beel shu sh hei .de [30] hair.sh bair .d'a? Sh beel hei-shu [31] hair.sh beel bair-shu .a?
A: Jey-been shu way.tou hei, kee.sh lii.tou bu hei, lii.tou bu chyuan.sh [32] hei .de.
B: Tzeem .ne?
A: Inwey shu .de jyy sh bair-jyy .è! Jyy.shanq .de tzyh tsair sh hei .de .ne; *suoo*.yii shu .de way.tou gen lii.tou *bu*sh *i*yanq .de.
B: .Èh, lii-way [33] bu *i*yanq. .E — tzar.men ren [34] shianntzay tzay [35] way.tòu hair.sh tzay lii.tou .a?
A: Tzar.men tzay lii.tou .a.
B: Tzay sherm .de lii.tou?
A: Tzay farngtz.lii, tzay i-suoo farngtz [36] .lii.tou, yee.sh tzay i-jian utz .lii.tou, tzay i-jian kehtarng [37] .lii.tou.
B: .Oh. Ren tzay kehtarng way.tou shuo-huah, kehtarng lii.tou .de ren ting.de-jiann .ting.bu.jiann .a?
A: *Woo* sheang [38] ting.bu-jiann.
Way.tou. Iu, yu, yeu, yuh!
A: Kee.sh yeou shyr.howl *yee* sheu [39] ting.jiann ideal.
Way.tou. Tu, twu, tuu, tuh!
A: Nii ting, way.tou yeou ren raang, yeou ren .tzay.nall dahshengl [40] raang .ne.[41]
Way.tou: Mha, ma, maa, mah!
B: *Bu*sh .ba? Sh bye.de [42] kehtarng.lii .tzay.nall shanq-keh [43] .ne .ba?

NOTES

1. *Shanq, shiah, tzuoo, yow, chyan,* and *how* are normally bound words. In this heading, they are mentioned as special terms for discussion, in which case any monosyllable can be hypostatized as a free word. Note that in reading the title, no pause is necessary between terms.

2. **Localizers.** — This lesson deals chiefly with localizers, also called postpositions. A localizer is a bound word forming the second component of a subordinate compound, resulting in a time or place word. In translation, however, it usually involves the use of a preposition (p. 53). Thus:

Form	Structure	Translation
Juol.shanq	'desk-top,'	'on the desk.'
Utz.lii	'room-inside,'	'in the room.'
Yiitz-how.tou	'chair-backend,'	'behind the chair.'
Jyy-dii.shiah	'paper-bottom,'	'under the paper.'
Hei.shiah	'dark-below,'	'under darkness, at night.'

The suffix *-.nall* is a general localizer. When it is not necessary to specify whether the relation is 'on' or 'in' or 'beside' or something else, then *-.nall* (or *-.jell* for near reference) is used, as *juotz.nall* 'desk-place, — at the desk.'

A one-syllable localizer is always bound, while a two-syllable localizer can occur as a free word, as *shanq.tou mei ren* 'top-end has no people, — there is nobody up there'; *juotz .de yow.bial* 'the right side of the desk.'

3. The noun suffix *-.tou* (< *tour* 'head, end') is less frequent than *-tz*.

4. Note that *juo-* (or *juol-*) can be used before *-.shanq*, but that the full word *yiitz* must be used before *-.shanq*.

5. ' **There-is-A-on-B** ' **Forms.** — In general, ' There is *A* on (at, in, etc.) *B*' takes the form of *B.shanq yeou A*, lit. '*B*-top has *A*.' When the location is extended to the whole universe, then it need not be specified, hence *Yeou A* '(the universe) has *A*, — there is *A*.'

6. When *tzay* precedes noun + localizer, it can be translated by 'to be' or left untranslated according to the following conditions:

(a) If it is a main predicate, the verb 'to be' must be expressed, as

Shu tzay juol.shanq 'The book is on the desk.'
Jyy tzay yiitz .de dii.shiah 'The paper is under the chair.'

(b) If *tzay* + noun + localizer occurs *before* another verb, no verb 'to be' will appear in the translation, as

Ta tzay jyy.shanq shiee jiig tzyh 'He writes a few words on the paper.'

7. *Duey* 'to match'; 'correct'; 'to face'; 'toward'; 'opposite.' *Miall* (< *miann* + *-l*) 'face, side.' *Dueymiall* 'opposite side.'

8. *Dii.shiah* (often weakened to *dii.shie* and *dii.hie*) 'bottom-down, — below.'

9. It would also be possible to use *yeou* 'there is' here. *Jyy dii.shiah sh juotz* means 'It is understood that there is something under the paper, and it is a desk.' *Jyy dii.shiah yeou juotz* means 'There might or might not be anything under the paper, but actually there is something — a desk.' *Sh* 'is' tells what it is, while *yeou* 'there is' tells *whether* there is anything.

10. *Tzyh* 'word'; 'character'; 'writing.'

11. In rapid speech, the localizer *–.shanq* is underarticulated, sounding like *–.ranq*.

12. A full 3rd Tone on the vowel *è* forms an interjection for hearty agreement: 'You are quite right.'

13. The AN *–kuay* is used with words for things in blocks, lumps, masses, and pieces of woven things.

14. On the use of *.leangg* in the sense of 'a few,' see Note 50, p. 146.

15. Verbal Expressions in Series. — When two phrases, especially of the verb-object type, occur in succession, the first can often be translated by an adverbial phrase. Thus, *na yowshoou shiee-tzyh* 'take right hand write words, — using the right hand, write words, — to write with the right hand.' (See pp. 38–39.)

On the use of a verb + object construction (*shiee-tzyh*) for an action denoted by an intransitive verb in English ('to write'), see Note 20, p. 137.

16. Omission of Possessive Pronoun. — In translating *woo yonq yowshoou shiee-tzyh* as 'I write with *my* right hand,' note that it is the English idiom that is peculiar in requiring the possessive *my*, since obviously I do not write with *your* hand. In general, the possessive is used only when necessary for clearness.

17. In the series of syllables *tzuooshoou shiee-tzyh*, the first two would normally both change into the 2nd Tone. Here, because of the contrasting stress on *tzuoo–*, *shoou* is weakened into a Half 3rd or completely unstressed and only *tzuoo–* has the 2nd Tone. (See also Note 4, p. 109.)

18. *È* (very short and high) 'Say!'

19. *Neng* 'able, can,' as distinguished from *huey* 'can, know how to.'

20. Complement and Predicate. — In Lesson 4, we had constructions like *ting.de-doong* 'can understand (from hearing),' in which we called *–.de-doong* a 'potential complement,' also *ting.de-ching.chuu* 'can hear clearly,' in which *–.de-ching.chuu* is a potential complement. Similarly, *shiee.de-hao* can mean 'can write well,' with *–.de-hao* as potential complement.

But *shiee .de* (text Lesson 3, between Notes 34 and 35) can also mean 'that which is written, the quality or style of writing, etc. and *Ta shiee .de hao* can mean 'What he writes is good, the way he writes is good, — he writes well,' where *Ta shiee .de* is the subject and *hao* is the predicate. In actual speech, there is no difference between *shiee.de-hao* 'can write well' and *shiee .de hao* 'write well, wrote well.' We distinguish the two constructions by varying the spacing and the hyphenation. Which is the meaning in speech will have to come out from the sense or the context.

The same ambiguity exists with questions formed by adding .ma or .a to a statement: *Ta shiee.de-hao .ma?* 'Can he write well?' *Ta shiee .de hao .ma?* 'Does he write well?' Both sound alike.

When, however, the question is put in the disjunctive form of A-not-A, then the two are different. Thus,

Ta shiee.de-hao shiee.bu-hao? 'Can he write well?'
Ta shiee .de hao .bu.hao? 'Does he write well?'

The negatives of these forms are also different. Thus,

Ta shiee.bu-hao 'He cannot write well.'
Ta shiee .de buhao 'He does not write well.'

21. The final particle *.è* indicates obviousness, 'you know, of course!'

22. In real laughter, of course, the *h* has the same glottal sound as in English and not the tongue-back fricative sound of Mandarin *h*.

23. *Wanq* 'toward,' often pronounced *wann* before consonants in rows *d, tz, j_r,* and *j_i*.

24. Note that *sh* does not correspond to 'are' of the passive voice in the translation. It is the 'are' in 'Foreign words *are* something which is written how?' For the *sh* can be omitted and the passive-voice 'are' would still be there: *Way.gwo-tzyh tzeem shiee?* 'Foreign words *are* written how?' The reason is that Chinese verbs can be taken in either the active sense or the passive sense according to context. (Cf. Note 35, p. 132.)

25. *I–* followed by AN can be omitted, in which case the AN is unstressed and has the meaning of 'a' rather than 'one.' This occurs only after verbs.

26. After personal pronouns, *.de* is omitted before free localizers or words for relationship.

27. *B tzay A (gen) C .de jongjiall* '*B* is between *A* and *C*.'

28. A complement (after a verb) usually expresses a result, while an adverb (before a verb) usually expresses a condition, manner, etc. Thus, *tzoou .daw yiitz how.tou* 'walk reach chair back, — walk to the back of the chair,' but *daw yiitz how.tou tzoou* 'reach chair back walk, — go to the chair and walk, — do walking after getting behind the chair.'

29. Between a pronoun and a noun, *gen* is not omitted.

30. Adjectives. — Chinese adjectives are verbs (pp. 47–48) and can therefore be full predicates, as *Jey-been shu hao* 'This book is good.' No verb 'to be' is normally used before an adjective, since it is already a verb.

Forms like *hei .de shu* 'books that are black, — black books' are just like *lai .de ren* 'one who comes.' Similarly, *hei .de* can also mean 'something that's black,' just as *lai .de* can mean 'he who (or that which) comes.' Similarly, *Jeh.sh hei .de* 'This is something black,' more simply, 'This is black,' just like *Ta sh Tsorng Meei.gwo lai .de* 'He is one who comes from America,' more simply, 'he comes from America.'

The rule about the use of *sh* with adjectives is then: either use both *sh* and *.de* or omit both.

31. A monosyllabic adjective immediately followed by a noun is closely bound to it as a compound. There is often (*heibaan*), but not always (*hei-shu*), a specialized meaning attached to the compound. But forms with *.de* like *hei .de shu* 'books that are black' are more likely taken in a general sense.

32. *Chyuan.sh* 'entirely, completely.'

33. *Lii-way* 'in-out.' Two bound words having opposite meanings can usually be combined to make one word.

34. *Tzar.men ren* or *tzar.men .de ren* does not mean 'we the people,' but 'our persons, our bodies.'

35. On the use of *tzay* instead of *sh* see Note 18, p. 130.

36. Although *farngtz* means 'house, building' and *utz* means 'room,' the bound forms *-farng-* and *-u-* as found in many compounds can both mean either 'house' or 'room.'

37. *Kehtarng* 'lesson-hall, — classroom.'

38. Never follow the English idiom 'I don't think so' in speaking Chinese, since the intended meaning is 'I think it is not so.'

39. *Sheu* 'permit'; 'may'; 'perhaps.'

40. *Dahshengl* 'big-sound, — loudly.'

41. *.Tzay.nall . . . .ne* 'right there,' form for expressing progressive action, '-ing.'

42. *Bye.de* 'other (not this one),' *not* to be used in the sense of 'an additional one.'

43. *Shanq-keh* 'take up lesson, — holding a class.'

44. (Exercise 4, Example.) Here is a case of the S–P predicate (p. 35): 'As for you, (your) Chinese is spoken well.'

45. (Exercise 4, (a).) If there is an object before forms like *.de hao* or *-.de-hao*, the verb is also repeated. The reason is that there is an aversion to breaking up the unity either of *shiee-tzyh* or of *shiee .de hao* (or *shiee.de-hao*, as the case may be).

EXERCISES

1. *Comment on the following:*

(a) Baw.shanq mei.yeou shinwen. (b) Jong.gwo .de baw .shanq mei.yeou way.gwo shinwen. (c) Way.gwo-shu .lii.tou yeou Jong.gwo-tzyh. (d) Heibaan.shanq shiee .de tzyh sh hei .de. (e) Yonq chian*bii* shiee .de tzyh sh hei .de. (f) Shianntzay kehtarng.lii mei ren. (g) Dihsan Keh tzay Dih'i Keh Dih'ell Keh .de jongjiall. (h) Woo shianntzay yonq yow*shoou* shiee-tzyh .ne. (i) Woo shianntzay shuo .de sh Jong.gwo-huah. (j) Ney-jaan deng tzay woo chyan.tou. (k) Menliengl sheang .de .shyr.howl way.tou mei ren. (l) Jey-suoo farngtz .lii *yeou* wuu.shyr-jii-jian utz.

2. *Answer the following:*

(a) Heibaan.shanq shiee hei-tzyh kann.de-jiann .kann.bu.jiann .a? (b) Weysherm .ne? (c) Nii sh yonq neei-jy shoou na kuaytz .de? (d) Jey-jian utz *yeou* jiig men .a? (e) Shyr*jii*-been shu gen shyr*jii*-been shu sh *jii*-been shu .a? (f) Yonq *feenbii* shiee.chu.lai ('write out') .de tzyh sh hei .de hair.sh feen .de ('pink')? (g) Shu bu kai .de.shyr.howl, lii.tou .de tzyh kann.de-jiann .kann.bu.jiann .a? (h) Jong.gwo-tzyh tsorng neei.bial wanq neei.bial shiee? (i) Shiee way.gwo-tzyh .de .shyr.howl .ne? (j) Jong.gworen shuo Liibayryh tzay Liibay'i .de chyan.tou .hair.sh how.tou .a? (k) Liibay'i daw Liibayryh jongjiall .de jiig ryhtz ('dates') jiaw sherm.me? (l) Hei-shu lii.tou weysherm *bu* wanchyuan sh hei .de?

3. *Example:*

Given:
Woo buneng shiee-tzyh;
Woo mei *jyy* bii:

Answer:
(1) Woo buneng shiee-tzyh.
(2) Nii tzeem (*or* weysherm) buneng shiee-tzyh .ne?
(3) Woo mei *jyy* bii .a.
(4) .Oh, nii inwey mei *jyy* bii, *suoo*.yii buneng shiee-tzyh, .sh .bu.sh?
(5) Duey .le.

(a) Wang San *bu* kann-baw; Wang San buhuey kann-baw. (b) Ta tzoou .daw men.nall; menliengl sheang .le. (c) Woo huey torngshyr ('simultaneously') *shiee* leangg butorng .de tzyh; *woo yeou* leang-jy shoou. (d) Tzar.men tzay lii.tou ting.de-jiann ren tzay way.tou raang; way.tou .de .ren raang .de sheang ('loud'). (e) (Woo tzwol ting shuo Lao Wang jiel lai, kee.sh) ta miengl .tsair lai .ne; ta jiel yeou-shyh. (f) Jiel tzay tzwol gen miengl .de jongjiall; jiel tzay tzwol .de how.tou, tzay miengl .de chyan.tou. (g) Bair-jyy .shanq shiee 'bair'-tzyh (the word 'bair') kann.de-jiann; bair-jyy .shanq shiee .de 'bair'-tzyh sh hei .de. (h) Renren dou gen woo shuo Jong.gwo-huah; woo shianntzay huey shuo Jong.gwo-huah .le. (i) Woo gen ta nemm dahshengl shuo-huah; ta shuo ta ting.bu-jiann woo shuo sherm.me. (j) Jeyg tzyh *woo* shiee.bu-chulai; woo bujydaw sh tzeem shiee .de. (k) Lao Wang sh yonq *tzuoo*.shoou shiee-tzyh .de; ta yonq yow.shoou shiee-tzyh .de shyr.howl shiee.bu-hao. (l) Woo bujydaw nii tzay way.tou nemm.shie shyr.howl .le; woom menliengl bu sheang .le.

UP, DOWN, LEFT, RIGHT, FRONT, BACK, AND MIDDLE   157

4. *Example:*

Given: Answer:

Nii Jong.gwo-huah shuo .de hao.   (1) Nii Jong.gwo-huah shuo .de hao .bu.hao?
  (2) Woo Jong.gwo-huah shuo .de buhao.
  (3) Tzeem .ne? (*or* Weysherm .ne?)
  (4) Inwey .a, inwey woo shuo.bu-hao, *suoo*.yii shuo .de buhao.
  (5) .Oh, inwey nii shuo.bu-hao, *suoo*.yii shuo .de buhao .a?
  (6) .Èh, duey .le.

(a) Ta yonq mau*bii* shiee-tzyh shiee⁴⁵ .de hao. (b) Jeyg way.gworen shuo Jong.gwo-huah shuo .de duey. (c) Yonq woo jey-jy gang*bii* shiee-tzyh shiee .de hei. (d) Jey-wey shian.sheng shuo-huah shuo .de ching.chuu. (e) Jong.gworen shuo Jong.gwo-huah shuo .de mann. (f) Na *feen*bii tzay bair-jyy .shanq shiee-tzyh .he.je na chian*bii* tzay heibaan.shanq shiee-tzyh shiee .de ching.chuu.

5. *Example:*

Given: Answer:

Nii kann.jiann feiji .le.   (1) Nii kann.jiann feiji .le .mei.yeou?
  (2) Mei.yeou, woo mei kann.jiann feiji.
  (3) *Nii* tzeem mei kann.jiann feiji .ne?
  (4) Inwey woo kann.bu-jiann feiji, *suoo*.yii woo mei kann.jiann feiji.
  (5) (*Ad lib.*) Feiji *yee* sheu wuh-dean .le .ba?

(a) Nii ting.jiann woo shuo .de sh sherm .le. (b) Woo ney-jiann shyh gen ta shuo-ching.chuu .le. (c) Wang Ell ting.chu ta sh Lao San .lai .le. (d) Ta.men tzwol kann.chu ('make out') ney-leang-jy sh sheir.de bii .lai .le. (e) Tzwol Lao Jang duey .woo ('to me') tzay diannhuah.lii shuo-ching.chuu .le. (f) Ta ting.chu nii sh Meei.gworen .lai .le.

LESSON 6
A SMOKE RING

Yesterday I finished up an important item of business, and I was very tired from working, awfully tired. After I came back, I didn't even want to eat supper, and couldn't even finish one bowl of rice. So I sat on a sofa to rest a while and smoke a little and so forth.

Just as I had finished smoking a cigarette, I saw, inside a smoke ring, there seemed to be something like a landscape painting. Well, how strange! This smoke ring just wouldn't dissolve. I blew at it, but couldn't blow it away either. After another moment it seemed as if I myself had walked into that smoke ring, too. Taking a look around, I could not see the things in my room, either. The sound of the clock which had been going 'ticktock ticktock' a while ago could no longer be heard either. The chair I was sitting on had also gone to I-don't-know-where. I just felt as if I were over a great sea and were flying there all the time. I looked below, and it seemed as if there were one very beautiful island after another.

I said, "Good, now this is fine! I always wanted to fly, but never could, this time I am really flying. I am flying both high and fast, what fun! Ha! It's real fun! But don't fall down, mind you! Otherwise I should either fall on an island and get smashed to death, or fall into the sea and get drowned.

"Let me fly down a little and take a look. Let me see, see if I can still fly down."

Well, it's true! I can still fly down. But once I went flying downwards, I kept straight on flying down, and when 1 wanted to fly up again, I couldn't fly up any more.

Meanwhile I dropped lower and lower, down to one thousand feet, nine hundred feet, eight hundred feet, seven hundred, six hundred, five hundred, ... straight on down to so low that I could see as if there were a great many people walking down there. So I shouted to them loudly and said, 'Hey, you, keep to one side, walk on one side! Stand aside! I am falling down, hey!

"No sooner said than done!" By that time, I began to see that what I had taken to be people a moment ago were not real people, but a lot of big trees. Bang! with a crash I fell on the top of one of the big trees.

I said, "What a mess, what a mess now! It won't matter if it only hurts a little from the fall, but if I got my eyes put out, what would I do then? Wonder if I can still open my eyes now."

. . . . . .

I opened my eyes and took a look, . . . Why, I had fallen asleep and had had a dream!

DIHLIOW KEH
IG IANCHIUAL

Tzwo.tian [1] woo tzuoh-wan.le [2] *i*-jiann [3] yawjiin .de shyh.chyng, kee.sh [4] tzuoh .de heen ley, tzuoh .de ley-jyi.le.[5] Hwei.lai .le lian woanfann yee [6] bu sheang chy, i-woan [7] fann dou chy.bu-wan. Woo .jiow tzuoh .tzay [8] *i*g dahyiitz .shanq shie.x,[9] chou.x ian [10] .sherm.de.[11] Gang chou-wan.le i-gel shiang'ian,[12] kann.jiann *i*g ianchiual.lii hao.shianq [13] yeou g shanshoei-huall [14] .shyh.de.[15] Èè? Jen [16] chyiguay! Jeyg ianchiual tzoong [17] *bu* sann.kai.[18] Woo chuei.x .ta, *yee* lao chuei.bu-sann. Yow guoh.le .i.hoel,[19] hao.shianq woo tzyhjii ren [20] *yee* tzoou .daw ianchiual.lii .chiuh [21] .le. Syhmiann *i*-kann,[22] yee kann.bu-jiann woo u.lii .de dong.shi .le. Gangtsair didadida .de jong tzoou .de sheng.in yee ting.bu-jiann .le. Woo tzuoh .de neyg yiitz yee bujydaw shanq naal .chiuh .le. Jiow jyuej [23] woo tzay *i*g dah-hae .shanq.tou lao .tzay.nall fei .shyh.de. Kann.x dii.shiah, hao.shianq yeou *i*-tzuoh .v.x .de [24] *heen* haokann [25] .de *hae*dao.

Woo shuo, "Hao .l'a, shianntzay hao .l'a! *Woo lao* sheang fei, lao fei.bu-chiilai,[26] jey.hwei kee [27] jen fei.chii.lai [28] .le. Fei .de yow gau yow kuay, fei .de jen haowal! [29] .Hah! Jen yeou yih.sy! [30] Kee.sh bye diaw.le.shiah-.chiuh, .ah! Buran [31] .a, *bu*.sh diaw .tzay *hae*dao.shanq shuai.syy, jiow.sh [32] huey diaw .de [33] *hae-shoei* .lii ian.syy .de.

"*Deeng* [34] .woo fei-shiah.chiuh .i.deal kann.x .ba. Ranq [35] .woo kann .a, ranq .woo kann hair fei.de.shiah.chiuh .fei.bu.shiah.chiuh."

Èr, jen.de! Hair fei.de-shiah chiuh. Kee.sh woo *i* wann-shiah fei, jiow ijyr [36] lao wann-shiah fei, tzay sheang fei.chii.lai yow [37] fei.bu-chiilai .le.

Nah .shyr.howl woo yueh diaw yueh di,[38] di .daw i-chian-chyy, *jeou*.bae-chyy, ba.bae-chyy, chi.bae, liow.bae, *wuu*.bae, ... ijyr di .daw kann.de-jiann [39] dii.shiah hao.shianq *yeou* sheuduo [40] ren .tzay.nall tzoou-dawl. Woo jiow duey .ta.men dahshengl raangj shuo, "Uai, nii.men kaw-bial tzoou, bial (.shanq) tzoou! [41] Jann .de parngbial .i.deal, woo yaw [42] diaw.shiah.lai .l'a, .hei!" ...

"Shuo shyr chyr, nah shyr kuay." [43] Daw nah .shyr.howl woo .tsair kann.chu.lai gangtsair *woo* yiiwei [44] sh ren .de, *bu*sh jen.de ren, sh sheuduo dah-shuh. Hualhalha! i-sheng, woo.de shentz diaw .de i-ke [45] dah-shuh .de dieengl.shanq.

Woo shuo, "Tzau [46] .le, j-h-eh [47] tzaugau .le! Yaw.sh jyy.sh shuai-terng.le hair *bu*yawjiin, kee.sh yaw [48] bae [49] .shuang yean.jing penq-shia.le, nah tzeem bann .ne? Buj(yd)aw [50] shianntzay woo.de yean.jing hair jeng.de-kai [51] .jeng.bu.kai .le." . . . . .

Jeng.kai.le yean.jing *i*-kann, ... Sheir j(yd)aw [52] gangtsair sh [53] shuey-jaur.lc, tz-h-uoh.le *i*g menq! [54]

NOTES

1. *Tian* 'sky'; *–tian* 'day.' *Tzwo.tian* = *tzwol*. Similarly, *jin.tian* = *jiel*, *ming.tian* = *miengl*. The *–.tian* forms for the names of days are slightly more formal than the *–l* forms.

2. *Tzuoh-wan* 'do to a finish, — finish doing.'

3. **Verb for Past Action with a Quantified Object.** — When a verb for an action in the past has an object containing a quantity word (including the case of 'one,' as *ig*, *i-baa*, etc.), the verb takes *.le* as a suffix. Thus, *Woo tzuoh.le leang-jiann shyh* 'I did two things.' However, when the verb is in the negative, with *mei* 'did not, have not,' no *–.le* is used.

4. *Kee.sh*, lit. 'but.' *Gen* cannot be used here, as it can only join substantives.

5. The complement *–jyi.le* 'to an extreme' corresponds in style to 'awfully.'

6. *Lian woanfann yee* 'including evening-meal too, — even my supper.'

7. *Woan* 'bowl,' an unrelated homonym of *woan* 'evening'; 'late.' *I-jy* or *ig woan* 'a bowl.' In *i-woan fann* 'a bowl of (cooked) rice,' *woan* is used as a temporary measure word (4(c), p. 46).

8. The phrase *.tzay ig dahyiitz .shanq* is a complement to *tzuoh*.

9. *Shie* 'to rest,' an unrelated homonym of the indefinite measure word *shie* 'some, amount.'

10. *Chou-ian* 'draw-smoke, — to smoke.'

11. *.Sherm.de* 'and so forth, and things.' Cf. 'what not.'

12. *Shiang'ian* 'fragrant-smoke, — cigarette,' also called *ianjeual* 'tobacco-roll.' The AN *–gel* (< *gen* 'root' + *–l*) is applied to rod-like objects.

13. *Hao₀shianq* 'well-like, — seem, as if.'

14. *Shanshoei* 'mountain-water, — landscape' (either the scenery itself or a painting of it). *Huah* 'to draw, to paint,' *huall* 'picture, painting.'

15. *.Shyh.de* '(so it) seems.' Either *hao₀shianq* ... alone, or ... *.shyh.de* alone, or both together (as used here) can be used for 'as if, it seems as if.'

16. *Jen* 'real, true.' When used as an intensive adverb, it usually still has an exclamatory force (cf. 'real good!'). It does not therefore correspond to the present status of the word 'very,' which no longer means 'true.'

17. *Tzoong* 'main'; 'all the time, always.' *Lao* 'old'; 'all the time, always.' *Tzoong bu*, or *lao bu* 'all the time not, — never.'

18. *Sann.kai* 'scatter-afar, — dissolve, disperse.'

19. *Yow guoh.le ihoel*, lit. 'again, having passed a moment.'

20. *Woo tzyhjii ren* or *woo tzyhjii .de ren* 'I self('s) person, — my own person, — I myself.'

21. *Tzoou .daw ianchiual.lii* 'walk to smoke-ring-inside, — walk into the smoke ring.' The additional complement *.chiuh* expresses direction away from the speaker. (See Note 28.)

22. *Syhmiann i-kann* 'four sides once look, — take a look around.'

23. *Jyuej* '(I) felt that, (I) found that . . .'

24. *I-AN i-AN .de X* 'one X after another.'

25. *Heen haokann* 'very good-looking, very beautiful.'

26. An unstressed directional complement is usually stressed again, with full tone, when –*.de–* 'can' or –*.bu–* 'cannot' is inserted.

27. *Kee* 'however': 'this time, however, I have really flown up.'

28. Directional Complements. — A number of verbs of motion *lai*, *chiuh*, etc., usually in the neutral tone, can be placed after a verb to indicate direction, as *na.lai* 'bring-come, — bring hither, — bring here,' *na.chiuh* 'bring-go, — bring thither, — take away,' *chu.lai* 'go-out hither, — come out,' *jinn.lai* 'enter hither, — come in,' *jinn.chiuh* 'enter hither, — go in,' *chii.lai* 'rise hither, — rise (in the direction of the speaker).' (There is no **chii.chiuh* in Northern Mandarin.)

A main verb plus directional complement can be attached, as a compound directional complement, to another main verb, as *na.chu.lai* 'take out (in the direction of the speaker),' *na.chu.chiuh* 'take out (away),' *fei.chii.lai* 'fly-rise-hither, — fly up.' In meaning, the directional complements –*.lai*, –*.chiuh*, –*.chu.lai*, –*.chu.chiuh*, –*.jinn.lai*, –*.jinn.chiuh*, and –*.chii.lai* are very similar to the German prefixes *her–*, *hin–*, *heraus*, *hinaus*, *herein*, *hinein*, and *heraus*, respectively.

29. *Wal* 'to play,' *haowal* 'good to play, — to be fun.'

30. *Yeou yih.sy* 'have meaning, — interesting, fun.'

31. *Buran* '(if) not thus, — otherwise.'

32. *Bu.sh A jiow.sh B* '(if) it is not a case of *A*, then it is a case of *B*, — either *A* or *B*.' (Cf. Note 23, p. 56.)

33. In complement position, *.de* (probably < *daw* 'arrive') 'to' is often used instead of *.tzay*, as *tzuoh .de juotz.nall* 'sit-at the table,' *diaw de shoei.lii* 'fall into the water,' *diaw .de shuh.shanq* 'fall on(to) the tree.'

34. *Deeng* 'wait.' *Deeng .woo . . .* 'wait for me to . . . , wait until I . . . .'

35. *Ranq* 'yield'; 'let.'

36. *Ijyr* 'one straight, — straight on, keep . . . –ing.'

37. In general *tzay* 'again' is used for considered events and *yow* 'again' for actual events. In most (but not all) cases, they correspond to future and past events, respectively.

38. *Yueh . . . yueh* 'the more . . . the more.' *Woo yueh diaw yueh di* 'the more I fell, the lower I (got), — I fell lower and lower.'

39. *Di .daw kann.de-jiann* 'low to the state of being able to see, — so low that I could see that. . . .'

40. *Duo* 'much'; 'many.' *Sheuduo* 'a great lot.'

41. *Kaw-bial tzoou* 'lean-side walk, — walk leaning to one side.' *Bial tzoou* is the expression a rickshaman often uses to warn off pedestrians.

42. *Yaw . . . .le* 'will (soon).'

43. *Shuo shyr chyr, nah shyr kuay* 'saying time slow, that (actual) time fast' is a common cliché in the style of novels. In ordinary speech it would be *Shuo .de shyr.howl mann, lai .de shyr.howl kuay.*

44. *Yiiwei* 'take-to-be, — take it (wrongly) that.'

45. *Ke* is the AN for all plants.

46. *Tzau* 'dregs, mess' (lit. and fig.). *Tzaugau* 'messy-cake' (fig. only).

47. The first *h* in *j-h-eh* is simply an indication for a laughed-out pronunciation, a sort of aspirated *cheh.*

48. *Yaw* (abbreviated from *yaw.sh*) 'if.'

49. Pretransitives. — When a verb has both a direct object and a complement, the usually preferred practice in Chinese is to break up the whole thing into two verbal constructions. The first part consists of the pretransitive *bae* (alternating with *bay* and the more formal *baa*) 'take hold of' and the object, while the second consists of the specific verb plus the complement.

Thus, instead of *penq-shia.le yean.jing* 'knock blind the eyes, — put out the eyes,' a more common way of saying this is *bae yean.jing penq-shia.le* 'take eyes, knock (them) blind, — have the eyes put out.' Similarly, *bae jey-woan fann chy-wan.le* 'take this bowl of rice, eat it up, — eat up this bowl of rice.' Cf. Exercise 3.

50. *Bujydaw* 'don't know' is often underarticulated into *buj'aw* or further into *b'r'aw*, especially, when followed by an A-not-A construction, in the sense of 'I wonder whether.'

51. *Jeng.kai* 'open up, open' limited to the eyes only.

52. *Sheir jy.daw* 'who knows (but that) . . . ,' expression of surprise.

53. *Sh* 'it is a case of.'

54. *Tzuoh-menq* 'do-dream, — to have a dream.' The spelling *tz-h-uoh* is to suggest a chuckled pronunciation (cf. Note 47).

EXERCISES

1. *Answer the following:*

(a) Nii chy-wan.le woanfann chou .deal sherm ian .a? (b) Nii jin.tian chy.le *jii*-woan fann? (c) Nii huey tzay *ig* ianchiual .lii tzay chuei .ig ianchiual .bu.huey? (d) Shuey-jaur.le .de .shyr.howl kann.de-jiann dong.shi .ma? (e) Shuey-jaur.le .de .shyr.howl shuo-huah .bu .shuo? (f) Hae .de jongjiall yaw.sh yeou dih, ney-kuay dih jiaw sherm.me?

(g) Feiji fei .de kuay .hair.sh chwan tzoou .de kuay? (h) 'Shianntzay' jey-leangg tzyh sh sherm yih.sy? (i) Yaw.sh ren tsorng shan.shanq shuai.shiah.lai, ta jiow tzeemyanql .a? (j) Nii yaw.sh ley .le, nah jiow tzuoh .deal sherm hao .ne? (k) Yaw.sh feiji diaw .de shuh.shanq, sh shermyanql .de sheng.in? (l) Yaw.sh nii yaw .ta *bu* nemm dahshengl shuo-huah, nii jiow tzeem duey .ta shuo .ne?

2. *Examples:*

Given:

I. Gangtsair woo ting-
.bu-jiann.

Answer:

(1) Gangtsair woo ting.bu-jiann.
(2) Nii shianntzay ting.de-jiann .ting.bu-.jiann .ne?
(3) Shianntzay .a, shianntzay woo ting.de-jiann .le.
(4) Jey.hoel ('this moment') .ne?
(5) Ér, jen chyiguay, jey.hoel yow ting.bu-jiann .le!

II. Woo tzwo.tian shuo-huah shuo .de mann.

(1) Woo tzwo.tian shuo-huah shuo .de mann.
(2) Nii jin.tian shuo-huah shuo .de mann .bu.mann .ne?
(3) Jin.tian .a, jin.tian woo shuo .de kuay .le.
(4) Shianntzay .ne?
(5) Ér, jen chyiguay, shianntzay woo shuo .de yow mann .le!

Apply form I or II, whichever is more suitable to the sense.

(a) Woo gangtsair lao fei.bu-chiilai. (b) Woo gangtsair ting.bu-chu nii shuo sherm .lai. (c) Woo tzwol Jong.gwo-huah shuo .de buhao. (d) Gangtsair hao.shianq ting.de-jiann neyg jong tzoou .de sheng.in. (e) Tzwol woo neyg ianchiual lao chuei.bu-sann. (f) Nah .shyr.howl woo *i* tzuoh-chwan jiow shuey.bu-jaur. (g) Woo jiel shanq.wuu ting.bu-jiann sheng.in. (h) Nii gangtsair shuo-huah shuo .de nemm kuay. (i) Tzwol jey-jiah feiji fei .de mann. (j) Woo gangtsair yiiwei (change *yiiwei* into *kann* 'see that' and *jyuej* 'felt that' in the successive answers) jey.shie shiang'ian tzar.men chou.bu-wan. (k) Woo gangtsair yiiwei neyg ren shuai .de *hae*.lii ian.bu-syy .de. (l) Tzwo.tian shanq.wuu ta shuo-huah shuo .de ching.chuu.

3. *Example:*

Given:

Jeh.sh *i*-shann men; chiing kuay.deal kai.kai .ta!

Answer:

Chiing kuay.deal bae jey-shann men kai.kai!

(a) Nah.sh jin.tian .de baw. Kuay kann-wan.le ('finish reading') .ta! (b) Jeh.sh i-utz .de ian; woo yaw chuei-sann.le .ta. (c) Jeh.sh nii.de fann; nii hair mei chy-wan .ta .ne. (d) Jeh.sh nii tzyhjii .de shyh.chyng. Nii jin.tian neng bann-wan.le .ta .ma? (e) Nah.sh .jiann yawjiin .de shyh; nii kuay.deal tzuoh-wan.le .ta! (f) Nah.sh ta.de yean.jing; ta neng.bu- .neng jeng.kai .ta? (g) Nah.sh nii tzwol tzuoh .de menq; *woo chiing* .nii tzay shuo .i.biann. (h) Jeh.sh nii gangtsair sheang .de yih.sy; shianntzay woo tsair doong-ching.chuu .le. (i) Jeh.sh 'gau'-tzyh; *chiing* nii shuo- ching.chuu.le .ta. (j) Nah.sh g Ing'wen-tzyh; nii mei.yeou shuo-duey .ta. (k) Jeh.sh g Jong.gwo-tzyh; nii weysherm bu *shiee*-hao.le .ta? (1) Nah.sh san-shuang kuaytz; *chiing* nii shianntzay bau-hao.le ('wrap well') .ta!

LESSON 7
MR. CAN'T STOP TALKING

A: I have a friend whose name is Talking, his full name is Can't Stop Talking.

B: (Chuckles.) 'Can't Stop Talking'!

A: This gentleman is most fond of talking, ...

B: Most fond of talking!

A: So people all call him the Talking Machine, ...

B: Phonograph, isn't it?

A: Sometimes they also call him the Broadcasting Station.

B: "Central Broadcasting Station, X G O A!"

A: Hey, quiet there! Don't keep interrupting me! Listen, listen to what I say.

B: Okay.

A: Well, about this man, when he goes to sleep at night, he talks in his sleep. In the morning, as soon as he wakes up, he starts to talk to himself. After he gets up and sees people — well, I don't have to tell you (what happens) then!

No matter what you talk about with him, no matter what you ask him, he always has something to say to you. When he finishes one sentence, he starts another, he finishes another, and then starts another, keeping on talking like that. He says, for example, what is big and what is small, which are bad and which are good. If that is more than this, then this is less than that. If I don't get up as late as you do, then you don't get up as early as I.

He says that steamships go faster than people, that automobiles, more-

4. *Translate into Chinese:*

(a) When I ate my supper, I ate three bowls of rice. (b) How strange! What I thought were pencils were not real pencils, but pairs and pairs of very beautiful chopsticks. (c) Did you come by plane? (d) Too bad! My book has dropped into the water. What shall I do? (e) Let me see if this paper has the item of news I have just heard. (f) The faster he talks the less I understand him (*yueh bu doong*). (g) There were many big trees on the island. (h) All around me not a man could be seen (*yee kann.bu-jiann*). (i) After another moment, he could indeed still open his eyes. (j) In less time than it takes to say it, a man fell overboard ('from on the ship') into the sea. (k) Shucks! I can't even write (out) the character 'i' any more. (l) My goodness! What are those things which are flying down from (on) the airplane?

DIHCHI KEH
TARN [1] BUHTYNG .SHIAN .SHENG

A: *Woo* yeou g perng.yeou shinq Tarn,[2] ming.tzyh jiaw Buhtyng.
B: .He.he, 'Tarn.bu-tyng'!
A: Jey.wey shian.sheng tzuey ay shuo-huah, . . .
B: *Diing* shii.huan [3] shuo-huah!
A: *Suoo*.yii ren.jia [4] dou goan [5] .ta jiaw huahshyatz, . . .
B: Lioushengji,[6] .sh .bu.sh'a?
A: *Yee* yeou shyr.howl goan .ta jiaw Goangboh Dianntair.[7]
B: 'Jongiang Goangboh Dianntair, X G O A!'
A: .Eh, bye naw! [8] Nii bye jinq [9] gen .*woo* daa-chah [10] .ia! Ting .a, ting .woo shuo!
B: .Oh, .hao.
A: .Ne.me — jeyg ren .a, ta woan.shanq [11] shuey-jiaw [12] .de .shyr.howl jiow shuo menqhuah. Tzao.chin [13] i-shiing jiow [14] chii-tourl gen tzyhjii shuo-huah. Chii.lai.le yiihow,[15] *i*-kann.jiann ren, nah dangran [16] genq buyonq [17] shuo .le.

Sweibiann [18] nii gen .ta shuo sherm shyh, bu*goan* nii wenn .ta sherm huah,[19] ta *tzoong* yeou huah gen .nii shuo .de. Shuo-wan.le *i*-jiuh, yow.sh *i*-jiuh, shuo-wan.le *i*-jiuh, yow.sh *i*-jiuh, lao nemm shuo. Bii.fang shuo sherm dah,[20] sherm sheau, neeig huay, neeig hao. Yaw.sh neyg bii [21] jeyg duo, jeyg jiow [22] bii neyg shao. Jearu *woo* chii.lai .de mei nii nemm chyr, *nii* chii.lai .de jiow mei woo nemm tzao.

Ta shuo luenchwan bii ren tzoou .de kuay, chihche tzoou .de yow bii

over, go faster than steamships, that trains are still faster than automobiles, that therefore trains are much faster than steamships. Furthermore, there are airplanes, which go faster than everything else, nothing else is as fast as an airplane, thus they are the fastest things in the world, so he says.

He also likes to discuss people. If he isn't talking about Jang San's good points, he is talking about Lii Syh's shortcomings. He says so-and-so and so-and-so are alike, so-and-so is a little better than so-and-so, so-and-so is worse than so-and-so, that so-and-so is not much good, so-and-so is actually pretty bad, so-and-so is bad no end, so-and-so really extremely bad. He says that there is no fear of there being too many good men; as for bad men, the fewer the better. There had better not be too many bad men; as for good men, however, the more the better. He says he hopes that the people of the world will get better day by day, so that good people will become more numerous every day and bad people will be day by day fewer.

B: Do you mean to say that this friend of yours always keeps talking from morning to night?

A: Although not quite so bad as that, it's almost like that. He starts from six o'clock in the morning, and once he has begun, he talks until twelve o'clock noon and never remembers to eat until he can no longer stand the hunger, or to drink until he can no longer stand the thirst.

But even when he eats, he does not eat properly either. When he starts eating, he eats either very, very fast, or very, very slowly. There is absolutely no certainty about the speed with which he eats. Sometimes, while he is talking, he will use his chopsticks to write on the table and then forgets to eat with them. Sometimes, he talks and eats at the same time, and the faster he talks, the more he eats, and the longer he talks, the less he can eat enough.

B: Then, is there no way to make him talk less?

A: There is simply nothing you can do about it. The more you interrupt him, the more he can't stop — unless you actually cover up his mouth. If you wait for him to talk until he stops talking himself, well, unless the sun rises in the western sky, there will never be a day when he finishes talking.

B: Have *you* finished talking?

A: Huh? ... Oh, me? I, I, I've finished — oh, *I* have finished!

NOTES

1. *Tarn* 'to talk, to chat'; 'to discuss.' *Buhtyng* 'Footstep-Pavilion,' a plausible *ming.tzyh*, homonymous with *bu tyng* 'not stop.' The translation 'Can't stop talking' comes out of the potential construction.

2. Object-Subject Constructions. — An object, especially after *yeou*,

MR. CAN'T STOP TALKING

luenchwan kuay, huooche bii chihche genq kuay, *suoo*.yii huooche bii luenchwan jiow kuay .de duo. Yow yeou feiji tzoou .de bii sherm dou [23] kuay, sherm dou mei.yeou feiji nemm kuay, nah .jiow.sh shyh.jieh.shanq [24] tzoou .de tzuey kuay .de dong.shi .le, .ta .shuo.

Ta yow shii.huan yih.luenn ren. *Bu*.sh [25] shuo Jang San charng,[26] jiow.sh shuo Lii Syh doan. Shuo sheir gen sheir *i*yanq, sheir bii sheir hao.i.deal,[27] sheir bii sheir huay.i.deal, shuo moouren [28] *bu*dah hao, moouren jeanjyr heen huay, moouren jen.sh huay .de buderleau,[29] *moou*moou-ren jen huay-jyi.le. Shuo hao-ren *bu*pah tay duo,[30] huay-ren jiow yuh shao yuh [31] hao. Huay-ren *bu*yaw tay duo; hao-ren .kee.sh yuh duo yuh hao. Ta shuo ta shiwanq shyh.jieh.shanq .de ren i-tian bii i-tian hao, .ne.me hao-ren jiow i-tian bii i-tian duo, huay-ren jiow i-tian bii i-tian shao .le.

B: Nii jey-wey perng.yeou nandaw [32] i-tian-daw-woan [33] lao .tzay.nall shuo-huah .ma?

A: Sweiran *bu*jyh.yu [34] wanchyuan tzemmyanql, dann.sh [35] yee chah.buduo [36] tzemmyanql .le. Ta tsorng tzao.chin liow-dean jong chiitourl, i-shuo jiow shuo .daw shaang.huo [37] shyr'ell-dean, bu deeng.daw duhtz eh .de buderleau, tzoong *bu* jihj chy dong.shi, bu deeng.daw *tzoei*.lii kee .de mei fartz,[38] tzoong *bu* jih.de he-shoei.

*Bu*guoh [39] ta lian fann yee bu haohaul.de [40] chy .è. Ta chy.chii fann .lai [41] .de .shyr.howl, *bu*sh chy .de tiing [42] kuay vx .de, jiow.sh tiing mann vx .de .nemm chy. Ta chy dong.shi .de kuay-mann [43] wanchyuan mei.yeou *i*dinq .de. Yeou.shyr.howl shuoj huah jiow yonq kuaytz tzay juol.shanq shiee-tzyh, jiow wanq.le [44] yonq .ta chy-fann .le. Yeou shyr.howl .ne, ta itourl [45] shuoj itourl chy, shuo .de yueh kuay jiow chy .de yueh duo, yueh shuo.bu-wan jiow yueh chy.bu-gow .le.

B: .Ne.me mei fartz jiaw .ta shao shuo .deal .ma?

A: Jeanjyr mei bann.faa. Nii yueh daa .ta.de chah,[46] ta jiow yueh shuo.bu-tyng — chwufei nii jen wuu.juh .ta.de tzoei. Nii yaw.sh [47] deeng .ta tzyhjii shuo .daw bu shuo .ia, nah chwufei shi-tian chu.le tay.yang,[48] yee *bu*huey [49] yeou g shuo-wan.le .de ryhtz .de.

B: Nii shuo-wan.le .ba?

A: Ar? . . . .Oh, woo .ia, .woo, .woo, woo shuo-wan.le. . . . .Ah, woo shuo-wan.le!

---

often serves also as subject to a following predicate. *Woo yeou g perng.yeou shinq Tarn* 'I have a friend (and this friend) has the surname of Tarn.' (See also p. 36.)

3. *Tzuey ay* 'most love,' *diing shii.huan* 'most like.' *Tzuey* and the slightly more colloquial *diing* (lit. 'top') are adverbs for the superlative degree, often used only as intensives.

4. *Ren.jia* 'people-family, — people, others (as against he himself).' Distinguish from *renjial* 'a family, a household,' with AN *–jia*.

5. *Goan* is the specific pretransitive (Note 49, p. 162) when the main verb is *jiaw* 'call.' It is also possible to omit it: *Ren.jia jiaw .ta huahshyatz*. In other dialects, *jiaw* is said twice, once as pretransitive and again as main verb: *Ren.jia jiaw .ta jiaw huahshyatz*.

Huahshyatz 'speech-box, — chatterbox,' old term for 'phonograph.'

6. *Lioushengji* 'retain-sound-machine, — phonograph,' AN *–jiah*.

7. *Goangboh Dianntair* 'broad-cast electric-terrace, — broadcasting station.'

8. *Bye* (< *buyaw*) 'don't . . .!' *Naw* 'to make noise, to make a disturbance.'

9. *Jinq* 'purely, all the time, keep . . . –ing.'

10. *Daa-chah* 'make-digression, — make interruptions.' *Gen woo daa-chah* 'to interrupt me.'

11. *Woan.shanq* is either 'evening' or 'night.' *Yeh.lii* is '(late) night' only.

12. *Shuey-jiaw* 'sleep nap, — to sleep,' *–jiaw* being AN for verbs.

13. The form *tzao.chin* is probably a blend of *tzao.chern* 'early-morning' and *tzao-ching 'early-clear.' The form *tzao.chern* occurs in Mandarin and other dialects, while *tzao-ching does not actually occur. Since there is no character for *–.chin* in *tzao.chin*, that for *chern* is used in the *Character Text*.

Observe that *tzao.chin* means just 'morning,' but *dah-tzao.chin* or *dahching tzao.chin* is used for 'early morning.'

14. *I . . . jiow* 'once . . . then, — as soon as.'

15. *Yiihow* 'thence-afterwards, — afterwards, after.'

16. *Dangran* 'right-ly, — of course.'

17. *Buyonq* 'not-use, there is no use, — need not.'

18. *Sweibiann* 'follow-convenience, as you please, — no matter . . . ,' *bugoan* 'not care-about, — no matter. . . .'

19. *Wenn i-jiuh huah* 'ask a sentence of speech, — ask a question.'

20. This and following sentences are illustrations of adjectives as predicates. Only in the English translation is it necessary to add a verb 'to be' before the adjective.

In Chinese, *sh* occurs before an adjective only under one of the following special circumstances:

(1) Before *.de*, as *jeh.sh hei .de* 'This is (something) black.'

(2) For contrasting different qualities, as *Ta sh gau, bu.sh dah*, 'He is tall, not big.'

(3) In emphatic assertion, as *Ta* **sh** *dah* 'He *is* big.'

(4) In the concessive *V-.sh-V* form (Note 12, p. 184). (See also p. 52.)

21. In explicit comparisons, superior, equal, and inferior degrees are expressed as follows:

Superior: *A bii B hao.*   '*A* is better than *B*.'
Equal: *A yeou B (nemm) hao.*   '*A* has *B* (that) good, — *A* is as good as *B*.'
Inferior: *A mei.yeou B (nemm) hao.*   '*A* has not *B* (that) good, — *A* is not so good as *B*.'

Equality can also be expressed by *iyanq* 'equally,' as:

A gen B iyanq hao.   '*A* with *B* equally good, — *A* is as good as *B*.'

For implicit comparison, *-.i.deal* or *-.deal* '(by) a little, more, -er' is used, as:

Jeyg hao (.i).deal.   'This is better.'

22. Note the position of *jiow* 'then,' which *never* precedes the subject.
23. *Sherm dou* 'anything'; *sherm dou bu, sherm dou mei.yeou* 'anything not, — nothing.'
24. Note that instead of 'in the world,' *shyh.jieh.shanq* means literally 'on the world.'
25. This *sh* has nothing to do with the 'is' in the translation. It is the unexpressed 'is' in 'if it *is* not a case of talking about Jang. . . .'
26. *Shuo Jang San charng, Lii Syh doan* is the usual idiom for 'to gossip.' Actually, *charng.chuh* 'long-points' is the term for 'good points' and *doan.chuh* 'short-points' for 'shortcomings.'
27. While in comparisons in English '-er' or 'more' is compulsory, *-.i.deal* is optional in comparisons. (Cf. Note 21.)
28. *Moouren* 'a certain person.'
29. *Buderleau* lit., 'no-getting-finish' and *-jyi.le* 'to an extreme' are here translated more nearly literally. In actual use, they correspond in style and force to 'awfully.'
30. *Bupah* 'don't fear' is an interpolated phrase: 'Good men, let's not be afraid, could be too many.' Note the preference for putting *duo* 'many' in the predicate. 'There are too many people here' is *Jell .de ren tay duo*, since the point is not that there are people here, but that the people here are too numerous.
31. *Yuh* 'the more' is a somewhat more literary word than *yueh*.
32. *Nandaw* 'hard-to-say, — do you mean to say?'
33. *I-tian-daw-woan* 'one day-to-night, — from morning to night.'
34. *Sweiran bujyh.yu* 'although not-reach-to.' As *bujyh.yu* is always used in a bad sense, it may be translated as 'as bad as.'

35. *Dann.sh* 'but,' slightly more formal than *kee.sh*.

36. *Chah.buduo* 'cannot differ much, — almost.'

37. Distinguish between *shaang.huo* (< *shaang-wuu*) 'toward noon, — around noon time' and *shanq.wuu* 'forenoon, A.M.'

38. *Mei fartz* 'have no way (out), — not to know what to do.'

39. *Buguoh* 'not past, not over, only, but.'

40. An adjective or adverb is often repeated, with change into 1st Tone (if not already in the 1st) and addition of *-l*, sometimes with addition of *-.de*, to give a more lively meaning. *Hao* 'good': *haohaul.de* 'goodly, well and properly.' *Kuay* 'fast': *Kuaykual.de* 'good and fast.'

41. Note the split complement by the object *fann*.

42. *Tiing* (< *diing* 'most,' with phonetic modification) 'pretty, rather.'

43. *Kuay-mann* 'fast-slow, — speed.'

44. *Wanq* 'forget' is used only intransitively. *Wanq.le* or *wanq.jih* can be used either transitively or intransitively.

45. *Itourl ... itourl* 'one end ... one end, — (doing one thing) while (doing another).'

46. *Daa-chah* is an intransitive verb, while 'interrupt' is a transitive verb. To translate the English object after 'interrupt,' one either puts another verbal expression before *daa-chah* or a possessive form before the internal object *chah*. Thus, 'interrupt him' may be translated as either *gen .ta daa-chah* (Note 10) or *daa .ta.de chah* 'make his interruption.'

47. *Yaw.sh* 'if' and other 'if' words can either precede or follow the subject.

48. *Shi-tian chu.le tay.yang* 'the western sky has produced a sun,' common figure for an impossibility.

49. A *chwufei* clause followed by a clause in the negative is 'unless,' but when followed by a clause in the positive containing *tsair ... .ne* it is to be translated as 'only if.' Thus, *Chwufei tial hao woo bu chu-men* 'Unless it is fine, I won't go out,' but *Chwufei tial hao woo tsair chu-men .ne* 'Only if it is fine will I go out.'

EXERCISES

1. *Answer the following:*

(a) Ta.men goan Tarn Buhtyng .Shian.sheng hair jiaw .shie sherm ming.tzyh .a? (b) Weysherm ta.men goan .ta jiaw ney.shie ming.tzyh .ne? (c) Ren shuo menqhuah .de .shyr.howl sh .bu.sh *i*dinq .tzay.nall tzuoh-menq? (d) Feiji tzoou .de *bii* huooche jyy kuay ideal .ma? (e) 'Huay'.tzyh sh sherm yih.sy .a? (f) 'Tay duo' leangg tzyh sh sherm yih.sy .ne? (g) Jey-keh .lii shuo .de ney-wey shian.sheng ta chy-fann chy .de kuay .bu.kuay? (h) Ta yeou shyr.howl na sherm shiee-tzyh? (i) Nii yaw.sh tzay .ta shuo-huah .de .shyr.howl gen .ta daa-chah, ta jiow tzeem .ne? (j) Tarn Buhtyng .Shian.sheng tarn .daw sherm ryhtz tsair huey

MR. CAN'T STOP TALKING

tyng .ne? (k) Tay.yang jii.shyr tsair huey tsorng shi.bial chu.lai? (l) Nii shuo-huah shuo .de duo .hair.sh Tarn .Shian.sheng shuo .de duo?

2. *Example:*

Given:
Woo bii ta dah.

Answer:
Yaw.sh *nii* bii ta dah, ta jiow mei.yeou nii nemm dah.

(a) I-ke shuh bii *ig* ren gau. (b) Yonq mau*bii* shiee .de tzyh bii yonq chian*bii* shiee .de tzyh haokann. (c) Huooche bii luenchwan tzoou .de kuay. (d) Baw*jyy* bii bau dong.shi .de jyy bair. (e) Ta chy-fann *bii* woo chy .de duo. (f) Ta Jongwen bii Ing'wen shiee .de ching.chuu. (g) Tarn Buhtyng shuo-huah .de shyr.howl bii chy dong.shi .de shyr.howl duo. (h) Woo.men *bii* woo.men .de shian.sheng lai .de tzao. (i) Nii shuo-huah .de sheng.in bii *woo* raang .de sheng.in hair genq gau. (j) Woo shanq.wuu bii shiah.wuu eh. (k) Huooche bii luenchwan charng, *yee* bii .ta kuay. (l) Denqtz bii juotz di, *yee* bii .ta sheau.

3. *Translate into Chinese:*

(a) They called him Mr. Non-stop, as well as The Broadcasting Station. (b) If he is not talking about one (this) thing, he is talking about another (that). (c) No matter at what time, he never remembers to eat his meals. (d) The more I thought of flying, the less I could fly. (e) He said he had seen such and such (sherm sherm) people and done such and such things. (f) The more people I see the more I like to see people. (See Note 30.) (g) After falling asleep, he still kept talking. (h) Do you mean to say that he never smokes? (i) Although I am not entirely ignorant of Chinese, I am almost like that. (j) Don't interrupt me! I am busy. (k) There is nothing certain about the speed with which people do things. (l) We simply didn't know what to do.

4. *Example:*

Given:
Ta kann.jiann.le ren tsair shuo-huah .ne.

Answer:
Ta hair mei kann.jiann ren .de .shyr.howl lao bu shuo-huah, dann.sh (*or* kee.sh) *i*-kann.jiann.le ren jiow shuo.chii huah .lai .le (*or* jiow chii-tourl shuo-huah .le.).

(a) Ta tzao.chin chii.lai.le tsair chy dong.shi .ne. (b) Tarn .Shian-.sheng shuey-jaur.le tsair shuo menqhuah .ne. (c) *Ig* ren tzuoh-shyh tzuoh .de duo tsair jyuej ley .ne. (d) Yeou ren tzay men way.tou .de .shyr.howl menliengl tsair sheang .ne. (e) Jey.wey shian.sheng lao.sh ting.jiann.le huooche .de sheng.in .le tsair jih.de ta sh yaw tzuoh huooche .de .ne. (f) Ta daw eh .de buderleau .le tsair chiuh chy-fann .ne. (g) Nii wuu.juh

.ta.de tzoei ta tsair bu gen .nii daa-chah .ne. (h) Woo chy-wan.le fann tsair chou-ian .ne. (i) Shiing.le tsair neng ting.jiann jong tzoou .de sheng.in .ne. (j) Woo pah woo daw.le Jong.gwo tsair huey na kuaytz chy dong.shi .ne. (k) Jell deeng.daw yeh.lii shyr'ell-dean jong yiihow tsair ting.de-jiann tsorng Jong.gwo goangboh.chu.lai .de shinwen .ne. (l) Shyh.jieh.shanq .de shyh.chyng deeng.daw tzuoh.le yiihow tsair neng jy.daw huey tzuoh .bu.huey .ne.

5. *Example:*

Given:
Ing'wen, lai, come.

Answer:
A. Ing'wen goan 'lai' jiaw sherm.me?
B. Ing'wen goan 'lai' jiaw 'come,' 'come' jiow.sh 'lai' .de yih.sy.

LESSON 8
ANTONYMS

Of the affairs of the world, of the things under heaven, there is not one that does not have two sides, a right and a reverse. No matter what the affair is, no matter what the thing is, if it has a right side, it always has a reverse side, if it has a reverse side, then it always has a right side. This is a fixed principle, which everyone knows and which everyone is clear about.

For example, the opposite of come is go, the opposite of buy is sell, the opposite of true is false, the opposite of good is bad. Moreover, 'not new' is 'old,' 'not long' is 'short,' 'not cold' is called 'hot,' 'not hard' is called 'soft.' If a thing is not easy to do, then we say that this thing is difficult, so to speak. If it is easily done, then we say this thing is easy. Therefore difficult and easy can also be regarded as antonyms. When a person is asleep, he is not being awake; when he is awake, he is not asleep. Thus, awake and asleep, again, are right and reverse words.

We now understand that all things in the world have a right and a reverse. In the use of words, there is also a right and a reverse. But sometimes, in speaking of an opposite thing, you do not need to use an opposite word; it will be all right just to add a 'not.' For example, the opposite of like is hate; if you put it more lightly, you just say 'don't like.' The opposite of good is bad, but ordinarily, you also say 'not good.' To be able to hear and get the idea is called 'to understand,' to be unable to hear and get the idea is called 'not to understand.' To be good fun is called 'interesting,' not to be good fun is called 'uninteresting.'

If you ask me, 'May I smoke here?' and if I let you smoke, then I say,

ANTONYMS 173

(a) Shianntzay ren, huahshyatz, lioushengji. (b) Ta.men dou, neyg *lao* shii.huan shuo-huah .de ren, Tarn Buhtyng. (c) Jong.gwo-huah, shuey-jiaw .de .shyr.howl shuo-huah, shuo menqhuah. (d) Jongwen, no matter how, sweibiann tzeem.me .huoh.jee bugoan tzeemyanql. (e) Jong-.gwo-huah, the people in the world, shyh.jieh.shanq .de ren. (f) Jey-wey shian.sheng, yueh kuay yueh hao, yuh kuay yuh hao. (g) Ing'wen, *bu*jyh.yu nemmyanql, not as bad as that. (h) Jell .de huah, shanq.wuu gen shiah.wuu (.de) jongjiall .de shyr.howl, shaang.huo. (i) Jong.gwo-huah, sheang he-shoei, kee. (j) Jong.gwo-huah, to find that . . . .he.je to notice that . . . , jyuej . . . (k) Jell .de ren, *bu*huey yeou .de shyh.chyng, shi-tian chu.le tay.yang. (l) Jong.gwo-huah, ren.jia shuo-huah .de .shyr.howl nii gen .ta naw, daa-chah.

DIHBA KEH
JENQFAAN-TZYH [1]

Tianshiah [2] .de shyh.chyng, tian-dii.shiah .de dong.shi, mei.yeou [3] *i*-yanql mei.yeou jenq-*faan* leang-miall .de. Wuluenn [4] sherm shyh.chyng, bugoan sherm dong.shi, yeou jenqmiall *tzoong yeou* faanmiall, *yeou* faanmiall jiow *tzoong* yeou jenqmiall. Jeh.sh *i*dinq .de daw.lii,[5] renren dou jy.daw, renren dou ming.bair [6] .de.[7]

Bii.fang shuo, lai .de faanmiall sh chiuh, mae .de faanmiall sh may, jen .de faanmiall sh jea, hao .de faanmiall sh huay. Hair yeou bu shin jiow.sh jiow,[8] bu charng jiow.sh doan, bu leeng [9] jiow jiaw reh, *bu* yinq jiow jiaw roan. Yaw.sh *i*-jiann shyh.chyng bu hao tzuoh, jiow shuo jey-jiann shyh.chyng heen [10] nan, .tzemm.yanql .shuo. Yaw.sh hao tzuoh [11] .de .ne, jiow shuo jeh shyh.chyng heen rong.yih, .tzemm.yanql .shuo. *Suoo*.yii nan-yih [12] yee *kee*.yii suann [13] sh jenqfaan-tzyh .le. Ren shuey-jaur.le .de .shyr.howl *bu*.sh shiingj; shiing .de .shyr.howl *bu*.sh shuey-jaur.le. .Ne.me shiing gen shuey-jaur yow.sh *i*-jenq i-faan [14] .le.

Tzar.men shianntzay yii.jing [15] ming.bair shyh.jieh.shanq .de dong.shi shyh.chyng [16] dou yeou-jenq *yeou*-faan. Tzay shuo yonq-tzyh, yee.sh yeou-jenq *yeou*-faan .de. Dann.sh yeou shyr.howl shuo faanmiall .de shyh, bu *i*dinq [17] deei [18] yonq faanmiall .de tzyh, jia *ig* '*bu*'-tzell [19] jiow shyng .le. Bii'ang [20] shuo, shii.huan .de faanmiall sh henn; shuo-ching.deal [21] jiow shuo bu shii.huan. Hao .de faanmiall sh huay, kee.sh pyngcharng [22] yee shuo buhao. Ting.de-chu yih.sy .lai jiaw ting.de-doong, ting.bu-chu yih.sy .lai jiaw ting.bu-doong. Haowal jiow jiaw yeou yih.sy, buhaowal jiow jiaw mei yih.sy.

Jearu nii wenn .woo, 'Jell *kee*.yii .bu.kee.yii chou-ian?' yaw.sh woo *sheu*

'You may smoke here'; if, however, I don't let you smoke, then I say, 'You may not smoke,' or 'Don't smoke!' If you keep asking me again, 'Will it be all right if I smoke?' then I must say, 'No, no! That won't do!' To put it more strongly, I will say, 'I forbid you to smoke, I won't allow you to smoke! I *told* you you were not allowed to smoke!'

If I have a rather difficult thing I want to ask you to do for me, I will ask you, 'Are you willing to do this thing for me?' If you say, 'I think this thing is very hard,' then I know that you are not willing to do it. If there is a very dangerous place, and I ask you, 'Do you dare to go to that place?' and if you say, 'I am afraid it's too dangerous there!' then I know that you don't dare to go.

There are many more two-sided things which, when you look at them, seem to be opposites, but are really correlatives, not really opposites. For example, the counterpart of man is woman, the counterpart of children is grownups. The counterpart of father is mother, the counterpart of son is daughter, the counterpart of parents, again, is offspring. The counterpart of elder brother is younger brother, the counterpart of elder sister is younger sister, therefore elder and younger brothers, again, are the counterparts of elder and younger sisters.

The counterpart of drink is eat, the counterpart of water is fire, the counterpart of here is there, the counterpart of you is I.

With your mouth you talk, with your ears you listen, with your hand you write, and for reading you have to use your eyes; so that talk, listen, write, and read, again, form two pairs of correlative terms. If you can neither speak, nor understand, nor write, nor read Chinese now, that means that you have not yet learned your Chinese. On the other hand, when some day you have mastered your Chinese, then you can both speak it accurately and understand it clearly, both write it correctly and read it intelligently.

NOTES

1. *Jenq* 'right, upright'; *faan* 'reverse, obverse.' *Jenqfaan-tzyh* '(a pair of) antonyms.'

2. *Tianshiah* 'under heaven, — the world' is a slightly more old-fashioned word than *shyh.jieh; tian-dii.shiah* 'under heaven.'

3. *Mei.yeou i-yanql mei.yeou* 'there is none that does not have ...' is an object-subject construction (p. 36).

Iyanq 'alike, same'; *i-yanq* or *i-yanql* 'one kind, one thing, one point.'

4. *Wluenn* 'no discussing, — no matter ...' is more literary than *sweibiann* or *bugoan*.

5. *Daw* 'way, road' is the 'tao' of Taoism; *lii* 'reason' is the 'li' of the Sung dynasty philosophers. *Daw.lii* 'principle, reason.'

.nii chou-ian, woo jiow shuo, 'Jell *kee*.yii chou-ian'; yaw.sh woo *bu* ranq .nii chou .ne, woo jiow shuo, 'Bu*kee*.yii chou-ian!' .he.sh shuo, 'Bye chou-ian!' Nii yaw.sh tzay lao wenn .woo, 'Chou-ian shyng .bu.shyng?' nah woo jiow deei shuo, 'Bushyng,bushyng! Tzemmyanql [23] bushyng!' Tzay shuo-jonq.deal jiow shuo, 'Bujoen chou-ian, busheu chou-ian! Woo gaw.sonq .nii busheu chou-ian .me!' [24]

Jearu *woo* yeou *i*-jiann heen nan tzuoh .de shyh.chyng *sheang chiing* .nii *geei* [25] .woo tzuoh .i.tzuoh, woo jiow wenn .nii, '*Nii* keen [26] *geei* .woo tzuoh jey-jiann shyh .bu.keen?' Yaw.sh nii shuo, 'Woo kann [27] jeh shyh heen nan .ba?' nah woo jiow jy.daw nii bukeen tzuoh .le.[28] Jearu yeou g heen weishean .de dih.fangl, woo wenn .nii, '*Nii* gaan shanq nall chiuh .bu.gaan?' yaw.sh nii shuo, 'Woo pah nall tay weishean .ba?' woo jiow jy.daw nii sh bugaan chiuh .le.

Hair *yeou* haoshie [29] leang-fangmiann [30] .de shyh.chyng, kann.chii.lai [31] hao.shianq sh jenq-*faan* leang-miall, chyishyr [32] *bu*guoh sh shiangduey [33] .de, binq *bu*.sh shiangfaan .de. Lihru [34] nan.ren .de dueymiall sh neu.ren, sheauharl [35] .de dueymiall sh dah.ren. Fuh.chin .de dueymiall sh muu.chin, erltz .de dueymiall sh neu.erl, fuh-muu [36] .de dueymiall yow.sh *tzyy*-neu. Ge.ge .de dueymiall sh dih.dih, jiee.jiee [37] .de dueymiall sh mey.mey, *suoo*.yii shiong-dih [38] yow.sh jiee-mey .de dueymiall .le.

He .de dueymiall sh chy, shoei .de dueymiall sh huoo, jell .de dueymiall sh nall, nii .de dueymiall sh woo.

Tzoei shuo-huah, eel.tou [39] ting, *shoou* shiee-tzyh, kann-shu hair deei yonq yean.jing; *suoo*.yii shuo, ting, shiee, kann, yow cherng.le [40] leang-duey dueymiall .de tzyh .le. Yaw.sh nii shianntzay Jongwen yee *bu*huey shuo, yee *bu*huey ting, yee *bu*huey shiee, yee *bu*huey kann, nah jiow.sh nii.de Jongwen hair mei shyue.de-huey. Faan.guoh.lai [41] shuo, gaanmiengl [42] *nii* bae Jongwen shyue-cherng.le [43] .de .shyr.howl, nah nii jiow yow shuo.de-joen, yow ting.de-ching, yow shiee.de-duey, yow kann.de-doong .le.

---

6. *Ming.bair* 'bright-white, — clear, to be clear about,' as distinguished from *ching.chuu* 'clear, distinct' (of things), as *Woo ming.bair jeyg lii, inwey jeyg lii heen ching.chuu*. Sometimes, however, *ming.bair* and *ching.chuu* are used interchangeably, except that *ching.chuu* cannot be used transitively, as *ming.bair* can.

7. The position of the clause *renren dou jy.daw, renren dou ming.bair .de* looks like an exception to the rule that a modifier must precede the modified. Actually, because of the final *.de*, it is not a modifier but a substantive construction in apposition to *daw.lii:* '(This is a fixed principle), a principle which everyone knows and understands.'

8. *Jiow* 'old' as a state, as distinguished from *lao* 'old' in age.

9. *Leeng* 'cold'; *reh* 'hot'; *liang* 'cool'; *noan.hwo* 'warm.' But *reh-shoei*

'hot (or warm) water'; *liang-shoei* 'cold water.' Some dialects have *leeng-shoei* for 'cold water.'

10. *Heen* is used much more frequently in Chinese than 'very' in English and consequently has a much weaker force. It can often be omitted in translation.

11. Of two pairs of opposites:

   (a) *hao* 'good,'   *huay* 'bad,'
   (b) *rong.yih* 'easy,'   *nan* 'difficult,'

only *hao* and *nan* are commonly compounded with a following verb, each covering both meaning (a) and meaning (b). Thus,

   (a) *haochy* 'good to eat,'   *nanchy* 'taste bad,'
   (b) *hao tzuoh* 'easy to do,'   *nan tzuoh* 'hard to do.'

We are spelling them differently — no space for (a) and space for (b) — but ambiguities do arise when the verb itself or the context cannot indicate which is meant, as *Jeyg her.taur nan chy* (same sound as *nanchy*) 'This walnut is hard to eat' or 'This walnut tastes bad.'

Certain combinations, however, have fixed idiomatic meanings, as *haokann* 'beautiful,' *haoting* 'beautiful (to hear),' *haoshow* 'good to receive, — feel good, comfortable,' *nankann* 'ugly,' *nanting* 'ugly (to hear),' *nanshow* 'hard to suffer, — uncomfortable, distressed, painful.'

12. In *nan-yih*, *yih* is the bound form of *rong.yih*. Dr. Sun Yat-sen's motto *Jy nan shyng yih* 'Knowing is difficult, doing is easy' is in the *wenli* style.

13. *Suann* 'reckon'; 'regard,' *Kee.yii suann sh* 'may be regarded as being,' the voice of the verb *suann* being neutral, as usual.

14. *I-jenq i-faan* is abbreviated form of *Ig jenq ig faan* 'One is right, the other is reverse.'

15. *Yii.jing* alternates with *yiijinq*.

16. Since there is no word in Chinese for 'things' to cover both 'objects' and 'affairs,' both *dong.shi* and *shyh.chyng* have to be mentioned. (There is a literary word *shyhwuh* to cover both, — because *shyh* means 'affair' and *wuh* means 'things.')

17. *Bu idinq* 'not necessarily': *idinq bu* . . . 'certainly not. . . .'

18. *Deei, deei yaw* or simply *yaw* 'must, have to.'

19. '*Bu*'-*tzell* (↗ ↘) '*Bu*-word, the word *bu*,' pronounced *bu(h).tzyh* (↘ ˙|) when the suffix *-l* is not used. Note that in close apposition, the specific word precedes the general. Cf. *Wang .Shian.sheng* 'Mr. Wang.'

20. *Bii'ang* is a frequent slurred form of *biifang*. Cf. 'f'rinstance.'

21. *Ching* 'light (opp. of heavy),' an unrelated homonym of *ching* 'clear.'

22. *Pyngcharng* 'level-constant, — average-ordinary, — ordinarily.'

23. Note use of *tzemmyanql* rather than *jeyg*. *Tzemmyanql bushyng*, lit.

'This way won't do!' Similarly, *Bye nemmyanql* or *Bye nemmj* means 'Don't do that!'

24. The particle *.me* is used to indicate an impatient tone, having the force of 'Can't you see?' or 'Why don't you understand?' It is really homonymous with the interrogative particle *.ma*, but the latter, because of sentence intonation, is usually longer and has a higher pitch. (See p. 59, and Ex. 3, p. 139.)

25. *Geei* 'give.' Since the phrase *geei .woo* is the first of two verbal expressions in series (p. 39e) it can be translated by an adverbial phrase and *geei* by a preposition, 'for, for the benefit of.'

26. *Keen* is an ordinary auxiliary verb like *neng* 'can,' *yaw* 'will.' There happens to be no corresponding English auxiliary verb meaning 'to be willing to.'

27. *Woo kann* 'As I look at it, — I think, I believe.'

28. This *.le* goes with the whole sentence, in which *jy.daw* is the main verb. 'Then I know that . . .' — a new development.

29. *Haoshie* (alternating with *haurshie*) 'a good lot, — a good deal, a lot.'

30. *Fangmiann* 'locality-side, — aspect, side.'

31. *Kann.chii.lai* '(when you) begin to look (at them), — at first sight.'

32. *Chyishyr* 'its reality, — as a matter of fact, really.'

33. *Shiangduey* 'mutually-facing, — opposite, relative.' *Shiangfaan* 'mutually opposed.' The distinction between *shiangduey* and *shiangfaan* is made only for discussion and not to be taken as serious philosophy. *Shiangduey-luenn* 'relativity theory.'

34. *Lihru* 'example-as, — e.g.,' much more formal than *bii.fang*.

35. *Sheauharl* (< *sheau-hair-l*) 'child.' *Sheau-sheauharl* 'small child'; *dah-sheauharl* or *dah-hairtz* 'big child.'

36. *Fuh-muu* 'father and mother.' *Shanq.ren* 'the person above, — a parent.'

37. *Jiee.jiee* has the tone pattern ⌐ ˈ|, the first *jiee* does not change into the second tone.

38. *Shiong* is the literary form for *ge.ge* 'elder brother.' Note the scopes of the following terms:

   shiongdih   'brothers (collec.)'
   shiong.dih   'brothers (collec.)'; 'a younger brother'; 'I' (polite form, in a speech)
   dih.shiong   'brothers (collec.)'
   dih.shiong.men 'brothers (collec.)'; 'brothers in arms, — the ranks, privates' (polite form, used by officers)

39. While *eel.tou*, *eel.dou* are the common forms for 'ear' and an illiterate speaker probably takes the second syllable for the same noun suffix *.tou* as in *how.tou*, the usual character written is that for *duoo*, AN for flowers.

40. *Cherng* 'to form, to become'; 'to complete.'
41. *Faan.guoh.lai* 'turning over in-my-direction, — contrariwise, on the other hand.'
42. *Gaanmiengl* 'hurry-on-to tomorrow, — by tomorrow, — some day.'
43. *Shyue-cherng.le* 'learn to completion, — have learned.'

EXERCISES

1. Make a list of all opposites or correlative words (without distinguishing them) that have appeared so far in Lessons 1–8.

2. *Comment on the following statements as to truth, paraphrasing the content in your own words. For example* — Jey-jiann shyh burong.yih tzuoh: Duey .le, jeh.sh *i*-jiann heen nan tzuoh .de shyh.chyng.

(a) Shyh.jieh.shanq .de dong.shi, yanqyanql dou yeou jenqmiall faanmiall .de. (b) Jey-jiuh huah .lii.tou .de daw.lii, mei.yeou ren bu ming.bair .de. (c) Dah gen doan sh *i*-jenq i-faan. (d) Shyue shuo Jong.gwo-huah sh heen rong.yih .de shyh.chyng. (e) *I*g ren shuey-jaur.le jiow ting.bu-jiann ren.jia shuo-huah .de sheng.in .le. (f) Weishean .de shyh.chyng renren dou gaan tzuoh. (g) Fuh-muu *tzyy*-neu sh leang-duey jenq-faan-tzyh. (h) Ting, shuo, kann, shiee sh *i*-jiann shyh. (i) Nii chwufei huey kann Jong.gwo-shu tsair neng shuo Jong.gwo-huah .ne. (j) Wang .Shian.sheng inwey bu pah weishean, *suoo*.yii bugaan tzuoh feiji. (k) Mei konql gen yeou shyh.chyng tzuoh sh *i*g jenqmiall *i*g faanmiall. (l) Ing'wen kann.chii.lai hao.shianq *heen* hao shyue, chyishyr ideal dou buhao shyue.

3. *Translate into Chinese:*

(a) Of the things in this room there is none that I do not know what to call. (b) Why are you not afraid to fall out from (inside) an airplane? (c) This is a statement one hears every day. (d) By today yesterday's news is already old. (e) When one is standing (*jannj*) one is not sitting, when one is awake one is not sleeping, but when one is sleeping one may also be talking, since some people talk in their sleep. (f) Can you write both Chinese and English words at the same time? (g) I do not like to use words which are both difficult to write and difficult to understand. (h) May I ask you a question? (i) Ask her to come here and sit on my left (side). (j) Were you unwilling to give this to him (*bae jeyg geei .ta*) or were you afraid to (.ne)? (k) I was neither (*yee bu.sh*) unwilling nor afraid, I simply did not see him. (l) Will it be all right if I tell him as soon as I see him?

ANTONYMS

4. *Example:*

Given:
Dih'i-tian, dih'ell-tian, dihsan-tian. Nii sh neei-tian kann-wan jey-been shu .de?

Answer:
Jey-been shu woo dih'i-tian hair mei chii-tourl kann; dih'ell-tian (*ad lib: nii* daa-diann-huah .geei .woo .de .shyr.howl) woo jenq ('just') .tzay.nall kannj .ne; daw.le dihsan-tian woo tsair bae jey-been shu kann-wan.le.

(a) Chyan.tian ('day before yesterday'), tzwo.tian, jin.tian. Nii.men sh neei-tian shanq-wan Dihba Keh .de? (b) Shyr-fen jong yiichyan ('ten minutes ago'), gangtsair, jey.hoel. Nii sh sherm shyr.howl chy-wan.le ney-i-dah-woan fann .de? (c) Liibaytian, Liibay'i, Liibay'ell. Nii sh neei-tian chu.chiuh mae.le ney-i-dahshie maubii .lai .de? (d) Liowg liibay yiichyan, guoh.le ig liibay, shianntzay. Jeyg way.gworen sh sherm shyr.howl shyue-huey.le Jong.gwo-huah .de? (e) Woo.men dou shiingj .de .shyr.howl, woo.men kuay yaw ('soon, about to') shuey-jiaw .de .shyr.howl, woo.men renren dou shuey-jaur.le .de .shyr.howl. Lao Tarn sh sherm shyr.howl shiee-wan jey-i-keh .lii .de Jong.gwo-tzyh .de? (f) Diannhuah hair mei sheang .de .shyr.howl, woo jenq .tzay.nall daa-diann-huah .de .shyr.howl, *woo* daa-wan.le diannhuah yiihow. Nii jy.daw woo sh sherm shyr.howl sheang.chu .ta jiaw sherm ming.tzyh .lai .de? (g) Woo jinn.chiuh .de .shyr.howl, woo chu.lai .de .shyr.howl, woo yow hwei.chiuh .de .shyr.howl. Shian.sheng sherm shyr.howl shanq shin-keh .de? (h) Tzwol yeh.lii shyr'ell-dean jong, guoh.le .i.hoel, yow guoh.le .i.hoel. Nii jy.daw woo sherm shyr.howl tzuoh-wan.le neyg heen chyiguay .de menq?

5. *Example:*

Given:
Shuo .de jonq.

Answer:
A. Shuo .de tzemm jonq, gow jonq .bu .gow .jonq .l'a?
B. *Bu* gow jonq, hair deei shuo-jonq.i.deal.
A. Tzemm jonq, shyng .bu.shyng .l'a?
B. Bushyng, vx! Tzay jonq.deal, woo gaw.sonq .nii hair .deei shuo· .de genq jonq.i.deal .me!

(a) Shiee .de dah. (b) Daa .de sheang. (c) Tzuoh .de hao. (d) Shuo .de ching.chuu. (e) Fei .de gau. (f) Tzoou .de kuay. (g) Chii.lai .de tzao. (h) Shiee .de jenq. (i) Shuo .de haoting. (j) Daw .de tzao. (k) Mae .de duo. (l) Shiee .de haokann.

LESSON 9
A GOOD MAN

A: I will tell you about a man.

B: What? About a man again? Is it about that — what is it? — Mr. Can't Finish Speaking?

A: What do you mean, 'Mr. Can't Finish Speaking'? There is no such name as Speaking.

B: No, no, I mean the, — the, the man with the name of — of — what-do-you-call-him? Oh yes, that's right, he's called Mr. Can't Stop Talking, is that right?

A: No, this time I am going to talk about another man, I am going to talk about a good man. Well, this man always says to people, "Every man in the world ought to 'Read good books, speak good words, be a good man, and perform good deeds.'"

B: Why, that's excellent, what else in the world could be better than that?

A: They are very good, to be sure, but although he wants to do these things, yet he has not the ability to carry out all these things.

B: How is that?

A: Well, take the matter of 'reading good books.' You see, he can't even recognize a character like 'dah,' what point is there in speaking of reading good books or bad books, then?

B: That's right, in that case there will be no point in saying whether books are good or bad then. Well, 'speaking good words' should be easy to manage.

A: It's easy, all right, but the words he says people often cannot understand very well. And it is not only strangers that can't understand him, you see, why, even those most intimate with him, those who are constantly with him from morning to night — be they his wife, the children in his own home, his servants, or his colleagues — they, too, often cannot understand him.

B: (*Laughs:*) Oh, I see, not Mr. Can't Stop Talking, but Mr. No Clear Speaking, what?

A: I told you there's no such name as Speaking!

B: (*Chuckles.*) What sort of dialect does he speak?

A: W-e-ll, I can't tell you either. The kind of language he speaks is really very special. You don't know whether his speech is the Peiping dialect or the Nanking dialect, neither like the Shantung dialect, nor like the Szechwan dialect, somewhat like the Cantonese dialect, but also a little like the Shanghai dialect, half like Chinese, but also half like a foreign language, as it were.

DIHJEOU KEH
IG* HAO REN

A: Woo geei nii jeang¹ ig ren.

B: Tzeemme? Yow jeang g ren l'a? Sh bush neyg — shermme Shuo Buwan Shg.?²

A: Sherm³ 'Shuo Buwan Shg.'? Meiyeou shinq Shuo de.⁴

B: Bush vx, woode yihsy sh shuo⁵ neyg⁶ vx, neyg shinq sherm.me — jiaw — jiaw sherm.me? Oh, duey le, jiaw Tarn .Butyng Shg., sh bush'a?

A: Bush, jey.hwei woo jeang de yowsh ig ren, woo jeang ig hao-ren. Jeyg ren a, ta tzoong duey ren shuo, "Farn.sh⁷ shyhjieh.shanq de ren a, dou inggai 'Dwu⁸ hao-shu, shuo hao-huah, tzuoh⁹ hao-ren, shyng¹⁰ hao-shyh.'"

B: Nah tzay hao meiyeou .lo,¹¹ shyhjieh.shanq hair yeou sherm bii jey-syh-yanql genq hao d'a?

A: Hao sh heen hao.¹² Buguoh ta sweiran sheang tzemm tzuoh, keesh ta mei been.shyh bae yanqyanql dou tzuoh-dawle.

B: Tzeem ne?

A: Ar, haobii shuo 'dwu hao-shu' de huah ba.¹³ Nii chyau ta lian ig **dah**.tzyh¹⁴ dou bu renn.de, hair tyi¹⁵ sherm¹⁶ dwu hao-shu dwu huay-shu ne?

B: Èè, nah yee shuo.bu-shanq¹⁷ .sherm shu hao shu huay¹⁸ le. Neme 'shuo hao-huah' tzoong¹⁹ gai hao bann .lo?

A: Hao bann sh hao bann, dannsh ta suoo²⁰ shuo de huah, ren.jia charngchangl ting.bu-dah-doong. Eh, budann sh shengren²¹ ting.bu-doong tade huah è, lian ta²² diing shour de i-tian-daw-woan gen ta lao tzay ikuall²³ de ren — naapah²⁴ ta tay.x a, ta tzyhjii jia.lii de sheauharl a, yonq.ren²⁵ a, torngshyhmen²⁶ a — tamen yee charngchangl yeou ting.bu-doong ta de shyrhowl.²⁷

B: O-h-oh,²⁸ bush Tarn Butyng Shg., sh Shuo Buching Shg., ar?

A: Woo gawsonq nii mei shinq Shuo de me!

B: Hèhè! Ta shuo de sh sherm dihfangl de huah²⁹ ne?

A: Eng — woo yee shuo.bu-shanqlai³⁰ le. Ta shuo de ney-joong huah jensh tehbye de heen.³¹ Ta shuo de yee bujydaw sh Beeipyng-huah, yee bujydaw sh Nan.jing-huah, bu shianq Shan.dong-huah, yee bu shianq Syh.chuan-huah, yeoudeal shianq Goangjou-huah, yow yeoudeal shianq Shanq.hae-huah, iball³² shianq Jonggwo-huah, yow iball shianq waygwo-huah shyhde.

---

* From Lesson 9 on, dots before neutral-tone syllables will be omitted. But in new compounds, before unstressed localizers and complements, and in special cases where there is possibility of doubt, the dot will be kept. (A dot before a compound localizer or complement goes for both syllables.) Tone sandhi will also be left unmarked.

B: It isn't anything in particular, and yet there's something of everything in it, is that right?

A: Yes, it's just a queer sort of language, which is neither Chinese nor Occidental, with a southern intonation and a northern accent.

B: If what he says is so difficult to understand, how do you know that he is a good man, then?

A: Uh — I think you can say — uh — there are two reasons. In the first place, he is the sort of man who, most of all, is willing to help people. So long as it is something beneficial to others, there is nothing that he is not willing to do, there is nothing that he is not glad to do. Not only can he do things others regard as difficult to do, but in addition he dares to do things others do not dare to do. If he believes that a certain thing is something a man ought to do, then he will certainly go right off and do it.

B: Then haven't the two things that you call 'being a good man' and 'performing good deeds' become identical things?

A: No, no! And that's just what I was going to — what I was going to call my second point.

B: And your second point is —?

A: Secondly, this man not only performs good deeds all his life, but also has a good heart. I think a man must have a good heart before he can be regarded as a good man.

B: But his heart is inside, how can you find out whether it is good or not?

A: There are ways to find out a little about it, too. Although I cannot understand very well what he says, still he seems to have a very good disposition. When others are happy, he is happy, too; when others are unhappy, he is also unhappy. When others laugh, he laughs, too; when others are feeling bad, he always goes to comfort them. Therefore, although I cannot see his heart, still I believe that, as a person, he certainly is good-hearted. That he is a good man is therefore absolutely beyond question.

B: Yeah, according to what you say, I think this man is pretty good, eh?

A: Isn't he, though?

NOTES

1. *Jeang* 'talk about, discuss, explain.' In other dialects *jeang* is often used for *shuo* 'say, speak' and *jeang-huah* for *shuo-huah*.

2. *Shg.*, abbreviation for *Shiansheng*.

3. Compare *Sherm jiaw* 'hao-ren'? "What do you mean by 'good man'?" with *Sherm* 'hao-ren'?! "What do you mean, 'good man'?!"

A GOOD MAN

B: Sherm dou [33] bush, sherm dou yeoudeal tzay .lii.tou, sh bush'a?

A: Duey le, jeanjyr sh i-joong bu-Jong-bu-Shi,[34] nan-chiang-beei-diaw [35] de guay-huah.[36]

B: Ta shuo de huah jihran [37] nemm nan doong, neme tzeem jydaw ta sh g hao-ren ne?

A: Eng — woo sheang keeyii shuo — yeou leangg yuan.guh. Dih'i-tserng,[38] ta jeyg ren a,[39] ta tzuey keen bang ren de mang.[40] Jyy yawsh [41] duey bye.ren yeou hao.chuh [42] de shyh.chyng, ta meiyeou bukeen gann de, meiyeou buyuann.yih [43] tzuoh de. Ta budann neng tzuoh renjia yiiwei nan tzuoh de shyh, binqchiee [44] gaan tzuoh renjia suoo bugaan tzuoh de shyh. Jearu ta shiangshinn i-jiann shyhchyng sh ig ren inggai tzuoh d'a, ta jiow idinq yaw chiuh tzuoh .chiuh de.

B: Neme nii suoowey [45] 'tzuoh hao-ren, shyng hao-shyh' — leang-yanql shyh, bush biann-cherngle [46] iyanq de le ma?

A: Bush vx! È, jeh jiowsh woo jenq yaw [47] shuo de — suoowey dih'ell-tserng le.

B: Dih'ell tserng tzeem ne?

A: Ell-lai [48] a, jeyg ren budann ibeytz [49] tzuoh hao-shyh, erlchiee ta shin hao.[50] Woo sheang ig ren feideei [51] shin hao, tsair neng suann hao-ren.

B: Keesh ta shin tzay liitou nii tzeem kann.de-chu ta [52] hao buhao lai ne?

A: Yee yeou fartz kann.de-chu ideal lai. Ta shuo de huah sweiran woo ting.bu-dah-doong a, keesh tade shinq.chyng [53] haoshianq feicharng [54] hao. Bye.ren gaushinq ta yee gaushinq; bye.ren bukuay.hwo ta yee bukuay.hwo. Ren.jia shiaw [55] ta tzoong shiaw; ren.jia nanshow de shyrhowl ta jiow tzoong chiuh an.wey .ren.jia. Suooyii woo sweiran kann.bu-jiann tade shin, keesh woo shiangshinn jeh ren idinq [56] shin hao. Suooyii shuo ta sh hao-ren a, nahsh jyueduey [57] meiyeou wenntyi [58] de.

B: Èr, jaw nii jehyanql jeang de, woo sheang jeyg ren daw [59] hair butsuoh,[60] ar?

A: Keebush ma?

The omission of *jiaw*, like the omission of 'by' in the English, makes the question much stronger.

4. Literally, 'There is no one who is surnamed *Shuo*.'

5. *Woode yihsy sh shuo*, usually spoken very rapidly, is the regular expression for 'I mean' in correcting oneself. Another common form is *Woo sh yaw shuo*.

6. *Neyg*, often with repetition, is a common form of hesitation. *Jeyg*

is even more common than *neyg* as a filler-in, especially in an extemporaneous speech. (See Lesson 24, p. 293.)

7. *Farn.sh* 'whoever is,' 'whatever is,' 'all.'
8. *Dwu* 'read (aloud),' slightly more formal than *niann* 'read (aloud).'
9. *Tzuoh-ren* 'act (as) a person, be a person, conduct oneself.'
10. *Shyng* 'perform,' as a transitive verb, is a more formal word than *tzuoh* 'do.' As an intransitive verb, meaning 'will do, okay,' it is an everyday word.
11. *Tzay hao meiyeou*, lit. 'anything still better does not exist.' The particle *.lo* (pronounced like English 'law') means 'obviously, of course, it goes without saying.' It is used more frequently in Southern Mandarin than in Peiping, where a simple *le* would more commonly be used here.
12. **V-sh-V Constructions.** — When a verb (including adjectives) is repeated with *sh* inserted in between, the construction has a concessive force, which can be translated as 'to be sure,' 'all right,' or merely a rising-falling-rising intonation on the last stress group. Thus, *Hao sh hao* '(as for being) good, it *is* good,' 'it's good, to be sure,' 'it's good, all right,' 'it's good (with ˦ ˧ over 'good'), but . . . .'
13. *Haobii . . . ba* 'For instance, let us talk about the matter (*huah*) of reading good books.'
14. If pronounced *dah-'tzyh*, with stress on *tzyh*, then the sentence would mean 'He does not recognize a single big character,' an equally common way of describing illiteracy.
15. *Tyi* 'lift (from above), raise'; 'raise the point of, — mention.'
16. The form verb + *sherm* + object is often used as a rhetorical question implying 'What's the use for, what's the point in . . . ?' Thus, *Nii buhuey shuo Jonggwo-huah shuo sherm Jonggwo-huah ne?* 'If you can't speak Chinese, what's the point in speaking (i.e. pretending to speak) Chinese, then?'
17. *Shuo.bu-shanq* 'cannot speak so as to come up (within range of relevancy), — there is no point in saying . . . .'
18. Note the predicative position of the adjectives *hao* and *huay*.
19. *Tzoong* 'always,' here used in the extended sense of 'should anyway, surely.' The final particle *.lo* is translated by pronouncing 'manage' with a low pitch on 'man-' and a rising pitch on '-age,' something like ˩ ˧.
20. *Suoo* is an emphatic adverb, with the force of 'actually, indeed, do . . . ,' occurring, like other adverbs, after the subject (if any) and before the verb. Because *suoo* is used mostly in *de*-constructions, which are usually translatable by relative clauses using 'whom, which, what,' it will be useful to associate it, for translation purposes, with such relatives, although grammatically it is still an adverb. Thus, *woo suoo jeang de ren* 'I-actually-talk-about man, — the man (whom) I am talking about'; *ta suoo chy de dongshi* 'the thing (that) he eats.'

21. *Sheng* 'unripe'; 'uncooked'; 'unfamiliar, unknown,' opp. of *shour* 'ripe'; 'cooked'; 'familiar.' *Shengren* 'stranger'; *shourren* 'an acquaintance.'

22. A *de* is understood here. When there is a string of *de*'s, one or more of them may be omitted.

23. *Ikuall* 'one-lump, — together.'

24. *Naapah* 'what-fear, — no matter if they are, be they . . . .'

25. *Yonq-ren* 'to employ people'; *yonq.ren* 'servant.'

26. *Torngshyh* 'same-job, — colleague, fellow-worker,' also used like a verb-object construction as *Woo gen ta torngle sheuduo shyrhowl shyh* 'I have worked with him for a long time.'

27. *Tamen yee . . . de shyrhowl* 'they, too, often have times when they cannot understand him.'

28. The spelling *O-h-oh* is to suggest a slight laughter superimposed on the vowel of *Oh* 'I see.'

29. There is a learned term *fangyan* 'locality-speech' for 'dialect.' Ordinarily, the word *huah* is used in referring to dialects and languages.

30. *Shuo.bu-shanqlai* 'cannot speak up (from my memory or limited knowledge), — cannot tell for sure.' Distinguish from *shuo.bu-shanq* 'there is no point in saying.'

31. Note the use of *heen* as complement here.

32. *Bann* 'half' can be used either as an AN, as in *iball* ($<$ *i* + *bann* + *-l*) 'one half,' or as a determinative, as *bann-kuay chyan* 'half a piece of money, — half a dollar,' *bann-dean jong* 'half an hour.'

33. Interrogative-Plus-Dou Constructions. — An interrogative plus *dou* (or *yee*) has the meaning of 'any, every.' *Sheir dou jydaw* 'everybody knows'; *neeig dou shyng* 'any one will do'; *naal dou kann.bu-jiann ta* 'can't see him anywhere'; *ta sherm dou chy* 'he eats anything.' So, with a negative, *sherm dou bush* 'it isn't anything in particular.' (See also p. 52.)

34. *Bu-Jong-bu-Shi de* 'neither Chinese nor Occidental' is used in a derogatory sense.

35. *Nan-chiang-beei-diaw* 'southern-tone-northern-tune, — mixed accent.'

36. *Guay* 'queer,' as against *chyiguay* 'strange.' *Chyi* as a free word is a more literary word, meaning 'exotic, marvelous.'

37. *Jihran* 'since, if (i.e., if, as you claim),' Fr. *puisque*.

38. *Tserng*, AN for things in layers or tiers, like *bey.uo* 'bedding,' *lou* 'storied house,' *yuan.guh* 'reasons,' which are thought of as being in layers.

39. *Ta jeyg ren a* 'This man (like) him, — he as a person.'

40. *Bang-mang* 'help-busy, — help' is an intransitive verb. An object in English is translated by a possessive form, as *bang woode mang* 'help me.'

41. *Jyy yawsh* 'if only, so long as.' Contrast with *jyy yeou* 'only if.'

42. *Yeou hao.chuh* 'have point of advantage, — advantageous, beneficial.'
43. *Yuann.yih* 'willing to, glad to,' has a more positive implication than *keen* which merely indicates absence of aversion.
44. *Binq₀chiee* 'moreover.'
45. *Suoowey* 'that which is called,' *nii suoowey* 'that which you call.' *Wey* 'call, speak of' is not a free word in the spoken style.
46. *Biann* 'change'; *cherng* 'to form.' As complement, *cherng* can be translated as 'into.'
47. *Jenq yaw* 'just going to.'
48. *I-lai, ell-lai,* etc. 'in the first place, in the second place,' etc.
49. *Ibeytz* 'one-generationful, — all one's life.'
50. **S–P Predicates.** — *Ta shin hao* is not to be analyzed as *Tade shin hao,* although the latter means about the same thing. *Ta* is the subject of *shin hao* and *shin* is the subject of *hao:* 'As for him, the heart is good.'

Forms like *shin hao* are subject-predicate predicates or S–P predicates (p. 35). In the following comparison, any one of the two Chinese constructions can be translated into any one of the three English constructions, but only the forms with *tade* and 'his' correspond grammatically.

Ta shin hao:	(No such form in English.)
Tade shin hao:	'His heart is good.'
(Not idiomatic in Chinese):	'He has a good heart.'
(No such form in Chinese):	'He is good-hearted.'

51. *Feideei* 'must, necessarily'; *feideei . . . tsair* 'must . . . before . . . .'
52. Although *ta* refers to an inanimate object (*shin*) and is the subject of *hao buhao,* the fact that it comes after *kann.de-chu* (*lai*) makes its use possible.
53. See Note 50.
54. Although *feicharng* means literally 'un-usual,' it actually means, when used adverbially, 'extremely.' The word for 'unusually' is *yihcharng* (*de*), lit. 'different from usual.'
55. *Shiaw* 'laugh'; 'smile.'
56. Since *shin hao* is a predicate, it can take a modifier *idinq,* which would not be possible if a *de* were understood between *ren* and *shin.*
57. *Jyueduey* 'exclude (the) relative, — absolutely.'
58. *Wenntyi* 'inquiry-topic, — problem, question.'
59. *Daw* 'inverted'; 'contrariwise'; 'rather (to my surprise),' a homonym of *daw* 'reach'; 'to.'
60. *Butsuoh* 'not wrong'; 'not bad, pretty good,' a favorite show-off word with foreign speakers of Chinese.
61. *Exercise 3, Example.* *Huey* in *huey Shanqhae-huah* is used in the sense of 'have a practical command of.' Cf. *Können Sie Deutsch?*

EXERCISES

1. *Examples:*

Given:
Hao bu hao? Duo bu duo?
Huey tzuoh buhuey? Jiel idinq tzuoh.de-wan ma?

Answer:
Hao sh hao, keesh (*or* dannsh, *or* buguoh) bu duo.
Tzuoh sh huey tzuoh (*or* huey sh huey, *or* huey tzuoh sh huey tzuoh), buguoh jiel bu idinq tzuoh.de-wan.

(a) Sheang chiuh ma? Shianntzay chiuh ma? (b) Chy le meiyeou? Chy de dongshi gow bu gow? (c) Nii shiihuan dwu Jonggwoshu ma? Nii rennde de Jonggwo-tzyh duo buduo? (d) Nii shuey-jaurle tzuoh-menq bu tzuoh? Shuo menqhuah bu shuo?

2. *Example:*

Given:
Jey-wey shiansheng yow ay shuo hao-huah, yow shiihuan tzuoh hao-shyh.

Answer:
Jey-wey shiansheng budann ay shuo hao-huah, erlchiee (*or* binqchiee) shiihuan tzuoh hao-shyh.

(a) Jeyg ren shin yow huay, shin.lii yow bu chingchuu. (b) Wang Tay.tay yow huey shuo waygwohuah, yow huey shiee waygwotzyh. (c) Ta shuo de huah yow chyiguay, sheng'in yow nan doong. (d) Na gangbii shiee-tzyh, yow bii chianbii hao shiee, yow bii ta haokann.

3. *Example:*

Given:
Ta buhuey [61] Shanqhae-huah buyawjiin è, ta huey Goangjou-huah è!

Answer:
Ta sweiran buhuey Shanqhae-huah, keesh ta huey Goangjou-hua.

(a) Woo mei daw.guoh Nanjing buyawjiin è, woo daw.guoh Beeipyng è! (b) Ta shuo-huah shuo de bu haoting buyawjiin è, ta shiee-tzyh shiee de heen haokann è! (c) Woo bujydaw ta mingtzyh jiaw sherm buyawjiin è, woo jihde ta haw jiaw sherm è! (d) Meiyeou shinq Shuo de buyawjiin è, yeou shinq Tarn d'è!

4. *Example:*

Given:
Jeyg dongshi heen hao.

Answer:
Jeyg dongshi hao de heen. Tzeem tzemm hao? Jen hao-jyile!

(a) Ta shuo de ney-joong huah heen tehbye. (b) Jeyg ren heen chyiguay. (c) Jeyg neuharl ('girl') heen haokann. (d) Jey-beel shu .lii.tou de shyhchyng heen haowal.

5. *Example:*

Given: Answer:

Jihran bu rennde tzyh, dangran genq buhuey dwu-shu lo!   Lian tzyh dou bu rennde, nah hair dwu sherm shu ne?

(a) Jihran buneng tzuoh sheau-shyh, dangran genq buneng tzuoh dah-shyh lo! (b) Jihran bugaan tzuoh chihche, dangran genq bugaan tzuoh feiji lo! (c) Jihran kann.bu-jiann baw, dangran genq kann.bu-jiann baw.shanq de shinwen lo! (d) Ta jihran buhuey chou-ian, dangran genq buhuey chuei ianchiual lo!

LESSON 10
THE TAILLESS RAT*

Once upon a time there was a rat who could not make up his mind about anything. No matter what you asked him, he never had anything definite to answer you. For example, if you were to say, "The weather is very fine today, isn't it?" he would perhaps say, "Maybe it is, the weather today is not bad, but maybe it isn't particularly good either — I am afraid it isn't a very fine day today — w-e-ll — I don't know whether this kind of weather is to be regarded as good or bad after all."

If you asked him, "Will you be free this afternoon to go out and take a stroll with me?" he would say, "Oh, I am sorry, I have no time in the afternoon, I am free in the morning though — oh, no, no, what I mean to say is, I am busy in the morning, but there's nothing in the afternoon — but what if it rains in the afternoon? We had better wait until we have had lunch before we decide; besides, I don't think this is anything of great urgency, you don't have to decide right away, why must we decide immediately? Why such a hurry?"

Sometimes, someone would ask him, "Mr. Rodens, how many sons and daughters have you?" and he would say, "Oh — I — I — uh — I believe I have seven sons and eight daughters — uh — well, let me see, perhaps it's eight sons and seven daughters maybe — anyway I have ten-odd children all told — or, or maybe it's twenty-odd or thirty, or thereabouts, I can't say for sure. Yes, I guess I have at least twenty-odd children."

One midnight, there was a great storm, which was on the point of blowing down the dilapidated house Mr. Rat was living in. The friends who lived with him all were startled out of their sleep and called to him, "Hurry up and run, don't lie sleeping there! Wake up, hey, get up!"

* This story appeared first in Henry Sweet's *Primer of Spoken English*, later was used by William Cabell Greet in his *American Speech* recordings. It has been modified and very much expanded here.

6. *Translate into Chinese:*

(a) What he said was very interesting, to be sure, but once he started talking, then he couldn't stop. (b) That he is an educated man ('read-book-man') is beyond question. (c) Since you cannot very well understand what he says, how do you know whether he is kind-hearted or not? (d) These men are not even afraid of death, not to speak of fire or water. (e) He doesn't understand anything. (See Note 33.) (f) Any time will do. (g) What I know is really not much. (h) This is the thing I am most afraid of. (Use *suoo* in (g) and (h).)

DIHSHYR KEH
WUWOEI SHUU [1]

Tsorngchyan [2] yeou g hawtz, ta sherm shyhchyng dou daa.bu-dinq jwu.yih.[3] Sweibiann nii wenn ta sherm huah, ta tsornglai meiyeou [4] idinq de huah hweidar nii de. Biiru nii shuo, 'Jiel tian.chih jen hao, ar?' ta jiow yee sheu shuo, "Sh de ba, jintian tian.chih butsuoh, keesh yee sheu butzeem [5] hao, woo pah jiel jeh tial budah hao ba, — ss [6] — woo yee bujydaw jey-tzoong [7] tial dawdii [8] suann hao suann huay le."

Yawsh nii wenn ta, "Nii jiel woan.bann.tial [9] yeou meiyeou gong.ful [10] gen woo shanq jie.shanq [11] .chiuh tzooux a?" ta jiow shuo, 'Aiia, dueybu-juh,[12] woo shiahwuu mei gong.ful, shanqwuu dawsh yeou konql — èh bush vx, woo sh yaw shuo shanq.bann.tian [13] mang, shiah.bann.tian mei shell — keesh shiahwuu yawsh shiah-yeu [14] ne? Tzarmen diing hao hairsh [15] deeng chy-guohle [16] wuufann [17] tzay daa-dinq jwu.yih ba; woo sheang jeh yow bush sherm diing jyi de shyhchyng, buyonq maashanq [18] jiow jyuedinq d'è, herbih [19] lihkeh jiow jyuedinq ne? Gannma tzemm jau-jyi [20] a?

Yeou shyrhowl yeou ren wenn ta, "Lao Shuu Shg. a, Nin Fuu.shanq [21] yeou jii-wey shaw.ye,[22] jii-wey *sheau*.jiee a?" ta jiow shuo, "Eng — woo — woo ia, woo sheang woo yeou chig erltz bag neu.erl — ss — eng, ranq woo kann a, meijoel [23] sh bag erltz chig neu.erl ba? Herng.sh [24] woo igonq yeou shyrjiig sheauharl — hesh, hesh yeesheu yeou ell-sanshyr-geh shanq-shiah yee shuo.bu-dinq. Èè, woo tsai woo jyhshao yeou ellshyr.laig [25] sheauharl ne."

Yeou i-tian bannyeh, dah-feng dah-yeu;[26] bae jey-wey Lao Shuu Shg. juh de ney-suool poh-farngtz [27] dou kuay chuei-ta [28] le. Gen ta torng-juh de i-ban [29] perng.yeoumen dou shiah-shiing le [30], jiow chiilai jiaw ta shuo, "Kuay.deal pao ba, bye shuey de .nall l'a! Shiing le, hei, chiilai l'a!"

The rat said lazily, sort of half awake and half asleep, "It is not yet light now, what are you getting up so early for? Oh, it seems to be raining out, that's right, it is actually raining."

"Hurry up and go, don't delay any more! What are you waiting for? The house is going to collapse! And if you won't go, we'll have to go without you."

"The house will collapse? This house is perfectly good! It has not collapsed, has it? I have stayed here for so long and this house has never collapsed before."

While he was talking, the wind was blowing harder and harder and the rain was falling more and more heavily. Fortunately, this Mr. Rat was the kind of person that never could make up his mind. He had just said that the house could not collapse, but after thinking it over, he said again, "Oh, my, this house is shaking so badly, there's no telling it may collapse after all. No, I am going to run for it, too."

Just as he walked out the door, he said again, "Goodness, gracious! such a heavy rain! I had better not go after all." Hardly had he finished his sentence, when suddenly Bang! with a crash, a whole great big house collapsed.

"Squeak, squeak, squeak, squeak!" Was that rat crushed to death, I wonder? No, he was not. For this indecisive Mr. Rat could not even make up his mind whether to die or not. Just as he had gone out of the front door, the house collapsed. Luckily, his body had already reached the outside and therefore did not get crushed after all. But while he was standing at the doorway, he left his tail inside the room, and it was cut off by a pillar which had fallen down.

From that time on, he became a rat without a tail. But since he had his tail cut off, he has also become a rat with decision and has never again been so indecisive as before.

NOTES

1. *Wu*, literary word for *meiyeou* 'have not.' In spoken Chinese, *wu–* is a bound word, meaning 'without, –less.' *Woei* is the bound stem word in *woei.ba* 'tail,' more colloquially, *yii.ba*. *Shuu* is the bound stem word in *Laoshuu* 'rat, mouse,' more colloquially *hawtz*, lit. 'consumer, waster.' *Wuwoei-shuu = meiyeou yii.ba de hawtz*.

2. *Tsorngchyan* 'from before, — formerly, once upon a time.'

3. *Jwu.yih* 'intention, decision, idea (for action).' *Daa-dinqle jwu.yih* 'make definite one's idea, — make up one's mind.'

4. *Tsornglai bu, tsornglai meiyeou* 'never before.'

5. *Butzeemme* 'not in any way, not particularly.'

6. *Ss,* pronounced with air sucked in between the teeth, expresses

Ney-jy hawtz jiow bann-shiing-bann-shuey de nemm laanlhalde [31] shuo, 'Jey.hoel tian hair mei lianq,[32] gannma tzemm tzao jiow chiilai a? Aiia, waytou haoshianq shiah-yeu ne ba, butsuoh, dyichiueh sh shiahj-yeu ne.'
"Kuay tzoou .b'ou! [33] Buneng tzay chyr .l'ou! Hair deeng shermme ia? Farngtz dou kuay dao .l'ou! Nii bu tzoou woomen deei shian [34] tzoou le."
"Farngtz yaw dao? [35] Jeh farngtz hair haohaulde me! Ta binq mei dao a! Woo tzayjell daile tzemm jeou, jeh farngtz tsornglai yee mei dao.guoh ia."

Ta shuoj-huah de shyrhowl, feng yueh gua yueh lih.hay,[36] yeu yueh shiah yueh dah. Haotzay [37] jey-wey Shuu Shg. sh lao daa.bu-dinq jwu.yih de. Ta gang shuole farngtz buhuey dao, keesh ta sheangle sheang yow shuo, "Aiia, jeh farngtz yau de tzemm lih.hay, meijoel jen huey dao ba? Derle [38] ba, woo yee tzoou le."

Gang tzoou-chule menkooul,[39] ta yow shuo, "Hao-jia.huoo! [40] Tzemm dah de yeu! Hairsh bye tzoou derle." Huah hair mei shuo-wan, hurande konglonglong! i-sheng, i-dah-suoo [41] farngtz jeenggehlde [42] ta le.

'Tzel, tzel, tzel, tzel!' Nah hawtz yah.syyle meiyeou? Meiyeou, mei yah.syy. Inwey jey-wey mei jwu.yih de Lao Shuu Shg. a, ta lian syy bu syy dou daa.bu-dinq jwu.yih de. Ta gang i tzoou-chule dahmen, nah farngtz jiow ta.shiahlai le. Shinq.kuei ta shentz yiijinq dawle waytou, suooyii dawdii mei yah-jaur.[43] Keesh ta jann de menkooul de shyrhowl bae i-tyau yii.ba geei [44] lah de utz liitou le, — suooyii bey [45] i-gen dao.shiah-lai de dah-juhtz geei tzar-duann le.

Tsorng tsyy [46] yiihow, ta jiow biann-cherngle i-jy wuwoei-shuu le. Dannsh ta tzyhtsorng dioule yii.ba guohhow a, ta yee biann-cherngle i-joong yeou jyueduann de hawtz le, bu tzay shianq [47] yiichyan nemm mei jwu.yih le.[48]

---

hesitation or thinking over. It is different from the Japanese sucked in *ss*, which is pronounced very long and expresses politeness.

7. *Jey-tzoong* 'this kind,' *-tzoong* being a blend between *joong* 'kind' and *tzong* 'lot, group' (as in *dahtzong* 'large lot'). *Tial* 'day (as to weather).'

8. *Dawdii* 'to bottom, at bottom, — after all.'

9. *Woan.bann.tial* 'late half day, — late afternoon.'

10. *Gong.ful* = *konql* 'leisure time.' *Gong.fu* means either 'leisure time' or 'time during which one has had a special training, — proficiency.'

11. *Jie.shanq* 'on the street, in town.'

12. *Dueybujuh* 'cannot face (you) and stay there, cannot maintain my face towards you, — I am sorry.'

13. *Shanq.bann.tian* = *shanq.wuu*; *shiah.bann.tian* = *shiah.wuu*.

14. **Impersonal V–O Constructions.** — A Chinese sentence not only may have a subject understood, but may not have any subject at all. Thus, *shiah-yeu le* 'downs rain, — it is raining.' Most weather phenomena are expressions in the verb-object sentence form as *gua-feng le* 'blows wind,' *shiah-wuh le* 'downs fog, — there is a fog,' *jaur-huoo le* 'kindles fire, — there is a fire.' The *le* indicates that it is usually a new situation that one notices while making such remarks.

15. Instead of *hao.i.deal*, the usual expression for 'had better' is *diing hao* 'best' or *diing hao hairsh* 'best after all.'

16. *Chy-guohle* 'have already eaten,' should be distinguished from *chy.guoh* 'have once eaten before.'

17. *Wuufann* 'noon meal.' In Peiping the term *tzaofann* 'morning meal' is often used for the second of three meals, as distinguished from *dean.shin* 'dot the heart, — refreshment,' used for breakfasts, teas, snacks or for articles of food other than regular dishes. To avoid ambiguity, *tzao-dean* or *tzao-dean.shin* is often used for 'breakfast.' The term *woanfann* 'evening meal' is used in practically all dialects.

18. *Maashanq* (with full tones) 'on horse, — right away, at once,' the horse being the fastest means of transportation in the old days.

19. *Herbih* 'why must?' *Lihkeh* 'standing-moment, the moment while you wait, — immediately.'

20. *Jau-jyi* 'get nervous.'

21. *Fuu.shanq* 'up at the mansion,' polite term for 'your family'; 'your house'; 'your native place.'

22. *Shaw.ye* 'young squire, Master,' here used for 'your son.' *Sheau.jiee* 'little maiden, — Miss,' here used for 'your daughter.'

23. *Joen* 'accurate,' *meijoel* 'there is no certainty, there is no telling but that . . . .'

24. *Herng.sh* (< *herng-shuh*) 'horizontal or vertical, — anyway.' *Igonq* 'all together, in all.'

25. The form *-.lai* has a different range from *-jii*. While *ellshyr-jiig* means from 21 through 29, *ellshyr.laig* has a more indefinite range from about 20 to not much over 25.

26. *Dah-feng dah-yeu* 'great wind and great rain' is a noun predicate in absolute position, that is, without a subject or verb. *Bae jey-wey* . . . starts a new sentence.

27. *Poh* 'broken'; 'worn.' *Kuay* 'fast'; 'on the point of.'

28. *Ta* 'to collapse,' unrelated homonym of *ta* 'he, etc.'

29. *I-ban* 'a class, a group.'

30. *Shiah* 'scare, startle,' unrelated homonym of *shiah* 'down.'

31. *Laanlhalde* reduplicated form of *laan* 'lazy.'

32. *Tian lianq* 'the sky brightens, — the day breaks, it's light.'

33. The particle *.ou* indicates a lively, but mild, warning or urging, 'mind you!' A preceding *.ba* plus *.ou* becomes *.b'ou* and *.le* plus *.ou* becomes *.l'ou*.

34. *Shian tzoou*, lit. 'go first.'

35. *Dao* 'topple over.'

36. *Lih.hay* 'fierce(ly).'

37. *Hao₀tzay* 'the good (thing) lies in, — fortunately.'

38. *Der* 'done, ready.' *Derle ba* 'consider that done, — let's call it a day, — I am going to change my mind.'

39. *Koou* 'mouth, opening'; *kooul* 'opening.'

40. *Hao-jia.huoo* 'good utensil, — goodness, gracious!' (See also p. 50.)

41. An adjective usually comes between an AN and the noun. When it is placed before an AN, there is a more lively meaning to it: *i-suoo dah farngtz* 'a large house'; *i-dah-suoo farngtz* 'a great, big house.'

42. *Jeeng* 'whole, integral.' *Jeenggehlde* 'the whole thing.'

43. The complement –₀*jaur* indicates the effect of 'getting at, touching, realized,' as *shuey-jaurle* 'sleep, so as actually to fall asleep,' *yah₀jaurle* 'crush so as actually to crush.'

44. *Geei* 'for the benefit of, for its benefit (or harm).' *Lah* 'to leave behind (through forgetfulness).'

45. Although any verb in Chinese may be taken in a passive sense, without any formal marker, the passive meaning can be made more explicit by mentioning the agent with *bey* or *bey . . . geei*, as *Yii.ba bey juhtz yahle* or *Yii.ba bey juhtz geei yahle* 'The tail was crushed by the pillar.'

An agent may also be introduced by *geei* or *geei . . . geei*, which however is ambiguous, since *geei* can also be used like *bae*. Thus, while *Yii.ba geei juhtz (geei) yahle* obviously means 'The tail was crushed by the pillar,' *Jang San geei Lii Syh daale* may mean either *Jang San bae Lii Syh daale* ('beat') or *Jang San bey Lii Syh daale* ('beaten').

46. *Tsyy*, literary word for *jeyg*. *Tsorng tsyy yiihow* 'from this afterwards, — from that time on.'

47. *Shianq* 'like,' *shianq yiichyan* 'like before.'

48. Uses of .le. — In this lesson, the progress of the story is often expressed by *.le* as a final particle. In general, *.le* expresses completed action or a new situation, the two often forming two sides of the same thing. For example, *yii.ba duann le* 'the tail is broken,' implies the completion of the breaking, resulting in a tailless rat. The uses of *.le* met with so far are summarized below:

(1) New situation:

Tzau le, shiah-yeu le!   'Too bad, it's raining!'
Derle, woo yee tzoou le.   'Call it a day, I am going, too.'

(2) Command in response to a new situation:
Shiing le, hei!   'Wake up, hey!'
Buneng tzay chyr le!   'Don't delay any more!'

(3) Completed action, especially in narration:
Tamen dou shiah-shiingle.   'They were all startled out of their sleep.'
Nah farngtz jiow ta le.   'Then the house collapsed.'

(4) Completed action with quantified object, as an isolated past event (Note 3, p. 160).
Ta biann-cherngle i-jy wuwoei-shuu.   'He became a tailless rat.'
Woo tzuohle i-jiann huay-shyh.   'I did something bad.'

(5) The same as a new situation:
Ta biann-cherngle i-jy wuwoei-shuu le.   '(And so, to go on with the story) he became, etc.'
Woo tzuohle i-jiann huay-shyh le.   'I have done something bad.'

(6) New situation in a consequent clause:
Nah woo jiow bu tzoou le.   'In that case I won't go any more.'
I-kannjiann ren genq buyong shuo le.   'As soon as he sees someone, I don't have to tell you (what happens) then.'

(7) Completed action in dependent clauses:
Shuole i-jiuh yowsh i-jiuh.   'After saying one sentence, he says another.'
Yawsh shi-tian chule tayyang, ...   'If the sun rises in the west, ...'

LESSON 11
WATCHING THE YEAR OUT

A: So cold in the room! I am getting colder and colder sitting here. It's miserably cold! Brr, how does it get so cold tonight? This stove hasn't got a particle of warmth in it, I bet it's getting out of coal.

B: Ah, how nice and warm! After all it's warmer inside the house, so warm it just makes you feel good! Yup, after all it's more comfortable here.

A: You call that comfortable! I am almost frozen to death sitting here. Gee! Is it snowing out?

B: And how! Just look at this all over me, my black hat has become a white hat and my black overcoat has become a white overcoat. There hasn't been such a heavy snow yet this year, has there?

(8) Obviousness:
Tzay hao meiyeou le (or *lo*).   'Nothing can be better than that.'
Jeyg nii dangran doong le (or *lo*).   'You understand this, of course.'
(9) Special idioms:
Duey le, hao-jyile.   'That's right, that's fine.'

Note that the negative form for completed action is *mei* or *meiyeou*, as *Farngtz mei ta* 'The house has not collapsed, *or* did not collapse.' The form *bu . . . le* usually indicates a new situation 'not . . . any longer.' (See also p. 58.)

EXERCISES

1. *Example:*

Given: Answer:

Woo chy-wanle fann le.   *A:* Neme *ta* chy-wanle meiyeou ne?
                           B: Meiyeou, ta mei chy-wan.

(a) Jeyg hawtz de *yiiba* yah-duannle. (b) *Dih'ig* ianchiual chueisannle. (c) Ta tzuoh de neyg *feiji* diaw de haelii le. (d) Woo bae '*dah*'-tzyh shiee-dueyle. (e) Lao *Jang* bae Ing'wen shyue-cherngle. (f) *Tzwol* woo chuchiuh le. (g) Tarn Shg. jiel *tzaochin* choule ellshyr-gen ian. (h) *Niide* shyhchyng woo gawsonqle ta le.

2. *Write down from listening to the teacher reading from the* Character Text *(p. 107) the same story in paraphrased form.* (The teacher may read very slowly, but should not stop for the student to catch up, but repeat the story as a whole several times for him to fill in the parts missed.)

3. *Translate the dictated text into idiomatic English.*

DIHSHYRI KEH
SHOOU [1] SUEY

A: Utzlii jen leeng! Woo yueh tzuoh yueh leeng. Leeng de jen nanshow! Ss [2] — jiel woanshanq tzeem tzemm leeng a? Jeh lutz ideal rehchiell [3] dou meiyeou me! Goanbao [4] sh meiyeou mei le ba?

B: Ha, jen noan.hwo! Dawdii sh farngtz liitou noan.hwo, noan.hwo de jen haoshow. Er, hairsh jell shu.fwu.

A: Hair shu.fwu ne! [5] Woo tzuoh de jell dou kuay [6] donq.syy le. He! waytou shiah-sheue l'a?

B: Kee bush ma? Nii chyau woo i-shen [7] de! Hei-mawtz biannle bair-mawtz, hei-dahchaang biannle bair-dahchaang le. Jin.nian hair mei shiah.guoh tzemm dah de sheue ne ba?

A: This year? Have you forgotten that big snow in March this year?

B: Mar — oh, I forgot *that* time, I meant *this* winter.

A: My, how fast the days go by! Before you know it, somehow another year has passed. The children have grown another year older, and the grownups have aged another year, too.

B: Sure! And this year is the —

A: The 37th year of the Republic, isn't it? It's the same as nineteen hundred forty-eight by the Western calendar. Last year was 1947, year before last was 1946. From tomorrow on it will be the year 1949. Year after next is 1950.

B: What day's today?

A: Huh?

B: What is the date today?

A: Oh, what day's today? Today is December 31st. Yesterday was the 30th, day before yesterday the 29th, the day before the day before yesterday the 28th. Tomorrow is the first of the next month, namely January first of next year; day after tomorrow is January 2nd, the day after the day after tomorrow is January 3rd.

B: Do you have a holiday?

A: We have only one holiday. Except for tomorrow, New Year's Day, we have no other holidays. Tomorrow being the anniversary of the inauguration of the Chinese Republic, it will be a holiday for the whole country.

B: What day of the week is today?

A: Today is Friday.

B: What date is next (week's) Saturday?

A: Uh — I can't tell for the moment. Why?

B: Oh, because I have some business a week from Saturday and shall have to go away. I wonder what day of January it will be?

A: Let me have a look at the calendar. Let me see, today's Friday, this Saturday is the first — one plus seven is eight — a week from Saturday will be the eighth.

B: What day was last Wednesday?

A: Last Wednesday? Let me think, this Wednesday was the 29th, last (week's) Wednesday was the 22nd — well, December 22nd, why that was the winter solstice!

B: Winter solstice?

A: That's right, the winter solstice always falls on December 22nd or thereabouts, and it's the day in the year with the shortest day and the longest night. The opposite of the winter solstice is the summer solstice, which always comes around June 22nd, and that day has the longest day and the shortest night in the year. Between the two solstices, there are also the vernal equinox and the autumnal equinox, thus forming the four seasons, spring, summer, autumn, and winter.

WATCHING THE YEAR OUT

A: Jin.nian? Jin.nian San.yueh.lii [8] ney-chaang dah-sheue nii wanqle ma?

B: San — oh, woo dou wanqle ney-hwei le, woode yihsy sh shuo **jey-hwei** Dong.tian.

A: .Ai,[9] ryhtz guoh de jen kuay, bu-jy-bu-jyue [10] de tzeem yow guohle i-nian le? Hairtzmen [11] dou jaang-dahle [12] i-suey, dahrenmen yee dou laole [13] i-nian le.

B: Sh a! Jin.nian sh Mingwo [14] —

A: Mingwo sanshyr-chi nian, bush ma? Jiowsh Gonglih [15] ichian jeou-bae [16] syhshyr-ba nian. Chiuh.nian [17] sh i-jeou-syh-chi, chyan.nian i-jeou-syh-liow. Jiee [18] ming.tian chii-tourl jiowsh i-jeou-syh-jeou-nian le. How-.nian sh i-jeou-wuu-ling.

B: Jiel jieel?

A: Ar?

B: Jin.tian sherm ryhtz?

A: Oh, jiel jieel a? [19] Jiel Shyr'ell.yueh sanshyri-haw. Tzwo.tian sanshyr, chyan.tian ellshyr-jeou, dah-chyan.tian ellshyr-ba. Ming.tian sh shiahg yueh [20] de i-haw,[21] jiowsh ming.nian de Jeng.yueh chu'i,[22] how.tian sh Jeng.yueh chu'ell, dah-how.tian sh Jeng.yueh chu-san.

B: Niim fanq-jiah [23] bu fanq?

A: Woomen jyy fanq i-tian jiah. Chwule [24] miengl Nian-chu'i fanq-jiah yiiway, woomen sherm jiah yee bu fanq. Miengl inwey sh Jonghwa [25] Mingwo Chernglih [26] jihniann-ryh, suooyii chyuan-gwo dou fanq-jiah.

B: Jintian Shingchi-jii [27] a?

A: Jintian sh Shingchi-wuu.

B: Shiah Shingchi-liow [28] sh sherm ryhtz?

A: .E — woo ishyr shuo.bu-shanqlai le. Nii gannma wenn?

B: Oh, woo sh inwey shiahg Shingchi-liow yeou-shyh, deei shanq bye.chull [29] .chiuh. Bujydaw sh Iyueh jii-haw?

A: Ranq woo kannx yueh.fenn-parl [30] .kann. Deeng woo sheang a, jiel Shingchi-wuu, jeyg Shingchi-liow sh i-haw — i jia chi sh ba — shiah Shingchi-liow [31] sh ba-haw.

B: Shanq Shingchi-san sh jii-haw?

A: Shanq Shingchi-san a? Deeng woo sheang a, jeyg Shingchi-san sh ellshyr-jeou, shanq Shingchi-san sh ellshyr'ell — è, Shyr'ell.yueh ellshyr-ell, gaan.chyng [32] jiowsh Dongjyh [33] .ou!

B: Dongjyh?

A: Duey le, Dongjyh laosh tzay Shyr'ell.yueh ellshyr'ell tzuooyow, sh i-nian liitou bair.tian tzuey doan yeh.lii tzuey charng [34] de ryhtz. Dongjyh de dueymiall sh Shiahjyh, tzoongsh tzay Liow.yueh ellshyr'ell tzuooyow, nahsh i-nian liitou tial tzuey charng yeh tzuey doan de ryhtz. Leang-jyh [35] de dangjiall ne, hair yeou Chuenfen Chioufen,[36] tzemmyanql jiow cherngle Chuen Shiah Chiou Dong [37] syh-jih le.

B: I seem to remember that as soon as the New Year holidays are over it is spring, isn't it?

A: Well, you must be thinking about the lunar calendar used in the old days. For New Year's in the old calendar comes about a month or a month and a half later than in the solar calendar, and so it is spring as soon as the New Year holidays are over.

B: Oh yes, that's right.

A: But since the revolution of the year Shinhay, we have abolished the lunar calendar and we have used the solar calendar as the national calendar. The year Shinhay was the year nineteen hundred eleven in Western chronology, the next year was 1912, which was the first year of the Chinese Republic, and by now it has been fully thirty-seven years.

B: Still a few moments to go.

A: That's right, still a few minutes to go. My goodness, it's already quarter to twelve, another quarter hour and it will be twelve midnight.

B: Your watch must be slow; according to my clock, it is now already eleven fifty-nine, forty-odd seconds, you see.

A: Yes, it's now fifty seconds, 51, 52, 53, 54, 55, 56, 57, 58, 59, —

Everybody: Twelve o'clock! Now it is 1949! This year is the thirty-eighth year of the Chinese Republic. Long live the Republic of China! Long live the United Nations!

NOTES

1. *Shoou* 'to watch, to guard'; 'to defend.' *Suey* measure word for 'years old'; 'year' in special compounds such as *shoou-suey* 'watch the year out.' The usual measure word for 'year' is *nian*.

2. *Ss*, pronounced with air sucked in between the teeth, is an interjection meaning 'Brr!' It is longer than the *ss* for hesitation (Note 6, p. 190).

3. *Reh-chih* 'hot air'; *rehchiell* 'warmth.'

4. ₀*Goan*₀*bao* 'to guarantee,' used here in the sense of 'I am sure, I bet.'

5. *Hair shu.fwu ne*, lit. 'Still (speaking of) comfortable? — you call that comfortable?' This form has about the same force as *Sherm 'shu.fwu'?* 'What do you mean, "comfortable"?'

6. *Kuay* 'fast (becoming), soon.'

7. *I-shen* 'whole bodyful, — all over oneself.'

8. The months in the year are named by number and –.*yueh* 'moon,' except that in the lunar calendar the first month is called *Jeng.yueh* (*jenq* 'right,' with modified tone, and –.*yueh*). By extension, *Jeng.yueh* is also sometimes applied to 'January.' The full word for 'moon' is *yueh.lianq*.

WATCHING THE YEAR OUT 199

B: Woo jihj haoshianq i-guohle nian jiowsh Chuen.tian le me?

A: Ah, nii idinq sh sheangj tsorngchyan yonq de inlih [38] le. Inwey inlih de Shinnian bii yanglih [39] lai de chyr, tzoong chyr ig yueh heje ig-bann yueh tzuooyow, suooyii i-guohle nian jiowsh Chuen.tian le.

B: Oh, butsuoh.

A: Keesh tzyhtsorng Shinhay [40] Germinq yiihow, jiow bae inlih geei feychwu le, jiow na yanglih danqtzuoh [41] gwolih yonq le. Shinhay nian sh Shilih [42] ichian jeoubae ishyr-i [43] nian, dih'ell nian i-jeou-i-ell, jiowsh Jonghwa Mingwo yuan-nian,[44] daw shianntzay tzwux sanshyr-chi nian le.

B: Hair chah ideal ba?

A: Butsuoh, hair chah jii-fen jong.[45] Aiia, shianntzay yiijing sh shyri-dean san-keh [46] le, hair yeou i-keh jong jiowsh bannyeh shyr'ell-dean l'a.

B: Niide beau mann l'ou; jaw woode jong kann.chiilai shianntzay yiijing yeou [47] shyri-dean wuushyr-jeou fen syhshyr-jii meau le, nii kann!

A: Èh, jehhoel wuushyr meau, wuushyri, wuushyr'ell, wuushyrsan, wuushyrsyh, wuushyrwuu, wuushyrliow, wuushyrchi, wuushyrba, wuushyrjeou, —

Chyuantii: [48] Shyr'ell-dean! Shianntzay sh i-jeou-syh-jeou l'a! Jin.nian sh Jonghwa Mingwo sanshyrba nian l'a! Jonghwa Mingwo wannsuey! [49] Lianher Gwo wannsuey!

The AN for *yeu* 'rain,' and 'sheue' is *-chaang*. The more general AN *-hwei* 'time' for events is also applicable, as in the next sentence.

9. *.Ai* is the sound of sighing, often with a voiced *h*-sound.

10. *Bu-jy-bu-jyue de* 'not knowing, not noticing, — unconsciously, without realizing it.'

11. *Hairtz* 'child, children,' term implying a little more personal interest in them than the colorless word *sheauharl* or *sheauhairtz*.

12. *Jaang-dahle* 'grown big, grown up.' In comparing ages, especially of children, *dah* is used for 'older,' as *Gege bii dihdih dah* 'The elder brother is older than the younger brother.'

13. An adjective with *.le* expresses change, as *ta lao le* 'he has aged'; *ta binq le* 'he is sick (has fallen ill)'; *ta hao le* 'he is well (again).'

14. *Mingwo* (with full tone on *gwo*) 'People's country, — republic.'

15. *Gonglih* 'public calendar, — years A.D.'

16. Thousands are never reckoned in tens of hundreds in Chinese.

17. *Chiuh.nian* 'the gone year, — last year.'

18. *Jiee* 'from.'

19. Speaker *A* repeats *Jiel jieel* in order to show that he is not ignorant of this typical Peiping expression, which had to be repeated before he caught on.

20. *Shiahg* 'next' is a determinative plus an AN. While *nian* is a measure word, before which a determinative is directly joined, *yueh* is a noun and therefore requires an AN. Thus, *i-nian* 'a year,' but *ig yueh* 'a month.' *Shiah₀nian* 'next (fiscal, academic) year,' *ming.nian* 'next (calendar) year.' (See also Note 28.)

21. *I-haw* 'number one, the first of the month (solar calendar only).'

22. *Chu'i, chu'ell, . . . chushyr* used to be limited to the names of the first ten days of a lunar month, now also used synonymously with *i-haw, ell-haw*, etc. Since two-syllable numbers are free words, simple numbers without AN, *shyri, shyr'ell*, etc., are usually sufficient as names of days from the 11th on.

23. *Fanq-jiah* 'to let go (for a) leave, — to have a holiday.'

24. *Chwule* 'besides, except, outside of.' If the phrase following is long, *yiiway* or *jy way* 'outside of that' is used as a terminal marker: 'end of exception.'

25. *Jonghwa* 'Middle Flowery' B is a formal term for 'Chinese.'

26. *Chernglih* 'form-establish, — establish, inaugurate.'

27. *Shingchi* 'star period, — week,' so called from the position of the moon among the stars, which returns to the same position very nearly once every four weeks. Since *liibay* means literally 'ceremony-bow, — worship,' there is a slight tendency for Christians to use *liibay* and its derivatives and others to use *shingchi* and its derivatives, but both forms are used by both. The *liibay*-forms, moreover, are a little more colloquial.

28. Words for 'week' and days of the week are either measure words or nouns. Hence it is possible to say either *shiah Shingchi-liow* or *shiahg Shingchi-liow*.

29. *Bye.chull* 'other place,' usually referring to a different locality, 'out of town.'

30. *Parl* (< *pair-l*) 'board, playcard.' *Yueh.fenn-parl* 'month-parts-board, — the calendar.'

31. *Shiah Shingchi-liow* does not necessarily refer to the next Saturday that comes along, but to the Saturday of next week. The expression may be regarded as a telescoped form of *shiah-shingchi de Shingchi-liow* 'next week's Saturday.' Similarly, the student should be careful not to misunderstand the reference of *jeyg* 'this' and *shanqg* 'previous, last' as applied to days of the week. (A further complication comes from the fact that Sunday is often regarded as the last day of the elapsing week rather than the first day of the coming week.)

32. *Gaan.chyng* 'indeed, why!'

33. *Dongjyh* 'winter-extreme, — time of winter when the sun is at an extreme position in celestial latitude.' Although *jyh* in the literary idiom also means 'arrive,' *dongjyh* has nothing to do with the idea of 'winter's arrival.'

34. On the translation of S–P predicates like *bair.tian tzuey doan* into an adjective-noun form 'shortest day,' cf. the form 'he has a good heart' (Note 50, p. 186).

35. *Leang-jyh* is a compound used in such a context only.

36. *Chuenfen* 'spring-divide, — vernal equinox,' *chioufen* 'autumn-divide, — autumnal equinox.'

37. A string of parallel bound words are often spoken together as if it were one compound (cf. title of Lesson 5). The full syntactic words for the names of seasons are *chuen.tian, shiah.tian, chiou.tian, dong.tian.*

38. *In–* 'the female principle, *yin*, lunar,' *inlih* 'lunar calendar.'

39. *Yang–* 'the male principle, *yang*, solar,' *yanglih* 'solar calendar,' specifically, 'the Gregorian calendar.'

40. *Shinhay* '1911.' There are two series of cyclical words, like A, B, C, X, Y, Z, used for arbitrary counters and for reckoning years, days, etc. One series consists of ten *tiangan* 'heaven's stems':

Jea   Yii   Biing   Ding   Wuh   Jii   Geng   Shin   Ren   Goei

and the other, twelve *dihjy* 'earth's branches':

Tzyy   Choou   Yn   Mao   Chern   Syh   Wuu   Wey   Shen   Yeou   Shiu   Hay.

The present cycle began with *Jeatzyy* for 1924, *Yiichoou* 1925, *Biing'yn* 1926, etc. Since there are ten *tiangan*, there is a constant correspondence between them and the last figure in the year number by Western chronology, thus:

Jea   Yii   Biing   Ding   Wuh   Jii   Geng   Shin   Ren   Goei.
'4   '5   '6   '7   '8   '9   '0   '1   '2   '3

41. *Na . . . danq* or *na . . . danq₀tzuoh* 'take . . . as.'

42. *Shilih* 'Occidental chronology.'

43. While numbers between 11 and 19 are called *shyri, shyr'ell*, etc., an optional *i–* may be placed before *shyri*, etc. in numbers involving hundreds, thousands, etc.

44. *Yuan–* 'primary, original,' used in naming the first year of an era. *Yuan-nian* 'the year 1.'

45. *Jii-fen jong* 'several divisions of clock, — several minutes.'

46. *Keh* 'quarter-hour.' Fractions of an hour, either in minutes or in quarters are named from the preceding hour, as *san-dean wuushyrsyh-fen* '3:54.'

47. *Yeou* 'have' is used instead of *sh* before quantity words in the sense of 'as much as, as late as,' etc.

48. *Chyuantii* 'whole body (of people present), — everybody.'

49. *Wannsuey* 'ten thousand years, — long live . . .!' *Wann* is the largest common unit of number used as a measure word. Numbers of

higher places are spoken of as so many *wann*, so many *chian, bae, shyr*, and unities. The method of saying Chinese figures is to divide them into groups of four, instead of three. For example,

14,000	1,4000	*Iwann syhchian*
271,000	27,1000	*Ellshyrchi-wann ichian*
450,000,000	4,5000,0000	*Syhwann wuuchian wann*
		(or *syhwannx wuuchian wann*)
2,000,000,000	20,0000,0000	*Ellshyr wannx* (or *ellshyr yih*)

Zeroes between figures are read as *ling*, as *ibae ling i* '101.'

CHRONOLOGICAL TABLE FOR LESSON 11

Syh-nian (yii)chyan:	Mingwo 33 nian = 1944
Dah-chyannian:	Mingwo 34 nian = 1945
Chyannian:	Mingwo 35 nian = 1946
Chiuhnian:	Mingwo 36 nian = 1947

JINNIAN   MINGWO 37 NIAN = 1948

San'g yueh (yii)chyan	= Jeouyueh
Leangg yueh (yii)chyan	= Shyryueh
Shanqg yueh	= Shyriyueh

JEYG YUEH   = SHYR'ELLYUEH

	Liibayryh	L'i	L'ell	L'san	L'syh	L'wuu	L'liow
Shanq(g) Liibay	19-haw	20	21	22	23	24	25
JEYG LIIBAY	26	27 Syh-tian (yii)chyan	28 Dahchyal	29 Chyal	30 Tzwol	31 JIEL	

Mingnian: Mingwo 38 nian = 1949

Shiahg yueh   = Jengyueh

(Hairsh JEYG LIIBAY)   1
                                                       Miengl

| Shiah(g) Liibay | 2 Howl | 3 Dahhowl | 4 Tzay guoh syh-tian | 5 | 6 | 7 | 8 |

(Tzay guoh leangg yueh) = Ellyueh

Hownian:	Mingwo 39 nian = 1950
Dah-hownian:	Mingwo 40 nian = 1951
Tzay guoh syh-nian⎫ : Syh-nian (yii)how ⎭	Mingwo 41 nian = 1952

EXERCISES

1. *Example:*

Given:

Woo tzoou-ley le;

woo shuo.bu-chu huah .lai le.

Answer:

Woo tzoou de jen ley, ley-jyile, woo ley de buderleau;

woo ley de jeanjyr huah dou shuo.bu-chulai le.

(a) Yeu shiah-dah le; ting.bu-jiann shuo-huah de sheng'in le. (b) Utz.lii leeng le; woo shuey.bu-jaur le. (c) Jeyg tial charng le; woan-shanq ba-dean jong hair lianq. (d) Ta deeng-eh le; ta kannjiann byeren de fann jiow sheang chy. (e) Jeyg tzyh shiee-sheau le; jeyg tzyh dou kann.bu-chingchuu le. (f) Ryhtz guoh de kuay; ryhtz shianq fei shyhde le. (g) Ta shuo-huah shuo de duo; ta lian chy-fann de gongful dou mei-yeou le. (h) Woo tzuoh-menq tzuoh de haowal; woo dou buyuannyih shiing le.

2. *Complete the following:*

(a) Jin.nian sh wuhtzyy nian, jiowsh Shilih ichian jeoubae syhshyrba nian. Chiuh.nian sh ____ (fill in the cyclical words from Note 40), jiowsh Shilih ____ (write out in words), chyan.nian sh ____, jiowsh ____, dah-chyan.nian sh ____, jiowsh ____. Ming.nian sh ____, jiowsh ____, how.nian sh ____, jiowsh ____, dah-how.nian sh ____, jiowsh ____. (b) Jintian i-haw, tzwotian ____, chyantian sh ____ g yueh de ____, dah-chyantian ____. Mingtian ____, howtian ____, ____ tian ____. (c) Jeyg yueh de ellshyrsan-haw sh shanq-liibay de Liibaysyh. Jeyg yueh ellshyrsyh-haw sh shanq ____. Jeyg yueh de ellshyrwuu-haw sh ____ liibay de Liibay ____. (*Continue through each day until:*) Shiahg yueh de ba-haw sh shiah-liibay de Liibayliow. *Use the chronological table.*

3. *Translate into Chinese:*

(a) Vernal and autumnal equinoxes are the two days of the year in which day and night are equally (*iyanq*) long. (b) I don't think so, I think it is only a few days before vernal equinox and a few days after autumnal equinox that the day is just as long as the night. (c) Ever since the 1911 Revolution, China has become a republic. (d) From last Monday, which was day before yesterday, to next Thursday is (*yeou*) fully a week and a half. (e) Gosh, I've forgotten what day of the week it is today. (f) I seem to remember that my car stopped as soon as I heard the train coming. (g) Although it is snowing so heavily outside, (yet) it is not cold at all. (h) Too bad, the watch I bought last month loses (*mann*) ten minutes a day.

LESSON 12
A RESCUE AT SEA

A: Hey! Come here and look, an airplane is falling down! There is an airplane accident!

B: Where?

A: There, over there, see it? The plane is falling. The motor has caught fire, look, it's emitting a lot of smoke. Gee, so quick, the fuselage starts to burn, too! Gosh, both the wings and the tail have started to burn. Gee, it's fallen into the sea, it's sinking little by little. I wonder if the people (*or* person) in the plane have (*or* has) escaped.

B: How could they (*or* he)? In such a short time?

A: Say! look, look, what's that over there floating in the air?

B: Where? I can't see it! Is it to the east or to the south?

A: I can't distinguish east, south, west, and north at all any more. Isn't our ship now (sailing) toward — ah, I see it now. It's over there, on the south side, where the sun is. Look, look, just above and to the right of that cloud.

B: I can't find it.

A: Well! It has suddenly disappeared again. Wonder where it has gone to.

B: What sort of thing was it that you saw, anyway? What shape was it? Was it square or round? How big was it? What color was it?

A: Because it was too far from here, so I couldn't distinguish whether it was red, green, yellow, green-blue, blue, or purple, or what. If it had been nearer, perhaps I could have — there, there, there, it's there again! Oh, so it was covered by a black cloud a while ago. Now it has reached the left side of the cloud, it's nearer now than at first, much nearer now.

B: Ah, I see it, too. Isn't that a parachute? Isn't that a man suspended from the parachute? That must be the pilot who flew that plane in the accident, I guess.

A: I bet it is — unless there was more than one person in the plane. Well, fortunately he escaped in time, otherwise I am afraid he would either be burned to death or get drowned.

B: Say, we had better go and rescue him at once, hadn't we? Otherwise he could still be drowned, you see.

A: Yeah, there's something in that. Hurry up and start the motorboat and go rescue him . . . Go this way! — Look out! Take it easy! Take it easy! Bear to the portside of the big ship! Don't bump against the rudder, mind you! Hey, look out for the screw!

DIH SHYR'ELL KEH
HAESHANQ JIOW-REN

A: Uai! Niimen kuaydeal lai kann, yeou [1] jiah feiji diaw.shiahlai le! Feiji chu-shyh [2] le!

B: Naal ne?

A: Neybial vx! Kannjiannle ma? Feiji diaw.shiahlai le. Fadonqji [3] jaur-huoo le, nii chyau, ta jinq maw-ial.[4] Aiia, jen kuay, feiji de shentz yee jaur-huoo le! Tzaugau, lian [5] chyhbaangl day woeiba dou shau-jaur [6] le. Ai — ia! diaw de *hae*.liitou le, ideal ideal de chern.shiahchiuh le. Feiji.lii de ren bujydaw taur.chulaile meiyeou?

B: Tzeem laidejyi [7] a, nemm ihoel gongful?

A: Ê! nii chyau vx, neybial yeou g sherm dongshi tzay bannkong jong piauj ne?

B: Neeibial a? Woo kann.bu-jiann me, tzay dongbial hairsh tzay nanbial a?

A: Woo yee fen.bu-chu [8] dong nan shi beei [9] .lai le. Tzarmen jehhoel chwan bush chonqj — ah, woo kann.chulai le. Tzay neybial, tzay nanbial, tzay tay.yang .ney.bial.[10] Chyau, nii chyau, gangx tzay ney-kuay yun.tsae de shanqtou yowbial.

B: Woo jao.bu-jaur [11] a.

A: Yee? [12] Huran yow meiyeou le. Bujydaw yow pao de naal chiuh le.

B: Nii kannjiann de dawdii sh tzeemyanql de ig [13] dongshi .lai.je? [14] Sh sherm yanqtz de? Sh fang de sh yuan de? Yeou dwo dah? Sh sherm yan.seh de?

A: I'wey [15] nah dongshi li [16] jell tay yeuan le, suooyii woo yee fen.bu-chu sh horng liuh hwang [17] ching [18] lan tzyy, hairsh sherm yan.shae [19] .lai le. Yawsh li jell jinn.deal me, yee sheu keeyii [20] — è, è, è, yow tzay.nall le! Oh, gangtsair gaan.chyng sh geei ney-kuay hei-yun geei daang.juh le. Shianntzay dawle ney-kuay yun.tsae de tzuoobial le, shianntzay bii chiitourl jinn.deal le, jinn de duo le.

B: A, woo yee kannjiann le. Nah bush g jianqluoh-saan [21] ma? Saan diishiah guahj de bush g ren ma? Nah idinq sh neyg [22] kai ney-jiah chule shyh de feiji de neyg jiahshyy-yuan le, .woo .tsai .sh.

A: .Goan.bao sh de ba? — chwufei [23] feiji.lii beenlai bujyy ig ren. Ah, shinq.kuei ta chenntzao [24] taurle.chulai, yawburan koongpah bush shau.syy yee deei ian.syy le.

B: Êh, tzarmen deei maashanq jiow chiuh jiow ta tsair shyng [25] n'è! Yawburan ta hairsh huey ian.syy d'è!

A: Èè, nii shuo de yeou dawlii.[26] Tzarmen kuay bae sheau chihchwal [27] kaile chiuh jiow ta chiuh. . . . Daa jeybial tzoou — Sheaushin! [28] Manndeal! Mannjdeal! Kawj dah-chwan de tzuoobial tzoou! Bye penq de duoh.shanq .chiuh, ah! Uai, sheaushin nah luoshyuan-jeang! [29]

B: What do you mean, 'screw'?

A: I mean that propeller that turns round and round.

B: Oh, that thing.

A: She's drawing deep, you can't see it now, but we'll have to go around a little to make sure not to collide. Not so fast! Okay, now you can open the throttle full.

B: What a nuisance, I've lost him again. Oh, he's already hit the water, right there.

A: Yeah, I see him too. Hey, there, you are all right! Don't worry, don't you worry, see! We'll be right over, we're coming right away! Oh bother, this stupid engine has to choose this of all times to get funny with you!

B: What's the matter?

A: What's the matter now?! I told you to put in some gas yesterday and you insisted on 'Wait a while, wait a while.' All right, now you can wait! Never mind now, take out the oars and row! Hurry up and row, row faster! Harder, row harder! That man is still afloat. Throw him the life-belt! No, that's no good, you threw it too far from him. Better throw him that rope from the bow. Did you make it? Good, hold on to it! Don't let go your hand, see! Let us pull you up this boat. Hey, this won't do! The boat is too light — say, don't you bother about that life-belt on the water, see — you put your weight on the other side. Don't move, don't you move! Let me pull him up from this side. — Oof! — all right now! Hurry up and row back to the ship and everything will be all right. (*Sound of whistle.*)

B: Listen, they must have seen us.

NOTES

1. **Definite and Indefinite Reference.** — There is a strong tendency to put nouns with an indefinite reference in the object position and nouns with a definite reference in the subject position or after a pretransitive. Thus, *Woo yeou i-jiah feiji* 'I have an airplane'; but *Feiji diaw.shiahlai le* 'The airplane is falling down.' For 'An airplane is falling down,' it is possible to say *I-jiah feiji diaw.shiahlai le*, but the preferred form is as given in the text here. Similarly, *Nii deei he-wanle shoei tzay tzoou* 'You must finish drinking some water (any water) before you go,' but, *Nii deei bae shoei he-wanle tzay tzoou* 'You must finish drinking the water (that you meant to drink, served on the table, etc.) before you go.'

2. *Chu-shyh* 'there comes out an event, — there is an accident,' an impersonal verb-object sentence.

3. *Fadongji* 'issue-motion-mechanism, — motor.' *Jaur-huoo* 'touch fire, — catch fire.'

B: Sherm 'luoshyuan-jeang'?
A: Jiowsh neyg huey juann [30] de neyg tueijinn-chih.
B: Oh, oh, neyg dongshi a.
A: Shianntzay chy-shoei [31] shen, kann.bu-jiann, keesh tzarmen deei rawyeuan [32] ideal tsair kawdejuh [33] bu penq ne. Mannmhalde! Hao! Shianntzay keeyii kai-tzwule maalih [34] le!
B: Jen taoyann! [35] Woo yow jao.bu-jaur ta le. Oh, yiijinq diaw.shiah-lai le. Tzay nall ne.
A: Ê, woo yee kannjiann le. Uai! nii fanq-shin! [36] bye jau-jyi, hei! Woomen jeh jiow lai! Maashanq jiow lai le! Dao-mei, [37] jeh huenn.janq [38] de ji.chih, pianpial [39] tiau tzemm g shyrhowl lai gen nii dao-luann.[40]
B: Tzeem l'a?
A: Hair 'tzeem le' ne? Woo tzwol jiaw nii shanq chihyou,[41] nii feideei yaw 'Deeng.hoel, vx.' Hao ba, shianntzay nii deeng ba! Berng [42] goan le, na jeang chulai l'a! Kuaydeal hwa, hwa kuaydeal! [43] Shyy-jinn,[44] shyy-jinn hwa! Neyg ren hair tzaynall piauj ne, nii bae jiowsheng-chiuan [45] rheng .geei ta! Bushyng, vx, nii rheng de li ta tay yeuan le. Bae chwan-tourl.shanq ney-tyau sherngtz rheng .geei ta ba. Nii rheng-dawle ma? Hao, lha.juh! Bye sa-shoou, ah! Deeng woom bae nii lha-shanq chwan.lai. Êh, bucherng [46] vx! Jeh sheauchwal tay ching — hai,[47] nii bye goan shoei.shanq de jiowsheng-chiuan le, hei — nii na shentz yahj neybial .i.deal. Bye donq, nii bye donq! Ranq woo jiee jeybial bae ta lha.shanqlai. — Ei! [48] — haol'a! Kuaydeal hwa-hwei dah-chwan .chiuh jiow hao le. (Du! Du!)
B: Nii ting, tamen idinq sh kannjiannle tzarmen le.

---

4. *Maw* 'send out, issue' is limited to a few words like *ial* 'smoke,' *shoei* 'water,' *pawl* 'bubbles.'

5. *Lian A day B* 'include A bring along B, — both A and B.'

6. *Shau-jaur* 'burn-touch, — burn to ignition, — kindle.'

7. *Laidejyi* 'have time (for),' *laibujyi* 'have no time for.'

8. The verb is *fen.chu.lai*, with *dong nan shi beei* as object.

9. There are three ways of naming the cardinal directions: *dong nan shi beei;* next in frequency, *dong shi nan beei;* and least often, *nan beei dong shi.* (Note 37, p. 201.)

Note the difference in word order between English and Chinese in the compounds for the intermediate directions:

Dongnan	*Dongbeei*	*Shinan*	*Shibeei*
'SE'	'NE'	'SW'	'NW'

10. The meaning of *tayyang neybial* depends upon the stress. When pronounced *tay.yang .ney.bial*, as it is here, it means 'the side where the

sun is.' If pronounced *tay.yang ney.bial*, with full tone on *ney-*, it would mean 'on that (yonder) side of the sun, — beyond the sun.'

11. *Jao* 'look for,' *jao₀jaur* 'find.' Cf. *kann* 'look at,' *kann.jiann* 'see.'

12. *Yee?* sound of surprise.

13. Compare *tzeemyanql de ig* and *tzemmyanql de ig* with the English word order in 'such a.'

14. The double particle *.lai.je*, usually applied to events of recent past, gives a slightly lively effect.

15. *Inwey* is often slurred into *i'wey* or even into a nasalized *.iuⁿ* [ỹ].

16. Distance 'from' is rendered by *li* 'leave' or *li.kai*. *Jell li nall yeou san-chyy* 'it is three feet from here to there.'

17. There being no color word for 'brown,' the word *hwang* 'yellow' often takes the place of 'brown,' as *hwang-mawtz* 'brown hat,' *hwang-shye* 'tan shoes.' The phrase *tzongseh de* 'palm-colored' is used only when one wishes to be very specific.

18. The color word *ching* has a very wide use. Its hue includes some greens and some blues and its value is light. The use of the word is to be learned in connection with the words it goes with, as *ching-tian* 'blue sky,' *ching-tsao* 'green grass.'

19. *Yan.shae* is an alternate form of *yan.seh*.

20. In Chinese there is no difference in form between an ordinary supposition and a supposition contrary to fact.

21. *Jianqluoh-saan* 'descend-fall-umbrella, — parachute.' While the AN for *saan* is *–baa* 'handle,' that for *jianqluoh-saan* is the general AN *–g(eh)*, since a parachute has no handle.

22. The first *neyg* modifies *jiahshyy-yuan*, but is resumed after the long *de*-construction (which contains another *de*-construction in it). This repetition is very common in unpremeditated speech.

23. A dependent clause comes after the main clause only when it is added as an afterthought.

24. *Chenntzao* 'taking the opportunity of earliness, — in good time.'

25. *Tsair shyng* 'only then will it do.'

26. *Yeou dawlii* 'there is something in what you say.' Cf. Fr. *avoir raison*.

27. *Chihchwal* 'gas-boat, — motorboat.'

28. *Sheau.shin* 'small-mind, — put one's mind on details, — be careful, look out.'

29. *Luoshyuan-jeang* 'screw-revolve-oar, — screw propeller' *luo.sy* 'screw.'

30. *Juann* is 'to turn around' or 'to revolve' and *joan* is 'to turn' to a different angular position. *Juann* also means '(to cause) to turn (through any angle).' *Tueijinn-chih* 'push-advance instrument, — propeller.'

31. *Chy-shoei* 'eat water, — to draw (of a ship).'

32. *Rawyeuan* 'go-around-far, — make a detour.'
33. *Kawdejuh* 'can lean so as to stay, — dependable(-ly).'
34. *Kai-tzwu maalih* 'open-full horsepower.'
35. *Taoyann* 'invite-loath, — to be a nuisance,' often used as an expletive of exasperation.
36. *Fanq-shin* 'let-mind (rest), — rest assured.'
37. *Dao-mei* 'to be out of luck,' a verb-object compound of obscure etymology; also used as an expletive.
38. *Huenn.janq* 'mixed-account,' term of abuse.
39. *Pian* 'one-sided,' *pianpial(de)* 'this of all things.'
40. *Dao-luann* 'stir-disturbance, — make trouble.'
41. *Shanq chihyou* 'put up gas-oil, — put in gasoline.' Cf. *shanq-keh* 'take up lessons.'
42. *Berng* is a phonetic fusion of *bu-yonq* 'don't need.' It means 'don't, because it is not necessary, — you don't have to.'
43. *Kuaydeal hwa* means either 'row faster' (with stress on *kuay*) or 'hurry up and row' (with stress on *hwa*), but *hwa kuaydeal* can only mean 'row faster.'
44. *Shyy-jinn* 'use strength, — hard.'
45. *Jiowsheng-chiuan* 'rescue-life-ring.'
46. *Cherng* 'formed, — okay' = *shyng*.
47. *Hai* as an interjection of disapproval has the regular tongue-back rough *h* of Mandarin.
48. *Ei*, sound of effort.
49. Exercise 1. In *mei . . . yiichyan* 'before . . . not' and *yiijinq . . . yiihow* 'after . . . already' the frequently used redundant *yiichyan* and *yiihow* serve as 'unquote' markers or markers of scope.

EXERCISES

1. *Example:*

Given:	Answer:
Feiji mei diaw.shiahlai de shyrhowl hair neng taur.chulai; feiji diaw.shiahlaile jiow taur.bu-chulai le.	Feiji mei diaw.shiahlai yiichyan,[49] hair laidejyi taur.chulai; feiji yiijinq diaw.shiahlaile yiihow kee jiow laibujyi taur.chulai le.

(a) Farngtz mei ta.shiahlai de shyrhowl hair pao.dechulai, farngtz tale.shiahlai jiow pao.bu-chulai le. (b) Jiahshyy-yuan mei ian.syy de shyrhowl, hair neng bae ta jiow-hwole ('revive'), yawsh ian.syyle jiow jiow.bu-hwo le. (c) Mei chu-shyh, tzao shanqle chihyou, hair neng gaan.de-shanq ('can catch') jiow-ren, chule shyh tzay chiuh shanq-you, nah jiow gaan.bu-shanq jiow-ren le. (d) Jey-tzoong huah ia, nii mei shuo-tsuoh de shyrhowl hair neng gae ('to correct'), shuo-tsuoh le jiow buneng gae le.

2. *Translate into Chinese:*

(a) Why, that thing floating on the water over there is the airplane which, we saw a while ago, was on fire. (b) Why, what I thought was a pilot suspended from a parachute was a black cloud under a white cloud. (c) At the vernal equinox, when the sun is due (*jenq*) east, it is exactly six o'clock in the morning. (d) I have looked for it for a long time but have not found it yet. (e) His eyes must have become blind, for he cannot tell the size or length of things far away from him. (f) The reason why I

LESSON 13
INQUIRING AFTER A SICK MAN

A: Hello, Shwuliang, you have come!

B: Well, well, Ell Ge, you here too!

Nurse: Say there, a little quieter, please!

A: That's right, we can't talk so loud here, otherwise we might wake the patients.

B: Is he better today? Is he still running a fever? Has he still got a fever?

A: He is much better today than yesterday. There is still some fever, it's true, but since this morning his temperature has gradually come down. I heard the nurse say that yesterday his highest temperature was as high as 41.3°, but today at 8:30 A.M., it had dropped to 38.5°.

B: I can never get used to the Centigrade thermometer. Is what you call 38.5° really to be regarded as high or not?

A: This slight fever is not considered serious in any way. You see, 37° Centigrade is equal to 98.6° Fahrenheit. Ordinarily, when there is no sickness, the body temperature is about around there. Now he has got 38.5°, that in Fahrenheit is — uh — 3 × 5 = 15, 3 × 9 = 27, 98 + 2 = 100, 7 + 6 = 13 — yes, it's 101.3° Fahrenheit.

B: One hundred and one point three, oh, that's not to be considered very high. Is his mind clear?

A: Yesterday, when his fever was at its height, his mind was a little clouded, and he kept talking delirious words, not even knowing where he was or recognizing people very well.

B: What did he say?

could not pull him up was that he was too heavy. (g) It won't do unless we go and wake him up at once, otherwise he might get crushed under the collapsing house. (h) Damn it, where have the oars gone to? (i) Beware the propellers! (j) I am afraid you have driven your motorboat too far from the ship; can you still throw him the rope on the starboard side of the boat? (k) Pshaw! I have lost sight of him again. (l) If you see a couple of oars floating on the water, don't pay any attention to them.

3. *Condense the story to about one-third of the original length from the point of view of the pilot, and prepare to tell the story in class as rewritten, or with variations.*

DIH SHYRSAN KEH TANN [1] BINQ

A: Ê, Shwuliang, nii lai le!

B: Ê, Ell Ge,[2] nii yee tzay jell!

Kanhuh:[3] Uai, dueybujuh, chiing niimen sheng'in sheau ideal!

A: Duey le, jell tzarm buneng tzemm dahshengl shuo-huah, hweitour[4] bae binq-ren[5] geei naw-shiing le.

B: Ta jintian haodeal le ma? Hair fa-shau[6] bu fa le? Hair yeou shau meiyeou?

A: Jintian bii tzwotian hao de duo le. Shau dawsh[7] hair yeou deal shau, keesh jintian tsorng tzaochin chii rehduh[8] jiow jiannjialde di.shiahlai le.[9] Woo ting neyg kanhuh shuo tzwotian tzuey gau gau daw[10] syhshyri-duh-san ne, jintian shanqwuu ba-shyr[11] sanshyr-fen de shyrhowl jianq daw sanshyr-ba-duh-bann le.

B: Woo tsornglai yee yonq.bu-guann[12] Shehshyh[13] de rehduhbeau de. Suoowey sanshyr-ba-duh-bann dawdii suann bu suann sh reh de ne?

A: Jey-deal shau bu suann tzeem lihhay de le. Nii sheang, Shehshyh de sanshyr-chi-duh sh deengyu Hwashyh[14] de jeoushyr-ba-duh-liow. Pyngcharng mei binq[15] de shyrhowl, shen.tii de uenduh[16] jiowsh chahbuduo tzemmyanql shanqshiah le. Shianntzay ta sh[17] sanshyr-ba-duh-wuu, sh Hwashyh — san[18] wuu i-shyr-wuu, san jeou ellshyr-chi, jeoushyr-ba jia ell sh ibae, chi liow shyrsan — èh, sh Hwashyh ibae-ling-i-duh yow shyr-fenn jy san.[19]

B: Ibae-ling-i-deal-san, ah, nah bu suann tzeem gau le. Ta ren[20] hair chingchuu ba?

A: Tzwotian fa-shau fa de lihhay de shyrhowl ren jiow yeoudeal hwu.twu,[21] jinq shuo hwu-huah,[22] lian tzyhgeel[23] ren tzay naal yee bujydaw, ren yee budah rennde.

B: Ta shuole shie sherm laije?

A: I don't know. It was they who told me. Later, when the fever had subsided a little, his mind was much clearer.

B: I see. What did the doctor say? Is it necessary to set the bone or operate or something?

A: He said according to his opinion it wasn't necessary to set any bones or do any other operation. The patient did have some burns and a good many external injuries. He said that he was at first afraid that his thighbone had been broken, but found out that it hadn't been. At the shoulder it was probably only the muscles that were injured, but fortunately no bones were broken anywhere, he said.

B: Even if they are only external injuries, they must be terribly painful anyway.

A: Of course. When we were getting him into the boat, he was still swimming hard. We gave him some brandy and he was still able to drink, but after getting on the big ship, he passed out and didn't know any more. He didn't say a word all the way.

B: Weren't there doctors on board?

A: There were, but the equipment was none too complete, so the only thing to do was just to give him first some — uh — some anesthetic to relieve the pain, apply some iodine to prevent infection — measures for emergency first aid — and as soon as the ship docked, they telephoned for an ambulance and sent him to this hospital. Look, that's Dr. New coming out of that ward; he is the most famous surgeon around here. He is not only a good doctor and a very learned man, but also a very charming person, and very approachable, so whether it's the nurses, or the patients, or his associates, everybody likes him and admires him.

B: Now that the doctor has come out, we can go in, I suppose?

A: Just let me ask that nurse first. Uh — excuse me, Miss, may we go in now?

Nurse: Please wait another moment, will you, gentlemen? Let me tidy up the room a little first! It'll be ready in a minute.

NOTES

1. *Tann* 'to probe, to spy around.' *Tann-binq* 'to inquire about sickness' L.

2. *Ell Ge* 'Second Brother (older than oneself).'

3. *Kan* 'to watch'; *huh* 'to protect' B. *Kanhuh* (alternating with *kannhuh*) 'a (hospital) nurse.'

4. *Hweitour* '(with a) turn (of the) head, — in a moment, by and by.'

5. *Binq₀ren* 'sick person, patient.'

INQUIRING AFTER A SICK MAN 213

A: Woo bujydaw. Sh tamen gawsonq woo de. Howlai shau tuey [24] le ideal, ren jiow chingchuu duo le.

B: Oh. Day.fu tzeem shuo laije? Yonq buyonq jie-guu [25] huohjee kaidau [26] shermde?

A: Ta shuo jaw tade yih.jiann kann.chiilai, keeyii buyonq jie-guu, yee buyonq yonq sherm bye-joong [27] de shooushuh. Yeou sh yeou jii-chuh shau-shangle [28] de dihfangl, gen haojii-chuh way-shang. Ta shuo ta chiitourl pah dahtoei de gwutou sher [29] le, howlai char.chulai [30] binq mei sher. Jianbaangl nall dahgay yee jyy yeou jinrow [31] showle deal shang,[32] shinqkuei naal de gwutou yee mei duann, ta shuo.

B: Jiow guangsh way-shang yee idinq terng de yawminq [33] lo.

A: Tzyhran [34] le. Woomen geei ta nonq.shanq [35] chwan .lai de shyrhowl, ta hair tzaynall shyy-jinn fuhj shoei.[36] Woomen geeile ta deal borlandih he, ta hair jydaw he, shanqle dah-chwan yiihow, ta jiow iun.guohchiuh [37] le, sherm shyhchyng yee bujydaw le, i-luh i-jiuh huah yee mei shuo.

B: Chwanshanq meiyeou i.sheng [38] ma?

A: Yeou dawsh yeou, keesh shehbey bu suann tay wanchyuan, suooyii jyy hao [39] shian geei ta shanq deal shermme — e — geei ta daa deal jyytonq de maafei-jen [40] a, shanq deal shiau-dwu [41] de deanjeou [42] a — nah-i-ley de linshyr [43] jiow-jyi [44] de bannfaa — gaan chwan i kawle ann [45] jiow daa-diannhuah jiawle i-lianq jiowshang-che [46] bae ta sonq.jinn [47] jeyg iyuann [48] .lii .lai le. È, nii chyau, tsorng ney-jian binqshyh.lii [49] tzoou.chulai de neyg jiowsh Niou Day.fu; ta sh jell tzuey chuming [50] de wayke-i.sheng [51] le. Ta budann beenshyh hao,[52] shyuewenn [53] hao, ren yee feicharng her.chih,[54] ideal jiahtz [55] yee meiyeou, suooyii wuluenn sh kanhuh a, binq-ren a, torngshyhmen a, renren dou shiihuan ta, pey.fwu ta.

B: Jehhoel day.fu chulai le, tzarmen keeyii jinnchiuh le ba?

A: Ranq woo shian wennx ney-wey huhshyh [56] .kann.[57] E — chiing wenn Nin, Sheaujiee, woomen shianntzay keeyii jinnchiuh le ma?

Kanhuh: Chiing niimen ell-wey tzay *deeng*.deengl, ah! Deeng woo bae binqshyh shian shyr.dou-vx-hao! Ihoel jiow der! [58]

---

6. *Fa-shau* 'develop fever, — to have a fever.'

7. *Shau dawsh yeou shau* is a stronger form than *shau sh yeou shau*. (See Note 12, p. 184.)

8. *Rehduh* 'heat-degree, — temperature.'

9. *Di.shiahchiuh* would also be possible, *-.lai* being preferred since the normal temperature is being taken as the speaker's standpoint.

10. *Tzuey gau gau daw* '(at the) highest (so) high (as to) reach.'

11. *Shyr* 'time, o'clock.' The speaker is apparently reading from a temperature chart, in which the more formal terminology is used.

12. *Guann* 'get used.'

13. *Shehshyh* 'Mr. Ce(lsius), — Centigrade.' Foreign names are transliterated into Chinese by using characters which the person doing the transliteration pronounces approximately like the original. Consequently, speakers of a different dialect reading the transliteration in characters will give a pronunciation deviating still further from the original.

The word *shyh* is used for 'Mr.' with foreign names in newspapers, scientific writings, etc.

14. *Hwashyh* 'Mr. Fah(renheit), — Fahrenheit,' no doubt transliterated by someone whose dialect had *f* for *hw* or *hu*.

15. *Mei binq* here is verb-object. In another context, the same expression might also mean 'have not been sick' or 'was not sick.'

16. *Uenduh* 'warm-degree, — temperature' is any temperature, while *rehduh* refers to high temperatures.

17. **Meaning of Subject-Predicate Relation.** — The subject in a Chinese sentence is literally the subject matter about which something is said. It does not necessarily denote the performer of the action denoted by the verb or to be equated to the term after a *sh*. Thus, although one must say in English 'He has 38.5°, or 'His temperature is 38.5°,' it is possible to say in Chinese *Ta sh 38.5°* 'As for him, (the temperature) is 38.5°.' (See also § 4, p. 35.)

18. The figuring is done as follows:

Spoken	*Implied*
'Now 38.5° is Fahrenheit —'	(The excess of 38.5° over the normal 37° is 1.5°, to be divided by 5 and multiplied by 9 to convert it to degrees Fahrenheit.)
'3 × 5 = 15.'	(Therefore the quotient is .3.)
'3 × 9 = 27.'	(Therefore the figure to add to the normal 98.6° is 2.7.)
'98 + 2 = 100.'	(So much for adding the integers.)
' 7 + 6 = 13.'	(The decimals, .7 of the 2.7, and .6 of the 98.6 add up to 1.3, which, when added to 100,)
'makes 101.3.'	

19. *Shyr-fenn jy san* 'three of ten parts, — three tenths.' In general, a fraction n/m is spoken of as *m-fenn ₒjy n*, *ₒjy* being the literary equivalent of *.de*.

20. *Ren* '(state of his) person, — mind.' *Hair chingchuu* 'rather clear' (not 'still clear').

21. *Hwu.twu* 'indistinct, muddled, confused.'

22. *Hwu-huah* 'nonsensical words.'
23. *Tzyhgeel* is a more colloquial form for *tzyhjii*.
24. *Tuey* 'retreat, subside.'
25. *Jie-guu* 'join bones.'
26. *Kai-dau* 'open (with a) knife,' popular expression for *yonq shoou-shuh* 'use hand-art, — to perform an operation.'
27. *Bye-joong* 'other kinds.'
28. *Shau-shangle* 'injured through burning, — burned.'
Note that both *-chuh* and *dihfangl* mean place, but *-chuh* is an AN and *dihfangl* is a noun.
29. The various words for breaking are used as follows:
Poh 'broken, of solids or surfaces.'
Lieh 'cracked, split.'
Sher, or *duann* 'broken, of legs, ropes, tails, etc.'
Suey 'broken to small pieces.'
30. *Char* 'to investigate.'
31. *Jinrow* 'muscle-flesh, — muscle.' The scientific term *jirow* 'muscle-flesh' is avoided in ordinary speech, since it is homonymous with 'chicken-meat.'
32. *Show-shang* 'receive injury.'
33. ... .*de yawminq* 'wants life, — killing, — terribly.'
34. *Tzyhran* 'self-ly, — of course,' = *dangran*.
35. *Nonq* is a very general verb meaning 'to do something with,' *nonq.shanqlai* 'got (him) up.'
36. *Fuh-shoei* 'to swim.'
37. *Iun* 'dizzy'; *iun.guohchiuh* 'to faint away.'
38. *I.sheng* 'heal-er, — physician.' Like 'doctor,' *day.fu* is the more popular term.
39. *Jyy hao* '(the) only good (thing, to do was).'
40. *Daa-jen* 'administer needle, — to give a hypodermic'; *maafei* 'morphine.' The general word for 'anesthetic' is *matzuey-yaw* 'numb — intoxicate drug.'
41. *Shiau-dwu* 'do away with poison, — sterilize.'
42. *Deanjeou* '(Io)dine-wine, — tincture of iodine.'
43. *Linshyr* 'impending-time, — for the time being, temporary.'
44. *Jiow-jyi* 'rescue-emergency, — first aid, to give first aid.'
45. *Kaw-ann* 'to lean against the shore, — to dock.'
46. *Jiowshang-che* 'rescue-injury-vehicle, — ambulance.'
47. The verb is *sonq.jinnlai* 'send into.'
48. *Iyuann* 'medical institution, — hospital.'
49. *Binqshyh* (or *binqshyy*) 'sick room' (either room or ward).
50. *Chuming* 'come out with a name, — famous.'
51. *Wayke* 'outside department, — surgery'; *neyke* 'internal medicine.'

52. See Note 50, p. 186.
53. *Shyue₀wenn* 'learn-inquire, — learning, erudition.'
54. *Her.chih* 'harmonious-air, — kindly, pleasant, charming.'
55. *Jiahtz* 'framework, scaffolding, — a front.'
56. *Huhshyh* 'protect-or, — nurse,' a more formal and polite term than *kanhuh*.
57. *Kann* (usually unstressed) 'and see.' *Wennx .kann* 'just ask and see.' Similarly, *kannx .kann* 'just take a look and see.'
58. *Der* 'done,' as applied to dishes of food, tailor's work, and, less frequently, to making of the bed, etc.

EXERCISES

1. Write eight sentences using a split complement, such as *sonq.jinn neyg utz.lii .chiuh*.

2. *Example:*

Given:
Niou Dayfu jiee ney-jian binq-shyh.lii chulai le; ta tzay jell diing chuming le.

Answer:
Jiee ney-jian binqshyh.lii chulai de ney-wey jiowsh (neyg —) jell diing chuming de (neyg —) Niou Dayfu.

(a) Lii Sheaujiee tzay jeyg iyuann.lii tzuoh-shyh; ta tzayjell tzuey haokann le. (b) Neyg Hwashyh-beau tzay ney-jang juotz.shanq; jeyg

---

LESSON 14
CONVERSATION WITH THE DOCTOR

A and B: Good morning, Doctor!
Doctor: Good morning!
A: Is the patient better today?
D: I can report today that the — he is much better.
B: There is no question about his life now, is there?
D: No, you can say that the critical stage has already passed. What I was afraid of yesterday was that when his fever was so high and his pulse was so fast, I was not sure whether his heart could take it. So I gave him a few injections to strengthen his heart. When I saw that his fever actually subsided gradually, I knew that he had already passed the crisis safely.
A: Well, it was fortunate! Did he have any internal injuries?
D: I examined him thoroughly inside and out and I don't think he looks like having had any internal injuries.
A and B: Oh, that's good.

CONVERSATION WITH THE DOCTOR 217

woo diing bu shiihuan yonq le. (c) Neyg jiahshyy-yuan diaw de hae.lii le. Tade feiji chule shyh. (d) Tarn Buhtyng Shg. shianntzay tzaynall itourl tzoouj itourl chy dongshi; Tarn Buhtyng Shg. renjia dou goan ta jiaw Lioushengji huohjee Goangboh Dianntair. (e) Lii Shiansheng tzay neyg kehtarng.lii dahshengl shuo-huah; ta geei woomen jeang Ingwen. (f) Neyg sheauharl shianntzay gen woo iyanq jonq; ta chiuhnian bii woo ching de duo. (g) Nii chyau, woo jeyg dahtoei shianntzay keeyii sweibiann ('freely') tzemm donq le; woo jeh dahtoei ney-hwei feiji chu-shyh shuai-duann le. (h) Ney-wey isheng yow gau yow dah; ta tzwol geei neyg binq-ren jie-guu le.

3. *Translate into Chinese:*

(a) Well, well, how is it that you have come to this hospital too? (b) I came to see whether the patient, after having had such a high fever yesterday, is better today. (c) The fever is not to be regarded as very high, to be sure, but there is still a degree and half of fever. (d) Well, that is not to be considered very serious, I guess. (e) Is it necessary to have a major (*dah*) operation before he can get well? (f) It will not be necessary to use much anesthetic for the operation. (g) The most important thing in such operations is to have everything sterilized. (h) The doctor will come in a moment, you won't have time to tidy the things in the room, I am afraid.

DIH SHYRSYH KEH
GEN DAYFU TARN-HUAH

A and B: Nin tzao a,[1] Dayfu!
Dayfu: Tzao a!
A: Jintian binqren hao.deal le ma?
D: Jintian dawsh [2] keeyii bawgaw — ta hao de duo le.
B: Shianntzay shinq.minq [3] dahgay meiyeou wenntyi le ba?
D: Sh de,[4] shianntzay weishean shyrchi keeyii shuo sh yiijing guohchiuh le. Woo tzwotian suoo [5] pah de jiowsh — fa-shau fa de nemm gau, may [6] tiaw de yow nemm kuay, bujydaw tade shintzanq [7] chydejuh [8] chybujuh. Suooyii geei ta daale jii-jen [9] chyang-shin de yaw. Howlai kann tade shau jiuran [10] mannmhalde tueyle.shiahlai le, woo jiow jydaw ta yiijing pyngx-anxde [11] jingguohle jeyg — weiji [12] le.
A: Ai, jen yunn.chih.[13] Ta neybuh [14] show-shang le meiyeou?
D: Woo geei ta *lii*xwayxde shihshide [15] char-guohle i-biann. Woo kann [16] ta bu shianq yeou sherm ney-shang de yanqtz.
B and A: Ah, nah hao!

D: The lungs, the intestines, and stomach, the liver, the kidneys, all seem to be in good shape. His bowels and urine are also in normal order. His breathing is quite even, too, and his throat isn't swollen, either. The only thing is that he is thirsty all the time, always clamoring for water to drink. That, of course, is because he is having a fever.

B: Was there much loss of blood?

A: Yes, that's why the first thing we did, as soon as he entered the hospital, was to give him a blood transfusion.

B: Were you able to find a blood-donor right then?

D: We did not have to look for any donor, there was ready plasma stored in the hospital, so that it could be taken out and used as needed.

A: Ah, that's really wonderful!

B: I wonder how many injuries he received in all, over his whole body?

D: Counting all the light injuries, there must have been — at least forty places — so many you couldn't count them exactly. The scalp was abraded, but fortunately nothing happened to the skull. The right ear, the right side of the face — from the temple to the cheek — and the nose were all abraded badly; luckily the eyeballs were not injured. His teeth, moreover, had bitten through his tongue and lip. The shoulders, the back, the chest, the abdomen, the arms, the elbows, the wrists, — those places only had skin injuries. His eyebrows and hair were almost half burnt off.

B: The places that were burnt must be pretty bad, I suppose?

D: Yes, I was going to say. The right thumb, as well as the index finger, and the middle finger were burnt very badly, and even the finger nails were scorched. But the ring finger and the little finger were not injured. The right knee cap and the right ankle were also burnt most seriously.

B: Gosh, how terrible!

D: Fortunately, modern medicine has progressed so fast, especially with those very effective drugs discovered most recently —

A: Such drugs as sulfanilimide and penicillin, is that right?

D: Yes, and there are others, too. So that at present, so long as the patient is treated early enough — the important thing is early — so long as the treatment is early enough, you can guarantee that there will be no danger of infection. Ten years ago, if you had happened upon a man with such serious injuries, it would be very difficult to predict what the result would have been.

B: Well, if we hadn't found you, Doctor New, I don't know whether we would have had such excellent results.

D: Oh, thank you! It's very kind of you to say so! We are only doing what we practitioners are supposed to do, that's all.

Nurse: Now you can go in, gentlemen. Third door to your right.

A and B: Good! — Thank you very much, Doctor!

D: Oh, don't mention it.

CONVERSATION WITH THE DOCTOR

D: Fey [17] a, charngtz a, wey a, gan a, shenntzanq a, dou hair haohaulde. Dahbiann [18] sheaubiann dou tong.[19] Hu.shi [20] yee heen yun de, saangtz yee bu joong. Jiowsh lao kee, lao nawj yaw he-shoei, nah dangran sh fa-shau de yuan.guh [21] le.

B: Shiee lioule [22] bu shao ba?

D: Duey le, suooyii i-ruhle yuann,[23] woomen touri-jiann [24] shyh jiowsh geei ta shu-sheue.[25]

B: Shu-shiee danqshyr [26] jiow jao.de-jaur ren ma?

D: Buyonq jao-ren d'è, iyuann.lii tswenj jiow yeou shiannchernqde sheuejiang, sweishyr [27] keeyii na.chulai yonq.

A: Tz! [28] jen miaw!

B: Bujydaw ta chyuan-shen igonq yeou dwo.shao-chuh [29] de shang?

D: Yawsh lian ching-shang yee suann.chiilai me, tzoong yeou — syhshyr-jii-chuh ne — duo de jeanjyr shuu.bu-ching le. Tour-pyi mo-poh [30] le, shinqkuei tour-guu mei-shyh.[31] Yow-eeltou, yow-lean — tsorng tay-yang [32] ijyr daw tzoeibahtz — gen byitz, dou tsa de heen lihhay; haotzay ycanjutz [33] mei huay. Ya yow bae tzyhjii de shertou gen tzoeichwen [34] geei yeau-poh le. Jianbaangl, bey.jyi,[35] shinkoou,[36] duhtz, ge.bey, ge.bey-jooutz, shoouwanntz, — ney-jii-chuh jiow guangsh pyi.fu [37] showle shang. Mei-.mau gen i-tour de tour.fah dou shaule chahbuduo i-bann.

B: Bey huoo shau de jii-chuh idinq shang de heen lihhay ba?

D: Jiow(sh) jeh huah lo. Yowshoou de dahjyy,[38] lian elljyy, jongjyy, dou geei huoo shau de heen lihhay, lian shooujy.jea dou shau-hwu le. Keesh wumingjyy [39] gen sheaujyrtou daw mei show-shang. Yowtoei de ker-.shigall, yowjeau de jeauwanntz yee shau-shang de diing lihhay.

B: Heh, jen tsaan! [40]

D: Kueide shiannday de ishyue, jinnbuh [41] de jemm [42] kuay, youchyish yeoule tzueyjinn fashiann [43] de jii-joong heen ling de yaw —

A: Lihru liouanjih [44] gen parnnishilin ney-i-ley de yaw, sh bush'a?

D: Duey le, yee hair yeou byede. Suooyii shianntzay jyy yawsh jyh de gow tzao — yawjiin de jiowsh tzao — jyyshiu [45] jyh de gow tzao, keeyii bau nii nenggow wanchyuan bihmean chwanraan dwu-jiunn de weishean [46] de. Taangruohsh [47] shyr-nian chyan penq.jiann le jemmyanq jonq-shang de ig ren a, nah — jyeguoo ruher,[48] jiow heen nan yuhliaw le.

B: Ah, yawsh woomen mei jao.daw Niou Dayfu,[49] nah yee bujydaw nengbuneng yeou tzemm lianghao de jyeguoo ba?

D: Ae,[50] haoshuo vx! naal lai de huah! [51] Woomen yee buguoh jiowsh jinn [52] woomen shyng-i de inggai jinn de tzer.renn jiowshle.

Kanhuh: Jehhoel niimen ell-wey keeyii jinnchiuh le. Yowbial dihsan'g men.

A and B: Hao! — Laujiah [53] vx, Dayfu!

D: Ai, bukeh.chih! [54]

NOTES

1. *Nin tzao a* is really a compliment 'you are so early (in getting up).'
2. *Daw* 'up-side-down,' same word, with tonal modification, as *dao* 'to topple over.' *Daw* or *dawsh* 'contrary' (to what a pessimist may think), hence 'I am glad to say ....'
3. *Minq, shinq.minq* 'life (vs. death)'; *shengminq*, same, learned term; *sheng.hwo* 'life (as activity)' or 'livelihood.'
4. Note use of *sh de* where one would say 'no' in English. (See p. 59.)
5. *Suoo* often has the force of 'all': *suoo pah de* 'that which I was afraid of, — all I was afraid of.'
6. *May* (alternating with *moh*) 'pulse'; *tiaw* 'jump, — beat.' The scientific term for 'pulse-beat' is *mohbor*.
7. *Shintzanq* 'heart organ,' medical term. (See also Note 17.)
8. *Chy* 'eat, absorb.' *Chydejuh* 'can absorb (the strain and) stay, — can stand the strain, can take it.'
9. *Jen* 'needle,' here used as a temporary measure word 'syringeful.' *Chyang-shin de yaw* 'drug for strengthening the heart.'
10. *Jiuran* 'actually, indeed.'
11. *Pyng'an* 'level-peaceful, — peaceful, safe.' *Pyngxanxde* 'safe and sound.' *Jing₀guoh* 'pass over, pass through.'
12. *Weiji* 'peril-situation, — crisis.'
13. *Yunn.chih* 'lucky-air, — luck, lucky.'
14. *Neybuh* 'interior parts.'
15. *Shih* 'fine (of thread, powder, etc.)'; *shihshielde* 'in great detail.' The doctor speaks a more formal language and uses fewer *-l* forms.
16. *Woo kann* '(The way) I look at it, — I think.'
17. The names of the chief internal organs are as follows:

	Of human beings:	As food:	Medical term:
'lungs'	fey	fey	fey
'stomach'	wey, duhtz	duutz	wey
'abdomen'	duhtz	—	fuh(buh)
'liver'	gan	gal	gan(tzanq)
'kidney'	shenntzanq, iautz	iautz	shenn(tzanq)
'intestines'	charngtz	charngl	charng(tz)
'heart'	shin	shin	shintzanq
'brains'	naotz	naol, naotz	nao

18. *Dahbiann* 'major convenience,' *sheaubiann* 'minor convenience,' can be used as nouns (action or result) or as intransitive verbs. Although they were originally euphemisms, they are now plain-speaking, though quite proper, words. Somewhat more decorous verb-object forms are *chu-gong*

and *jiee-shooul*, respectively. *Shanq tsehsuoo* (or *maufarng*) *.chiuh* is equivalent to 'go to the toilet.' The blunt verb-object forms are *lha-shyy* and *sa-niaw*.

19. *Tong* 'go through,' here used in the sense of 'not stopped up.'
20. *Hu.shi* 'exhale-inhale, — breath, to breathe.'
21. *Sh . . . de ₀yuan.guh* 'it is (for) the reason of . . . .'
22. *Liou* 'flow' an unrelated homonym of *liou* 'retain' (in *lioushengji*).
23. *Ruh-yuann* 'enter the hospital.'
24. *Touri-* 'head-one, — first, the very first.'
25. *Shu-sheue* 'transfer blood, — transfuse blood.' *Sheue* and *shiueh* are more learned forms of *shiee*.
26. Distinguish between *danqshyr* 'right then and there' and *dangshyr* 'at the time (I am talking about).'
27. *Sweishyr* = *sweibiann sherm shyrhowl*.
28. *Tz!* pronounced with a click, 'Tsk!' One *Tz* expresses either approval and admiration or disappointment and hesitation, but a succession of two or more *Tz!* expresses disgust or scandalousness.
29. *Duo-shao* 'much or little, many or few'; *duo.shao* or *dwo.shao* 'how much or many?'; *dwo shao* 'so little or so few!' *dwo.shao-chuh* 'how many places?'
30. *Mo* 'rub,' *tsa* 'scrape.' *Motsa* 'friction' (lit. or fig.).
31. *Mei-shyh* 'nothing the matter with it.'
32. *Tay.yang* 'the sun'; 'the temples.'
33. *Jutz* 'pearl, bead'; *yeanjutz* 'eyeball.'
34. *Tzoeichwen*, less formally, *tzoeichwel*.
35. *Bey.jyi* 'back-ridge, — the back.'
36. *Shinkoou* 'heart's opening, — the chest.'
37. *Pyi* 'skin' in the widest sense. *Pyi.fu* 'the surface of human skin.'
38. The names for the fingers given here are slightly formal. More common names are *dahjyrtou, elljyrtou, dihsan'g jyrtou, dihsyhg jyrtou, sheaujyrtou*. Still more familiar names are *dah.muge, ell.mudih, jongguulou, huhgwosyh, sheaunhioux* (no neutral tone on last syllable). Note the forms *jyr-* in *shooujyrtou* 'finger' and *jy-* in *shooujytou* 'finger' or *(shoou)jy.jea* 'finger nails.' In other combinations 'finger' is *jyy*. The verb 'to point at with the finger, to refer to' is also *jyy*.
39. *Wumingjyy* 'nameless finger, — ring finger,' also called *syhjyy* or simply *dihsyhg jyrtou*.
40. *Tsaan* 'tragic,' also used, in student slang, for any trivial thing that has gone wrong.
41. *Jinnbuh* 'advanced-step, — progress, to make progress.'
42. The doctor uses the more formal *jemm* instead of *tzemm*.
43. In speaking of drugs, *faming* 'develop-clear, — invent(ion),' is often also used instead of *fashiann* 'discover(y).'

44. *Liouanjih* 'sulphor-an-dose, — sulfanilimide.' *Parnnishilin* is also called *piannnisylin*.

45. *Jyyshiu*, a more literary form of *jyy yaw*.

46. So far as the words are concerned, *bihmean chwanraan dwu-jiunn de weishean* could either be analyzed as 'the danger of avoiding infection with poisonous germs' (*weishean* modified by all the preceding) or as 'avoid the danger of infection with poisonous germs' (*weishean* as object of *bihmean*). The former would of course not make sense here.

47. As we have seen, there is no formal feature in Chinese to indicate supposition contrary to fact; however, the use of a less common 'if'-word *taangruohsh* gives a suggestion of such an implication.

48. *Ruher* 'like what, how?' literary equivalent of *tzeemyanq*.

49. In very polite or respectful language, the term of address is used instead of *nii* or even *Nin*. *Woo na woode, Shiansheng na shiansheng de* 'I take mine, you take yours, sir.'

50. *Ae*, interjection of disagreement or mild disapproval. In China one does not say *shieh.x* 'thank you' or *duo-shieh* 'many thanks' for a compliment, which would imply an immodest admission of one's merits. The proper thing to do is to deny it.

51. *Naal lai de huah!* 'Whence such words (of over-praise)?'

52. *Jinn* 'to exhaust.' *Jinn-tzer, jinn-tzer₀renn* 'perform (exhaustively) one's duty.'

53. *Laujiah* is said to thank the doctor for his information.

54. *Keh.chih* 'guest-air, — polite, to stand on ceremonies.'

EXERCISES

1. *Complete the following sentences:*

(a) ____ tian shanq ____ binqren fa ____ fa de nemm ____, yawsh ta ____ tzanq chybu ____, jiow deei geei ta ____ deal ____ de jen, yawburan koong ____ jiow yeou ____ de ____ shean ba. (b) Dahbiann bu tong sh inwey ____ buhao de yuanguh, ____ biann tay duo sh inwey ____ tzanq yeou binq de ____. (c) Ren mei binq de shyr ____ shentii de uenduh sh Hwa ____, jiow deengyu ____ shyh ____. (d) ____ le jiow sheang ____ shoei, ____ le jiow sheang ____ fann. (e) Yawsh ig ren de ____ tzanq buhao, jiow buneng ranq ta shyy-jinn de pao, yawsh pao de tay ley le, jiow ____ pah yeou ____ tzanq ____ bu ____ de wei ____. (f) Jeyg iyuann.lii sweibiann sherm isheng ____ sherm binq dou huey ____. (g) Haotzay ta ____ mei show-shang, yawburan shianntzay kann.bu ____ dongshi le. (h) Renren deei jinn tzyhjii ing ____ de ____.

2. *Example:*

Given:
Ta chiitourl bu fa-shau de shyrhowl hair jihde tzyhjii tzay naal.

Answer:
Howlai fa-shau fa de lian tzyhjii tzay naal dou bu jihde le.

(a) Chii-tourl bu ley de shyrhowl woo yeanjing hair jeng.de-kai. (b) Jintian tzaochin yuntsae shao de shyrhowl hair kanndejiann tayyang. (c) Tzwotian saangtz bu terng de shyrhowl hair he.de-shiah shoei. (d) Shanq liibay ya bu terng de shyrhowl woanshanq hair neng tzuoh shyh-chyng. (e) Ta chii-tourl shyue Jonggwo-huah de shyrhowl shuo de mei Jongworen nemm kuay. (f) Beenlai ney-suoo farngtz bu yau de shyrhowl neyshie ren hair jann.de-juh. (g) Gangtsair ney-jy chwan tzoou de heen jinn de shyrhowl keeyii tingdejiann sheng'in. (h) Shiahtian ryhtz charng de shyrhowl ba-dean jong hair kanndejiann niann-shu.

3. *Example:*

Given:
Ta fa-shau, suooyii lao kee.

Answer:
Ta weysherm lao kee? Ta suooyii lao kee ia, sh inwey fa-shau de yuanguh.

(a) Gangtsair bey hei-yun geei daang.juh le, suooyii kannbujiann. (b) Jeyg ren sweiran showle shang, keesh mei chwanraan dwu-jiunn, suooyii hao de kuay. (c) Neyg ren duey ren tay bukehchih, suooyii renren dou taoyann ('loathe') ta. (d) Ta bannluh.shanq ('midway') meiyeou chihyou le, deei i-luh hwaj lai, suooyii lai-woan le. (e) Yeou jiig ren tzay utz.lii jinq dao-luann, suooyii woo ideal yee tingbujiann nii shuo de huah. (f) Woo pyngcharng tzoongsh yonq yowshoou shiee-tzyh de, suooyii tzuooshoou shiee-tzyh shiee.bu-hao. (g) Woo lao goan feiji chyantou huey juann de neyg dongshi jiaw 'fengshann' ('fan') laije, suooyii nii shuo 'luoshyuan-jeang' woo bu doong. (h) Shianntzay shooushuh shiau-dwu bii tsorngchyan shiau de hao, suooyii bii tsorngchyan weishean yee shao de duo le.

4. *Write out the conversation of the visit with the patient.*

LESSON 15
WORLD GEOGRAPHY

Teacher: Today we shall talk about the geography of China. But before we talk about today's lesson, we ought just to review first the world geography we had last time, shall we? Chyan Tian'i, do you remember what continents there are in the world?

Chyan: Uh — the largest continent in the Eastern Hemisphere is Asia, of course. The one joining Asia on the west is Europe. South of Europe, separated by the Mediterranean Sea, is Africa.

T: What is the relation between Africa and Asia?

Ch: What relation? Oh, Africa is to the southwest of Asia. Originally the three continents of Europe, Asia, and Africa were all connected. Afterwards they opened the Suez Canal and opened up the Red Sea to the Mediterranean Sea, so that Africa and Asia are now separated.

T: Correct, that's correct. And then?

Ch: Oh, then there is — uh — in the Eastern Hemisphere there is Australia, in the Western Hemisphere there are the two continents of North and South America, with a Panama Canal between them. Then there is — uh — there is — oh, Teacher, is Antarctica in the Eastern or the Western Hemisphere?

T: Since the name means 'South Pole Continent,' then there would be no point in speaking of East or West.

Ch: I see.

T: Lii Shoouchyang, can you recite for us the names of the several oceans in the world?

Lii: Well, the largest one is of course the Pacific Ocean, which is between Asia and America. And the next is the Atlantic Ocean, to the west of Europe and east of America. Next to that is the Indian Ocean, to the south of Asia. Then there is the Arctic Ocean at the North Pole and the Antarctic Ocean at the South Pole —

T: Chyan Tian'i, what were you going to ask?

Ch: Teacher, if there is already an Antarctica at the South Pole, how can there be room for an Antarctic Ocean?

T: The Antarctic Oc — uh — well — the, the, we'd better talk about that next time, shall we? Today we still have to review the names of various countries in the world, you see. Wang Shyrshan, what are some of the large countries in the world, where are they all located, can you recite them?

Wang: Of the large countries, China is in Asia. Then there is India, and Russia — a part of Russia is in Europe. But in Europe, outside of Russia, the remaining countries are all pretty small ones.

DIH SHYRWUU KEH
SHYHJIEH DIHLII [1]

Shiansheng: Jintian jeang Jonggwo dihlii. Dannsh tzay meiyeou jeang jintian de gongkeh yiichyan ne, woomen [2] inggai shian baa shanq-tsyh suoo jeang de shyhjieh dihlii uenlii i-biann, a! Chyan Tian'i, nii jihde shyhjieh.shanq yeou shie sherm dahluh [3] bu jihd'a?

Chyan: Eng — Dong Bannchyou tzuey dah de dahluh dangran jiowsh Yahjou [4] le. Gen Yahjou Shi-buh lhianj de jiowsh Oujou. Tzay Oujou de Nanbial, ger-kaile ig Dihjong Hae, jiowsh Feijou.

Shg: Feijou gen Yahjou sh sherm guan.shih ne?

Ch: Sherm guan.shih a? Oh, Feijou tzay Yahjou de shinan. Beenlai Ou–, Yah–, Fei– san-jou doush lhianj de. Howlai kaile i-tyau Suyishyh Yunnher,[5] bae Horng Hae gen Dihjong Hae daa-tong le, suooyii Feijou gen Yahjou jiow fen.kai le.

Shg: Duey, shuo de duey. Hair yeou ne?

Ch: Oh, hair yeou me [6] — Dong Bannchyou me hair yeou Awjou, Shi Bannchyou yeou Beei Meeijou gen Nan Meeijou leang-piann [7] dahluh, dangjong yeou i-tyau Banamaa Yunnher. Hair yeou me — hair yeou —, èh, Shiansheng, Nanjyi [8] Jou sh tzay Dong Bannchyou hairsh tzay Shi Bannchyou a?

Shg: Jihran jiaw Nanjyi Jou, nah jiow wusuoowey [9] dong-shi lo.

Ch: Oh.

Shg: Lii Shoouchyang, nii neng buneng baa shyhjieh.shanq jiig dah-yang de mingtzyh bey [10] geei woomen dahjia [11] ting.x .kann?

Lii: Tzuey dah de me — dangran jiowsh Taypyng Yang [12] lo, tzay Yahjou Meeijou de dangjong. Chyitsyh [13] me — sh Dahshi [14] Yang, tzay Oujou jy [15] shi, Meeijou jy dong. Chyitsyh me sh Yinn.duh Yang, tzay Yahjou yii-nan.[16] Hair yeou Beeijyi de Beei Bingyang [17] gen Nanjyi de Nan Bingyang —

Shg: Chyan Tian'i, nii yaw wenn sherm laije?

Ch: Shiansheng, Nanjyi jihran yeoule g Nanjyi Jou, hair linqway [18] ge.de-shiah [19] ig Nan Bingyang ma?

Shg: Nan Bingy — e — ng — jeyg vx — jeyg shiah-hwei tzay jeang ba, ah! Jintian tzarmen hair deei baa shyhjieh.shanq geh-gwo de mingtzyh uenshyi vx n'è. Wang Shyrshan, shyhjieh.shanq yeou shie sherm dah de gwojia, dou tzay naal, nii bey.de-chulai ma?

Wang: Dah de gwojia ia, Jonggwo tzay Yahshihyah lo. Hair yeou Yinn.duh, gen Eh.gwo [20] — Eh.gwo i-buh.fenn sh tzay Oujou de. Oujou chwule Eh.gwo jy way, chyiyu de gwojia doush tiing sheau d'è!

T: But some small countries, like Holland, Belgium, Denmark, and so forth are fairly important, though.

W: Yes. Europe has Great Britain, France, Germany, Spain, those are the comparatively large ones. The two northernmost countries are called Norway and Switzerland —

T: You've got it wrong, Wang Shyrshan. Switzerland is a republic to the north of Italy.

Ch: Is that the country where the Red Cross Association and the former League of Nations are located?

T: That's right! Wang Shyrshan, what you had in mind was Sweden, which is a constitutional monarchy. All right, will you continue?

W: To continue, the largest country on the American continent is of course the United States. Next to that is Canada, then Mexico. As to South America, then there is Brazil, Argentina; Africa has Egypt, Australia has Austria —

T: Come, come, you've got things mixed up again! Austria is a European country, you see. The one that was once annexed by nazified Germany some years ago was Austria. *Australia* is one of the British dominions, with an independent government, and is also a democratic country, just like Canada.

L: Wang Shyrshan forgot that Asia has Japan.

W: I did not! What Teacher asked was, what *large* countries there were in the world!

T: (*Laughs.*) That's logical, too. Chyan Tian'i, do you remember the names of the capitals of the various countries?

Ch: The capital of China is in Nanking, it was moved to Chungking for several years during the war. The capital of U.S.S.R. is at Moxico —

T: What?!

Ch: (*Chuckles.*) I mean Moscow. The capital of Russia is at Moscow, Poland at Warsaw, Germany at Berlin, Italy at Rome, Greece at Athens, Turkey at Angora, France at Paris, England at London, America at New York —

Class: What?!

Ch: Oh, no, no, the capital of the United States is Washington!

Class: Ah, that's better!

NOTES

1. *Dihlii* 'earth-principles, — geography.'

2. The teacher uses a somewhat more formal style of diction and pronunciation than in ordinary conversation. Thus, *woomen* is used in the sense of *tzarmen*, *baa* instead of *bae*. He also uses fewer *-l* forms, as *beeibian* for *beeibial*.

Shg: Keesh yeou jiig sheau-gwo, biifang shianq Herlan,[21] Biilihshyr, Danmay, deengx,[22] tamende dih.wey [23] shiangdangde [24] jonqyaw è.

W: Eng. Oujou yeou Inggwo,[25] Fah.gwo, Der.gwo, Shibanya, sh biijeaude dah.i.deal de. Diing beeibial de leang-gwo jiaw Nuouei, Rueyshyh —

Shg: Nii nonq-tsuoh le, Wang Shyrshan. Rueyshyh sh Yihdahlih [26] beeibial de neyg gonqhergwo.

Ch: Sh bush jiowsh neyg — Horng Shyrtzyh [27] Huey gen tsorngchyan de Gwojih [28] Lianmeng suoo tzay de dihfangl?

Shg: Duey le vx! Wang Shyrshan, nii shin.lii [29] sheangj de neyg sh Rueydean, sh g jiunjuu lihshiann [30] de gwojia. Hao, nii tzay jiej shuo ia!

W: Hair yeou, Meeijou tzuey dah de me, jiowsh Meeigwo le. Chyitsyh sh Jianadah, Mohshige. Nan Meei me jiow yeou Bashi, Agentyng; Feijou yeou Aijyi; Awjou yeou Aw.gwo —

Shg: Hai, nii yow nonq-hwu.twu le! Aw.gwo sh Oujou de gwojia è. Chyan jii-nian tserngjing bey nahtsuey-huah [31] de Der.gwo binqtuen-.guoh [32] de neyg sh Aw.gwo. Awjou sh Inggwo de lianbang jy i,[33] yeou g dwulih [34] de jenqfuu, yeesh g minjuu-gwojia,[35] gen Jianadah iyanq de.

L: Wang Shyrshan wanqle Yahjou hair yeou Ryhbeen [36] ne.

W: Woo naal wanq l'a? [37] Shiansheng wenn de sh shyhjieh.shanq yeou sherm **dah**-gwo è!

Shg: He he, nemm shuo yee tong.[38] Chyan Tian'i, nii jihde geh-gwo de jingcherng [39] de mingtzyh bu jihde?

Ch: Jonggwo de shooudu [40] tzay Nanjing, daa-janq de shyrhowl tserngjing ban daw Chorngchinq chiuh le jii-nian. Su Eh Lianbang de shooudu tzay Mohshige —

Shg: Ar? shermme?

Ch: He he, woo sh yaw shuo Mohsyke. Eh.gwo sh Mohsyke; Polan [41] sh Hwasha; Der.gwo sh Borlin; Yih.gwo sh Luomaa; Shilah sh Yeadean; Tuueelchyi sh Angelha; Fah.gwo me Bali; Inggwo Luenduen; Meeigwo Neouiue —

Chyuantii: Erng?!

Ch: Oh, bush vx, Meeilihjian [42] de shooudu sh Hwashenqduenn.

Chyuantii: Êh, nah tsair duey a!

---

3. *Luhdih* 'land (as opposed to water)'; *dahluh* 'great land — continent.'

4. The full names for the continents, rarely used at present, are *Yahshihyah* or *Yeashihyea* 'Asia,' *Ouluoba* 'Europe,' *Afeilihjia* 'Africa,' *Awdahlihyah* (or *-yea*) 'Australia,' *Yahmeeilihjia* (or *Yea-*) 'America.' *Jou* 'land surrounded by water, — islet (in a river), a continent.' In the sense of 'continent,' *jou* is a bound form, with optional neutral tone.

5. *Yunnher* 'transport-river, — canal.'

6. The particles *me*, *ne*, and *a* (or *ia* after vowels) can all be used for pauses. But while a pause with *ne* or *a* is made to give the listener time to understand, a pause with *me* is made to give the speaker time to think what to say next.

7. *Piann* 'slice,' AN for thin things or surfaces.

8. *Nanjyi* 'south extremity, — South Pole.'

9. *Wusuoowey* 'nothing to be called, — there is no point in speaking of.'

10. *Bey* '(to turn one's) back (to the teacher), — to recite by heart.'

11. *Dahjia* 'big-family, — everyone present.'

12. *Tay₀pyng Yang* 'Grand-Peaceful Ocean, — Pacific Ocean.'

13. *Chyitsyh* 'its next, — next to that.'

14. *Dahshi Yang* 'Great-West Ocean, — Atlantic Ocean.'

15. *Oujou jy shi* = *Oujou de shibial*. *Jy*, the literary equivalent of *de*, is often used in learned discussions.

16. While *tzay Yahjou jy nan* or *tzay Yahjou de nanbial* may mean either 'in the south of Asia' or 'to the south of Asia,' *Yahjou yii-nan* means only 'to the south of Asia.' On the other hand, *tzay Yahjou de nanbuh* (*-buh* 'part') means only 'in the south of Asia.'

17. *Bingyang* 'ice-ocean.'

18. *Linqway* 'separately, additionally, extra.'

19. *Ge* 'to place, put'; *-.de-shiah* 'have room for,' *ge.de-shiah* 'have room for (placing),' *chy.de-shiah* 'have room (in the stomach) for eating, — to have an appetite for.'

20. Also called *Er.gwo*, the full transliteration being *Ehluosy* or *Erluosy*. 'U.S.S.R.' is *Su Eh Lianbang*, *Su* being short for *Suweiai* 'Soviet.'

21. *Herlan* alternates with *Heh.lan*; *Biilihshyr* alternates with *Bii.gwo*; *Danmay* alternates with *Danmoh*.

22. *Deengx* 'et cetera'; 'such things (or persons) as.'

23. *Dih.wey* 'place-seat, — position (usually fig.).'

24. *Shiangdang* 'correspond'; *shiangdangde* 'moderately, fairly.'

25. The full names of these countries, rarely used, are *Ingjyilih* 'England,' *Fahlanshi* 'France,' *Deryihjyh* 'Germany.' 'Great Britain' is *Dah Buliehdian*.

26. Less commonly, *Yih.gwo*.

27. *Shyrtzyh* 'the character *shyr* (十), — a cross.'

28. *Gwojih-*, bound compound for 'international.'

29. Distinguish between *shinlii* 'mind principles, — psychology,' and *shin.lii* 'mind's inside, — in the mind (or heart).'

30. *Jiunjuu lihshiann* 'sovereign-rule-establish-constitution, — monarchial constitutional, — constitutional monarchy.'

31. *Huah* 'transform,' as suffix '-fy, -ize,' as *Ouhuah* 'Europeanize.'

WORLD GEOGRAPHY 229

32. *Binqtuen* 'combine-swallow, — annex.'

33. *Jy i*, often used in precise language, is the literary equivalent of *de ig* 'one of.'

34. *Dwulih* 'alone-stand, — independent,' to be distinguished from *gulih* 'alone-stand, — stand alone, isolated.'

35. *Minjuugwo* or *minjuu-gwojia* 'people-master country, — democracy.'

36. *Ryhbeen* 'sun-origin, — Japan.'

37. In doubting a statement, one challenges the speaker by demanding him to specify the place or time. *Woo naal wanqle?* 'Where did I forget?' *Woo jiishyr wanqle?* 'When did I forget?' Merely saying *Naal a?* is equivalent to saying 'No!'

38. *Tong* 'it goes through, — logical, grammatically correct.'

39. *Jingcherng* 'capital-city.'

40. *Shoou-* 'head,' an unrelated homonym of *shoou* 'hand.' *Shooudu* 'head city, — capital,' a more formal term than *jingcherng*.

41. *Polan*, also pronounced *Bolan*.

42. The full name *Meeilihjian* or *Meeilihjian Herjonqgwo* 'The United States of America' is used only in classrooms and official documents.

EXERCISES

1. *Example:*

Given:	Answer:
Tzarmen deei shian baa shyhjieh dihlii uenlii-wanle,	Yaw deengdaw tzarmen yiijing shian baa shyhjieh dihlii uenlii-wanle jy how,
ranhow woo tzay (*or* tsair) geei niimen jeang Jonggwo dihlii.	woo tsair chii-tourl geei niimen jeang Jonggwo dihlii ne;
	woode yihsy (jiow)sh shuo: tzay woo hair mei geei niimen jeang Jonggwo dihlii yiichyan a, tzarmen deei shian baa shyhjieh dihlii uenlii-wanle tsair shyng (*or* hao, *or* cherng).

(a) Woo deei shian baa fann chy-wanle, ranhow tsair neng geei nii tzuoh-shyh. (b) Tsorngchyan Dergwo sheang shian baa neyshie jinn.deal de sheau-gwo binqtuen le, ranhow tzay baa shyhjieh.shanq suoo yeou de dah-gwo dou geei binqtuen le. (c) Nii deei shian daw Neouiue, ranhow tsair daw Hwashenqduenn. (d) Chwan.shanq de isheng shian geeile ta deal jiowjyi de yaw, ranhow iyuann.lii de isheng tsair geei ta kai-dau. (e) Woo deei shian bae ney-jian binqshyh shyrdou vx hao, ranhow niimen tsair neng jinnchiuh kann binq-ren. (f) Nii shian gawsonq woo niide yihsy, ranhow woo tzay gawsonq nii woode yihsy. (g) Ta shian shyue-hueyle shuo Jonggwo-huah, ranhow tzay shyue dwu Jonggwo-shu. (h) Tade perngyeou shian tsorng binqshyh.lii tzoou.chulai, ranhow ta tzyhgeel tzay mannmhalde tzoou.chulai.

2. *Example* — Suyishyh Yunnher de dongbian yeou Horng Hae, shibian yeou Dihjong Hae, yee tzay Yahjou Feijou de jongjiall.

Similarly, or with variations, describe the positions of (a) The United States, (b) Panama Canal, (c) Australia (say 'Southocean' for the South Seas), (d) France, (e) Russia (say 'Small-Asia' for Asia Minor), (f) Atlantic Ocean, (g) Africa, (h) Antarctica.

3. *Translate into Chinese:*
(a) Do you know what important countries there are in Europe?

LESSON 16
CHINESE GEOGRAPHY

Teacher: Have you any other questions? ... Good, I shall now begin to lecture on the geography of this country. China is the country with the largest population in the world, comprising almost one-fourth of the population of the world. The majority of the Chinese population, however, lives in the eastern and southern parts of China. As for Tibet in the southwest, Kokonor in the west, Sinkiang Province in the northwest, and Inner Mongolia in the north, — in those regions, the population is comparatively sparse. The northernmost provinces are the provinces of the northeast, namely the nine provinces of Liaoning, Liaopeh, Antung, Kirin, Sungkiang, Hokiang, Lungkiang, Nunkiang, Hsingan, which foreigners sometimes call Manchuria.

Wang: Are the people there what they call Manchus?

T: There, you are talking nonsense again, it's not like that at all. Listen, let me explain it to you slowly. More than three hundred years ago, when the Manchus entered the Pass, they dispersed to live in various places in the interior, and since the Republic they have gradually become assimilated to the Chinese, so that now it is frequently impossible to distinguish between Manchus and Chinese —▸ they are all Chinese, that's all. As for the inhabitants of the Northeast, they are almost all Chinese, the great majority of whom have moved there from Shantung.

Lii: Is Jehol also a province?

T: Yes, and Jehol, Chahar, and Suiyuan, these three provinces together are called Inner Mongolia. Down further south are the northern provinces of the Yellow River Basin, — Shantung, Hopeh, Honan, Shansi, Shensi, Kansu, Ninghsia. Sometimes we call this region 'the North,' the place of

(b) It is very difficult to explain the relation between the United Nations and the various countries of the United Nations. (c) Since he was not (at all) seriously ill, there is no point in saying whether the crisis has passed. (d) You were going to ask me something, Teacher? (e) I was going to ask you if you could still recite the 'heaven's stems' and the 'earth's branches.' (f) Since you have already eaten two big bowls of rice, can you still eat that big piece of meat? (g) These words we are learning, except for perhaps one-third of them, are all fairly important, you know. (h) What's the matter with you? If you are not getting one thing wrong, you are getting another thing mixed-up. (i) What you had in mind was not the America of former times, but a modern America.

DIH SHYRLIOW KEH
JONGGWO DIHLII

Shiansheng: Niimen dahjia hair yeou sherm wenn de meiyeou l'a? ... Hao, shianntzay kaishyy[1] jeang beengwo[2] dihlii. Jonggwo sh shyhjieh-shanq renkoou tzuey duo de gwojia, chahbuduo jann[3] chyuan-shyhjieh renkoou de syh-fenn-jy-i. Dannsh Jonggwo de renmin, duoshuh juh tzay Jonggwo de dongnan-buh. Jyhyu[4] shinan de Shitzanq, shibial de Chinghae, shibeei de Shinjiang Sheeng, gen beeibial de Ney Mengguu — neyshie dihfang ne, renkoou biijeaude shishao ideal. Tzuey beeibial de jii-sheeng jiowsh dongbeei jii-sheeng, jiowsh Liau.ning,[5] Liaubeei, Andong, Jyi.lin, Songjiang, Herjiang, Longjiang, Nuennjiang, Shing'an, jeou-sheeng, waygworen yeou shyrhowl goan ta jiaw Maan.jou.

Wang: Nall de ren sh bush jiowsh suoowey Maan.jouren a?

Shg: Ai, nii yow shia-shuo[6] le, wanchyuan bush nemm hwei shyh! Ranq woo lai mannmhalde jiee.shyh[7] geei niimen ting, ah! Sanbae-duo-nian chyan, Chyiren[8] ruhle Guan[9] yiihow, tamen jiow fensann daw Guanney geh-sheeng juhj, tzyhtsorng Mingwo yiilai, jiow jiannjiannde yiijing gen Hannren[10] tornghuah[11] le, suooyii shianntzay woangx fen.bu-chu sherm[12] Chyiren Hannren le — faan.jenq[13] doush Jonggworen jiowshle. Jyhyu shianntzay Dongbeei de jiumin a, chahbuduo chyuansh Hannren, tamen dahduoshuh doush tsorng Shan.dong banle[14] chiuh de.

Lii: Rehher'l sh bush yeesh i-sheeng[15] a?

Shg: Sh de, Rehher, Charhaeel, Sweiyeuan jey-san-sheeng her.chiilai jiaw Ney Mengguu.[16] Tzay wann nan ideal jiowsh Hwangher liouyuh[17] de beei jii-sheeng — Shan.dong, Herbeei, Her.nan, Shan.shi, Shaan.shi, Gan.suh, Ningshiah. Yeou shyrhowl woomen goan jey-i-day[18] dihfang yee the earliest development of the ancient culture of China. Confucius was born in Shantung, of course.

Ch: Wasn't Confucius a native of the state of Lu?

T: Yes, the state of Lu is part of present day Shantung, you see. The capitals of the most flourishing dynasties in ancient China — those of the Shang dynasty, the Chou dynasty, the Ch'in dynasty, the two Han's, the T'ang, the Sung, the Yuan, the Ming, the Ch'ing — the capitals of these dynasties were for the most part in the region of the Yellow River basin. But the Yangtze basin is the center of modern China. From Sikang, Szechwan, Hunan, Hupeh, Kiangsi, Anhwei, down to Kiangsu, and Chekiang — these provinces are considered the richest. The southernmost provinces are Fukien, Taiwan (Formosa), Kwangtung, Kwangsi, Kweichow, and Yunnan. These provinces also occupy extremely important positions from the political, strategic, economic, and cultural points of view. Uh — can any of you think of some prominent men who are southerners?

L: President Chiang is a southerner.

Ch: No, he is from Chekiang, and Chekiang is in the eastern part of central China, you see.

L: (*Interrupts.*) That's not the way to say it, because —

T: Quiet, please! You are both right and both wrong. In the first place, since Kiangsu and Chekiang, compared with the northern provinces, are in the south, there are actually people who call the two provinces of Kiangsu and Chekiang 'the South.' For instance, when a man from Shanghai asks you if you can speak the southern dialect —

W: (*In Shanghai dialect.*) Gan you zbeak the zouthern dialect? (*All laugh loudly.*)

T: Yes, the real Shanghai dialect should of course be spoken with a Shanghai accent — what I meant to say was, what the Shanghai people call the southern dialect simply means the speech of the Shanghai region. So what Lii Shoouchyang said was not entirely without reason. Why then were you both wrong? Well, since the chairman of the government of a country represents the whole country, there is fundamentally no point in speaking of east, west, south, or north —

Ch: He is just a Chinese, is that it?

T: Yes, that's just it.

W: I have thought of a famous man from the south.

T: Who?

W: Dr. Sun Yat-sen was a native of Kwangtung, wasn't he?

L: Didn't you hear what we were all just discussing —

T: Uh — Chyan Tian'i raised his hand first.

Ch: Teacher, Dr. Sun Yat-sen was the Father of the Chinese Republic,

jiaw Beeibian, jehsh Jonggwo guu.shyr.howl wenhuah fadar tzuey tzao de dihfang. Koong Tzyy [19] jiowsh sheng tzay Shan.dong de lo.

Chyan: Koong Tzyy bush Luu.gworen ma?

Shg: Sh a, Luu.gwo jiowsh shianntzay Shan.dong sheeng de i-buh.fenn [20] a. Jonggwo guuday [21] tzuey shingwanq [22] de jii-chaur [23] de gwodu [24] — Shang.chaur a, Jou.chaur a, Chyn.chaur a, leang-Hann, Tarng, [25] Sonq, Yuan, Ming, Ching — jey-jii-chaur de jingcherng chahbuduo doush tzay Hwangher liouyuh de. Dannsh Charng Jiang [26] liouyuh sh shiannday Jonggwo de jongshin. Tsorng Shikang, Syh.chuan, Hwu.nan, Hwubeei, Jiang.shi, An.huei, daw Jiang.su, Jeh.jiang — ney-jii-sheeng yaw suannsh tzuey fuh de jii-sheeng le. Tzuey nanbial de jii-sheeng jiowsh Fwu.jiann, Tair.uan, Goang.dong, Goang.shi, Guey.jou, Yun.nan. Jey-jii-sheeng tzay [27] jenqjyh.shanq, gwofarng.shanq,[28] jingjih.shanq, wenhuah.shanq, yee doush jann feicharng jonqyaw de dihwey de. E — niimen sheir sheang.de-chulai yeou naa-shie [29] chuming de ren sh nanfang ren a?

L: Jeang Juushyi [30] sh Nanbian ren.

Ch: Naal a? Jeang Juushyi sh Jeh.jiang ren, Jeh.jiang tzay Jonggwo de jongbuh dongbial è!

L: (*Daa-chah.*) Bush nemm shuo de, inwey —

Shg: Bye naw vx! Niimen leangg ren shuo de dou duey, yee dou bu-duey. Dih'i-tserng, inwey Jiang.su Jeh.jiang gen Beeibian bii.chiilai sh tzay nanbial, suooyii dyichiueh sh yeou ren goan Jiang– Jeh– leang-sheeng jiaw 'Nanbian.' Biifang ig Shanqhae-ren wenn nii shuo, Nii huey shuo Nanbian-huah buhuey —

W: Nong weyte kàang Népie hhèwoh va? [31] (*Chyuantii dah shiaw.*)

Shg: Duey le, jende Shanqhae-huah dangran sh yonq Shanqhae koouin [32] shuo de lo — woode yihsy sh shuo Shanqhae-ren suoowey Nanbian-huah, jiowsh Shanqhae ney-i-day de huah de yihsy. Suooyii Lii Shoouchyang shuo de huah yee bush chyuan meiyeou dawlii. Tzeem yow buduey ne? Inwey i-gwo jenqfuu de juushyi sh daybeau chyuan-gwo de, genbeen [33] jiow wusuoowey dong shi nan beei —

Ch: Tan [34] yahgel [35] jiowsh Jonggworen sh bush'a?

Shg: Duey le, jiow(sh) jeh huah lo.

W: Woo sheang daw g Nanbian de mingren le.

Shg: Sheir?

W: Jongshan Shiansheng [36] sh Goangdong Jongshan-ren è.

L: Nii mei tingjiann tzarmen dahjia gangtsair jeang de —

Shg: E — Chyan Tian'i shian jeu-shoou.

Ch: Shiansheng, Jongshan Shiansheng sh Jonghwa Mingwo de Gwofuh, nah bush yee jiow 'wusuoowey dong shi nan beei' le ma?

wouldn't that then also be a case of 'no point in speaking of east, west, south, or north'?

T: Yes, you are right. That's a good point.

L: (*Grumbles.*) That was just what I wanted to say, but Teacher wouldn't give me a chance! (*Bell rings.*)

T: It's time. Today's lesson on Chinese geography is at an end. Prepare your lessons well, will you? Tomorrow examination!

Class: Gee!

NOTES

1. *Kaishyy* 'open-begin, — to begin,' a more formal term than *chiitourl.*

2. *Been–* 'this' is a formal term. *Beengwo* 'this country' and *been-gongsy* 'this company' are neutral as to politeness; *been-juushyi* 'I, the chairman,' has a very superior air; *been-ren* 'this person' is a humble form for 'I,' used in speeches. *Been-ren* also means 'the person himself.'

3. *Jann* 'to occupy.'

4. *Jyhyu* 'reach-to, — as to.'

5. The indicated neutral tones on the second syllables in the names of the provinces are all optional.

6. *Shia* 'blind' before a verb means 'at random, nonsensically.' *Shia-shuo* = *hwu-shuo* 'to talk nonsense.'

7. *Jiee* 'unfasten, untie,' *shyh* literary equivalent of *jiee*; *jiee.shyh* 'explain.' Cf. 'unfold, unravel.'

8. *Chyiren* 'bannermen.'

9. *Guan* 'Pass,' short for *Shanhae Guan* 'Shanhaikuan.' *Ruh Guan* 'enter the Pass.'

10. *Hannren* 'the Han people, — Chinese in the narrower sense.'

11. *Tornghuah* 'same-ize, — assimilate.' It does *not* mean 'identify.'

12. *Sherm Chyiren Hannren* may be regarded as an indirect rhetorical question *Sherm Chyiren Hannren?* (Note 3, p. 182.)

13. *Faan.jenq* 'right or reverse, — anyway.' Cf. *herngsh < herng-shuh.*

14. *Ban* 'to move (furniture or house).'

15. *Sheeng* 'province' is either noun (with *ig*) or quasi-AN (with *i–*).

16. Sometimes Ninghsia is regarded as part of Inner Mongolia.

17. *Liouyuh* 'flow-region, — (river) basin.'

18. *Day* 'region, belt.'

19. *Koong Tzyy* 'K'ung Philosopher, — Confucius,' more popularly, *Koong.futzyy* 'K'ung Master,' whence the latinized form.

20. *Buh.fenn* 'part, fraction.'

21. *Guuday* 'ancient generations, — ancient times.'

22. *Shingwang* 'rise-flourish, — flourish.'

Shg: Ëh, nii shuo de duey. Jeyg yihsy heen hao.
L: (*Ji.guj.*) Nah jiowsh woo jenq yaw shuo de huah, Shiansheng bu geei woo ji.huey shuo me! (*Daa shiah-keh-ling.*[37])
Shg: Daw shyrhowl le. Jintian Jonggwo dihlii-keh wanbih.[38] Niimen dahjia dou yuh.bey hao.deal, ah! Mingtian kao!
Chyuantii: Oh!

---

23. *Chaur₀day* is the full word for 'dynasty'; *chaur* is quasi-AN or combining form in names of dynasties.
24. *Gwodu* 'country's metropolis, — capital,' more formal than *jingcherng*.
25. The teacher is tired of saying –.*chaur* in each case. (See Note 37, p. 201.)
26. The term *Charng Jiang* 'Long River' is much more frequently used than *Yangtzyy Jiang* 'Yangtze River.'
27. *Tzay* . . . –.*shanq* 'in regard to, –ically.'
28. *Gwofarng* 'national defense.'
29. The teacher uses the formal pronunciation *naa-shie* for *neei-shie*.
30. Nobody speaks of *Jeang Jiehshyr Dah Yuanshuay*, which would be a literal translation of 'Generalissimo Chiang Kai-shek' (the form *shek* is Cantonese), but usually refers to him as *Jeang Woeiyuan Jaang* 'Chairman of the (Military) Commission Chiang,' or *Jeang Juushyi* 'Chairman Chiang' (of the Nationalist Government).
31. In this notation for the Shanghai pronunciation, the vowel *à* is a very broad *a* or open *o*, *hh* is a voiced *h*, and *t*, *k* and *p* are unaspirated, harder than Mandarin *d*, *g*, *b*. The sentence in Mandarin would be, word for word, *Nong hueyde jeang Nanbian shyanhuah bu a?*, i.e. *Nii huey shuo Nanbian-huah buhuey?*
32. *Koou₀in* 'mouth-sound, — accent.'
33. *Genbeen* 'root-origin, — fundamentally.'
34. *Tan* : *ta* = *Nin* : *nii*, but *tan* is much less frequently used, even in the Peiping region.
35. *Yahgel* 'bearing down to the root, — to start with, in the first place.'
36. Dr. Sun (*Suen*) is usually referred to as *Jongshan Shiansheng*, also as *Gwofuh*. *Yatsen* is the Cantonese pronunciation of his style *Yihshian*. His *mingtzyh* was *Wen*.
37. *Shiah-keh* 'to dismiss class.' *Ling* is used instead of *liengl*, in the style of stage directions, which are usually in *wenli*.
38. *Wanbih* 'finish-complete,' a very formal term for 'finished.'

EXERCISES

1. *Complete each of the following sentences in two different ways (each dash stands for one or several words):*

(a) Yawsh niimen ____, tzarmen shianntzay jiow kaishyy ____ le. (b) ____ jann chyuan- ____ de ____ -fenn-jy- ____. (c) ____ de ____, dahduoshuh ____. (d) Sh bush bush ____ jiowsh ____, sh bush a? (e) Tzyhtsorng ____ yiilai, jiow jiannxde i ____ bii i ____ le. (f) Nii sheang-de chu ig ____ de ____ lai ma? (g) ____ bu geei woo ____ shuo-huah. (h) ____ goan ____ de ____ jiaw ____.

2. *Translate into Chinese:*

(a) After the patient entered the hospital two weeks ago, he lived in

LESSON 17
TALKING ABOUT INDUSCO

A: Oh, pshaw!

B: What's the matter?

A: Simply ridiculous! It's already half past seven! I told you to get up early and you just lay there in bed and snored away.

B: Who did? I got out of bed as soon as it was morning, how much still earlier did you expect me to be?

A: Then you spent too much time dallying. Washing your face, brushing your teeth, and rinsing your mouth, putting on your clothes and socks, tying the shoe-strings, — spending so much time at each —

B: But you insisted on waiting for the water to boil, and for making tea with boiling water for breakfast, we had to wait so much longer.

A: Well, stop blaming this and blaming that! What's the good of arguing about it? Better hurry up and go!

B: It'll be faster if we call some rickshas.

A: A good idea! Where are the rickshas coming from in these parts? There are neither vehicles nor donkeys to ride here. You just have to walk with your feet. I think we still have time, though. It's over five *li* from here to the factory. Our appointment with them is to arrive there for the visit before eight. I heard that the country roads here are not too bad. I think we shall have time if we walk fast.

B: Okay, let's go.

A: Here we go! . . .

B: They all call those factories 'Indusco.' How do you explain the term 'Indusco'?

various parts of the hospital, and after these many days, he has gradually become no different from a well man (*hao-ren*). (b) The T'ang dynasty is actually one of the most flourishing dynasties (*chaur.day*) in ancient times. (c) What I had in mind was only the names of the most important dynasties. (d) The provinces which occupy the most important positions politically, strategically, economically, and culturally are the southernmost provinces. (e) It is an actual fact that they do call the southeastern part of the United States 'The South.' (f) The reason that he gave (*shuo*) out was not entirely groundless. (g) The people here are frequently unable to distinguish the cardinal directions. (h) As for those who live in that dilapidated house, the majority were those who moved in there afterwards.

DIH SHYRCHI KEH TARN GONGHER

A: Aiia, tzaugau!
B: Tzeem l'a?
A: Jeanjyr shiaw.huah! Chi-dean-bann le .dou![1] Woo jiaw nii tzao.deal chiilai, nii jiow lao taang de chwang.shanq [2] tzaynall daa-hu.lu.
B: Naal a? Woo i-dah-tzao jiow chii-chwang le, nii hair yaw jyy.wanq woo dwo tzao a?
A: Neme nii dan.wuh de shyrhowl tay duo le. Shii-lean le,[3] shua-ya shuh-koou le, chuan [4] i.shang, chuan wahtz, jih shyedall le — meei-jiann shyh dou fey nemm dah gongful —
B: Keesh nii feideei deeng shoei kai le, weyle yaw na kai-shoei chi-char [5] chy dean.shin, yow deei deeng nemm banntian![6]
A: Ai, bye guay[7] jeyg guay neyg le. Jeh yeou sherm jeng.toul?[8] Hairsh kuay tzoou b'ou!
B: Jiaw yangche [9] chiuh kuaydeal.
A: Hao?! Jell naal lai yangche ia? Jell yee mei che tzuoh yee mei liu chyi, yinqsh [10] deei na jeau tzoou. Keesh woo sheang hair laidejyi, .dawsh. Jell li gongchaang yeou wuu-lii-duo dih. Tzarmen gen tamen iue [11] de sh ba-dean chyan.ideal daw nall tsanguan,[12] jell shiang.shiah [13] de dawl ting shuo hair bu tay huay. Kuaydeal tzoou laidejyi, .woo .sheang.
B: Hao ba, tzarmen jiow tzoou ba!
A: Tzoou l'a!...
B: Tamen dou goan neyshie gongchaang jiaw 'Gongher,'[14] 'Gongher' leangg [15] tzyh tzeem jeang a?

A: 'Indusco' is just a simplified way of saying 'Industrial Cooperatives' or 'Light Industrial Cooperative Movement.'

B: I see. How was the Light Industrial Cooperative Movement started?

A: The history of this movement begins in the 27th year of the Republic [1938]. You remember the 26th year was the year in which the war of resistance began, wasn't it? At that time, our government, as well as the people, already realized that the fighting this time was not likely to be that of a short war. Everybody was determined on long-term resistance, so they took from the factories machines, trained workmen, and experienced technicians — both equipment and personnel —

B: I heard that a good many took their families along, too —

A: Yes, and they all suffered a lot — they endured I-don't-know how many hardships and suffered I-don't-know how much misery, before they arrived in the provinces in the interior and finally set up their industries again. Thus, it was possible, on the one hand, to help those workers who had lost their jobs to solve their problem of livelihood, and at the same time, too, they were able to manufacture a lot of articles needed for daily use.

B: Yes, that's killing two birds with one stone, isn't it?

A: That's it, that's where the advantage lies.

B: What's the meaning of '*Light* Industry Cooperatives?'

A: Well, light industries don't need large capital; everybody can put up money and set up for himself, you see?

B: Then what's the difference between this and ordinary small trade or handicraft?

A: Well, this is just the distinction between what you call industry and ordinary handicraft. Although what they are doing now is not heavy industry, and not even basic industry, yet the way they manufacture things and run their affairs is entirely according to scientific method. Wherever machines can be used they use machines; where there is room for improvement on the old methods, they change them into new methods; thus, on the one hand, they can increase their power of production, and at the same time, they can also raise the standard of living of the people.

B: Well, that's wonderful! But the majority of the common people have no knowledge of science.

A: That doesn't matter. In the Indusco there are many specialists who can help them. They have a good many engineers who are returned students from abroad. They are constantly doing research to find out what kinds of simplified machinery and what kinds of native materials can be used to make what kinds of goods that will be both useful and can sell cheaply.

B: Say, we have walked quite a while, are we half way yet?

A: Oh, where are we? I'm afraid we have taken the wrong road. Better ask somebody. Oh, excuse me, sir!

C: Huh?

TALKING ABOUT INDUSCO

A: 'Gongher' jiowsh 'Gongyeh Hertzuoh' heje 'Ching Gongyeh Hertzuoh Yunndonq' de jeandan shuo.faa.

B: Oh. Ching Gongyeh Hertzuoh Yunndonq sh tzeem fachii d'a?

A: Jeyg yunndonq de lihshyy sh tsorng Mingwo ellshyrchi-nian chiitourl de. Nii jihde ellshyrliow-nian ney-nian, bush kanqjann [16] kaishyy de ney-nian ma? Nah shyrhowl tzarmen de jenqfuu gen renmin jiow yiijing liaw.daw ney-tsyh de daa-janq a,[17] bujiannde [18] sh ig doan-shyrchyi de jannjeng. Renren dou shiahle charngchyi diikanq de jyueshin,[19] suooyii bae [20] gehchuh gongchaang.lii de jichih a, yeou shiunnliann de gong.ren a, yeou jingyann de jihshy a — lian jichih day ren —

B: Ting shuo hair yeou haoshie dayj jia.jiuann tzoou de ne —

A: Duey le, tamen dou kuu de heen — tam bujydaw chyle duo.shao kuu, showle duo.shao tzuey, tsair ban-dawle neydih geh-sheeng hao rongyih [21] tsair bae gongyeh yow jiannsheh.chiilai. I-fangmiann ne, keeyii bangjuh neyshie mei shell gann mei fann chy de gong.ren, hao [22] ranq tamen jieejyue sheng.hwo de wenntyi, torngshyr ne,[23] yow keeyii tzaw.chu [24] sheuduo ryhyonq bihshiu de wuhpiin .lai —

B: Èè, tzemmyanql dawsh 'i-jeu leang-der,' [25] ar?

A: Èh, jiow jeh huah lo, hao.chuh jiow tzay jell lo.

B: '**Ching** gongyeh' tzeem jeang ne?

A: Ching gongyeh me, keeyii buyonq dah tzybeen a; renren dou neng tzyhjii chu-chyan [26] lai bann a.

B: Neme jeyg gen pyngcharng tzuoh sheau mae.may [27] de heje tzuoh shoou.yih de yeou sherm butorng ne?

A: Ah, jeh jiowsh suoowey gongyeh gen puutong shoou.yih de fen.bye le. Tamen shianntzay bann de sweiran bush jonq gongyeh, binqchiee yee bush jibeen gongyeh, dannsh tamen jyh.tzaw dongshi gen bann-shyh, chyuansh jawj keshyue fangfaa de. Farnsh keeyii yonq jichih de dihfangl jiow yonq jichih; keeyii bae jiow-fartz gaeliang de dihfangl, jiow gaecherngle shin-fartz; tzemmyanql i-fangmiann keeyii tzengjia shengchaan de lih.lianq, torngshyr ne, yow keeyii bae renmin de sheng.hwo cherng-.duh [28] geei tyi-gau [29] le.

B: Tz, jen hao! Keesh pyngcharng laobae.shinq [30] duoshuh sh meiyeou keshyue jy.shyh d'a!

A: Nah mei guanshih a, Gongher.lii yeou sheuduo juanmen de rentsair [31] keeyii bang-mang a. Liitou yeou haoshie gongcherngshy sh tsorng waygwo hweilai de liouxhyuesheng.[32] Tamen i-tian-daw-woan yanjiow yonq tzeem vx jeandan-huah de jichih, yonq neeishie vx beendih de tsair.liaw, ranhow tzaw.de-chu [33] shermvx yow yeou yonq yow may de pyan.yi de huohwuh .lai.

B: È, tzarmen tzooule tzemm banntian, kee yeou iball luh l'a?

A: Aiia, tzarmen dawle naal l'a? koongpah tzoou-tsuoh le luh le ba. Diinghao wennx ren ba. È, laujiah, Nin a!

C: Erng?

NOTES

1. This *dou* is an afterthought word. *Chi-dean-bann le dou* 'half past seven, as late as.' It is also possible to put *dou* both before and after, *Dou chi-dean-bann le dou*. There is usually no pause between *le* and final *dou*.

2. Note the use of *.shanq* 'on' where the English has 'in.'

3. This *le* is a particle of enumeration used when the speaker has 'and what not' attitude toward the things enumerated.

4. *Chuan* 'pierce,' used as 'put on' or 'wear' for articles in which some part of the body goes through. But *day* 'put on top,' is used for *shooutawl* 'gloves,' as well for *mawtz* 'hat' and *yeanjienql* 'eye-glasses.'

5. *Chi-char* 'infuse tea, — make tea.'

6. *Banntian* 'half a day'; 'a long time' (which may be a few seconds or many minutes). Cf. 'Don't be all day about it!'

7. *Guay* 'to find queer, — to blame.'

8. *Yeou . . . -.toul* 'worth . . . -ing'; *mei . . . -.toul* 'not worth . . . -ing.' *Jeng* 'fight over, wrangle'; 'argue.'

9. *Yangche*, abbreviated form of the now obsolete word *dongyang-che* 'east ocean vehicle, — Japanese vehicle, — ricksha.'

10. *Yinqsh* 'the hard fact is that . . . .'

11. *Iue* 'to make an agreement.'

12. *Tsanguan* 'to visit (museums, factories, schools, etc.).'

13. *Shiang.shiah* 'the country'; *shiah-shiang* 'go to the country.'

14. The popular translation of *gongher* (or *kung-ho* in the Wade system) as 'work together' is opposed to the spirit of Chinese grammar, since the modifier must precede the modified. The word for 'work together' or 'cooperate' is *hertzuoh* 'together work.'

15. *Gongher*, or any other disyllabic compound is spoken of as *leangg tzyh* (see p. 33).

16. *Kanqjann* 'resistance-war,' *n.* or *v.*

17. The *a* marks a pause after the subject, in preparation for a difficult predicate.

18. *Bujiannde* 'not seen as likely' has no positive form **jiannde*, except in playful contradiction to *bujiannde*.

19. *Shiah jyueshin* 'lay down determination, — to be determined.'

20. After *bae*, the specific verb gets lost when the speaker is interrupted. Presumably he would have said something like *dou ban daw neydih chiuh le* 'moved them all to the interior' to complete his sentence.

21. *Haorong.yih* 'how easy?! — finally, after great difficulty.'

22. *Hao* 'good (for), — in order to.'

23. The *ne* is to be translated by an upswing of the voice on 'time' in 'at the same time, ...'

24. The verb is *tzaw.chulai*.

25. *I-jeu leang-der* 'one effort two results,' a commonly quoted literary phrase. *Jeu* 'raise,' *der* 'get.'
26. *Chu-chyan* 'put out money, — put up money.'
27. *Mae.may* 'buy-sell, — a trade.' *Tzuoh mae.may de* 'tradesman.'
28. *Cherng.duh* 'degree of advancement, standing, level.'
29. *Tyi-gau* 'lift up, — raise.'
30. *Laobae.shinq* 'old hundred surnames, — the common people.'
31. *Rentsair* 'human material, talents.'
32. *Lioushyue* 'to remain (abroad) to study.' *Lioushyuesheng* 'a student studying abroad'; 'one who has studied abroad, returned student.'
33. The verb is *tzaw.de-chulai*, with a long inserted object.

EXERCISES

1. *Answer the following:*

(a) Daa jell daw nall yeou ibae ellshyr-lii dih. Yawsh tzuoh chihche nii sheang deei tzoou duoshao shyrhowl? Yawsh na jeau tzoou, i-luh yow deei shiex chyx dongshi shermde, nah yaw duoshao shyrhowl ne? (b) Nii tzaochern shian tzuoh shie sherm shell ranhow tsair chii-tourl chy deanshin? (c) Shoei tzay haemiall.shanq kai de kuay hairsh tzay gau-shan-.shanq kai de kuay? (d) Sherm jiaw 'laibujyi'? 'Laibujyi' jeyg huah sh tzeem jeang de? (e) Hertzuoh yeou sherm haochuh? (f) Jaw niide yihjiann kann.chiilai, dih'ell-tsyh shyhjieh jannjeng yiihow, hair huey yeou dihsan-tsyh buhuey l'a? (g) Jonggwo tzueyjinn jey-tsyh kanqjann, chwule gongren yiiway, hair yeou sherm yee dou ban daw neydih chiuh le? (h) Jiannsheh gongyeh yeou sherm yonqchuh? (i) Ing'wen goan tzuoh i-jiann shell yeou leangg yonqchuh jiaw sherm a? Jongwen ne? (j) I-jiann shell yawsh yonq jiow-fartz tzuoh tzuoh.bu-hao, nah jiow tzeem bann ne? (k) Sherm jiaw sheng.hwo cherng.duh di a? Shuo ig ren de sheng.hwo cherng.duh di sh sherm yihsy a? (l) Sherm jiaw lioushyuesheng? Lioushyuesheng gen byede shyue.sheng yeou sherm butorng ne?

2. *Example:*

Given:	Answer:
	A: Nii (ta, *etc.*) shanq jell lai gannma (tzuoh sherm.me, weysherm lai, *etc.*)?
Jell yeou shyh meiyeou?	B: Woo lai wennx jell yeou shyh meiyeou; woo sh lai jao-shyh tzuoh de.
Woo lai jao-shyh tzuoh.	A: Jell naal yeou shyh a? Jell yee mei shyh tzuoh, yee mei fann chy.

(a) Ta nall yeou char meiyeou? Woo chiuh jao char he. (b) Niimen jia.lii yeou shu meiyeou? Woo lai jao shu niann. (c) U.lii yeou reh-shoei meiyeou? Woo lai jao shoei shii-lean. (d) Chwan.shanq yeou isheng meiyeou? Woo lai jao isheng kann-binq. (e) Niimen gongchaang.lii yeou huey kai chihche de meiyeou? Woo lai jao kai-che de kai chihche. (f) Niimen jell yeou jyy meiyeou? Woo lai jao jyy shiee-tzyh. (g) Jell yeou huey shuo Jonggwo-huah de meiyeou? Tamen lai jao ren gen tamen shuo Jonggwo-huah. (h) Niimen jell yeou maa meiyeou? Woo lai jao maa chyi. (i) Niimen yeou hao-shinwen gawsonq woo meiyeou? Woo lai jao shinwen ting. (j) Jey-beel shu .lii yeou huall meiyeou? Woo lai jao huall geei sheauharl kann. (k) Jeyg iyuann .lii yeou ney-joong shin-faming de yaw meiyeou? Woo lai jao shin-yaw geei binqren daa-jen. (l) U.lii yeou joen.ideal de jong meiyeou? Woo lai jao g joen.ideal de jong kann shyrhowl.

3. *Translate into Chinese:*

(a) I have made an appointment with the doctor to visit the Red

LESSON 18
TO THE MINSHENG WORKS

A: Excuse me, sir, could you tell me how to get to the Minsheng Works?

C: (*In Chungking dialect:*) Eh? Whut deed you say?

B: Oh, he doesn't understand what you say. Let me ask him. Uh — we want to go to the Minsh — we want to reach the Minsen Works, to the Minsen Factory, and we don't know — uh — we do not know how to get there.

C: Oh, the Minsen Warks? Teke this rawd and torn to the lift, —

A: I see, turn to the left.

C: Go past the second bridge, then turn to the right, walk something like two li, then there will be a gross road —

A: A what?

B: He says there will be a crossroad.

C: That's right, a gross road, but you don't pay any attention to that. Walk a little further on and you will get to a T-junction. Turn in there, and then you will see a foreign-style building, with a triangle sign on the door, and that will be the Minsen Warks. You can't mess it!

A: Much obliged!

B: Thank you, sir!

Cross Hospital at a quarter of four. (b) As there is no certainty about the speed of the boat, we had better (say 'best') start as soon as we get up. (c) How do you explain the name Tarn Butyng? What do they call him that for? (d) Soon after the war of resistance started, technicians and workmen in various kinds of industries, one after another, moved into the provinces in the interior. (e) The injuries which he received in that airplane accident have almost completely healed (*hao le*). (f) By this cooperative method, one can both help those who have no job to do and at the same time make a great many extremely useful articles. (g) The most important thing in learning Chinese or any other language is to use everyday the words which you have already learned. (h) In this school there are a good many returned students doing research in various (*geh-joong*) sciences. (i) Have we still time to arrive there at eight? (j) I read this lesson God-knows-how-many times before (*tsair*) I could recite the names of the provinces. (k) Well, the difference between what you call a physician and a surgeon just lies in (say 'on') this. (l) The reason that these things can sell so cheaply is that native material is used.

DIH SHYRBA KEH
TSANGUAN MINSHENG [1] CHAANG

A: Laujiah, Nin a! Chiing wenn [2] shanq Minsheng Chaang sh tzeem tzoou d'a?

C: Enq? Nii sor sahtz a? [3] (Erng? Nii shuo shermme?)

B: Êh, ta bu doong niide huah. Ranq woo lai wenn ta. Eng — woomen yaw sanq [4] Minsh — woomen yaw daw Minsen Tsaang chiuh, daw Minsen Gongtsaang chiuh. Butzydaw — e — busheaude [5] syh tzeem tzoou dih?

C: .Or, Minsen Tsaang a, tsorng tzeh-tyau luh shianq tzoo tzoan, —
(.Oh, Minsheng Chaang a, tsorng jey-tyau luh wann tzuoo joan, —)

A: Oh, wann tzuoo goai.

C: Tzoou-guohle [6] dih'ellg chyau, tzay shianq yow tzoou, tzooule leanglii luh de yanqtz, jiow yeou ig syr-tzyh-luhkeel — [7]

A: Yeou ig shermme?

B: Ta shuo yeou ig shyr-tzyh-luhkooul.

C: Duey le, ig syr-tzyh-luhkeel, buguoh nii buyaw chiuh goan ta. Tzay tzoou-guoh.chiuh ideal, yow daw ig din-tzyh-luhkeel.[8] Tsorng din-tzyh-luhkeel joan.jinnchiuh, nii jiow kann-dao [9] i-tzuoh [10] yang-farngtz, menshanq yeou g sanjeaul-shyng [11] de jau.pair,[12] nah jiowsh Minsheng Chaang le. Buhuey tsuoh de.

A: Laujiah vx!

B: Dueybujuh, ah, Shiansheng!

C: Oh, don't mention it!....
A: Uh — Has Mr. Liou, the manager, come in yet?
D: Are you lucking for Mr. Liou, the ungineer?
A: Oh, yes, Mr. Liou, the engineer.
D: He hasn't arrived yet, but he will be here soon — oh, here he is. Mr. Liou, there are some people lucking for you.
Liou: Excuse me, gentlemen, I am late.
A: Oh, we have only just arrived ourselves. Uh — Mr. Liou, allow me to introduce my friend, this is Mr. Shyu Ryhshin, who has come with me to visit your factory.
B: I'm glad to meet you.
L: Delighted to meet *you.*
B: Is this factory entirely devoted to manufacturing textiles?
L: Yes, originally we did specialize in this line. Afterwards we gradually enlarged our scope, and now, besides towels, blankets, sheets, and things like that, we have added a department of chemical articles, including alcohol, soap, ink —
A: I heard that in Indusco they also manufacture weapons, is that right?
L: Yes, that's in another factory. Here, other than uniforms, overcoats, and (leather) shoes, we do not make military goods. There are some — ha ha! — small trifles, such as airplanes, tanks, aircraft carriers —
B: Dear me, 'small trifles'?!
L: Oh, just toy models for children to play with.
B: Oh, they are just —
L: What we produce are mostly articles needed for ordinary living.
B: Oh, that's why it's called the 'People's Livelihood Factory,' isn't it?
L: That's right. Not far from here there is another factory called the Mintzwu Works. They can make rifles and guns, cartridges, electric batteries, radio receivers; they can also refine kerosene and gasoline. Since we must have national defense in order to preserve our national freedom, therefore the factory where they manufacture weapons is called the National Works.
B: There is still the Principle of Democracy in the Three Principles of the People, isn't there? Is there a factory called Democratic Works?
A: I heard that they are preparing to set up a Democratic Press, aren't they?
L: Yes, there is such a plan. This press is going to be used for promoting popular education and for giving expression to public opinion. For if you want the people to be self-governing, you must at the same time raise the level of popular knowledge; that's why it's called the Democratic Press. — Oh, it's eight now, they are starting work at the factory. Oh, Ding! Ding!
D: Yes.

C: Ah, bukehchih, bukehchih! . . .
A: E — Liou Jinglii lai le ba?
D: Nii shiansheng [13] sh bush jao Liou Gongcherngshy [14] a?
A: Ah, butsuoh, Liou Gongcherngshy.
D: Ta hair mei lai, dannsh jiow yaw lai le — oh, ta lai le. — Liou Shiansheng, yeou keh.ren jao nii.
L: Ah, dueybujuh, dueybujuh! Woo daw-chyrle.
A: Ai, woomen yee buguoh gangtsair daw de. E — Liou Shg., ranq woo jiehshaw i-wey perngyeou. Jehsh Shyu Ryhshin Shg., gen woo ikuall lai tsanguan de.
B: Jeouyeang [15] vx!
L: Ah, bii-tsyy [16] vx!
B: Jeyg chaang .lii sh bush juanmen jyhtzaw faangjy-piin [17] d'a?
L: Êh, beenlai juan tzuoh [18] jey-i-harng. Howlai baa fannwei jiannxde kuoh-dahle, shianntzay chwule shoou.jin a, taantz a, beydal [19] a, nah-ley dongshi jy way, woomen yow tianle [20] i-men huahshyue [21] yonqpiin, baukuoh jeoujing [22] a, yitz a, mohshoei [23] a, —
A: Ting shuo Gongher.lii hair tzaw bing.chih ne, sh bush a?
L: Butsuoh, tzay linqway ig chaang .lii. Woomen jeh.lii chwule jyhfwu, dahchaang, pyishye [24] jy way, bu tzuoh jiunyonq-piin de. Yeou shie — he he! — sheau-wanyell,[25] haobii feiji le, jannche [26] le, harngkong muujiann [27] le, —
B: He, hao-jiahuoo! 'Sheau-wanyell'?!
L: He he, nah buguoh doush geei sheauharlmen wal de mushyng jiowshle.
B: Oh, gaanchyng jiowsh —
L: Woomen chu de dongshi dahduoshuh sh puutong [28] sheng.hwo bihshiu de yonqpiin.
B: Oh, suooyii jiaw Minsheng Chaang, ar?
L: Duey le vx. Li jeh.lii buyeuan [29] hair yeou i-jia [30] jiaw Mintzwu Chaang de. Tamen neng tzaw chiang-paw, tzyydann, diannchyr, wushiann-diann shouinji,[31] binqchiee hair neng liann meiyou [32] gen chihyou. Inwey yaw baotswen mintzwu [33] de tzyhyou jiow deei yeou gwofarng, suooyii jyhtzaw wuuchih de gongchaang jiow jiaw Mintzwu Chaang lo.
B: Sanmin Juuyih [34] bush hair yeou Minchyuan [35] Juuyih ma? Yeou meiyeou jiaw Minchyuan Chaang d'a?
A: Ting shuo tamen jenq tzaynall yuhbey yaw kaibann [36] ig Minchyuan Yinnshua Suoo [37] ne, sh bush a?
L: Duey, sh yeou jeyg shyh.[38] Jeyg yinnshua-suoo sh yuhbey [39] tyichanq pyngmin jiaw.yuh,[40] gen fabeau renmin de yanluenn [41] yonq de. Inwey ruguoo yaw renmin tzyhjyh [42] me, torngshyr jiow deei baa renmin

L: If anybody looks for me, tell him that I have gone with two guests on a tour of inspection and shall be back in about an hour.

D: Vury goad, sir.

NOTES

1. *Minsheng* 'the people's livelihood.'

2. *Chiing wenn* 'please (allow me to) ask, — may I ask . . .? Could you please tell me . . .?'

3. Speakers C and D are from Chungking and speak a variety of Southwestern Mandarin spoken in several provinces with remarkable uniformity. The main features of the Chungking dialect are as follows:

(1) The four tones are 55:, 11:, 42:, 35:, that is, ˥, ˩, ˦, ˧. They correspond for the most part to the four tones of Northern Mandarin, such as that of Peiping. (The orthography used here for the Chungking tones is on the basis of word-classes and not of actual musical tune. This makes words meaning the same things look very much alike.)

(2) The retroflex initials j_r, ch_r, sh_r, and r become dentals *tz, ts, s, z*. (The palatals j_i, ch_i, sh_i remain unchanged.)

(3) Initials *n* and *l* merge into one, sounding more like *l* than *n*, but Northern *n* before *i* or *iu* becomes *gn* (as in French).

(4) Finals *-eng* and *-ing* (for all tones) merge with *-en* and *-in*, respectively.

(5) Finals *e* and *uo* mostly become *é* and *o*.

Since most of the changes consist in coalescence of different sounds, it is easier for a speaker of Northern Mandarin to speak Southwestern Mandarin than vice versa.

4. Speaker B has a smattering of the dialect. He realizes that *shanq . . . chiuh* 'to go to . . .' should be *daw . . . chiuh*.

5. *Sheaude* 'to know' is more frequently used than *jydaw* in the central dialects; *dih* reading pron. and dialectal pron. of particle *de*.

6. In order not to complicate the text too much, the words of Speaker C (and D) from here on will be given mostly in Standard Mandarin. In the Chungking dialect, these sentences (with suitable substitution of tone values) will be as follows:

C: Tzoou-gohle dih'ellg chyau, tzay shianq yow tzoou, tzooule leang-lii luh .li yanqtz, jiow yeou ig syr-tzyh-luhkeel — . . . Duey le, ig syr-tzyh-luhkeel. bwugoh nii bwuyaw chiuh goan ta. Tzay tzoou-goh-de jyshyh cherngduh tyi-gaule tsair shyng a;⁴³ suooyii tsair jiaw Minchyuan Yinnshua Suoo. — Ȇ, shianntzay daa ba-dean le, chaang.lii kaigong le. Lao Ding! Lao Ding!

D: Uei! ⁴⁴

L: Ruguoo yeou ren lai jao woo, nii jiow shuo woo peirj ⁴⁵ leang-wey laibin ⁴⁶ daw chaang.lii tsanguan .chiuh le, dahiue guoh ig jongtourl jiow hweilai ba.

D: Hao, yawde ⁴⁷ vx!

---

chiuh yideal, yow daw ig din-tzyh-luhkeel. Tsorng din-tzyh-luhkeel tzoan-jinnchiuh, nii jiow kann-dao yi-tzoh yang-farngtz, mensanq yeou goh sangor-shyn .ni tzaupair, nah jiows Minsen Tsaang le. Bwuhuey tsoh.li ... .Or, bwukérchih, bukérchih! ...

D: Nii Shiansen s bus tzao Liou Gongtsernsy a? ... Ta hair mhei lai, danns jiow yaw lai le — .or, ta lai le. — Liou Shiansen, yeou kérzen tzao nii.

7. Cf. *Horng Shyrtzyh Huey.*

8. The character for *ding* (*din* in SW Mandarin) is 丁 . *ding-tzyhluhkooul* 'T-junction'; *dingtzyh-chyy* 'T-footrule, — a T-square.'

9. The complement *-dao* in the central and some southern dialects correspond to Mandarin *-.jiann* and *-.jaur.*

10. Words for large buildings take the AN *tzuoh* 'seat.'

11. *Sanjeaul-shyng* 'triangle-shaped.'

12. *Jau.pair* 'beckon-board, — signboard.'

13. *Nii Shiansen* 'you, sir,' there being no word like *Nin* in SW Mandarin.

14. *Gongcherngshy* is not a very common term of address, but not quite so strange as a form like 'Engineer Liou' would be in English.

15. *Jeouyeang* '(I have) long looked up (to you),' — used in first meeting a well-known person.

16. *Bii-tsyy* 'that-this, — mutually.' *Bii-tsyy vx* 'the compliment is mutual.' A more modest reply would be *Haoshuo vx.* (See Note 50, p. 222.)

17. *Faangjy* from *faang-sha* 'spin yarn,' *jy-buh* 'weave cloth.'

18. *Juan tzuoh* 'specially make, specialize in making.'

19. *Bey.uo* 'bedding'; *dantz, dal* 'singlet, sheet'; *beydal* 'bed sheet.'

20. *Tian* 'to add,' an unrelated homonym of *tian* 'sky, day.'

21. *Huahshyue* 'transformation-science, — chemistry.'

22. *Jeoujing* 'wine-spirit, — alcohol.' *Jeou* is the most general and only common word for 'alcoholic drink.'

23. *Mohshoei* 'ink-water, — (liquid) ink,' less formally *mohshoel.*

24. Since ordinary Chinese shoes are made of cloth, leather shoes are called *pyishye*.

25. *Wanyell* 'toy.' Since *wanyell* is often used in the sense of 'trifle,' speaker B does not realize at first that they are actual toys.

26. *Jannche* 'war-vehicle, — tank,' popularly called *taankehche*.

27. *Harngkong muujiann* 'sail-void mother-vessel, — aircraft carrier.'

28. *Puutong* 'general, ordinary.'

29. *Li jeh.lii buyeuan*, less formally, *li jell buyeual*.

30. Stores, firms, etc. take the AN *–jia* or *–jial*.

31. *Wushiann-diann shouinji* 'wireless-electricity receive-sound-machine, — wireless (or radio) receiver.'

32. *Meiyou* 'coal-oil, — kerosene'; *chihyou* 'gas-oil, — gasoline'; *shyryou* 'stone-oil, — petroleum.'

33. *Mintzwu* 'people-race, — nation'; *tzyhyou* 'free, freedom.'

34. Distinguish between *juuyih* '-ism' and *jwu.yih* 'intention, decision.'

35. *Minchyuan* 'people's (political) rights.'

36. *Kaibann* 'open-manage, — set up.'

37. *Yinnshua* 'print-brush, — printing,' from the brushing process in woodblock printing. *Yinnshua-suoo* 'printing establishment.'

38. *Sh yeou jeyg shyh* 'there is this affair.'

39. *Yuh.bey ... yonq* 'to prepare for the use of ....'

40. *Pyngmin jiaw.yuh* 'ordinary-people education, — popular education.'

41. *Fabeau yanluenn* 'publish opinion (as expressed in speech).'

42. In the literary style, *tzyh* 'self,' like French *se*, precedes the verb, *tzyhjyh* 'se régir.' Taken over into the spoken language, *tzyhjyh* is an inseparable intransitive verb, 'to practice self-government.'

43. *Tsair shyng a* 'before it will do, you see.'

44. *Uei!* in answer to one's name. *.Ei!* in Peiping.

45. *Peirj* 'keeping company with.'

46. *Laibin* 'come-guest, — a formal visitor.'

47. *Yawder* (pron. like *yaudeei*) 'desirable, fine' is a typical southwestern expression, which has been carried down the river by returned refugees.

EXERCISES

1. *Example*:

Given:	Answer:
Woomen chii-tourl jyy tzuoh wanyell; deeng daw fannwei kuoh-dahle yiihow, shianntzay budann tzuoh wanyell, binqchiee yee tzuoh jen-dongshi le.	Woomen beenlai guang tzuoh wanyell; howlai baa fannwei kuoh-dahle, suooyii jehhoel chwule tzuoh wanyell yiiway (*or* jy way), erlchiee hair tzuoh jen-dongshi le.

(a) Jey-jia gongchaang .lii chii-tourl jyy jyhtzaw jeoujing; deeng daw fannwei kuoh-dahle yiihow, shianntzay budann jyhtzaw jeoujing, binq-chiee yee jyhtzaw bye-joong de huahshyue-piin le. (b) Woomen chii-tourl jyy shyue shuo Jonggwo-huah; deeng daw cherngduh tyi-gaule yii-how, shianntzay budann shyue shuo Jonggwo-huah, binqchiee yee shyue shiee Jonggwo-tzyh le. (c) Ney-i-jial yinnshua-suoo chii-tourl jyy huey yinn hei-bair de dongshi; deeng daw fartz gaeliangle yiihow, shianntzay budann neng yinn hei-bair de dongshi, lian yeou yanseh de yinnshua-piin dou huey yinn le. (d) Jell chii-tourl jyy geei ren jyhx sheau-binq; deeng daw shehbey jiannxde jia-duole yiihow, shianntzay· budann neng jyh sheau-binq, binqchiee yee neng kai-dau, jie-guu shermde le.

2. *Example:*
Given: Answer:
Kaibann jeyg yinnshua-suoo,   Kaibann jeyg yinnshua-suoo yeou sherm yonq.chuh?
keeyii tyi-gau renmin de jyshyh   Kaibannle jeyg me, hao tyi-gau ren-cherngduh.   min de jyshyh cherngduh a.

(a) Shehlih Minsheng Chaang keeyii jyhtzaw ryhyonq bihshiu de dongshi. (b) Shyue Jonggwo-huah keeyii gen Jonggworen hertzuoh. (c) Woo mae jehshie diannchyr keeyii tzuoh diannchyr de mae.may. (d) Shyhjieh.shanq famingle sheuduo-joong jichih keeyii tzuoh ren de lihlianq suoo buneng tzuoh de shyhchyng. (e) Pyi pohle shanq deanjeou keeyii shiau-dwu. (f) Tzaw-chyau keeyii guoh-her. (g) Tzaw feiji keeyii tzay tian.shanq fei. (h) Rennde tzyh keeyii dwu-shu.

3. *Translate into Chinese:*
(a) Excuse me, sir, will you please tell me the way to the Long Life (*Charngsheng*) Hospital? (b) Take the second turn to the north over there, turn east at (*dawle*) the second traffic light ('red-green lamp'), go straight on for about two miles (*Inglii*), and as soon as you have gone over a little hill, you will be able to see the hospital right in front of you. You can't miss it. (c) Mr. Suen, this is my friend Mr. Jang Tiantsair, who has just arrived here from New York to visit your hospital (*Guey Yuann*). (d) We very much like to have visitors come from a distance (*yeuan.chull*). (e) The people must first have freedom of speech before (*tsair*) there can be political freedom. (f) I hope there will be a good factory in every city. (g) The things this factory specializes in are chemical articles, especially various kinds of newly discovered drugs. (h) The machinery used in the heavy industries is very hard to move to the interior; that was why the light industries were the earliest to get started.

LESSON 19
RENTING A HOUSE

Mr.: Say! 'For Rent,' 'For Rent,' 'Vacancy for Rent'! Oh, please make a stop! Will you make a stop at the next station, please?

Mrs.: You must be seeing apparitions; where, pray, can there be houses for rent nowadays?

Mr.: It's true, I saw it with my own eyes. If you don't believe it, we'll get off and go take a look. And it's a pretty big house, too.

Mrs.: All right, wait until the car stops and we'll go and see.

Mr.: Really, I must have been 'seeing apparitions,' as you said. Why, I saw a perfectly clear 'For Rent' sign a while ago!... Oh, there, there, there it is!...

Mrs.: Well, there's nobody in. Ring some more!

Mr.: Maybe the bell is out of order. Let's knock on the door. Hey, open the door! Open the door, hey there! Is there anybody in?... Well? Still nobody.

Keeper: Coming! coming! coming right away. You people have come to see the house, I suppose?

Mr.: Yes, how many rooms has this house?

K: Thirty-two rooms all together. Come in, please, I'll lead the way. This side is the gateman's room, the other side is the ricksha room, and on the other side of the courtyard is a three-room size reception hall.

Mr.: Where are the main rooms?

K: The main rooms are in an inner apartment, there are two more courtyards inside, both larger than this one....

Mr.: Gee, what big rooms! Well, there are even echoes, too. Yoohoo! (*Echo:* Yoohoo!) Who are you? (*Echo:* ... you?)

Mrs.: The roof is so high.

K: It's good to be high, cool in the summer.

Mr.: But cold in the winter!

Mrs.: Where are the kitchen and the servants' quarters?

K: They are in the backyard, look, you can see them from this window here in the back.

Mr.: Yes, each of these courtyards is bigger than the last, the backyard is still bigger than the main court; and there are two pine trees, and there are a lot of bamboos there, and that pond over there may perhaps be used for raising fish.

K: It was originally a goldfish pond.

Mrs.: Say, there's a vegetable garden over there, too. Look, look, you can plant vegetables there. I think we can plant some cabbages, spinach, radishes, tomatoes, ...

DIH SHYRJEOU KEH
TZU FARNGTZ

Shiansheng: È, 'Jau-tzu,' 'Jau-tzu,' 'Jyifarng jau-tzu'![1] Èh, laujiah, tyng i-tyng! Chiing nii dawle shiah-i-jann tyng i-tyng!

Taytay: Jiann-goei le, chiing wenn nii jeh niantourl naal yeou jau-tzu de farngtz?

Shg: Jende me, woo chinyean[2] kannjiann de me. Nii bu shinn tzarmen shiahchiuh kannx chiuh. Hairsh i-suool tiing dah de farngtz ne.[3]

Ty: Hao, deeng che tyngle, tzarmen shiahchiuh kannx chiuh.

Shg: Jensh, nii shuo de 'jiann-goei le,' tzeem woo gangtsair kannjiann chingxchuux[4] de ig jau-tzu de goanggaw[5] me!... Oh, yeou le, yeou le, tzay jell....

Ty: Tzeem mei ren a? Nii tzay duo enn .leang.shiall![6]

Shg: Yee sheu diannliengl huay le ba? Tzarmen chiaux men kann. Uai, kai-men! Kai-men, hei! Yeou ren meiyeou?... Yee? hairsh mei ren.

Kan Farngtz de: Lai le, lai le! Shuo-huah jiow lai.[7] Niimen leang-wey sh lai kann farngtz de, sh bush a?

Shg: Duey le, jeh farngtz yeou duoshao-jian?

K: Igonq sanshyr'ell-jian.[8] Nin jinnlai woo liing Nin chyaux. Jeybial sh menfarngl, neybial sh chefarng,[9] yuanntz neybial sh ig san-kaijian de dah-kehting.

Shg: Shanqfarng[10] ne?

K: Shanqfarng tzay liitou i-jinn,[11] liitou hair yeou leangg yuanntz ne, dou bii jeyg yuanntz dah....

Shg: He! Hao[12] dah de farngjian.[13] È, hair yeou hweisheng[14] ne. Uai! (*Hweisheng:* Uai!) Nii sh sheir? (*Hweisheng:* ... sheir?)

Ty: Jeh farngdieengl jen gau.

K: Gau hao, shiahtian liang.kuay.

Shg: Keesh dongtian leeng è!

Ty: Chwufarng gen shiahfarngl tzay naal?

K: Tzay howyuall, Nin chyau, jiee howtou jeyg bo.li[15] chuang.huh jell jiow kann.de-jiann.

Shg: Èè,[16] jehshie yuanntz ig bii ig dah, howyuall bii jenq-yuanntz hair genq dah le; hair yeou leang-ke songshuh, nall hair yeou sheuduo jwutz, neybial neyg chyrtz.lii meijoel hair keeyii yeang-yu[17] ne.

K: Beenlai sh g jinyu-chyr.

Ty: È, neybial hair yeou g tsayyuan ne. Nii chyau, nall keeyii jonq-tsay. Woo sheang tzarmen keeyii jonq deal bairtsay,[18] bortsay, luo.bo, shihorngshyh,[19] ...

Shg: Èh, tzarmen farngtz hair mei kann-hao,[20] shian bye mang nonq

Mr.: Well, we haven't yet decided on the house, don't be in such a hurry to fix the vegetables yet! Let me see. Yes, the doors, windows, floors, and the ceilings and so forth are in rather good shape, aren't they? Oh, Keeper! Has this house electric lights and water supply from pipes?

K: There is wiring, but the electricity is not connected. We do have water supply from pipes.

Mrs.: Have you a new-style bathroom?

K: There was one, it was installed by the former occupant, but when they left, they had the enameled bathtub and the flush toilet and those things dismantled and removed.

Mr.: Oh, so long as the pipes are still there, we can buy the things and have them put in again. Uh — What price is this house rented for?

K: The rent is fifty-two dollars a month.

Mr.: That's not expensive, is it?

Mrs.: No, I find it very cheap, too. Is it far from here to go marketing, shopping, and so forth?

K: It isn't far. This is Old Riverside, you see. You turn north from the corner and walk something like fifteen minutes and there will be markets and general stores there; if you take a bus, a street car, a pedicab, or something, it will be still faster.

Mrs.: Yes, the location is quite central, isn't it? Let's take this.

Mr.: Good, let's decide to take it.

K: What is your name, please?

Mr.: My name is Jang, Jang Tiantsair: 'tian' as in 'tian-shiah,' 'tsair' as in 'rentsair,' — I'll leave my card with you. — Hadn't I better pay some deposit first? How much shall I pay?

K: Just as you please, Mr. Jang.

Mr.: Suppose I pay twenty-five dollars first — five, ten, fifteen, twenty, twenty-five — twenty-five dollars.

K: All right, I will make out a receipt for you; in the afternoon I will go and report to the landlord to make out a contract.

Mr.: Oh, what's the number of this house?

K: That's all right, it's just the second door on the north side from the east end of the street.

Mr.: Will you tell me what the number is, so that I can make a note of it?

K: It's — uh — it's — uh — number thirteen.

Mr.: I see, number thirteen — (*writes*) 'Number thirteen Old Riverside' — 'Number thirteen Old Riverside'! Say, wait a minute! Thirteen Old Riverside — isn't this one of the Four Great Haunted Houses of this place? Ah, that's why the rent is so cheap! So that's where the cheapness lies! By and by, when the ghosts start to haunt you every night, then it's going to be wonderful!

tsay a! Ranq woo kannx. Èè, jeh farngtz de men, chuang,[21] dihbaan,[22] diingbaan,[23] shermde, dou hair buhuay, ar? Èh, kan-farngtz de! Jeh farngtz yeou dianndeng tzyhlai-shoei [24] meiyeou?

K: Diannshiann [25] dou yeou, jiowsh mei jie-diann. Tzyhlai-shoei yee yeou.

Ty: Yeou shinshyh de shiitzao-farng [26] meiyeou?

K: Beenlai dawsh yeou, sh chyantou de farngkeh [27] tzyhjii juang de, keesh tamen ban-tzoou de shyrhowl jiow bae tsyrtiee [28] de tzaopern, choushoei-maatoong [29] shermde dou geei chaile.shiahlai ban-tzoou le.

Shg: Oh, jyy yaw shoei-goantz hair yeou, woomen keeyii mae le tzay juang.chiilai. E — jeh farngtz tzu sherm jiah.chyan? [30]

K: Tzu.chyan sh wuushyr'ell-kuay chyan [31] ig yueh.

Shg: Jeh daw buguey, ar?

Ty: Èè, woo yee jyuej jeyg heen pyanyi. Jell shanq-jie [32] mae-tsay shanq puhtz .chiuh [33] shermde yeuan buyeuan?

K: Buyeuan. Jell bush Lao Heryall ma? Chu-kooul wanq beei, tzoou shyrjii-fen jong jiow yeou shie shyhchaang gen tzarhuoh-pull;[34] yawsh da gonggonq-chiche,[35] diannche, hesh sanluenche shermde nah jiow genq kuay le.

Ty: Èè, dihdean dawsh heen jongshin de, ar? Tzarmen jiow idinq yaw ba.

Shg: Hao, nah tzarmen jiow jyuedinq yaw ba.

K: Nin Gueyshinq a?

Shg: Woo shinq Jang, Jang Tiantsair: 'tianshiah' de 'tian,' [36] 'rentsair' de 'tsair,' — woo liou g pianntz geei nii. Shian fuh deal dinq.chyan ba? Fuh duoshao?

K: Sweibiann Nin le, Jang Shg.

Shg: Fuh ellshyrwuu-kuay chyan ba, — i-wuu,[37] i-shyr, shyrwuu, ellshyr, ellshyrwuu—ellshyrwuu-kuay.

K: Hao, woo geei Nin kai g shoutyaul; [38] shiahwuu woo jiow chiuh bawgaw farngdong chiuh geei Nin yuhbey jertz.[39]

Shg: Oh, jell sh menpair [40] jii-haw?

K: Mei guanshih, jiowsh dongkooul luhbeei dih'ellg dahmel.

Shg: Nii gawsonq woo sh jii-haw, woo hao [41] jih.shiahlai.

K: Sh — sh — shyrsan-haw.

Shg: Oh, shyrsan-haw — (*shieej*) 'Lao Heryan [42] shyrsan-haw' — 'Lao Heryall shyrsan-haw'! È, ranq woo kann! Lao Heryall shyrsan-haw — jeh bush jeh dihfangl de Syh-dah Shiongjair lii de ig shiongjair ma? Oh, suooyii tzu de nemm pyanyi ou! Yuanlai [43] pyanyi jiow pyanyi tzay [44] jeyg .shanq! Hweilai yeh.lii naw.chii goei [45] .lai tsair miaw ne!

Ty: Ch! [46] Nii yow jiann-goei le. Naj g [47] nantzyy-hann, itourl tzaynall tyichanq pohchwu mishinn, itourl hair pah goei ne, hair! [48] Yee bu pah shiou!

Mrs.: Come on! You are seeing apparitions again. A big he-man like you, promoting the abolition of superstitions and being afraid of ghosts on the side! Aren't you ashamed of yourself?
Mr.: I am not afraid of ghosts, I am afraid *you* are afraid of ghosts, you see!
Mrs.: Not me!
Mr.: If you are not afraid, I am not afraid either.
Mrs.: I am not.
Mr.: Then we still want the house?
Mrs.: We do.

NOTES

1. *Jyifarng jau-tzu* 'propitious-house solicit-rent, — vacant house for rent.'

2. After *chin–* 'with one's own . . . ,' either the bound word *–yean* or the syntactic word *yean.jing* can be used. Similarly, *woo chin'eel(tou)* 'with my own ears.'

3. *Hair . . . ne*, which occurs many times in this lesson, expresses interest in new aspects of a thing being looked over. The implication is: I thought that was all there was to it, but here is something more about it *still*.

4. In a reduplicated word like *chingxchuux*, the relative stresses of the syllables are in the order of first, fourth, third, second, but usually no one is so entirely unstressed or toneless as in the *–.chuu* of the simple form *chingchuu*. (Cf. p. 40.)

5. *Goanggaw* 'broad-tell, — advertisement.'

6. *Enn .leang.shiall* 'press a couple of times'; *shiall* 'stroke,' AN for verbs.

7. *Shuo-huah jiow lai*, cf. 'before you can say "A, B, C."'

8. A *jian* 'room' in Peiping housing means the space between columns, including even the open spaces under a porch. Thirty-two *jian* therefore may amount to only about twelve actual rooms.

9. *Chefarng* may be either a space for a ricksha or a garage.

10. *Shangfarng* 'upper room(s), — master's room(s).'

11. *Jinn* 'advance, enter,' AN for rows of rooms (sometimes with *shiangfarng* 'wings'), separated from other units of courtyards.

12. *Hao* 'how, what a!'

13. *Farngjian* 'room' as space to use or live in, as distinguished from *utz* 'room' as a thing.

14. *Hweisheng* 'return sound, — echo.'

15. *Bo.li* 'glass.'

Shg: **Woo** bu pah goei è, woo sh pah **nii** pah goei è!
Ty: Woo tsair bu pah goei ne! [49]
Shg: Nii bu pah woo yee bu pah.
Ty: Woo bu pah.
Shg: Neme jeh farngtz hairsh yaw le?
Ty: Yaw.

---

16. Distinguish Èè, sound of hearty approval; È, calling attention with some excitement; .Èh, general agreement or calling attention.

17. *Yeang* 'rear, cultivate, keep.'

18. *Bairtsay* 'white-vegetable, — (Chinese) cabbage,' also applied to Chinese green.

19. *Shihorngshyh* 'western-red-persimmon, — tomatoes.'

20. The complement *–hao* means 'to a satisfactory conclusion.'

21. The bound word *chuang* (for *chuang.huh*) can be used in an enumerated list.

22. *Dihbaan* 'ground-board, — floor, flooring.' 'The floor' as a place is '*dih*' or '*dih.shiah*.'

23. *Diingbaan* 'top-board, — ceiling.' Because ceilings in Peiping are often made of papered matting, a common term for 'ceiling' is *diing.perng* 'top-shed.'

24. *Tzyhlai-shoei* 'self-coming water, — automatic water, — water from a pipe system.'

25. *Diannshiann* 'electric thread, electric line, — wire.'

26. *Shii-tzao* 'wash-bath, — take bath.'

27. *Farngkeh* 'house-guest, — tenant.'

28. *Tsyrtiee* 'porcelain-iron, — enameled ware.'

29. *Choushoei-maatoong* 'pullwater-commode, — flush toilet.'

30. *Jiah.chyan* 'price-money, — price.' *Chyan* in words for money for specific uses is usually in the neutral tone.

31. Fifty-two dollars for such a big house would be cheap even for prewar prices.

32. *Shanq-jie* 'go to street, — do shopping.'

33. *Shanq puhtz .chiuh* 'go to the stores.'

34. *Tzar₀huoh-pull* 'miscellaneous-goods store, — general store.'

35. *Gonggonq-chihche* 'public automobile, — bus.'

36. Characters are identified by mentioning well-known combinations in which they occur.

37. The Chinese count things by fives. (Cf. p. 147.2b.)

38. *Shoutyaul* 'receipt-slips, — receipt.'

39. *Jertz* 'folder.' For rent and charge accounts with stores, etc., the Chinese custom has a long strip of stiff paper folded back and forth into a small pad called *jertz*. On a *farng-jertz*, the terms of the lease is written at the beginning, with space for monthly entries.

40. *Menpair* 'door-signboard, — house number.'

41. *Woo hao* 'in order that I can . . . .'

42. The reading pronunciation *–yan* '(river)side' is used here instead of *–yall*, as the diminutive suffix is never actually written on street signs or in addresses.

43. *Yuanlai* 'originally, — so the explanation is . . . .'

44. *Pyanyi jiow pyanyi tzay* 'as for being cheap, the cheapness lies in . . . .'

45. *Naw-goei* 'ghosts make disturbances' is an impersonal verb-object construction, like *shiah-yeu*.

46. *Ch$_i$!* sound of contempt.

47. *Naj (i)g* 'in spite of being a . . . , with all the dignity of a . . . .' *Hann* 'man, vir' B; *nantzyy-hann* 'he-man.'

48. On . . . *ne hair*, cf. . . . *le dou*, Note 1, p. 240.

49. *Woo tsair . . . ne!* 'It is only I that . . . , — I certainly . . . .'

EXERCISES

1. *Example:*

Given:	Answer:
Huaychuh tzay naal ne? (*or:* yeou sherm huaychuh ne?)	Duey le (*or:* èh, *etc.*), huay jiow huay tzay ta buhuey shuo Jonggwo-huah,
Tzuey huay de jiowsh ta buhuey shuo Jonggwo-huah.	Èh, huay jiow huay tzay jeyg-.shanq.

LESSON 20

THE WALRUS AND THE CARPENTER*

<blockquote>
The sun was shining on the sea,
  Shining with all his might:
He did his very best to make
  The billows smooth and bright —
And this was odd, because it was
  The middle of the night.
</blockquote>

* From *Through the Looking-Glass and What Alice Found There*, by Lewis Carroll (Charles Lutwidge Dodgson), London (Macmillan), 1871.

(a) Haochuh tzay naal ne? Tzuey hao de jiowsh ta shentii neybuh meiyeou show-shang. (b) Yeou sherm nanchuh ne? Tzuey nan de jiowsh tamen lea bii-tsyy kannjiann le lao bu shuo-huah. (c) Yeou sherm tzaugau ne? Tzuey tzau de jiowsh woo wanqle ta juh de naal le. (d) Yeou sherm haowal ne? Tzuey haowal de jiowsh keeyii yeang jinyu. (e) Tsuohchuh tzay naal ne? Tzuey tsuoh de jiowsh bu gai tzule i-suool yehyeh naw-goei de farngtz. (f) Yeou sherm taoyann ne? Tzuey taoyann de jiowsh yueh jiaw tam bye naw tamen naw de yueh lihhay. (g) Yeou sherm guay ne? Tzuey guay de jiowsh torngshyr yow chu tayyang yow shiah-yeu. (h) Miawchuh tzay naal ne? Tzuey miaw de jiowsh woo kann.de-jiann ta, ta kann.bu-jiann woo.

2. *Example:*

Given:
Gwutou shuai-duannle deei jie.chii-lai.

Answer:
Gwutou shuai-duannle me, keeyii bae shuai-duannle de gwutou geei jie.chiilai a.

(a) Huah shuo-tsuohle deei gae-dueyle. (b) Shyuesheng shuey-jaurle deei jiaw-shiingle. (c) Diannshiann lha-sherle deei jie-chiilai. (d) Ney-ke syy-shuh dao.shiahlaile deei ban-tzoou. (e) Gangtsair huah mei shuo-chingchuu, deei tzay shuo i-biann. (f) Jey-jii-joong gongyeh hair mei heen fadar, deei jiannsheh.chiilai. (g) Jeyg yueh de farng.chyan hair mei fuh, deei kuaydeal fuhle. (h) Yeou g ren diaw de her.lii le, deei kuaydeal jiow.shanqlai.

3. *Write down, from listening to the teacher's reading in the* Character Text *(p. 126), the Keeper's version of the story.*

4. *Translate the dictation, after correction, into idiomatic English.*

DIH ELLSHYR KEH [*]
HAESHIANQ [1] GEN MUH.JIANQ [2]

Tayyang jaw tzay dah-hae .shanq,
 Ta pinminq [3] shyy-jinn d' gann:
Ta sheang bae lanqtou guei.jyh-hao,[4]
 Yaw yow guang yow bu luann — [5]
Keesh jeh heen guay, i'wey [6] nah jenq sh
 Tzay bannyeh san-geng-bann.[7]

[*] For the text of Alice's conversation with Tweedledee and Tweedledum before and after the poem, as recorded on Folkways Records, FP8002, see p. 298.

The moon was shining sulkily,
    Because she thought the sun
Had got no business to be there
    After the day was done —
"It's very rude of him," she said,
    "To come and spoil the fun!"

The sea was wet as wet could be,
    The sands were dry as dry.
You could not see a cloud, because
    No cloud was in the sky:
No birds were flying overhead —
    There were no birds to fly.

The Walrus and the Carpenter
    Were walking close at hand;
They wept like anything to see
    Such quantities of sand:
"If this were only cleared away,"
    They said, "it *would* be grand!"

"If seven maids with seven mops
    Swept it for half a year,
Do you suppose," the Walrus said,
    "That they could get it clear?"
"I doubt it," said the Carpenter,
    And shed a bitter tear.

"O Oysters, come and walk with us!"
    The Walrus did beseech.
"A pleasant walk, a pleasant talk,
    Along the briny beach:
We cannot do with more than four,
    To give a hand to each."

The eldest Oyster looked at him,
    But never a word he said:
The eldest Oyster winked his eye,
    And shook his heavy head —
Meaning to say he did not choose
    To leave the oyster bed.

THE WALRUS AND THE CARPENTER 259

Yueh.lianq kannle jiueje tzoei,[8]
    Ta shin.lii sheang, gangtsair
Hair daangje [9] i-tian guoh-wanle,
    Tzeem Tayyang hair yaw lai?
"Ta jeanjyr mei guei.jeu," [10] ta shuo,
    "Tzemm pao.lai chai wood' tair." [11]

Nah hae sh shy d' shianq sherm nemm shy,
    Nah shatz jiow gan d' shianq gan.[12]
Nii kannb'jiann tianshanq i-piann yun,[13]
    I'wey binq mei yun tzay tian: [14]
Yee meiyeou neaul tzay [15] chuan-kong guoh — [16]
    Sh binq mei neaul tzay chuan.

Haeshianq gen ig Muh.jianq
    Tam lea rel mannmhald' pao;
Tamen kannjiannl' nemmshie shatz
    Jiow ku de g buderleau:
"Yawsh jeh dou sao-ching le," tam shuo
    "Nah chiibush [17] feicharng hao?"

"Yawsh chig laomhatz na chig duenbuh [18]
    Lai sao ta dahbann-nian,[19]
Nii tsaitsai kann," nah Haeshianq shuo,
    "Kee [20] nenggow sao.de-wan?"
Nah Muh.jianq diawje yeanlell [21] shuo,
    "Ai, woo kann jeh heen nan."

"Êh, Lihhwangmen," nah Haeshianq shuo,
    "Lai gen woom sannsann-buh.[22]
Lai shuoshuo-huah, lai daadaa-chah,
    Tzay haetal'nq [23] tzooutzoou luh:
Woom lea rel syhg shoou chan [24] syh-wey,
    Tzay duol' pah chan.bu-juh." [25]

Nah lao lihhwang yee bu yuan.yi,[26]
    Yee bu na shoou chiuh chan:
Nah lao lihhwang jyy yauyau-tour,
    Bae yeanjing fan i-fan — [27]
Ta yihs' sh shuo, shianq ta jeh yanql,
    Hair tzay chiuh shanq haetan? [28]

But four young oysters hurried up,
    All eager for the treat:
Their coats were brushed, their faces washed,
    Their shoes were clean and neat —
And this was odd, because, you know,
    They hadn't any feet.

Four other Oysters followed them,
    And yet another four;
And thick and fast they came at last,
    And more, and more, and more —
All hopping through the frothy waves,
    And scrambling to the shore.

The Walrus and the Carpenter
    Walked on a mile or so,
And then they rested on a rock
    Conveniently low:
And all the little Oysters stood
    And waited in a row.

"The time has come," the Walrus said,
    "To talk of many things:
Of shoes — and ships — and sealing-wax —
    Of cabbages — and kings —
And why the sea is boiling hot —
    And whether pigs have wings."

"But wait a bit," the Oysters cried,
    "Before we have our chat;
For some of us are out of breath,
    And all of us are fat!"
"No hurry!" said the Carpenter.
    They thanked him much for that.

"A loaf of bread," the Walrus said,
    "Is what we chiefly need:
Pepper and vinegar besides
    Are very good indeed —
Now if you're ready, Oysters dear,
    We can begin to feed."

Yeou syhg sheau lihhwangl heen sheang lai,
  Tam sheang [29] de buderleau:
Tam shuale ishang shiile lean,
  Bae shyedall yee jih-hao — [30]
Keesh jeh heen guay, i'wey nii jydaw
  Tam yahgel jiow mei jeau.

Yow syhg lihhwang genje lai,
  Yow syhg genje tzoou;
Yueh lai yueh duo — nii ting woo shuo —
  Hair yeou, hair yeou, hair yeou —
Tam dou jiee shoei.lii tiaw.shanq ann,[31]
  Nemm chilhikualhad' [32] tzoou.

Nah Haeshianq gen neyg Muh.jianq
  Yow tzooule leang-san-lii,
Tam jaole i-kuay dah shyrtou
  Lai [33] danqtzuoh chiuanshen-yii: [34]
Nah igeh igehl d' sheau-lihhwangl
  Jiow dahhuool [35] wann chyan jii.[36]

Nah Haeshianq shuo, "Lai tarn-huah ba,
  Tzarm shuo doan hair shuo charng:
Shuo shye — shuo chwan — hair shuo huoochi —
  Shuo bairtsay — gen gwowang —
Wenn hae tzeem juu [37] de goengoen-tanq — [38]
  Wenn ju kee neng shanq-farng." [39]

"Chiing deeng i-deengl," tam lianmang [40] shuo,
  "Woom jeanjyr gaan.bu-shanq; [41]
Woom yeou de choanb'-guoh chih [42]
  .Lai, mm gehgehl dou heen panq!"
"Niim berng tzemm mang," nah Muh.jianq shuo,
  Tam shuo, "Nin jen tiilianq!" [43]

Nah Haeshianq shuo, "Tzarm tzuey yawjiin d'
  Sh lai [44] g dah-miannbau: [45]
Hair yeou heen hao d' hao-tzwo.liaw [46]
  Sh suan-tsuh [47] gen hwujiau — [48]
Eh, Lihhwangmen, niim hao le ba?
  Hao, tzarm jiow donq-shoou tiau." [49]

"But not on us!" the Oysters cried,
    Turning a little blue.
"After such kindness, that would be
    A dismal thing to do!"
"The night is fine," the Walrus said.
    "Do you admire the view?

It was so kind of you to come!
    And you are very nice!"
The Carpenter said nothing but
    "Cut us another slice:
I wish you were not quite so deaf —
    I've had to ask you twice!"

"It seems a shame," the Walrus said,
    "To play them such a trick,
After we've brought them out so far,
    And made them trot so quick!"
The Carpenter said nothing but
    "The butter's spread too thick!"

"I weep for you," the Walrus said:
    "I deeply sympathize."
With sobs and tears he sorted out
    Those of the largest size,
Holding his pocket-handkerchief
    Before his streaming eyes.

"O Oysters," said the Carpenter,
    "You've had a pleasant run!
Shall we be trotting home again?"
    But answer came there none —
And this was scarcely odd, because
    They'd eaten every one.

NOTES

1. *Haeshianq* 'sea-elephant, — the walrus.'
2. *Muh.jianq* 'wood-artisan, — carpenter.' Similarly, *woa.jianq* 'tile-artisan, — mason,' *tiee.jianq* 'blacksmith,' *torng.jianq* 'coppersmith,' *yn.jianq* 'silversmith.'
3. *Pinminq* 'stake-life, — with all one's strength.'
4. *Guei.jyh* 'put in order.'

THE WALRUS AND THE CARPENTER

"Keesh tiau sheir a?" tam raangje shuo,
  Tam shiah d' dou [50] biann le shae.
"Niim gangtsair day mm nemmyanql hao,
  Tzeem ihoel yow tzemm — tz! — Ae!"
"Jiel tial jen hao," nah Haeshianq shuo,
  "Êh, Muh.jianq, nii chyau nah hae!

Nii jiel neng lai, woo jen gaushinq!
  Woo heen sheang jiann niid' miann!" [51]
Nah Muh.jianq jyygoan [52] chyje shuo,
  "Êh, tzay g'woom [53] chie i-piann:
Woo yuannyih nii bye nemmyanql long —
  Woo jiawl' nii hao-jii-biann!"

"Jeh gai [54] bugai," nah Haeshianq shuo,
  "Tzemm geei tam shanq jeyg danq? [55]
Tzarm jiaw tam gen woom pao tzemm yeuan,
  Sh gen woom chulai guanq!" [56]
Nah Muh.jianq naje miannbau shuo,
  "Jeh hwangyou [57] moo.bu-shanq!" [58]

Nah Haeshianq shuo, "Woo wey niim ku a,
  Ai! niim jen keelian!" [59]
Ta yeanley-uang'uangld' [60] tzaynall tiau,
  Bae dah de dou jao-chyuan,
Hair tau.chu [61] doul.liid' [62] sheau-shooujiuall
  Lai daang [63] tzay yean-miannchyan.[64]

"Hwei-jia le, hei!" nah Muh.jianq shuo,
  "Niim wal de kee hair hao?
Tzeem b'yuan.yi a?" Kannkann shianq
  Sh lihhwang feicharng shao —
Keesh jeh nan guay,[65] i'wey tam ge'l-lea [66]
  Bae gehgehl dou chy-leau.[67]

---

5. *Luann* 'disordered.'
6. This is pronounced as one syllable. (See Note 15, p. 208.)
7. *Bannyeh san-geng-bann* 'midnight third watch and half, — the small hours of the night.'
8. *Jiue-tzoei* 'to pout.'
9. *Daangje, daangj = yiiwei* 'to take for, to think (wrongly).'
10. *Guei.jeu* 'rule, manners'; *mei guei.jeu* 'without manners, rude.'

11. *Chai ig ren de tair* 'to pull down the scaffold from under someone, — to spoil someone's plans.'

12. *Gan d' shianq gan* is of course as un-Chinese as 'dry as dry' is un-English. The usual expression would be *shianq sherm nemm gan* 'as dry as anything.'

13. The usual full word for 'cloud' is *yun.tsae*.

14. *Binq mei yun tzay tian*, in ordinary prose, *binq mei yun.tsae tzay tian.shanq*.

15. *Tzay*, very often used in current prose, is short for *.tzay.nall*, indicating progressive action. (See p. 55.)

16. *Chuan-kong guoh* 'pass while piercing space.'

17. *Chiibu, chiibush* 'isn't it . . .?'

18. *Duenbuh* 'stomp-cloth, — mop.' The specific AN is *-baa*.

19. *Dah₀bann-nian* 'the greater half of a year.'

20. *Kee* 'whether' interrogative adverb.

21. *Diawje yeanlell* 'dropping (eye) tears.'

22. *Sann-buh* 'loosen steps, — to take a walk.'

23. *Haetal'nq*, slurred form of *haetal.shanq*.

24. *Chan* 'to take by the hand.'

25. *Chan.bu-juh* 'cannot hold fast.'

26. *Yuan.yi* 'to say a word.'

27. *Fan-yeal, fan-yean.jing* 'to roll one's eyes.'

28. Lit. 'in such a state, would he still go up the beach?'

29. *Sheang* 'desire, to be eager.'

30. *Bae shyedall yee jih-hao* 'tie up the shoestrings, too.'

31. *Tiaw.shanq ann* 'jump up the shore,' would have a split complement *.lai* in ordinary prose.

32. *Chilhikualhade* 'clatter-clatter.'

33. On the use of *lai* to indicate purpose, see p. 56.

34. *Chiuanshen-yii* 'surrounding-body-chair, — armchair.'

35. *Dahhuool = dahjia* 'everybody (present).'

36. *Jii* 'to crowd.'

37. *Juu* 'to boil, to cook.'

38. *Goen-tanq* 'rolling-hot, — boiling hot.'

39. *Shanq-farng* 'go up the house(top).'

40. *Lianmang* 'hurriedly.'

41. *Gaan.shanq* 'catch up.'

42. *Choan-chih* 'to pant,' *choan.bu-guoh chih .lai* 'cannot catch one's breath.'

43. *Tii₀lianq* 'considerate.'

44. *Lai*, here used in a causative sense 'to cause to come,' often so used in ordering dishes.

45. *Miannbau* 'flour-wrap, — bread.'

46. *Tzwo.liaw* 'making-material, — seasoning.'
47. *Suan-tsuh* 'sour-vinegar,' central dialect term for *tsuh* 'vinegar.'
48. *Hwujiau* 'barbarian pepper, — black pepper.'
49. *Donq-shoou tiau* 'Set about to pick out.'
50. *Shiah d' dou* 'so scared that . . . .'
51. *Jiann-miann* 'to meet face to face'; *jiann niide miann* or *gen nii jiann-miann* 'to meet with you.'
52. *Jyy₀goan* 'only care about . . . .'
53. *G'woom* is weakened form of *geei woomen*.
54. *Gai* and *inggai* are mostly interchangeable, but *gai* is used more often as a predicate 'right, the way things ought to be,' while *inggai* is used more often as an auxiliary verb 'should, ought to.'
55. *Shanq-danq* 'go up the pawn counter, — to be tricked.'
56. *Guanq* 'to have an outing, to take a pleasure trip.'
57. *Hwangyou* 'yellow oil, — butter.'
58. *Moo.shanq* 'to smear on,' *moo.bu-shanq* 'cannot smear on.'
59. *Kee-* '-able,' *keelian* 'pitiable.'
60. *Uang.chulai* 'to ooze'; *yeanley-uang'uanglde* 'tearfully.'
61. *Tau.chulai* 'fish out.'
62. *Doul* 'pocket.'
63. *Daang* 'to screen, to shield.'
64. *Miann₀chyan* 'forefront, front.'
65. *Nan guay* 'hard to wonder, — no wonder.'
66. *Ge'l-lea* 'brothers two, — the two chums.'
67. *Chy-leaule* 'eat up.'

EXERCISES

1. *Example:*

Given: Answer:
Tam lean.shanq de yanshae yee   Tam shiah de lihhay de lian lean-
biann le, sh inwey shiah de heen   .shanq de yanshae dou biann le.
lihhay de yuanguh.

(a) Tam bae shyrhowl yee wanqle, sh inwey wal de heen gaushinq de yuanguh. (b) Woo yeanjing jeng.bu-kai, sh inwey tayyang jaw de heen lianq de yuanguh. (c) Bu pah tanq de ren yee buneng he jey-woan char, sh inwey jeh char juu de heen tanq de yuanguh. (d) Bu shinn goei de ren yee bukeen juh jey-suoo farngtz, sh inwey yehlii shengin naw de heen sheang de yuanguh. (e) Ta sherm shyhchyng yee bujydaw, sh inwey fa-shau fa de heen gau de yuanguh. (f) Sheir yee kannbujiann heibaan- .shanq de tzyh, sh inwey shiansheng tzay heibaan.shanq shiee-tzyh shiee de heen sheau de yuanguh. (g) Nii choan.bu-guoh chih lai le, sh inwey nii gangtsair pao de heen kuay de yuanguh. (h) Jeyg Meeigworen shuo-huah, ta beengwo-ren yee ting.bu-doong sh inwey tade koouin shuo de heen guay de yuanguh.

LESSON 21
LISTENING AND LISTENING IN
ACT I. DICTATION

Teacher: Today I am going to give you a new exercise to do. You have all done your studies pretty well, but your ability in listening to speech is still inadequate. I shall say a few sentences at the speed at which a Chinese ordinarily speaks. After listening, write down the sentences one by one. Do you all have your paper and pencils ready? All right, now the dictation begins:

Sentence 1: Excuse me, sir, how do you go from here to the railroad station?
Sentence 2: Will this suitcase be in the way if I put it here?
Sentence 3: Say, please move this bundle over a little, will you?
Sentence 4: Mr. Wang says that he has an engagement tomorrow evening and begs to be excused.
Sentence 5: I heard that you were not feeling well yesterday, are you better today?
Sentence 6: Yeah, I think I like this best.
Sentence 7: If he hadn't abused me, would I have hit him without cause or reason?
Sentence 8: With all his variations, isn't he always harping on the same thing?

A: Professor, you talk too vast.
T: What? Too what?
A: No, no, I mean you talk too fast.
T: That's right, I talk too *fast* — oh, no, who said fast? I talk too slowly!
B: Please say the sentences once more, Professor.
T: All right, I will say them once more: Sentence 1: Excuse me, how do you go from here to the railroad station? Sentence 2: Will this ....

ACT II. VISITING A CLASS

Visitor: Professor Lii and gentlemen. Coming to visit your class in Chinese today, I find it extremely interesting. When I watched you practice conversation, heard you pronounce the sounds with such accuracy, and talk with such fluency — by the way, Mr. Lii, can they understand

2. Rewrite the story of 'The Walrus and the Carpenter' in prose and prepare to tell it in class.

DIH ELLSHYRI KEH
TING YEU[1] PARNGTING[2]
DIHI MUH.[3] TINGSHIEE

Shiansheng: Jintian woo geei niimen ig shin de liannshyi tzuohx. Niimen shu dou hair niann[4] de butsuoh, keesh niimen ting shuo-huah[5] de beenshyh dou hair bushyng. Woo shianntzay jaw[6] Jonggworen pyngcharng shuo-huah de kuay-mann shuo jiig jiuhtz. Niimen tingle geei woo i-jiuh i-jiuh de dou shiee.shiahlai. Niimen dou yuhbey-haole jyy-bii le ba? Hao, shianntzay kaishyy tingshiee:

Dih'i-jiuh:[7] Lau Nin jiah, jiee jell shanq huooche-jann sh tzeem tzoou d'a?

Dih'ell-jiuh: Woo bae jeyg shoou-tyibau ge de jell ay-shyh[8] bu ay-shyh?

Dihsan-jiuh: Ėh, chiing nii bae jeyg dah-bau.fwu[9] geei nuo-guohchiuh deal, hao ba?

Dihsyh-jiuh: Wang Shiansheng shuo ta miengl woanshanq yeou iuehuey,[10] ta shiehx le.[11]

Dihwuu-jiuh: Tingshuo Nin tzwol bushufwu le, jiel jyuej hao.deal le ma?

Dihliow-jiuh: Ėh, woo sheang woo hairsh diing shiihuan jeyg.

Dihchi-jiuh: Ta yawsh mei mah woo, woo huey wu-yuan wu-guh[12] de daa ta ma?

Dihba-jiuh: Ta shuo-lai shuo-chiuh[13] hair bush ney-jiuh huah?

A: Shiansheng, nii shuo de tay guay.[14]
Shg: Ar? Tay shermme?
A: Bush bush, woo sh yaw shuo nii shuo de tay **kuay**.
Shg: Duey le, woo shuo de tay **kuay** — ah, buduey, sheir shuo kuay laije?. Woo shuo de tay mann!
B: Chiing Shiansheng tzay shuo i-biann.
Shg: Hao, tzay shuo i-biann: Dih'i-jiuh: Lau Nin jiah, jiee jell shanq huooche-jann sh tzeem tzoou d'a? Dih'ell-jiuh: Woo bae ....

DIH'ELL MUH. TSANGUAN SHANQ KEH

Laibin: Lii Jiawshow, geh-wey shiansheng. Woo jintian lai tsanguan niimen shanq Jongwen-keh, jyuej feicharng de yeou chiuh.wey.[15] Woo kann niimen gangtsair tzuoh huey-huah[16] liannshyi de shyrhowl, ting niimen dwu-in[17] dwu de nemm joen, shuo-huah shuo de nemm liou.lih —

me if I talk like this? Is my use of words and so forth not too difficult for them?

Teacher: Oh, they can understand you all right. They can now converse with you on any topic. You can chat with them quite freely, joke with them, or even discuss learned subjects with them — it would be all right if you just regard them as no different from the Chinese.

V: Well, then their accomplishment must be quite remarkable. Uh — Professor Lii just told me that you can understand anything that is spoken to you and speak anything you want. Well, that's really wonderful. When you get to China and are able to speak freely with the Chinese people, that must be very convenient for carrying on your work there.

T: Mr. Wu says that if you have anything to ask him about China, he will try to answer you the best as he can.

A: Professor, what dialect was it that you were using in talking with Mr. Wu? Was it Cantonese or the Shanghai dialect?

ACT III. IN SHANGHAI

C: Why, this place is lately getting to be more and more lively, it seems to me. The streets are not only full of accents from other provinces, but there seems to be quite an increase in the number of Occidentals, too, do you notice?

D: (With Shanghai accent:) Yez, I didn'd notise id ad all ad virst; now thad you have mentioned id, really id's rather — esbesially Amerigans, zo many, zuch a lod of them!

C: That's right, and I have heard that some of them can speak a few words of Chinese, too.

D: The Jhinese they sbeak must be vull of sdrange and gueer zounds, isn'd thad zo?

C: Hey, not so loud! Two foreigners are coming. How do you know they don't understand what we say? If they hear you laugh at them they may take offence at you.

D: Ah, whad does id madder. Don'd you worry, id would be all righd even if you dalked sdill louder. That's all right!

C: Don't speak Mandarin!

D: Esbesially the gind of Mandarin like mine — the nasional language with a Zhanghai agsent — when a voreigner hears id he will zerdainly nod know wad id's all aboud. They are all zo derribly sdubid.

A: Gan you sbeak the Zhanghai dialect?

B: Hm! Lesson Sixteen!

èh, Lii Shg., woo tzemmyanql shuo-huah tamen keeyii ting.de-doong ba? Yonq-tzyh shermde dueyyu tamen bu tay nan ba?

Shg: Ti—ng.de-doong.[18] Tamen shianntzay sherm tyi.muh dou neng gen nii tarn. Nii keeyii jiingoan [19] sweibiann gen tamen liau-tial [20] a, kaiwanshiaw [21] a, shenn.jyh.yu [22] taoluenn shyueshuh [23] a — jeanjyr keeyii na tamen danq Jonggworen iyanq jiow der le.[24]

Lai: Oh, nah tamen cherngji heen keeguan [25] le. E — Lii Jiawshow gangtsair gaw.suh [26] woo shuo, niimen shianntzay sherm huah dou ting.dedoong, sherm huah dou huey shuo le. Hao, nah jensh leau.bu.de.[27] Niimen jianglai [28] dawle Jonggwo yiihow, nenggow sweibiann gen Jonggworen shuo-huah, nahsh duey.yu [29] niimen fwuwuh [30] .shanqtou idinq feicharng fangbiann de.

Shg: Wu Shg. shuo niimen yaw yeou sherm guanyu [31] Jonggwo shyhchyng de wenntyi, ta yawsh jydaw de, keeyii sheang fartz [32] hweidar niimen.

A: Shiansheng, gangtsair nii gen Wu Shg. shuo de sh naal de huah? Sh Goangdong-huah hairsh Shanqhae-huah?

DIHSAN MUH. DAWLE SHANQHAE

C: Jinnlai [33] jeh dihfangl tzeem yueh biann yueh reh.naw [34] le, haoshianq. Jie.shanq tingjiann de budann jinqsh shuo wayluh-koouin [35] de, woo jyuej haoshianq Shi.yangren [36] yee duo.chu le bushao .lai [37] le shyhde, nii kee jyued'a?

D: (*Yonq Shanqhae-koouin:*) Èè, woo chiichu [38] ideal meiyeou liou-shin,[39] shianntzay nii tyi.chiilai, jende dawsh — youchyish Meeigworen, duo de ia, duo-jyile.

C: Duey le, woo ting shuo tamen dangjong yeou de hair huey shuo leang-jiuh Jonggwo-huah ne.

D: Tamen jeang [40] de Jonggwo-huah idinq doush chyichyiguayguay de sheng'in, sh bush a?

C: Uai, sheng'in sheau.deal! Yeou leangg waygworen lai le. Nii tzeem jydaw tam bu doong tzarmde huah ne? Tamen tingjiannle nii shiaw.huah [41] tamen, hweitour bu da.yinq [42] nii.

D: Yeou sherm yawjiin? Nii fanq-shin hao le,[43] tzay sheang.deal yee mei guanshih! Buyawjiin de.

C: Nii bye shuo puutong-huah! [44]

D: Tehbyesh woo jey-tzoong — Shanqhae sheng'in de Gwoyeu [45] — waygworen tingjiann le idinq genq.jia [46] moh-ming-chyi-miaw [47] de. Tamen doush benn de yawminq.[48]

A: Nong weyte kààng Zànqhé-hhèwoh va?
(Nii huey shuo Shanghae-huah ba?)

B: Hng! Dih Shyrliow Keh!

C: Goodness me, this man really can speak the Shanghai dialect! Where did you get such a good Shanghai accent!

B: Ha ha ha, he really can't, he has learned just that one sentence.

D: My, this Mandarin you are speaking sounds even more polished!

A: Oh, thank you for the compliment, I don't speak well at all! What I say is full of 'sdrange and gueer zounds.'

C: Gracious, what have we done!

D: Isn'd id embarrazzing!

C: How embarrassing! So they have heard everything we were discussing about them all that time, gee!

D: Gozh!

NOTES

1. *Yeu* is the literary equivalent of *gen* 'with, and,' often used in titles of articles, books, etc.

2. *Parngting* 'lateral-listen, — listen in, audit.'

3. *Muh* 'curtain (of a stage)'; AN 'an act'.

4. Since *niann-shu* 'read-book' means also 'to study,' *shu niann de butsuoh* means 'study pretty well.'

5. *Ting shuo-huah* 'listen to speaking.' *Ting-huah* could be used here, too, but *ting-huah* often also means 'to listen to (to obey) instructions.'

6. *Jaw* 'following, according to.'

7. The times in seconds for saying these sentences at ordinary conversational speed are approximately as follows:

Sentence:	(1)	(2)	(3)	(4)	(5)	(6)	(7)	(8)
Seconds:	2.5	2.5	2.5	2.5	2.5	1.5	3	2

8. *Ay* 'hinder'; *ay-shyh* 'hinder matters, — to be in the way.'

9. *Bau.fwu* 'bundle wrapped with a square cloth with opposite corners tied together.'

10. *Iuehuey* 'engage-meet, — engagement, appointment.'

11. *Ta shiehx le* 'he sends his thanks.'

12. *Wu-yuan wu-guh de*, a lively form of *meiyeou yuanguh*.

13. *Shuo-lai shuo-chiuh* (with full tones on the complements) 'talk back and forth, after all that talk.'

14. *Guay* 'queer.' Student A is still not sure of his aspirated and unaspirated initials.

15. *Chiuh.wey* 'interest-flavor, — interest,' *yeou chiuh.wey* 'interesting,' more colloquially *yeou yihsy, yeou chiuell.*

16. *Huey-huah* 'meet-speech, — conversation (as a language exercise).'

17. *Dwu-in* 'to pronounce sounds, pronunciation.'

LISTENING AND LISTENING IN   271

C: Aiiau! Jeyg ren jende huey shuo Shanqhae huah! Nii tzay naal shyue de tzemm i-koou [49] Shanqhae-huah?
B: He he he, ta binq buhuey, ta jiow shyue-hueyle jey-i-jiuh.
D: A'ia,[50] niimen jey-leang-jiuh Gwoyeu jeang de genq piaw.lianq![51]
A: Ae, haoshuo vx, shuo de bu hao, ideal yee bu hao! Woo shuo de doush 'Chyichyiguayguay de sheng'in.'
C: Aiiau,[52] tzaugau!
D: Tzeng nèweizing [53] lei!
   (Jen nanweichyng!)
C: Dwo buhaoyihsy,[54] hai! Nah tzarmen gangtsair yihluenn le tamen nemm banntian de huah, dou geei tamen ting le chiuh [55] le, aiiau!
D: A'ia!

---

18. A long, breathy *ti—ng* gives the air of 'ostentatious confidence.'
19. *Jiin* 'all the way'; *jiin₀goan* 'all you want.'
20. *Liau-tial* 'chat about the weather, — to chat.'
21. *Kai-wanshiaw* 'to open fun and laughter, — to joke' *Gen ta kai-wanshiaw* 'to joke with him' or 'to make fun of him,' but *kai tade wanshiaw* 'to make fun of him.'
22. *Shenn* is the literary equivalent of *heen* 'very'; *shenn₀jyh₀yu* 'so extreme as to reach, — in extreme cases, even.'
23. *Shyueshuh* 'learning-art, — learning, *wissenschaft*.'
24. *Jiow der le* 'it will be all right.'
25. *Guan* 'behold,' *kee-* '-able,' *keeguan* 'remarkable.'
26. *Gaw.suh* is a more formal word than *gaw.sonq*.
27. While *buderleau* 'no end, awful(ly)' has a neutral sense, *leau.bu.de* is always used in a good sense: 'great, grand, wonderful.'
28. *Jianglai* 'will-come, — future, in the future.' Cf. Fr. *avenir*.
29. *Duey.yu . . . .shanq(tou)* 'with regard to' is used with verbs, while *tzay . . . .shanq* (Note 27, p. 235.) is used with nouns.
30. *Fwuwuh* 'undertake-service, — to carry on work,' usually applied to public service.
31. *Guanyu* 'relating to, — concerning.'
32. *Sheang fartz* 'think of a way, try to.'
33. *Jinnlai* (with full tone on *lai*) 'near-come, — recently,' to be distinguished from *jinn.lai* 'come in.'
34. *Reh.naw* 'hot-noisy, — bustling, full of life.'
35. *Wayluh-koouin* 'outroute-accent, — foreign accent,' usually applied to that of other provinces.
36. *Shi.yangren* 'West-ocean-people, — Occidentals.'
37. *Duo.chu.lai* 'come out with an excess, — to increase.'
38. *Chiichu* 'begin-beginning, — at first.'

39. *Liou-shin* 'leave a mind (on the matter), — to notice, to pay attention (to).'

40. *Jeang* in the sense of *shuo* is dialectal.

41. *Shiaw.huah,* 'laugh-word, — joke,' here used as a transitive verb, 'to laugh at.'

42. *Da.yinq* 'to answer to (some one's call)'; 'to agree to.' *Bu da.yinq* 'to take offence at.'

43. *... hao le* 'it will be all right to ....' This use is more common in the central dialects. In Northern Mandarin, ... *der le* is more commonly used.

44. *Puutong-huah* 'general speech, — Mandarin (in the wider sense).'

45. *Gwoyeu* 'National Language.'

46. *Genq.jia* 'still-additionally, — all the more.'

47. *Moh-ming-chyi-miaw* 'nobody (can) name its mystery, — at a loss to understand,' a commonly spoken literary cliché.

48. *Yawminq* 'demanding (your) life, — awful,' usually after *de*, in predicative position.

49. *Koou* is AN for *huah* in the phrase *shuo i-koou ... huah.*

50. *A'ia* is the Shanghai form for *aiia.*

51. *Piaw.lianq* 'bleached-bright, — elegant, smart, polished.'

52. *Aiiau* is used more often by women than by men (speakers C and D being presumably women).

53. *Nan₀weichyng* 'hard to make (equanimity of) feeling, — to be em-

---

LESSON 22
STUDYING

Waiter: What kind of tea will you two gentlemen have?

A: Dragon well!

B: Have you chrysanthemum?

W: Chrysanthemum? Yes, we have chrysanthemum tea.

B: What time shall we be able to arrive tomorrow?

W: We arrive the first thing in the morning. (*The train whistles.*) — One order dragon well, one order chrysanthemum!

B: Ah, here we go!

A: Ryhshin, I've known you so long, and I've never asked you where your ancestral home is. I thought at first that you were from Shanghai, then, again, when I heard you speak such pure Mandarin, too, I had the impression that you were a northerner.

B: Well, if you start talking about this, it's going to be a long story.

STUDYING 273

barrassed.' A more frequently used expression in Mandarin is the following:

54. *Buhaoyihsy* 'not well felt, — embarrassed, diffident.' *Haoyihsy* 'to have the nerve to.'

55. *Geei tamen tingle chiuh le* 'let them hear and get away with it.'

EXERCISES

1. *Make six sets of four sentences each illustrating the uses of the following words:*

(a) Duey 'to, towards,' *as* Ta duey ren heen herchih.

(b) Dueyyu . . . (shanq *or* shanqtou) 'towards, for, with regard to,' *as* Gongher yunndonq dueyyu renmin de shenghwo (shanq *or* shanqtou) yeou heen dah de yonqchuh.

(c) Guanyu 'concerning, about,' *as* Guanyu jeyg tyimuh woo yiijing duey ta jeang.guohle haojii-biann le.

(d) Shennjyh(yu) 'in extreme cases, even,' *as* Keesh ta bu mingbair jeyg dawlii, shennjyh(yu) genq jeandan.deal de dawlii ta yee bu doong.

(e) Jyhyu 'as to, as for,' *as* Jyhyu chy-fann shuey-jiaw, . . .

(f) Bujyhyu 'not as bad as, will not probably come to,' *as* ta dawsh bujyhyu wanqle.

2. *Write down from dictation a paraphrase of a part of the story as dictated by the teacher from the* Character Text *(p. 128).*

3. *Translate the dictated text into idiomatic English.*

DIH ELLSHYR'ELL KEH
NIANN SHU

Char.farng:[1] Leang-wey shiansheng chy [2] sherm char?
A: Longjiing.[3]
B: Yeou jiuhual [4] meiyeou?
Char: Jiuhua [5] ia. Jiuhua-char yeou.
B: Miengl jii-dean jong keeyii daw?
Char: Miengl tian i-lianq jiow daw. (*Huooche chihdyi-sheng.*)[6] I-keh [7] longjiing, i-keh jiuhua!
B: Ah, kai-che le!
A: Ryhshin ah, woo renn.shyhle nii tzemm jeou, woo tsornglai mei wenn.guoh nii yuanjyi [8] sh naal. Woo yuanshian [9] hair yiiwei nii sh Shanqhae-ren, howlai tingjiann niide Gwoyeu yowsh shuo de nemm chwenjenq,[10] jyuede nii yow shianq sh g Beeifang-ren.[11]
B: Ah, jeyg guh.shyh [12] shuo.chiilai charngj ne.[13] Woomen yuanjyi sh

Our place of origin is Changchow — (*Sound of striking a match.*) — Oh, I have some here — thank you! — Uh — by origin, I am from Changchow;* but I was born and brought up in the north, and I not only could not speak the southern dialect, but could not even understand it very —

A: Isn't the Changchow dialect a Southern Mandarin dialect, like that of Nanking, Yangchow, and other places of that region?

B: Oh no, it sounds like the Soochow or Shanghai sort of dialect.

A: Oh, then I have had it wrong all along.

B: Well, as soon as we children were ready for school, my grandfather engaged a teacher from the south who spoke our home dialect to teach us, that's why as a child I always read in a southern pronunciation.

A: Didn't you go to school when you were in the north?

B: I didn't. I was saying, wasn't I? that we only studied in the family school at home. Starting from four years old, I began to learn characters; at five I began to read the 'Three-character Classic,' the 'Hundred-family Surnames,' the 'Thousand-character Text,' then right after that, I read the 'Great Learning,' 'Doctrine of the Mean,' the 'Analects,' 'Mencius.' After I finished the Four Books, there were the Five Classics. Well, of the Five Classics, I only read the 'Book of Odes,' 'Book of History,' — uh — 'Tso's Chronicles,' and the 'Book of Rites.' That leaves the 'Book of Changes,' which I didn't read.

A: But why didn't you read any poetry?

B: I did, but I didn't read it in the school. My mother was very fond of poetry, and —

A: Really?

B: Yes, and every night she would teach us brothers and sisters to read the 'Three Hundred T'ang Poems,' and we studied them until we could recite every poem from memory.

A: When you read poetry aloud, did you chant it?

B: Yes, we did. For instance — let me see, for instance — take Chang Chi's 'Mooring by the Maple Bridge at Night.'

A: Say, won't you chant it in your own dialect?

B: Well, all I learned *was* in my local melody, you see! Uh — um — it's about like this. Uh —

"The moon goes down, a raven cries, frost fills the sky.
River maples, fishing lanterns, — facing sadness I lie.
Outside of Ku Su [Soochow] City the Han Shan Temple.
At midnight a bell rings; it reaches the traveler's boat." **

— something like that. (*The train whistles.*)

* This story is largely autobiographical of the author.
** Translated by C. W. Luh in his *On Chinese Poetry*, Peiping, 1935.

Charng.jou [14] — (*Gua* [15] *yanghuoo* [16] *sheng*.) — Ȅ, woo.jell yeou! Shiehx xx! — E — woo beenlai sh Charng.jou-ren; keesh woo isheaul [17] shengjaang tzay Beeibian, budann buhuey shuo Nanbian-huah,[18] lian ting dou ting budah —

A: Charng.jou-huah bush shianq Nanjing, Yang.jou ney-i-luh [19] de Nanfang Guanhuah ma?

B: Bu—sh, sh shianq Su.jou, Shanqhae ney-i-ley de sheng'in.

A: Oh, nah woo ishianq dou gao-tsuoh [20] le.

B: Eh, keesh woomen sheauharlmen i-kai-meng [21] de shyrhowl, woo tzuufuh [22] jiow jiee Nanbian chiing [23] le i-wey shuo jiashiang-koouin [24] de shiansheng lai jiau woomde shu,[25] suooyii woo sheau.shyrhowl [26] tzoongsh yonq Nanfang'in dwu-shu de.

A: Nii tzay Beeifang de shyrhowl nandaw mei jinn.guoh shyueshiaw [27] ma?

B: Mei jinn.guoh. Bush woo gangtsair shuo de, woomen jiow tzay jia.lii de syshwu.lii niann-shu è. Woo tsorng syh-suey chii jiow chii-tourl renn fangkuall-tzyh; [28] wuu-suey chii-tourl jiow niann *Santzyh Jing*,[29] *Baejia Shinq*,[30] *Chiantzyh Wen*,[31] howlai jiej niann *Dah.shyue*,[32] *Jong.iong* [33] *Luen.yeu*,[34] *Menq .Tzyy*.[35] Syh Shu dwu-wanle me, jiowsh Wuu Jing. Neme, Wuu Jing littou woo jiow niann le *Shy.jing*,[36] *Shangshu* [37] — e — *Tzuoojuann*,[38] gen *Liijih*.[39] Jiow shenqle *Yih.jing* [40] mei niann.

A: E, nii tzeem bu dwu shy [41] a?

B: Shy dwu a, keesh bush tzay shufarng.lii niann de. Woo shian-muu [42] tzuey ay shy tsyr ge fuh,[43] —

A: Jend'a?

B: Ȅh, meei-woanshanq jiau woomen tzyy.mey [44] jiig ren niann *Tarng Shy Sanbae Shoou*,[45] shooux dou niann daw bey.de-chulai.

A: Niimen dwu-shy heng [46] bu heng a?

B: Heng a. Biifang — ranq woo kann a, biifang — Jang Jih de 'Feng Chyau Yeh Bor' ba!

A: Ȅ, nii yonq niimde jiashiang'in hengx kann!

B: Woo shyue de jiowsh jiashiang-diawl è! E — m — chahbuduo sh tzemmyanql de. E —

"Yueh luoh u tyi shuang maan tian,[47]
Jiang-feng yu-huoo duey chour mian.
Gusu cherngway Harn Shan Syh,
Yehbann jongsheng daw kehchwan."

— .tzemm.yanql .niann. (*Chihdyi-sheng*.)

A: Well, that's really beautiful, isn't it? Then there is the antique style of poetry, how is that chanted?

B: Well, as for antique poetry, that's a different type of melody again. Antique poetry — let me see — oh, Li Po's 'Night Thought,' of course.

'In front of my bed is the moon's light.
I thought it was frost on the ground.
Lifting up my head, I gaze at the moon,
Lowering my head, I think of home.'

Vender: All-spice tea eggs! All-spice tea eggs! Want some all-spice tea eggs?

A: Ah, it makes me homesick to hear that!

B: Doesn't it?

A: Well, then afterwards where did you go to school after all?

B: Afterwards? Well, afterwards, our whole family returned home in the south, and I entered high school there. At that time, I began to study English, history, geography, as well as natural sciences, like physics and chemistry.

A: How about mathematics?

B: Mathematics and Chinese we had, of course.

A: What subject did you like best?

B: I think I still like Chinese best, that's why I am in the department of Chinese now.

A: Yeah, since you have such a good foundation in Chinese, you naturally find it more interesting.

B: That's not the reason, or rather you can say it's for an exactly opposite — (*Coughs.*)

A: Waiter! Waiter!

B: Waiter! Porter!

W: Coming, sir!

B: Will you bring us some more boiling water! I have talked myself hoarse. (*Sound of whistle.*)

NOTES

1. *Char.farng* 'tea-room, — waiter, attendant.' (Cf. Note 57.) The word for 'tea house' is *chargoal* or *chargoan-diann*.

2. The waiter is presumably from some central province, where *chy* is used for *he* 'drink' and *chou* 'smoke,' as well as *chy* 'eat.'

3. *Longjiing* 'dragon well,' brand of green tea from the place of that name near Hangchow; loosely, any high-grade green tea.

4. *Jiuhual* or *jyuhual* 'chrysanthemum-flower,' a variety of small chrysanthemum flower used as tea.

5. As a drink, the suffix *-l* is often omitted.

A: Ha, jen meei, ar? Neme hair yeou guushy, yowsh tzeem heng de ne?
B: Oh, guushy nah yowsh i-joong diawl le. Guushy ranq woo sheangx kann a — oh, Lii Bor [48] de 'Yeh Sy' lo:
"Chwang-chyan mingyueh [49] guang,
Yi sh dihshanq shuang.
Jeu-tour wanq mingyueh,
Di-tour sy guhshiang."
May dongshi de: Wuushiang charyeh-dann! [50] Wuushiang charyeh-dann! Wuushiang charyeh-dann yaw ba?
A: Ay. woo tingle dou sheang-jia le!
B: Kee bu?
A: Neme howlai nii dawdii jinn de sherm dihfangl de shyuetarng ne?
B: Howlai a? Howlai me, woomen chyuan-jia ban-hwei daw Nanbian, woo jiow tzay Nanbian jinnle jongshyue.[51] Nah shyrhowl woo jiow kaishyy shyue Ing'wen, lihshyy, dihlii, hair yeou wuhlii,[52] huahshyue, neyshie tzyhran-keshyue.
A: Shuhshyue [53] ne?
B: Shuhshyue gen Jongwen dangran yeou lo.
A: Nii tzuey shiihuan dwu neei-i-men gongkeh?
B: Woo sheang woo hairsh diing shiihuan dwu gwowen.[54] Suooyii woo shianntzay tzay gwowenshih a.
A: Èè, nii Jongwen jihran yeou nemm hao de gendii,[55] dueyyu ta dangran genq gaanjyue shinqchiuh [56] le.
B: Bush jeyg yuanguh, huohjee keeyii shuo sh inwey ig chiahx shiangfaan de — (*Ker.sow.*)
A: Char.farng! Char.farng!
B: Char.farng! Huoo.jih! [57]
Char: Ei,[58] jeh jiow lai, shiansheng!
B: Tzay g'woom lai ideal kai-shoei! Woo saangtz dou shuo-yeale.[59]
(*Chihdyi-sheng.*)

---

6. *Chihdyi-sheng* 'steam-flute-sound,' stage direction language for *chuei-shawl de sheng'in* 'sound of blowing the whistle.'

7. *Keh* 'guest, customer,' here used as AN 'an order of.'

8. *Yuanjyi* 'original registry, — place of origin.' In China, a person is said to be a native of whatever place his near ancestors (in some cases even distant ancestors) have come from.

9. *Yuanshian* 'original-previous, — originally.'

10. *Chwenjenq* 'pure and correct.'

11. *Beeifang* 'northern locality, — the north.'

12. *Guh.shyh* 'old-story, — story.'

13. An adjective with *-j ne* is a common lively intensive, as *haoj ne, dahj ne, lihhayj ne.*

14. There are two places usually romanized 'Changchow' on the map, one in Fukien and the other in Kiangsu, which is the place referred to here. (In the full Wade orthography, the latter should be 'Ch'angchow,' but many maps omit the aspiration signs.)

15. *Gua* 'scrape.'

16. *Yanghuoo* 'foreign-fire, — matches,' in Peiping popularly called *cheudengl* or *yangcheudengl* 'foreign-getter-lighter.'

17. *Isheaul* 'from childhood.'

18. On the meaning of *Nanbian*, see text before Note 31, p. 233.

19. *Ney-i-luh* 'that route, — that type.'

20. *Gao* is a central-dialect word for *nonq.*

21. *Kai-meng* 'open up ignorance, — begin school.'

22. *Tzuufuh* 'grandfather' and *tzuumuu* 'grandmother' are mentioning terms. There is much variation in the forms for direct address. *Ye.ye* 'grandpa' and *nae.nae* 'grandma' are the most frequently used forms in Peiping.

23. *Chiing* 'ask, invite' is the term used in connection with engaging teachers and professional people. For clerks, unskilled workers, etc. the word is *guh* 'hire.'

24. *Jiashiang* 'homestead.'

25. *Jiau-shu* 'teach-book, — to do teaching'; *jiau tade shu* 'to give him instruction.'

26. *Woo sheau.shyrhowl* 'when I was small, in my childhood.'

27. *Shyueshiaw*, or the more old-fashioned term *shyuetarng*, is applied to modern schools, as opposed to *shufarng* 'book-room, — the study, family school.' *Syshwu* 'private-school, — family school' is the technical term for the same.

28. *Fangkuall-tzyh* 'square-piece characters, word cards.'

29. *Santzyh Jing* (or . . . *Jiengl*) 'Three-character Classic,' a 13th century elementary reader in which each phrase has three syllables.

30. *Baejia Shinq* (or . . . *Shienql*) 'Hundred-family Surnames,' anonymous, 11–13th century, rimed list of 438 surnames, with four syllables to each phrase.

31. *Chiantzyh Wen* (or . . . *Wel*) 'Thousand-character Text,' by *Jou Shingsyh*, 6th century, A.D., rimed reader with four syllables to a phrase, each of the 1000 characters occurring only once in the book.

32. *Dah₀shyue* 'the Great Learning,' a chapter in *Liijih* (see Note 39).

33. *Jong₀iong* 'Doctrine of the Mean,' by *Koong Jyi*, grandson of Confucius, 5th century B.C. This is also a chapter in *Liijih*.

34. *Luen₀yeu* 'the (Confucian) Analects,' 5th century B.C.

35. *Menq ₀Tzyy* 'Mencius,' 4th century B.C.

36. *Shy.jing* 'the Poetry Classic, — the Book of Odes,' anonymous, 6th century B.C. and earlier.

37. *Shanqshu*, also called *Shu.jing* 'the Book of History,' anonymous, before the 6th century B.C., with many later additions.

38. *Tzuoojuann* 'Tso's Chronicles, the *Tso Chuan*, ca. 6th century B.C.

39. *Liijih* 'Record of Rites, — Book of Rites,' compiled by *Day Shenq*, 1st century B.C.

40. *Yih.jing* 'Change-Classics, — the Book of Changes,' of uncertain authorship, probably pre-Confucian.

41. *Shy* refers to the more usual kind of poetry, as speaker A does not regard the poems of *Shyjing* as ordinary poetry.

42. *Shian–* 'former, — deceased,' limited to reference to relatives older than oneself.

43. *Shy* in current usage refers to poems usually with five or seven syllables to the line. *Tsyr* is a poem with lines of unequal length following rather rigid patterns of succession of tones. *Ge* as a literary form is either *shy* or *tsyr* where there is more obvious rhythm and repetition of words to lend itself to singing. (An actual song is called *ge'l*.) *Fuh* is a form of descriptive essay in which there is much use of assonance, alliteration, onomatopoeia, internal rhymes, end rhymes, and other sound effects.

44. *Tzyy.mey*, literally 'elder and younger sisters,' is used by some people to include brothers. Cf. Germ. *Geschwister*. *Jiee₀mey*, however, always means 'sisters' only.

45. *Shoou* 'stanza,' also AN for poems.

46. *Heng* or *heng.x* 'to hum (a tune).'

47. Ancient *shy* or current *shy* written in the traditional style of five- or seven-syllable lines are chanted by improvising on definite types of melodies. The first poem given here belongs to a type called *liuhshy* 'metric poem.' Its melody has a range of low *mi* to high *mi* or the *sol* above it and ends on low *mi*, or *sol-mi* slurred over the last syllable. This melody type is almost universal for the whole country. The second poem belongs to the type called *guushy* 'antique poem.' Its melody varies from place to place. In Changchow, Kiangsu, it has a range of a low *la* to the *do* an octave and a minor third above and ends on the lower *do*. The nearly universal *liuhshy* melody for the first poem and the Changchow melody for the second poem are as follows:

'Feng Chyau Yeh Bor'.

Jang Jih

Yueh luoh u tyi shuang maan tian, Jiang-feng yu-huoo duey chour mian.

Gu-su cherng-way Harn Shan Syh, Yeh-bann jong-sheng daw keh-chwan.

"YEH SY"

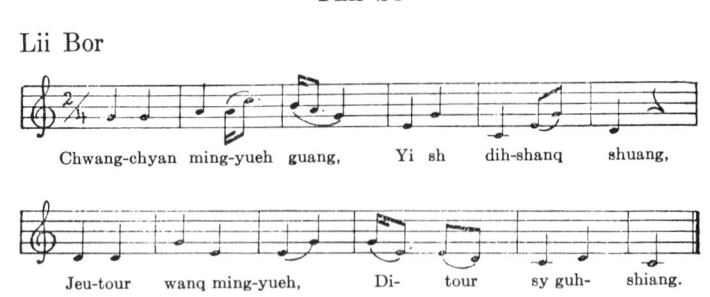

Lii Bor

Chwang-chyan ming-yueh guang, Yi sh dih-shanq shuang,

Jeu-tour wanq ming-yueh, Di- tour sy guh- shiang.

48. *Lii Bor* 'Li Po,' 8th century poet. There are many translations of his poems into English.

49. *Mingyueh* has often been over-translated as 'the bright moon' or even 'the dazzling moon.' At the time when the poem was written, the expression probably meant no more than just 'the moon' and was used instead of *yueh* when the meter called for two syllables. Cf. Modern colloquial *yueh.lianq*.

50. *Wuushiang charyeh-dann* 'five-spice tea-leaf eggs,' eggs boiled hard with tea leaves and spices.

51. *Jongshyue* 'middle school,' corresponding to the American high school.

52. *Wuhlii* 'things-principles, — physics.'

53. *Shuhshyue* 'number-science, — mathematics,' also called *suannshyue* 'reckoning-science.' Arithmetic is *suannshuh* 'reckoning-technique.'

54. *Gwowen* or *gwowel* 'national literature, — Chinese (as a school subject).'

55. *Gendii* 'foundation.'

56. *Gaanjyue shinq₀chiuh* 'to feel interest.'

57. *Huoo.jih* is more used for waiters in restaurants and tea houses, while *char.farng* more in hotels, on trains, and ships.

58. *Ei!* interjection in answer to a call.

59. *Yea* 'dumb, hoarse.'

60. *Exercise 1 (f)*. *–Buh* is AN for *shu* as a work, while *–been* or *–beel* is AN for *shu* as a physical thing.

EXERCISES

1. *Example:*

Given:
Woo renn.shyhle nii nemm jeou le; shianntzay yaw wennx (nii) nii yuanjyi sh naal le.

Answer:
Woo sweiran renn.shyhle nii nemm jeou, keesh tsornglai mei wenn-.guoh nii yuanjyi sh naal; shianntzay deei chii-tourl wennx nii le.

(a) Woo shyue-hueyle shuo sheuduo Jonggwo-huah le; shianntzay yaw shyuex dwu Jonggwo-shu le. (b) Ta dawle Jonggwo yeou shyrjii-nian le; jinnian yaw shanq Beeipyng chiuh guanqx ('do some sightseeing') le. (c) Woo sh Charngjou-ren; shianntzay inggai yaw daw tzyhjii de jiashiang chiuh kannx le. (d) Niimen renndele sheuduo goanggaw.shanq de tzyh le; miengl yaw chii-tourl rennx shu.lii de tzyh le. (e) Woode erltz shiihuan nonq jichih shermde; ta shianntzay yaw chii-tourl niann deal jeang tzyhran-keshyue de shu le. (f) Woo duey ren jintian yee jeang Sanmin Juuyih, mingtian yee jeang Sanmin Juuyih; shianntzay woo deei mae beel *Sanmin Juuyih* ney-buh [60] shu lai dwux le. (g) Woo kannjiann-.guoh haoduo Jonggwo neydih de shanshoei; shiahg yueh woo sheang daw Anhuei de nan-buh chiuh guanqx Hwang Shan chiuh le. (h) Jey-i-jial gongchaang bannle tzemm sheuduo nian; jinnian yaw bann i-leang-joong jonq-gongyeh le.

2. *Example:*

Given:
Woo sheau.shyrhowl buhuey shuo Nanbian-huah.

Answer:
Oh, nemm nii Nanbian-huah sh dahle yiihow tsair shyue-hueyle de ma?

(a) Woo mei ruh shyueshiaw yiichyan mei niann Ing'wen. (b) Che mei kai yiichyan sh jiaw.bu-jaur char de. (c) Woo tzwotian mei tingjiann jey-jiann dah-shinwen. (d) Woomen shiongdih jiig ren tzay shyueshiaw de shyrhowl bu dwu *Tarng Shy Sanbae Shoou* de. (e) Woo mei daw Meeigwo lai yiichyan mei chy-guoh waygwo-fann. (f) Mei ban-jinn jcy-suoo farngtz liitou lai de shyrhowl woo bujydaw naw-goei. (g) Woo mei tingjiann nii niann guushy yiichyan yiiwei Jonggwo niann-shy chuhchull doush iyanq de diawl. (h) Woo tzwol woanshanq shuey-jiaw de shyrhowl hair mei jyuej tour-terng.

3. *Write out and practice telling Ryhshin's early language experience, with variations on the places and circumstances.*

LESSON 23
THE VERNACULAR LITERATURE MOVEMENT

Child: (*Cries.*)
Traveler I: Hey, there, look where you're going! What's the matter with you? You, you, you look how you've spilled it all over me!
Lady: Look how you've scalded the poor child, hands burned all red! — Darling, don't cry, it's all right, it's all right, I'll wipe it for you with my hankie.
Waiter: I am so sorry, please, please forgive me!
Trav I: Look at this new gown of mine, damned if it isn't all ruined by you!
W: I am so sorry sir! I was really too careless. I hadn't thought the train would stop with such a jerk. With a lurch, and I —
Trav I: That won't do, that's not enough!
Child: My new dress is all wet! Boo hoo!
Lady: There, there, don't cry any more, dear!
Traveller II: Come, come, it's a good thing the water wasn't dirty. Uh — waiter!
W: Yes sir, yes sir!
Trav II: Hurry up and bring a clean cloth and wipe it for this gentleman!
Trav I: All right, just to be courteous to this gentleman, I'll let you go this time.
Lady: Does it still hurt, precious?
Child: Um-m — doesn't any more.

. . . . . .

A: Well, what's happened to our pot of tea? He's been gone a long time!
B: Yes, what's the matter? Ah, here he comes. Uh — as I was saying a while ago, when I was young I didn't like to read serious books very much. Outside of 'Mencius,' 'Tso Chuan,' and the poems of Li Po, I didn't care at all for reading the other classics. As for books like 'Lao Tzǔ,' 'Chuang Tzǔ,' and such like, which I did enjoy reading, our teacher would not teach us to read them.
A: Is that so?
B: Yes. I was especially fond of reading novels, which our teacher called 'idle books' and which he forbade us to read, and we would get scolded if we were found out by him. Sometimes I secretly hid the novels in my desk drawer, — books like 'Water's Strand,' 'Dream of the Red Chamber,' 'Informal History of Literary Men,' 'History of the Three Kingdoms,' —

DIH ELLSHYRSAN KEH
BAIRHUAH WEN [1]

Sheauharl: (*Ku.*)
Leukeh I: Ê, è, è, nii yeanjing kann de naal chiuh le? Nii tzeem gao de sha? [2] Nii, nii, nii kann, nii saa de woo i-shen de!
Neukeh: Nii chyau nii bae hairtz tanq de, shoou dou tanq de tonghorng [3] de! — .Guai.guai,[4] bye ku, buyawjiin, buyawjiin, woo na woo shooujiuall geei nii tsax.
Charfarng: Dueybujuh, chiing Nin, chiing Nin yuan.lianq!
Leu I: Nii kann woo jey-jiann shin-dahguall,[5] hair bush dou geei nii nonq-huay le!
Char: Dueybujuh, Nin a! Woo shyrtzay sh tay tsushin [6] le. Naalii sheaude [7] huooche huran de i-tyng sha? Woo ig jann.bu-woen,[8] jiow —
Leu I: Nah bucherng, nah buneng suann! [9]
Sheau: Woode shin-ishang dou geei nonq-shy le! E-heh!
Neu: Hao, hao, bye ku le, ah!
Leukeh II: Der le, der le! Haotzay shoei bu tzang. Êh, Charfarng!
Char: Sh, sh,[10] Nin a!
Leu II: Kuay na .kuay [11] gan.jinq jaan.buh lai! Geei jey-wey shiansheng tsax!
Leu I: Hao, kann jey-wey shiansheng de mianntz,[12] jey-hwei raule [13] nii!
Neu: Hair terng bu terng l'a, .bao.bey?
Sheau: M — bu terng le.

. . . . . .

A: Êr, tzarmen ney-hwu char tzeem l'a? Ta tzooule banntian le me!
B: Êè, tzeem hwei shell? Ah, lai le. E — woo gangtsair jenq tzay shuo woo sheau.shyrhowl budah shiihuan niann jenq.jing shu. Chwule *Menq Tzyy, Tzuoojuann,* gen *Lii Bor* de shy jy way, chyiyude jing-shu woo ideal ycc butzay.hu [14] niann. Woo suoo [15] shiihuan kann de *Lao Tzyy* [16] a, *Juang Tzyy* [17] a, — nah-ley de shu shiansheng yow bu jiau woomen niann.
A: Sh ma?
B: Êh. Woo youchyi ay kann sheaushuol,[18] shiansheng goan ta [19] jiaw shyanshu,[20] busheu woomen kann, char.jaur [21] le hair deei air-mah. Woo yeou shyrhowl toutoulde [22] bae sheaushuol-shu tsarng de shujuol chou.tih [23] lii — biifang *Shoeihuu Juann* [24] a, *Hornglou Menq* [25] a, *Rulin Wayshyy* [26] a, *Sangwo Jyh* a, —

A: Isn't 'History of the Three Kingdoms' an official history in the 'Twenty-four Histories'?

B: The book I am talking about is the 'Story of the Three Kingdoms,' the novel that the general public reads for amusement, you know.

A: Oh, I see.

B: Later, when I entered college, our professor of Chinese not only did not prohibit us from reading novels, but even told us to study them as lessons, so that we could actually display them right on the tops of our desks, and openly read 'idle books' in public; oh, what a pleasure!

A: From the way you talk, you must be in favor of this — uh — the, the New Literature Movement?

B: Yes, I am very much in favor of the Vernacular Literature Movement.

A: W-e-ll, for elementary education, or mass education, perhaps the colloquial language will be more suitable, but if you want to discuss somewhat advanced learned theories, the spoken idiom is perhaps not so accurate as the literary, I'm afraid. And aren't your 'Lao Tzǔ' and 'Chuang Tzǔ' books all written in the literary language?

B: But the T'ang dynasty records of lectures on Buddhism, —.

A: But —

B: — the Sung dynasty philosophers' —

A: But the currently used official documents of various kinds, such as international treaties, law statutes, —

B: But —

A: — the commercial contracts, articles in magazines, even the advertisements or news in the newspapers, or even ordinary correspondence, —

B: Well — uh —

A: — still take the literary language as the main —

B: Well, if we start to discuss this problem thoroughly, we wouldn't be able to finish even if we talked all night. Too bad I am not Hu Shih, and don't know how to argue with you properly. Why, I, I thought you were always in favor of *pai-hua*, aren't you?

A: So I am, I merely pretended that I was taking the opposite point of view in order to have a chat with you, that's all.

B: Aw, what a fool you made of me!

A: There's nothing to do on the train anyway, so I was looking for a subject to talk about, just to kill time. (*Yawns.*) Oh, I still have some tea! — Thank you very much!

B: Why, he has just brought this tea and it's already gone! He didn't fill the pot to start with, I guess. (*Yawns.*) Oh, it's half past eleven already. I am sleepy and hungry, too.

W: Will the two gentlemen care for some refreshments?

A: Ah, you said you were hungry; I invite you to a midnight supper.

A: Sangwo Jyh [27] bush Ellshyrsyh Shyy .lii de i-buh jenq-shyy ma?
B: Woo shuo de ney-buh sh *Sangwo Jyh Yeanyih* è, sh neyg ibande ren kannj wal de sheaushuol è.
A: Oh.
B: Howlai woo ruh le dahshyue,[28] woomde gwowel jiawshow budann bu jinnjyy [29] woomen kann sheaushuol, hair jiaw woomen na ta danq gongkeh niann, — jiuran keeyii bae sheaushuol-shu bae [30] de shujuol de shanqtou, tzay dah-tyng-goang-jonq,[31] gongran de kann.chii shyanshu .lai, nii chyau jeh dwo guoh-yiin [32] a!
A: Ting nii jey-tzoong koou.chih,[33] nii syh.hu sh tzanncherng jeyg jeyg — jeyg jeyg Shin Wenshyue Yunndonq de lo?
B: Sh de, woo sh feicharng tzanncherng jeyg Bairhuah Wen Yunndonq de.
A: M — wey chujyi [34] jiawyuh, huohjee dahjonq [35] jiawyuh, huohjee bairhuah shiangyi .i.deal, dannsh ruguoo yaw jeang gaushen [36] .i.deal de shyuelii,[37] koongpah koouyeu [38] meiyeou wenyan nemm joenchiueh ba? È, nii neyshie Lao Juang de shu bu doush wenyan shiee de ma?
B: Keesh Tarng.chaur de Forjiaw de yeuluh [39] a, —
A: Buguoh —
B: Sonq.chaur liishyuejia [40] de —
A: Buguoh shianntzay tongshyng de geh-joong gongwen a, haobii gwojihde tyauiue a, faaliuh liitou de tyauwen a, —
B: Keesh —
A: — neyshie shangwuh de hertorng a, tzarjyh.lii de wen.jang a, naapah bawshanq de goanggaw torng [41] shinwen, shennjyhyu pyngcharng ren shiee-shinn, —
B: È —
A: — rengjiow sh yii wenyan wei juu —
B: Ay, jeyg wenntyi yawsh chehdii de taoluenn.chiilai, jiowsh i-yeh shuo daw tianlianq yee shuo.bu-wan de lo. Kee.shi [42] woo bush Hwu Shyhjy,[43] bujydaw tzeem gen nii biann hao.[44] Èr, woo, woo daangj nii shianqlai sh tzanncherng bairhuah de, bush ma?
A: Sh .sh sh [45] è! Woo buguoh jeajuangl de [46] jann tzay faanmiall de lihchaang gen nii shia-liaux [47] jiowshle.
B: Ch! woo shanq le nii nemm g dah-danq! [48]
A: Che.shanq herngsh mei shell gann, jao g tyimuh sweibiann tarnx, shiaumo [49] vx shyrjian [50] jiowshle. (*Daa-ha.chiann.*) — È, woo char hair yeou ne! — Bukehchih bukehchih!
B: Yee? Tzeem gang paw.lai [51] de char yow meiyeou le? Ta yahgel jiow mei bae charhwu geei daw-maan,[52] woo kann. (*Daa-ha.chiann.*) Shyridean-bann le dou. Woo yow kuenn yow eh.
Char: Leang-wey shiansheng jiaw deal sherm deanshin ba?
A: È, nii shuo nii eh le; woo chiing nii chy shiauyeh.[53] Ranq woo kannx

Let's have a look! (*Reads menu.*) 'Fried Noodles' — fried noodles are too rich for this time of the night — 'Soup Noodles,' say, I'll treat you to some ham and chicken noodles!

B: No, let me be host! Waiter, two orders of ham and chicken noodles!

A: Say, no, no, I ordered it!

B: I said it first, it was I —

A: Waiter, listen to what I say, let me —

B: Hey, hey, hey! (*The train whistles.*)

W: Two orders of ham and chicken noodl — es!

. . . . . .

Child: Ma! Mama!

Lady: Yes, darling! What is it?

Child: Ma, I'm hungry.

NOTES

1. *Bairhuah* 'plain-talk, — colloquial language, *pai-hua*,' as opposed to *wenyan* 'the literary language'; *bairhuah-wen* 'vernacular literature,' especially the currently used style of writing, which contains many new terms and literary expressions. (See p. 8.)

2. *.Sha* is a final particle used in very insistent questions. It is used much more frequently in central dialects, where it also occurs in emphatic statements.

3. Adjectives are often associated with one or more intensifying words of suitable figure, as

Tong-horng	'red through and through.'
Shiueh-bair (< *sheue-bair*)	'snow-white.'
Chiuh-hei (< *chi-hei*)	'black as lacquer, — pitch-black.'
Fei-baur	'flying-thin.'
Tiee-yinq	'hard as iron.'
Pih-ching	'light as (break)wind.'

4. *Guai* 'shrewd'; 'good (as a child).' *Guai.guai* 'darling baby.' Terms of direct address, like interjections, are spoken without, or almost without, tones.

5. *Dahguall* 'big-hanger, — unlined robe.' Robes with lining of cloth, wadding, or fur are called *paurtz*.

6. *Tsu* 'coarse, coarsed-grained'; *tsushin* 'careless,' opposite of *shihshin* 'careful, observant.'

7. *Naalii sheaude*, Southern Mandarin for *naal jydaw* 'how could one know . . . .?'

.kann, a! (*Kann tsaydantz*.⁵⁴) 'Chao-miann-ley' ⁵⁵ — jeh bannyeh sangeng de, chao-miann tay nih ⁵⁶ lo — 'Tang-miann-ley,' è, woo chiing nii chy huootoei-jisel-miann! ⁵⁷

B: È, ranq woo lai tzuoh-dong! Charfarng, leang-keh huootoei-jisy-miann!
A: È, bu, bu, sh woo jiaw d'è!
B: Woo shian shuo de, sh woo —
A: Charfarng, nii ting woode huah, ranq woo lai —
B: È, è, è! (*Chihdyi sheng*.)
Char: Leang-keh huootoei-jisy-miann!

. . . . . .

Sheau: Mha! Mha.mha!
Neu: Ei, .bao.bao! Shermme?
Sheau: Mha, woo eh le.

---

8. *Woen* 'steady'; *ig jann.bu-woen* 'a failure to stand steadily.'
9. *Nah buneng suann* 'that cannot be considered settled.'
10. *Sh*, repeated and not followed by *de*, is a very unctuous form of 'yes.'
11. This .*kuay* 'piece' is the AN for *jaan.buh* 'wiping-cloth.' (On omission of *i-* after a verb, see Note 25, p. 154.)
12. *Mianntz* 'face, courtesy.'
13. *Rau* 'to spare from punishment.'
14. *Tzay.hu* 'to care for'; *butzay.hu* 'not to care for.'
15. See Note 20, p. 184.
16. *Lao Tzyy* 'Lao Tzŭ,' 6th century B.C., founder of Taoism. The name of his book is properly called *Dawder Jing* 'Canon of the Way and Virtue,' loosely *Lao Tzyy*. Distinguish between *Lao Tzyy* and *laotz* 'father' (cf. 'the old man').
17. *Juang Tzyy* 'Chuang Tzŭ,' 5th century B.C., Taoist philosopher. The name of his book is properly called *Nanhwa Jing*, loosely called *Juang Tzyy*.
18. *Sheaushuo(l)* 'small talk(er), — a novel.'
19. Note the use of *ta* for 'them.' (See p. 47.)
20. *Shyanshu* 'idle book, leisure book,' old term for 'novel.'
21. *Char* 'investigate, inspect'; *char.jaur* 'find out (from investigation).'
22. *Tou* 'to steal'; *toutoulde* 'stealthily.'
23. *Chou.tih, chou.tiell* 'draw-tier, — drawer.'
24. *Shoeihuu* or *Shoeihuu Juann* 'Water's Strand (Chronicles),' by *Shy Nay'an*, 14th century, translated by Pearl S. Buck as 'All Men are Brothers,' New York, 1937; by J. H. Jackson as 'Water Margin,' Shanghai, 1937.

25. *Hornglou Menq* 'Red Upper-story Dream, — Dream of the Red Chamber,' by *Tsaur Sheuechyn*, 18th century, translated by Chi-chen Wang, London, 1927.

26. *Rulin Wayshyy* 'Scholars Outside-history, — Informal History of Literary Men,' a satirical novel by *Wu Jingtzyy*, 18th century.

27. *Sangwo Jyh* 'History of the Three Kingdoms,' properly the name of one of the 'Twenty-four (Dynastic) Histories'; it is commonly used as an abbreviated name for *Sangwo Jyh Yeanyih* 'Story of the Three Kingdoms,' by *Luo Guannjong*, 14th century, translated by Brewitt Taylor as 'San Kuo, or the Romance of Three Kingdoms,' Shanghai, 1925.

28. *Dahshyue* 'university, college'; *shyueyuann* 'college.'

29. *Jinnjyy* 'prohibit-stop, — prohibit.'

30. The second *bae* 'arrange, display,' is an unrelated homonym of the pretransitive *bae* or *baa*. In central dialects, it is often used for *ge* 'to put.'

31. *Dah-tyng-goang-jonq* 'great hall wide multitude, — public place,' a commonly spoken literary cliché.

32. *Yiin* 'habit (for smoke, drink, etc.)'; *guoh-yiin* 'habit-satisfying, — satisfying to a craving.'

33. *Koou.chih* 'mouth-air, — tone, expression.'

34. *Chujyi* 'beginning-grade, — elementary.'

35. *Dahjonq* 'great-multitude, — the masses.'

36. *Gaushen* 'high-deep, — abstruse, advanced.'

37. *Shyuelii* 'learned principles, — learned theories.'

38. *Koouyeu* 'word of mouth' is the literary term for *bairhuah* 'colloquial language.'

39. *Yeuluh* 'speech-records, — lecture notes (on Buddhism).' One of the earliest of Mandarin texts extant is *Shiyunn Yeuluh*, in the Japanese edition of the *Tripitaka* or *Daizō kyō*, case 31, vol. 2. *Shiyunn* died in 853 A.D.

40. *Liishyue* 'science of principles, — philosophy,' a term applied to the works of the Sung philosophers only. (The new term for 'philosophy' is *jershyue* 'wisdom-science.') The suffix *–jia* may be translated as '–ist, –er,' etc.; cf. 'to be at home in . . . .'

41. *Torng* 'same, together with,' used in central and southern dialects for *gen*.

42. *Kee.shi* 'regretable, — it's a pity, too bad.'

43. Hu Shih's *mingtzyh* is *Shyh* 'Shih'; *Shyhjy* is his *haw*, or courtesy name.

44. *Hao* is the predicate of the subject *tzeem gen nii biann*.

45. On the form *V sh V*, see Note 12, p. 184.

46. *Jeajuangl* 'falsely-makeup, — pretend.'

47. *Shia-liau* 'chat at random.'

48. The verb object expression is *shanq-danq* 'go up the pawn (counter), — to be fooled.'
49. *Shiaumo* 'consume-wear, — wear off.'
50. *Shyrjian* 'time-interval, — time,' a more formal expression than *shyrhowl*.
51. *Paw* 'steep.'
52. *Daw* 'to pour.'
53. *Shiauyeh* 'consume-night, — midnight supper, snack,' in some dialects used as a verb: 'to eat a midnight supper.'
54. *Tsaydantz* or *tsaydal* 'dishes-list, — menu.'
55. *Chao* is a characteristically Chinese form of cooking, somewhat similar to *sauté*. *Chao-miann-ley* 'the category of fried noodles.'
56. *Nih* 'greasy, too rich.'
57. *Huootoei* 'fire-leg, — (salt) ham'; *jisel* or *jisy* 'chicken threads, — chicken shreds.'

EXERCISES

1. *Example:*

Given:

Woo bu shiihuan niann jing-shu, keesh heen shiihuan niann *Menq tzyy* gen *Tzuoojuann*.

Answer:

Woo chwule heen shiihuan niann *Menq tzyy* gen *Tzuoojuann* jy way, chyiyude jing-shu woo i-yanql yee bu shiihuan niann.

(a) Woo bu shiihuan kann shen de yanshae, keesh shiihuan kann shen-horng gen shen-lan. (b) Jeyg shyuesheng pah shyue tzyhran-keshyue de gongkeh, keesh ta bupah shuhshyue. (c) Jensh moh-ming-chyi-miaw, shianntzay bawshanq de sheuduo wenjang chahbuduo wanchyuan sh yonq wenyan shiee de, dannsh suoowey 'wenshyue' ney-i-buhfenn dawsh yonq bairhuah shiee de. (d) Minsheng Chaang .lii chahbuduo sherm dou huey jyhtzaw, jiowsh buhuey jyhtzaw tsornglai mei tzay Jonggwo jyhtzaw.guoh de dongshi. (e) Ney-wey shiansheng chahbuduo tzoong tzaynall heng diawl, keesh ta tzoei.lii chyj dongshi de shyrhowl jiow bu heng le. (f) Shyhjieh.shanq de dahjou dahduoshuh doush tzay Beei Bannchyou, dannsh Awjou gen Nanjyi Jou sh jeenggehl tzay Nan Bannchyou de. (g) Jeyg farngtz geh-dihfangl dou heen gan.jinq, buguoh howyuall tzang de buderleau. (h) Yonq Jonggwo-tzyh shiee Goangdong-huah gen shiee Gwoyeu chahbuduo sh wanchyuan iyanq de, dannsh yeou shaoshuh de tzyh — haobii *ta*-tzyh a, *kann*-tzyh a, *jeh*-tzyh, *nah*-tzyh, *hair*-tzyh, *sh*-tzyh shermde — jeyshie tzyh Goangdong-huah gen Gwoyeu jiow butorng le.

2. *Translate into Chinese:*

(a) The reason why I like to read *Mencius* is that it is very like the modern Chinese literary language. (b) When our teacher forbade us to read the so-called idle books, we just hid them between volumes of serious books. (c) Not only did the teachers in the new schools permit us to read novels, but also told us to read as many novels as possible (*use 'the more the better' construction*). (d) We felt that to be able to read novels on our desks was more craving-quenching than being permitted to smoke in the classroom. (e) After hearing the history of the Indusco, I am sure you

LESSON 24
AN AMERICAN MAKES A SPEECH

A: Oh, gosh! We've arraived* late. Listen, they are already renging the bell for the meeting.

B: Sure thing! As I told you, since our train was late, we should have come straight to the auditorium —

A: How could you do thet? —

B: — and you insisted on going to the dorms first.

A: — we hed so much beggage. What could you have done if you hedn't set them down?

B: Say, they've started singing the national anthem! Let's go in quietly.

(*Singing of the national anthem.*)

'The three principles of the people
Are our party's aim
On these we build our Republic,
On these we advance to a world community.

Know ye all comrades,
As the people's vanguards,
From morn till night never relax,
Only the principles shall ye follow!

Resolve to be diligent, resolve to be brave,
Ye shall be faithful, ye shall be loyal,
With one heart, with one spirit,
Persevere from beginning to end!'

* The vowel shift in the English is to give a hint of Speaker A's dialect

will be very much in favor of this movement. (f) For convenience of marketing and shopping, perhaps it is better to live in a busy section of the city. (g) In the so-called vernacular literature, such as the novels of the Ming and the Ch'ing dynasties — even the books Hu Shih himself has written — they continue to take the literary language to be its mainstay. (h) Aren't you one of those who support the Literary Revolution?

3. *Summarize the arguments for and against the Vernacular Literature Movement.*

DIH ELLSHYRSYH KEH MEEIGWOREN YEANSHUO [1]

A: Huay le, huay le! Tzarmen daw-chyrle. Nii ting, yiijing daa-jong kai-huey le.

B: Keebush ma? Woo shuo de, tzarmen huooche jihran wuhle dean, jiow inggai ijyr daw dah-liitarng [2] —

A: Nah tzeem cherng a? —

B: — nii iseel [3] yaw shian daw suhsheh.[4]

A: — tzarmen shyng.lii nemm duo, nii bu shian geei ta fanq.shiahlai yee bushyng a.

B: E, tamen yiijing kaishyy chanq gwoge'l le! Tzarmen chingchienglde jinnchiuh.

(*Chanq Gwoge.*) [5]

"Sanmin juuyih,
Wu-daang suoo tzong,
Yii jiann mingwo,
Yii jinn dahtorng.

Tzy eel duo-shyh,
Wei min chyanfeng,
Suh-yeh feei shieh,
Juuyih sh tsorng!

Shyy chyn shyy yeong,
Bih shinn bih jong;
I-shin i-der,
Guanncheh shyy-jong!"

Woman Student I: (*Whispers.*) There's a foreigner sitting on the platform.
Woman Student II: Where?
W I: There, to the right of the president's seat.
W II: Oh, I see him now; he seems to be quite young!
W I: Hey, not so loud!
President: Today we welcome an American student, who has recently arrived in China. He is an exchange student from Harvard University of Cambridge, Massachusetts, to our university. Mr. Reim. (*Applause.*)
Reim: President Hu, my teachers, and fellow students. The proverb has put it very well, "Heaven is not to be feared, Earth is not to be feared, but a foreign devil talking Chinese, — that is fearful!" (*Laughter.*) I — uh — I don't know how to make a speech in the first place, still less to make a speech in Chinese. If I speak badly, I beg all of you — uh —
A: Well, his Mendarin is not bed, eh? —
R: — to forgive me! —
B: Yeah, the devil's devilish accent is better than your 'netional eccent,' what?
A: Ha ha ha!
R: — I have been wanting to come to China since my childhood, and so I have often bought English books and periodicals pertaining to China to read. Sometimes, too, I have gone to New York and Boston to buy Chinese things, go to Chinese restaurants, and so forth. I have also wanted to learn to speak Chinese, to learn Chinese characters, and study China's culture. But everybody warned me again and again what a difficult language Chinese was, and so I was frightened by them and never dared to try.

But last winter, I made a resolution and elected a Rapid Course in the Chinese Language at Harvard University; moreover, I met with good fortune and got a scholarship to come here as an exchange student. Now I have actually attained my object of coming to China to study, and I just don't know how to express my happiness.

And — uh — and above all, as a student from Harvard like myself — you know Harvard only takes men students — I am particularly glad to come to China and see that every university is — uh — uh — co-educational! (*Great laughter.*)

Uh — although I have not been here very long, I have received help and guidance in every way from all my teachers and all my fellow students, and I don't know how to thank you adequately. I hope that, in the future, you will all continue to give me your guidance from time to time. (*Applause.*)
B: Well, this foreigner's Chinese is really not bad, is it?
A: Yes, he speaks sech polished Mendarin, I even can't beat him et it.

AN AMERICAN MAKES A SPEECH

Neusheng I: (*Eelyeu.*)[6] Jeangtair.shanq[7] yeou g yangrel[8] tzuoh de nall.
Neusheng II: Naal a?
Neu I: Tzay nall, tzay shiawjaang weytz de yowbial.
Neu II: Oh, kannjiann le; haoshianq tiing nianching de ne!
Neu I: Êh, bye tzemm dahshengl!
Shiawjaang: Jintian woomen huan'yng[9] i-wey shinjinn daw Jonggwo lai de Meeigwo torngshyue.[10] Ta sh Meeigwo Masheeng[11] Jiannchyau[12] Haafor Dahshyue gen been-shiaw de jiauhuann shyuesheng. Limuh[13] Torngshyue. (*Guu-jaang-sheng.*)[14]
Limuh: Hwu Shiawjaang, geh-wey laoshy,[15] geh-wey torngshyue. Swuyeu shuo de hao, "Tian bu pah, dih bu pah, jiow pah yanggoeitz shuo Jonggwo-huah."[16] (*Shiaw-sheng.*) Shiongdih — jeyg — beenlai jiow bu- huey yeanshuo, genq buhuey yonq Jonggwo-huah yeanshuo. Shuo de buhao de .huah,[17] chiing dahjia jeyg —
A: Êr, tade gwoyeu shuo de buhuay è —
Limuh: — chiing dahjia yuanlianq —
B: Êh, goeitz de goeiyeu[18] bii niide gwoyeu shuo de hao deal, ar?
A: Ha ha ha!
Limuh: — Shiong.dih tsorngsheaul jiow sheang shanq Jonggwo lai, suooyii charngcharngl mae le shie jeang Jonggwo shyhchyng de Ing'wen- shu-baw[19] lai dwu. Hair yeou shyrhowl shanq Neouiue, Boshyhduenn chiuh mae Jonggwo dongshi, shanq Jonggwo fanngoal shermde. Woo hair sheang shyue shuo Jonggwo-huah, renn Jonggwo-tzyh, yanjiow Jonggwo de wenhuah. Keesh renren dou jiinggaw woo shuo Jongwen dwo nan dwo nan, suooyii bae woo shiah de tzoong bugaan shyh.

Keesh chiuhnian dongtian woo shiah le jyueshin, tzay Haafor Dahshyue sheuan le i-men Jonggwo Yeuyan[20] Suhcherng Ke;[21] yow penq.daw hao- yunn.chih, derle i-bii[22] jeangshyue-jin, shanq jell lai tzuoh jiauhuann- shyuesheng. Shianntzay jiuran dar-dawle daw Jonggwo chyou-shyue[23] de muhdih, woo jyuej jeanjyr kuay.hwo de shuo.bu-chulai le.

E — youchyish shianq woo tzemm ig tsorng Haafor Dahshyue lai de shyuesheng — niimen jydaw Haafor sh jyy shou[24] nansheng[25] d'è! — shianntzay dawle Jonggwo, kannjiann gehgehl dahshyue doush jeyg — jeyg — nan-neu torng-shiaw,[26] jeyg shyy woo jyuej[27] youchyi gaushinq! (*Hong-tarng dah-shiaw.*)[28]

E — shiong.dih daw le jehlii[29] hair mei dwo jeou, cherng[30] geh-wey shyjaang,[31] geh-wey torngshyue, chuhchuh de bang-mang jyydean,[32] bujydaw tzeemyanq gaanshieh[33] tsair hao. Yiihow hair shiwanq dahjia shyrshyr jyydao![34] (*Guu-jaang-sheng.*)

B: Êè, jeyg waygworen de Jonggwo-huah shuo de jen butsuoh, ar?
A: Êè, ta jey-i-koou de piawlianq gwoyeu lian woo dou shuo.bu-guoh[35] ta.

294 LESSON 24

B: Let's go meet him after the meeting.
A: Okey.

NOTES

1. *Yeanshuo* 'perform-speak, — to make a speech,' as distinguished from *jeangyean* or *yeanjeang* 'lecture.'
2. *Dah-liitarng* 'big ceremony-hall, — auditorium.'
3. *Iseel* (< *i-syy-l*) 'all the way to death, — insistently.'
4. *Suhsheh* 'lodge-residence, — dormitory.'
5. The national anthem was adopted from the Kuomintang's party song. The words were by Dr. Sun Yat-sen and the melody was composed by Ch'eng Mao-yun (*Cherng Mawyun*). The harmonization generally used is that of the present author. The words are in an archaic literary style, more literary than that of current *wenli*.
6. *Eelyeu* 'ear-speech, — whisper,' literary word for *daa-cha.chal*.
7. *Jeangtair* 'speech platform, — the platform.'
8. *Yangrel, yangren* 'foreigner, an Occidental.'
9. *Huan'yng* 'glad-receive, — welcome.' Be sure to avoid any linking of the first *n* with the *y* by not quite closing the *n*. (See p. 95h.)
10. *Torngshyue* 'same-school, — schoolmate, fellow student,' also used as a polite form, by the faculty, in speaking of students. *Woo gen ta torng.guoh shyue* 'I have been to the same school with him.' Cf. *torngshyh*.
11. *Masheeng* 'Ma(ssachusetts) State.' Note, however, that 'California' is *Jiajou* 'Ca(lifornia) State,' *jou* being the official term for a state of the United States.
12. *Jiannchyau* is half transliteration and half translation, the Cantonese pronunciation for *jiann* 'double-edged sword,' being *kimm*. The word was first applied to Cambridge, England.
13. *Limuh* — George Reim, who spoke the part of the American student in the first phonograph recording of this lesson in 1944.
14. *Guu-jaang* 'drum the palms,' literary and stage-direction term for *pai-shoou* 'clap the hands.'
15. *Laoshy* 'old teacher' is a respectful form of addressing teachers.
16. With appropriate substitutions, this is a common formula used when a native hears his language (or dialect) spoken by a foreigner. If a native of *X* tries to speak the language of *Y*, then a native of *Y* would remark, *Tian bu pah, dih bu pah, jiow pah X-ren shuo Y-huah*. Instead of *jiow pah*, one also says *jyy pah* or *tzuey pah*.
17. The form . . . *.de .huah* means 'if you are speaking of, — if it is a matter of, in case, if.' If *huah* were stressed, with full tone, then *shuo de*

AN AMERICAN MAKES A SPEECH 295

B: Dai.hoel [36] sann le huey [37] tzarm chiuh jiannx ta chiuh.
A: Hao a.

Chinese National Anthem

Dr. Sun Yat-sen
Translated by Tu T'ing-hsiu

Ch'eng Mao-yun
Harmonized by Y. R. Chao

buhao de hvah would mean either 'words badly spoken' or 'bad words which are spoken.'

18. Speaker A, presumably from Szechwan, pronounces *gwoyeu* like *guééyuh*.

19. *Baw* in a collective sense includes both magazines and newspapers.

20. *Yeuyan* 'language,' a learned term.

21. *Suhcherng-ke* 'rapidly completed course, — rapid course.'

22. *Bii* '(stroke of the) pen,' AN for *jeangshyue-jin* 'encourage-learning money, — scholarship, fellowship' and for other words for money. Note however that the AN for *jypiaw* 'draw-ticket, — cheque' is *-jang*.

23. *Chyou-shyue* 'seek-learning, — to pursue study.'

24. *Shou* 'receive, admit.'

25. *Nansheng* = *nan-shyuesheng*.

26. *Nan-neu torng-shiaw* 'men-women same-school, — co-educational.'

27. *Shyy woo jyuej* 'makes me feel.'

28. *Hong-tarng dah-shiaw* 'Resound-hall great-laugh, — he brought down the house.'

29. The speaker uses the formal *jeh.lii* for *jell* in order to return to a serious part of the speech.

30. *Cherng* 'to be favored by . . . -ing.'

31. *Shyjaang* 'teachers-elders, — faculty members (in relation to student).'

32. *Jyydean* 'indicate-point, — point things out to, guide.'

33. *Gaanshieh* 'feel and thank, — to be grateful, to express gratitude to.'

34. *Jyydao* 'point-lead, — guide.' *Jyydean* refers more to practical and specific things, while *jyydao* refers more to general principles.

35. *Shuo.bu-guoh* 'cannot surpass in speaking.'

36. *Dai.hoel* 'stay a while, — after a while.'

37. *Sann-huey* 'disperse meeting, — meeting adjourned.'

EXERCISES

1. *Translate the following into Chinese.*

Woman Student III: Hello, Tang Ryhshin, so you are back at school.

Tang: Hello, Yang Lihfen! Haven't seen you for a long time. Did you receive my letters?

III: Hm! Why were you so fond of saying such nonsense, writing such long letters?

T: Huh huh huh! I — I —

III: When did you arrive?

T: I just arrived, I arrived this morning, and I almost missed (could not catch) the meeting.

III: Missed the what?

T: The meeting, the meeting in the auditorium. Isn't today the —

III: Oh, today's Monday, that's right, and I forgot the whole thing. By the way, what happened at the meeting? Will you tell me about it?

T: I arrived late, too, because our train came in late, and our richshas were so —

III: 'You (*pl.*)'?

T: Yes, Old Wang and I came together.

III: Oh, Old Wang!

T: Yes, that's right. By the time when (*gaan*) we had put our baggage in the dormitory and then come to the auditorium, they had already started to sing the national anthem. So we just entered stealthily and sat on a couple of seats by the entrance. They were particularly restless (*naw de heen*) today; while the anthem was being sung, they kept whispering without stopping. I think maybe because there was a — oh, you guess who came to make a speech today?

III: Um — I can't guess. Who?

T: I will tell you. An American made a speech in Chinese. He was an exchange student from Yale (*Yeluu*) University of Cambridge, Mass.

III: Yale? Isn't Yale University in New Haven (*Shin Gaang*)?

T: Oh, I said it wrong, it was Harvard University of Cambridge, and his name was called — his surname seems to be Li — Li something, I can't remember very clearly, either.

III: How was the Chinese this foreigner spoke?

T: Not bad, he didn't speak badly at all, he spoke in a quite polished manner. He could use proverbs, make jokes and what not. As soon as he began, he said something like — "Heaven is not to be feared, earth is not to be feared, only fear a foreign devil learning the Chinese language!"

III: Ha ha, a foreign devil calling himself a foreign devil?

T: Yes, that's why he can joke, you see (*sha*)? I have heard that Americans always like to act this way, they frequently make jokes on themselves. When you hear them you don't know whether it is better to laugh together with them, or not to laugh. Anyway we all laughed out loudly (*ha ha*). Then he said something like — Harvard only took men students and no women students.

III: Oh? Really? This is the first time I have heard of it.

T: Yes, that was the first time I heard of it, too. He said that when he arrived in China and saw that of all the (*suoo yeou de*) universities in China there was not one that wasn't co-educational, he said, he felt awfully happy about it. At this (*shuo daw jell*) all of us laughed so loudly that the whole auditorium resounded. And the girl students giggled (*gelgelde shiaw*) especially loud.

III: I don't think so; I didn't laugh!

T: But you weren't there (use *chiuh*)! See if you wouldn't laugh if you'd been there! Afterwards he made some more polite remarks; he said that after arriving at school all the teachers and fellow students were so kind to guide and help him in everything, he was grateful to everybody beyond expression, and so on and so forth, with a great lot of polite words, just like a Chinese making a speech.

III: Is that so?

T: Yes. When he was through talking, everybody clapped for a long time. Then the meeting adjourned. After the meeting I walked out of the auditorium and met a good friend of mine.

III: Really?

T: Yup.

III: Who?

T: You.

III: Tut!

2. *Prepare to act out the conversation in class.*

APPENDIX

TEXT OF CONVERSATION BEFORE AND AFTER "THE WALRUS AND THE CARPENTER"

Toeideldih: Nii shiihuan shy ma?

Alihsy: Mm — tiing shiihuan de — **yeou de** shy. Êh, hao buhao gawsonq woo neei-tyau luh keeyii tzoou-chu jeyg shuhlintz?

Toeideldih: Woo bey neei-shoou geei ta?

Toeideldem: "Haeshianq gen Muh.jianq" diing charng.

Toeideldih: Tayyang jaw tzay dah-hae .shanq —

Alihsy: Yawsh **heen** charng de huah, kee hao chiing nii shian gawsonq woo neei-tyau luh —

Toeideldih: Tayyang jaw tzay dah-hae .shanq, (p. 257)

. . . .

Bae gehgehl dou chy-leau. (p. 263)

Alihsy: Woo hairsh shiihuan nah Haeshianq, inwey nii jydaw, ta duey neyshie keeliande lihhwang dawdii **yeou ideal** bu haoshow.

Toeideldih: Ta bii Muh.jianq chy de duo è, keesh! Nii chyau, ta naj kuay sheau-shooujiuall daang de yean-miannchyan, hao ranq Muh.jianq shuu.bu-ching ta chyle duoshao è: yaw faan-guohlai shuo.

Alihsy: Nah jen keewuh! Nah woo hairsh shiihuan Muh.jianq — ta jihran chy de mei Haeshianq nemm duo.

Toideldem: Keesh ta neng chy duoshao chy duoshao è.

Alihsy: Neme, tamlea herngsh doush been **taoyann** de **renwuh**!

(The English for the above may be found in
Through the Looking-Glass, Chapter IV.)

VOCABULARY AND INDEX

VOCABULARY AND INDEX

Figures following entries are page numbers. Figures following decimal points after page numbers are numbers of sections, notes, or exercises, whichever will apply. A superscript after a page number indicates the nearest superscript in the text preceding the word in question. Superscript 0 means that the word in question precedes superscript 1.

When no specific AN is given after a noun for individual things, the general AN -geh is understood to be applicable. For other symbols and abbreviations see list inside back cover.

A

.a (or .ia after open vowels) particle for pause 122.10, 228.6; for (new) questions 59d, 122.6; (high pitch) for expressing obviousness 123.13; (low pitch) for echo questions 129.3, 139.3
aan I, me (dialectal) 99
Ae! No, indeed! Oh, no! 50.27, 146.57, 222.50, 263[50]
ae short (of stature) 39.10f
Agentyng Argentina 227[30]
.Ah! Mind you! 159[30], 207[45]; Well! 205[9]; interjection to soften a command, etc. 146.60
ai sorrowful L 98
.Ai! sound of sighing 199.9
.Ai.ia! Goodness! 129[33]; Oh! 191[32]; Gosh! 203.3e
Aiiau! Goodness me! Gee! 272.52
Aijyi Egypt 227[30]
air-mah to receive a scolding 283[21]
an peace B 21.2
Andong Antung 231[5]
Angelha Angora 227[41]
An₀huei Anhwei 35.5b, 233[26]
ann dark 100
ann shore 215.45, 264.31
an.wey to comfort 183[55]
ao short heavy jacket AN -jiann 99
Ar? Huh? What (did you say)? 141[16]
..., ar? ..., isn't it? 277[47]
arng, ang lofty L 102
au to stew 98
Aw.gwo Austria 227[30]
Aw₀jou, Awdahlihyah, -yea Australia 227.4
ay love, love to 36.6b, 100, 167.3
ay-shyh to be in the way 270.8
ay-tsair love wealth,—avaricious 48e

B

ba eight B 142.4
... .ba particle for tentative statement: ..., I suppose? 92, 121[27]; warning about indecorous combinations with 144.18; interrogative particle 59d, 277[50]
baa pretransitive, see second bae
-baa AN for chair and things with handles 132.34
baan board AN -kuay 99
bae display 288.30
bae, bay, baa pretransitive 39.10g, 49.25, 162.49, 226.2
-bae hundred 141[3], 159[38]
Baejia Shinq (... Shienql) 'Hundred Family Surnames' 278.30
bag eight 189[22]
bah.bah papa 40.12
bair white 151[30]
bairhuah colloquial language 286.1
bairhuah-wen vernacular literature 286.1
bairshuu sweet potatoes 42g
Bairtaa Syh White Pagoda Temple 111
Bair.tian daytime 197[33]
bairtsay Chinese cabbage; Chinese green AN -ke 255.18
Bali Paris 227[41]
ban move (furniture, residence, etc.) 227[40], 234.14
-ban class, group 192.29
Banamaa Panama 225[7]
bang₀juh help 239[21]
bang-mang help 47.24, 185.40
bann manage, do (about it) 159[49]
bann half B 185.32
bannchyou hemisphere 225[3]
bann₀faa way to do about it; measures, action 167[45], 213[44]

301

bannkong-jong mid air 205⁷
bannluh.shanq midway 223.3d
bann-shyh to run business 239²⁷
banntian a long time 210.2d, 240.6
bannyeh midnight 189²⁵
bannyeh san-geng(-bann) (.de) middle of the night 263.7, 287⁵⁵
bao enough, full (from eating) 103
₀bao.bao baby, darling 287⁵⁷
₀bao.bey treasure; precious! 283¹³
bao-shean insure, insurance 37.8
baotswen preserve 245³²
Bashi Brazil 227³⁰
ba₀shyr eighty; ba.shyr- eighty- 142.4
bau to wrap 129³⁷; to guarantee 219⁴⁵
bau.fwu bundle 270.9
bau₀kuoh include, comprise 245²¹
baw newspaper AN -fell (issue), -jang (sheet) 131.28, 296.19
bawgaw report 217²
bawjyy newspaper 131.28
baw.shanq in the newspaper 132.31
bay *pretransitive, see second* bae
bay.wanq call on 52.30
beau a watch AN -jy 199⁴⁶
beau table, chart 103; -meter 111, 211¹³
Beei.bian, -.bial the North 233¹⁸
Beei Bingyang Arctic Ocean 228.17
Beeifang the North 277.11
Beeijyi North Pole 225¹⁶
Beeimen Jie North Gate Street 112
Beeipyng Peiping 181³¹, 187.3a
been root L 64; been- this, the present 234.2; -been, -beel *AN for books* 280.60
beendih local, native 239³²
beengwo this country 234.2
beenlai originally 205²³
been-ren I (in a speech); the person himself 234.2
been-shiaw this school, our university 293¹²
been.shyh ability, skill 181¹², 213⁵¹
beitz cup AN -jy 41.13
benn stupid 103, 269⁴⁷
benq to hop 92
berng... better not ... 57.37, 209.42
bey˙ recite by heart 228.10
bey ... (geei) by 49.25, 54.32, 193.45
beydal bed sheet AN -tyau 247.19
bey.de-chulai can recite, to know by heart 225¹⁹, 275⁴⁵
bey.jyi the back 221.35
bey.uo quilt AN -tyau 185.38, 247.19
-.bial, -.bian side 131.20
biann argue 285⁴³

biann change 186.46; become 269³³
-biann number of times *AN for verbs* 145.44, 263⁵³
biann₀cherng.le change into, become 186.46
biau mark, standard B 98
bih must B 291⁵
bihmean avoid 222.46
bihshiu necessary 239²⁴
bii compare; than 49.25, 53.30, 169.21
bii writing instrument (brush, pencil, pen, chalk, etc.) AN -jy, -goan 127⁹, 130.10; -bii *AN for funds, accounts* 296.22
bii'ang f'rinstance 176.20
bii.fang for instance 165¹⁹
Bii.gwo, Biilihshyr Belgium 228.21
biijeau.de comparatively 227²⁵
biing third heaven's stem 201.40
Biing'yn the year 1926 (± n × 60) 201.40
biiru for example 189⁴
bii-tsyy mutually 247.16
bing soldier 245²³
bing ice 36.6c
binq sick, sickness 211¹, 214.15
binq bu really not 189.6g
binq₀chiee moreover 49.26, 56.35, 186.44, 187.2
binq .le fall sick 199.13
binq mei....a! hasn't..., has it? 191³⁵
binq₀ren a patient 212.5
binqshyh, binqshyy ward, room (in a hospital) 215.49
binqtuen to annex 229.32
bo to push aside 97
Bolan, Polan Poland 229.41
bo.li glass AN -kuay 254.15
Bor to moor L 275⁴⁶
Borlin Berlin 227⁴¹
borlandih brandy 213³⁶
bortsay spinach AN -ke 251¹⁸
bortz neck 44.20
Boshyhduenn Boston 293¹⁹
bu not, un- 57.37; *tone sandhi of* 107; -.bu- *in potential complements:* cannot 145.39; Bu! No! 59d, 123.20, 139.3
bu....le not...any longer 195(9)
bucherng won't do 283⁸, 209.46
budah not very 167²⁸
budann not only 18 ⁴³
bu da.yinq to take offense at 272.42
buderleau no end, awful 259¹⁶
buduey wrong 59d, 107
bugaan dare not 175²⁸

bugaushinq not glad, don't care to 34.3
bugoan don't care, no matter (what) 168.18, 174.3
buguey inexpensive 253³¹
buguoh only; but 170.39
buh cloth AN -kuay (piece), -pii (bolt) 122.4
-buh footstep 166.1
-buh part, region 231³; *AN for books (as a work)* 280.60
buhao not good, bad 153.20
buhaoyih.sy embarrassed, diffident 273.54
-buh.fenn part, fraction 225²⁰; 234.20
bu idinq not necessarily 176.17
bujiann.de not likely 240.18; I don't think so 297
Bu.jie. No, not so. 59d, 107
bujoen not permit, prohibit 175²³
bu-Jong-bu-Shi neither Chinese nor Occidental, nondescript 185.34
bu-jy-bu-jyue .de without realizing it 199.10
bujydaw don't know 130.12; I wonder . . . 162.50
bujyh(₀yu) not as bad as 49 ftnt 17, 169.34, 273.1f
bujyy more than 205²³
bukeen unwilling (to) 57.37
bukee.yii must not 175²²
Bukeh.chih! Don't mention it! 222.54
bukuay.hwo unhappy 183⁵⁴
buneng unable, cannot 49.26, 156.3
bupah there is no fear that 169.30
buran if not, otherwise 161.31
bu.sh is not 121²⁴; it is not that . . . 58; Bu.sh! No!, Not so! 59d, 123.20; Bu—sh! No, indeed! 275¹⁹
bu.sh . . . jiow.sh . . . either . . . or . . . 56.35, 167⁴¹⁻⁴²
busheau.de don't know 246.5
busheu not permit, must not, forbid 175²³, 283²⁰
-.bu-shiah have no room for 228.19
bu shu.fwu indisposed, ill 267¹¹
bushyng won't do 176.23, 207⁴⁵
butorng different 107, 137.23
butsuoh not bad 186.60; that's right 199³⁹
butzay.hu not to care for 287.14
butzeem(.me) not particularly 190.5
buyaw not to want; will not 107; don't! 57.37, 167³¹
buyawjiin not important, it doesn't matter 146.56
buyeuan not far 248.29, 253³³
buyonq need not 168.17

buyuann.yih unwilling (to) 186.43
bye don't! 57.37, 175²²
bye.chull elsewhere, out of town 200.29
bye.de another (a different one) 52.29, 155.42
byejel a pin 43.17
bye-joong other kinds 215.27
bye.ren somebody else, others 183⁴¹
byitz the nose 219³²

C

Ch! *sound of contempt* 256.46
chaang factory, works 243¹
chah to differ, to lack 170.36, 199⁴⁴
chah.buduo almost 170.36; about, approximately 211¹⁶
chai dismantle 253²⁹
chai-tair to undermine (someone's) plans 264.11
chan to take by the hand 264.24; to mix (as liquid) 98
chan.bu-juh cannot hold fast 264.25
chanq sing 92, 291⁴
chanq-shih to sing (musical) plays 36.6d
chao fry, stir-fry 93
chao-miann fried noodles 289.55
char look up 34; investigate 215.30
char tea (the drink) 240.5
char.farng waiter 276.1
chargoal, chargoan-diann AN -jia(l) 276.1
Charhaeel Chahar 231¹⁵
charhwu teapot AN -baa 285⁵¹
char.jaur find out (from investigation) 287.21
charng long 111, 173⁸
charng constant B 176.22
charng, charngcha(r)ngl often 181²⁶
charng.chuh good point 169.26
charngch(y)i long-term 239¹⁸
Charng Jiang Yangtze River 235.26
Charng.jou Changchow, Kiangsu 278.14
charngl intestine, sausage AN -gel, -gen 220.17
charngtz intestines AN -tyau 220.17
charyeh tea (leaves) 280.50
-chaur *quasi-AN:* dynasty 235.23
chaur₀day dynasty 235.23
che vehicle, car AN -lianq 144.35
cheau skillful 56.35
chefarng ricksha room, garage AN -jian 254.9
chehdii thoroughly 285⁴¹
chenntzao in good time 208.24
chern to sink 205⁶
chern minister, official L 45.21

chern fifth earth's branch 201.40
cherng city 275⁴⁷
cherng to form, to complete 178.40; will do, okay 209.46
cherng to be favored by . . . -ing 296.30
Cherng *common surname* 294.5
cherng.duh extent, degree 36.6a; standard, level 241.28
cherng₀ji attainment, result 269²⁴
chernglih establish, inaugurate 200.26
cherng₀lii in town 47.23
cherntz orange 47.24
chetour locomotive 33 ftnt 2
cheudengl, yangcheudengl matches AN -gel 111, 278.16
chi seven B 142.4
chi wife L 20
chiahchiah exactly, precisely 277⁵⁶
-chian thousand 141³; *non-use of ten hundreds* 199.16
chian lead (the metal or graphite) 130.14
chianbii pencil AN -jy, -gen, -gel 130.14
chiang gun, rifle AN -gaan 93
chiang₀diaw intonation 185.35
chiang-paw rifles and guns, firearms 245³⁰
chianq to get something in one's windpipe 93
Chiantzyh Wen (. . . *Wel*) 'Thousand Character Text' 278.31
chiau to knock on 251⁶
chi-char make tea 240.5
chie to cut (with a knife) 263⁵³
chig seven 189²³, 259¹⁷
chih air, gas 100; -.chih *unvoicing of after 4th Tone* 28.11
chihche automobile AN -jiah, -lianq 113, 165²²
chihchwal, -chwan motorboat 208.27
chihdyi steamwhistle L 277.6
chihyou gasoline 209.41, 248.32
chii to rise B 49.26
chiibu(sh) . . . ? isn't it . . . ? 264.17
chiichu at first 271.38
chii.lai to rise, to get up (in the morning) 165¹⁴; -.chii.lai *directional complement:* up 161.28; to begin to 170.41
chiing request, please 145.42; engage (a teacher) 278.23
chiing-keh invite guests, to have company 49.25
chiing wenn may I ask . . . ? 246.2
chii-tourl begin to 165¹⁴
chilhikualha.de clatter-clatter 264.32
ching light green or blue 208.18
ching clear 175⁴³; 219²⁹
ching light (not heavy) 176.21

Ching.chaur the Ch'ing dynasty 233²⁵
chingchiengl.de quietly 291⁴
ching.chuu clear(ly) 141⁴¹, 175.6
Chinghae Kokonor, Tsing Hai 231⁴
ching-tian blue sky 208.18
ching-tsao green grass, grass 208.18
chinyean with (my) own eyes 254.2
chioufen autumnal equinox 201.36
chiou.tian autumn 201.37
chi₀shyr seventy; chi.shyr- seventy- 142.4
chiuann urge, advise 103
chiuanshen-yii armchair AN -baa 264.34
chiu.chiuel cricket 40.12
chiuh to go (to a place) 143⁴⁹, 175²⁸; ₀chiuh to, in order to 55–56.34; -.chiuh *directional complement:* away, off, Germ. *hin-* 161.28; *unvoicing of after 4th Tone* 28.11
chiuh-hei pitch-black 286.3
chiuh.nian last year 202
chiuhsheng 4th Tone 25
chiuh.wey interest 270.15
choan.bu-guoh chih .lai breathless 264.42
chonqj toward 205⁹
choou second earth's branch 201.40
Chorngchinq Chungking 227⁴⁰
chou-ian to smoke 59c, 160.10
chour gloom, worry, sadness 275⁴⁷
choushoei-maatoong flush toilet AN -taw 255.29
chou.tih, -.tiell a drawer 287.23
chow.chorng bedbug 43.17
chu *unvoicing of after 4th Tone* 28.11; out (see chu.chiuh, chu.lai)
chu- *prefix for dates* 200.22
chuan to put on, to wear 240.4
chuang.huh window AN -shann 251¹⁵
chuan-kong pierce space 264.16
chuanq create 100
chuay trample 34.2
chu.bu-lai cannot come out 92
chu.chiuh to go out 195.1f; -.chu.chiuh *directional complement:* out, Germ. *hinaus-* 161.28
chuei blow, blow at 159¹⁸, 192.28
chuei-shawl blow the whistle 277.6
chuenfen vernal equinox 201.36
chuen.tian spring 201.37
chu-gong to go to the toilet (for bowel movement) 220.18
-₀chuh place 70, 215.28
chu-hann to sweat 48d
chuhchuh in every way 293³¹
chuhchull everywhere 281.1g
chu'i the first (of the month) 107, 200.20

chujyi elementary 288.34
chu-kooul go around the corner 253[33]
chu.lai come out 179.4g; -.chu.lai *directional complement:* out, Germ. *heraus-* 161.28; *insertion of object*, 44.19, 144.24
chu-men go out (of the house) 170.49
chuming famous 215.50
chu-shyh there is an accident 206.2
chu tay.yang the sun comes out 170.48
chwan to hand on 40.12
chwan ship, boat AN -jy, -tyau 19, 144.35
chwang.shanq in bed 240.2
chwanraan infect(ion) 222.46
chwantourl bow (of a ship) 207[45]
chwenjenq pure and correct 277.10
chwufarng kitchen AN -jian 251[14]
chwufei unless 170.49
chwufei . . . tsair only if 170.49
chwu.le . . . jy way (*or* yiiway) except for . . . 200.24, 245[18], 248.1
chy, chyr foolish (dialectal) 97
chyal day before yesterday 202
chyan positive principle B 70
chyan money 241.26; Chyan *common surname* 225[2]
chyan front, before 152.1; . . . chyan . . . ago 202
chyanfeng vanguard 291[5]
chyang wall AN -daw, -duu 149[6]
chyang.nall where the wall is 149[6]
chyang-shin .de heart-strengthening 220.9
chyan.nian year before last 202
chyan.tian day before yesterday 160.1, 179.4a
chyan.tou front 151[24]
chyau bridge AN -daw 243[6]
chyau look 132.37
chy-bao.le to be full, to have eaten enough 43.19
chy.bujuh cannot stand, cannot take it 220.8
chy.dejuh can stand, can take it 220.8
chy.guoh have eaten (once) before 192.16
chy-guoh.le have already eaten 192.16
chyh wing B 94
chyhbaangl wing 205[5]
chyi his L (*forms of the script*) 67-68
chyi to ride (astride) 29.3, 237[9]
chyi exotic, marvelous 185.36
chyiguay strange 159[16], 185.36
chyi₀ren bannermen, Manchus 234.8
chyishyr as a matter of fact, really 177.32
chyitsyh next to that 228.13

chyiyu.de the remaining 225[20], 293[13]
chy-kuu endure hardship 239[20]
chyn diligent B 291[5]
chyn zither 103
Chyn.chaur the Ch'in dynasty 233[24]
chyng clear, clear up (of the weather) 57.36
chyong poor 52.30
chyou ball 38.10c
chyou-shyue to pursue study 296.23
chyr slow; late 162.43
chyr.tsuenn size 42.16
chyrtz pond 251[16]
chy-shoei draw water (of a ship) 208.31
chyuan.sh entirely 155.32
chyuantii everybody (in a group) 201.48
-chyy (Chinese) foot 42.16, 46b

D

da to take (streetcars, boats, etc.) 253[34]
daa strike, beat (and many uses) 142.1; from 49.25; smash 41.13; strike (of the clock) 247[43]
daa-cha.chal to whisper 294.6
daa-chah to make interruptions 47.24, 168.10, 170.46
daa.daa-chah to have some diversion 259[22]
daa diannhuah to telephone 142.2
daa-dinq.le jwu.yih make up one's mind 190.3
daa-ha.chiann to yawn 285[50]
daa-hu.lu to snore 237[2]
daa-janq to fight a war 227[40]
daa-jen to administer a hypodermic 215.40
daang (political) party 291[5]
daang, daang.juh to screen, to shield 205[20], 264.63
daangj(e) to think (wrongly), to take it (wrongly) 263.9
daa.shoou rioter 41.14c
dah large 165[19]; great 135[26]; big, old(er) 199.12
dah₀bann- the greater half of a 264.19
dahbiann stool, to go to stool 220.18
Dah Buliehdian Great Britain 228.25
dahchaang overcoat AN -jiann 195[7]
dahching tzao.chin early morning 168.13
dahchyal, dah-chyan.tian day before day before yesterday 202
dah-chyan.nian year before year before last 202
dahduoshuh the great majority 231[13]
dahgay probably 113, 138.34

dahguall (unlined) robe AN -jiann 286.5
dah-hairtz big child 176.35
dahhowl, dah-how.tian day after day after tomorrow 202
dah-how.nian year after year after next 202
dahhuool everybody (present) 264.35
dahiue approximately, about 95, 247⁴⁶
dahjia everybody (present) 228.11
dahjonq the multitude, the mass 288.35
dahjyy, dahjyr.tou, dah.muge thumb 221.38
dah-liitarng auditorium 294.2
dahluh continent, mainland 227.3
dahmen, dahmel front door 191⁴², 253⁴⁰
dah.ren a grownup 175³⁵
dah-sheau.jiee young lady 108
dahshengl loudly 155.40
dah-shiaw laugh loudly 49.26, 293²⁷
Dahshi Yang Atlantic Ocean 228.14
dahshyue university 95, 288.28
Dah₀shyue 'The Great Learning' 278.32
dahshyy ambassador 43.17
dahtoei thigh AN -tyau 213²⁸
dahtorng world community 291⁵
dah-tyng-goang-jonq public place 288.31
dah-tzao.chin early morning 168.13
dahtzong large lot 191.7
dahyang ocean 225⁹
dahyiitz sofa AN -jang 159⁸
dah-yuanshuay generalissimo 235.30
dai stay, remain 191³⁵
dai.hoel after a while 296.36
dangjong middle, between 225¹²; ... dangjong among 269³⁹
dangran of course 168.16
dangshyr at the time 221.26
Danmay, Danmoh Denmark 228.21
-dann eggs B 280.50
dann.sh but 170.35
danqshyr right then and there 221.26
dantz, dal sheet, list 247.19
dan.wuh to dally 237²
dao fall down, topple over 193.35, 220.2
dao-luann make trouble 209.40
dao-mei to be out of luck 209.37
dar-daw attain 293²²
dau knife AN -baa 38.10a
daw arrive 145.37; ....daw ...to 152²⁷
daw....chiuh to go to 246.4
daw up-side-down, contrary to expectation, rather 186.59, 220.2; to pour 289.52
daw way, *tao* 174.5
daw-chean to apologize 39.10e

Dawder Jing 'Canon of the Way and Virtue' 287.16
dawdii at bottom, after all 191.8
daw.guoh have been to 59c
daw.lii principle, reason 174.5, 208.26
dawl road AN -tyau 237¹³
daw.luh sheng not to know one's way about 35.5c
daw.sh though (*parenthetical*) 189¹², 213.7; ..., .daw.sh ..., though (*afterthought*) 237¹⁰
day to put on, wear 47.24, 240.4
day to treat 263⁵⁰
day bring (along) 56.34; -day region, belt 234.18; belt, string, lace (*see shyedall*)
daybeau represent(ative) 233³²
day.fu the doctor 213⁴⁹, 215.38
₀day.nall is ... -ing 55.33
da.yinq to answer 272.42
-.de *subordinative particle:* of (*with terms reversed*), 's 131.26; *examples of* 132.38; *substantive forms:* -er, one 136.11; *for past event with a specific point* 145.37; *apparent exception in word order* 175.7; *omission of after pronouns* 47.24, 154.26; *omission of in a string* 185.22; *predicative use of as disting. from potential complement* 153.20
-.de *suffix for possibility* 41.13; *in potential complements:* can 145.39
.de at, into 161.33
deal (decimal) point 211¹⁹; -₀deal some, a little 52.30; -.deal -er, more 53.30, 169.21
-dean (jong) o'clock 144.32
deanjeou tincture of iodine 215.42
dean.shin breakfast, tea, refreshment, snack 43.18, 237⁵, 192.17, 285⁵²
....de buderleau awfully... 169.29
....de duo much more, much ...-er 111, 167²²
deei, deei yaw must 176.18
deeng wait, wait for 161.34
deengdeeng etc., et al. 228.22
deeng.hoel wait a while 207⁴¹
deengyu equal to 211¹³
....de heen extremely 53.30
....de .huah if (it is a matter of)... 57.36; the matter of 184.13; in case ... 294.17
deng lamp AN -jaan 132.35
denqj yeal to be staring 58
denqtz stool AN -jang 129³³
der obtain, receive 241.25, 293²¹; done, finished 193.38, 216.58

der virtue, spirit 291⁵
Der.gwo, Deryihjyh Germany 228.25
Der .le, der .le! Call it a day! Let it go! 193.38, 283⁹
deryih proud, satisfied 52.30(2)
-.de-shiah have room for 228.19
....de ₀shyr.howl when..., at the time when... 57.36, 156.1k
....de yanqtz something like, about... 243⁶
....de yawminq terribly... 215.33
....de yih.sy (see sh....de yih.sy)
....de ₀yuan.guh (for) the reason that... 57.36, 221.21, 265.1
di low 161.38; to lower v.i. 277⁴⁹
dial .le to go away, beat it 40.13
diannche trolley, tramway AN -lianq 253³⁵
diannchyr battery, cell 245³⁰
dianndeng electric lamp AN -jaan 253²³
diannhuah telephone 142.2
diannliengl electric bell 143.8
diannshiann electric wire AN -gen, -gel 255.25
dianntair radio station 113, 168.7
diannyeengl motion picture 113
diaw drop, fall 161.38
diawl melody, tune 275⁴⁶
didadida ticktock ticktock 159²²
die dad 98
dieengl top, pinnacle 159⁴⁵
dih land 162.1f; the floor (as a place) 129²⁶
dih- *prefix for ordinal numbers* 120.1, 143.4
dihbaan the floor (as a thing) AN -kuay 76.11, 255.22
dihdean location 253³⁵
dih.dih younger brother 175³⁶
dih'ell second 127⁰; the next, the following 199⁴³
dih'ell-tian the second day, the next day 41.13
dih.fangl place 215.28
dih'i first 120.1
dih'i-tserng in the first place, firstly 185.38
dihjiig which? number what? 143.12
Dihjong Hae Mediterranean Sea 225⁴
dihjy earth's branch 201.40
dihlii geography 226.1
dih.shiong brothers (*collec.*) 177.38
dih.shiong.men brothers (*collec.*); the ranks, privates 177.38
dih.wey position 228.23
diikanq resist(ance) 239¹⁸

diing most, -est 53.30, 167.3
diingbaan ceiling 255.23
diing hao (....ba) had better 53.30, 192.15
diing.perng ceiling 255.23
dii.shiah, dii.shie, dii.hie below 152.2, 153.8
Ding *common surname* 121¹⁰; fourth heaven's stem 201.40
dingdang dingdong 41.13
dinglhing-danglhang jingling-jangling 41.13
ding-tzyh-luhkooul T-junction 247.8
dinq to subscribe for (magazines) 51.29
dinq decide 103
dinq.chyan deposit, good-faith money 253³⁶
diou lose 191⁴⁶
di.shiah.lai come down, subside 213.9
doan short 173⁸
doan.chuh shortcoming 169.26
dongbeei northeast 207.9
dong.bial the east 205⁷
dongjyh winter solstice 200.33
Dongjyu East (telephone exchange) 149.6
dongkooul eastern end (of a street) 253⁴⁰
dongnan southeast 110, 207.9
dong nan shi beei the (cardinal) directions 207.9
dong.shi thing, object, article AN -jiann 128.1, 176.16
dong-shi east and west 225⁹
Dong.tian winter 197⁸, 201.37
dongyang-che (*see* yangche)
donq to freeze 195⁶
donq move 100
donq-shoou to set about to 265.49
doong understand 148.5(1)
doong.shyh member of a board, trustee 43.18
-doou (Chinese) peck 46b
dou in all cases, uniformly, all 136.3 (*see* (*also* sherm dou, .le .dou)
dou to hold (as in a sack) 103; doul pocket 265.62
dow.funaol soft bean curd 113
dowyaltsay beansprouts 113
Du! Du! *sound of a steam whistle* 207⁴⁸
duann to break, to sever 215.29
duenbuh a mop AN -baa 264.18
duey match; correct; to face, opposite 152.7, 225.5; to, towards 39.10e, 273.1a
duey...shuo say to... 157.5e
Duey.bujuh! I am sorry, excuse me!

191.12, 211³, 283⁴; Duey.bujuh, .ah! Thank you! (*for a favor*) 243¹²
Duey .le. Yes., That's right. 59d, 92, 123.18
dueymiall counterpart, opposite side 152.7, 175³⁴
duey₀yu for, towards 269¹⁷
duey₀yu ... (.shanq *or* .shanq.tou) with regard to 271.29, 273.1b
-duh degree 80, 211¹⁰
Duh *common surname* 29
duhtz stomach; abdomen 167³⁷, 220.17
duo much, many 162.40; *predicative use of* 169.30; -duo over, more than 237¹⁰; *see also* .de duo
duo.chu.lai to be in excess, to increase 271.37
duoh rudder 205²⁸
duo.shao, dwo.shao how much or many? 221.29
duo-shao much or little, many or few 221.29
duoshuh the majority 231³
dwo how, to what degree 205¹⁴
dwom, dwo.me how, to what degree 40.13
dwo shao so little, so few 221.29
dwu read (aloud), to study 184.8
dwu-in pronunciation 270.17
dwu-jiunn poisonous germs 222.46
dwulih independent 229.34
dwu-shu to study 137.20
dwushu-ren educated man 189.6b
dyichiueh really, actually 191³²

E

e flatter L 98
.E— *sound of hesitation:* er—, uh— 138.25
Ê! (*short and high*) *interjection for calling attention:* Say! 153.18, 255.16, 275⁴⁶
.è *final particle:* you know, you see, of course! 137.19, 154.21
Èè! *interjection for approval:* You are quite right! 153.12, 255.16
Èè? *interjection of surprise* 159¹⁵
eel thou, ye L 30.13, 291⁵
eel near L 30.13
eel.tou, eel.dou the ear AN -jy 177.39, 219³¹
eelyeu whisper L 294.6
Eeng! Oh, no indeed! 50.27
ee.shin nauseated 42f
eh hungry 167³⁷, 203.1d, 285⁵²
.Èh! Hey! *interjection for calling attention* 124.25; (*half-low pitch*) *inter-jection of agreement:* Uh-huh, Yeah, Yup, Yes! 59d, 124.28, 139.3, 143⁵⁸, 255.16
E-heh! Boo hoo! 283⁹
Eh.gwo, Er.gwo, Ehluosy, Erluosy Russia 228.20
Ei! *sound of effort:* Oof! 209.48; *interjection in answer to a call:* Yes! 280.58
ell two B 124.22, 142.4
elljyy, elljyr.tou, ell.mudih index finger 221.38
ell-lai in the second place 186.48
ell₀shyr twenty; ell.shyr- twenty- 142.4
.Eng. Uh-huh, M-hm, Yeah. 59d, 130.4, 139.3
enn to press (upon) 21.2, 254.6
Èr! *interjection for conclusiveness:* Yup! 195⁴
Er.gwo, Erluosy (*see* Eh.gwo, etc.)
erl child B 30.13
erl while, moreover L 30.13
erl₀chiee moreover 56.35, 187.2, 248.1
erltz son 175³⁵
Erng? Huh? 239³³

F

faaliuh law AN -tyau 285⁴⁰
faan reverse, obverse 174.1
faang-sha spin yarn 247.17
faangjy-piin textile goods 247.17
faangsha-chaang cotton mill 112
faan₀guoh₀lai shuo on the other hand, contrariwise 178.41
faan.jenq anyway 234.13
faan₀miall reverse side 173⁴
fabeau publish, express 248.41
fachii originate, initiate 239¹⁵
fadar develope, flourish 233¹⁸
fadonqji motor AN -jiah 206.3
Fah.gwo, Fahlanshi 228.25
faming invent(ion) 221.43
fan turn over 264.27
fang square 205¹⁴; a (public) square 62
fangbiann convenient 269³⁰
fangfaa method, technique 239²⁷
fangkuall square piece 278.28
-fangmiann *quasi-AN:* aspect, side, phase 177.30
fang-yan dialect 185.29
fann (cooked) rice 160.7; meal AN -duenn 171.3c
fanngoal restaurant AN -jia(l) 293¹⁹
fannwei scope 245¹⁸, 248.1
fanq to let go 200.23; to put 291⁴
fanq-chiang set off a gun, shoot 38.10c
fanq-jiah to have a holiday 200.23

fanq-shin rest assured 209.36, 269⁴²
fan-yeal, fan-yean.jing to roll one's eyes 264.27
farng room, house B 155.36
farngdieengl roof 37.8, 251¹⁴
farngdong landlord 253³⁸
farng-jertz paper for lease, accounts, etc. 256.39
farngjian room 254.13
farngkeh tenant 255.27
farngtz house AN -suoo(l) 155.36, 251⁰
farn.sh ... dou all 184.7
fartz method 170.38
fa-shau to have a fever 213.6
fashiann discover(y) 221.43
feei bandit 86
feei shieh be not indolent L 291⁵
feen flour, powder 99
feenbii chalk AN -gel, -jy 129³⁸
feen.de pink 156.2f
fei to fly 86, 159²³
fei-baur flying thin 286.3
feicharng extremely 186.54
feichwan flying boat 42g
fei₀deei must 186.51
fei₀deei — tsair ... must — before ... 186.51
fei₀deei (yaw) insist on 207⁴¹
feiji airplane AN -jiah 145.36
Fei₀jou, Afeilihjia Africa 227.4
feir fat 86
-fell, -fenn portion, share; fraction 214.19; *AN for newspapers, etc.* 38.10a
fen, fen.chu.lai distinguish 207.8
fen.bye distinction, difference 239²⁷
feng wind 110
fengshann fan 223.3g
fengshuh maple AN -ke 275⁴⁷
fengyeu storm 192.26
-fen (jong) minute (of the clock) 179.4b, 201.45
... -fenn jy — —- ... th 214.19
fensann disperse 231⁹
fey lungs 220.17
fey expense 10.9; to waste 86
feychwu abolish 199⁴⁰
fey-shern to take trouble 38.9
fey-shyh troublesome, labor-costing 48e
Forjiaw Buddhism 285³⁸
fuh to pay 36.6d, 253³⁶
fuh rich 233²⁶
fuh a form of descriptive essay AN -piann 279.43
fuh(buh) abdomen 220.17
fuh father B 45.21
fuh-chin father 175³⁵
fuh-muu father and mother 177.36

fuh-shoei to swim 35.4, 215.36
fuhshoei-chyr swimming pool 113
fuu.shanq your house; your family; your native place 192.21
Fwu₀jiann Fukien 233²⁶
fwu.shoou bannister; doorknob 43.17
fwuwuh to carry on work, to perform service 271.30

G

g (= geh)
g *use of for* ig 36.6d, 261⁴⁴
gaan dare 175²⁸
gaan by the time when 297
gaan.bu-shanq cannot catch up; gaan-.de-shanq can catch up 209.1c, 264.41
gaan.chyng indeed, why! 200.32, 205²⁰
gaan.ji grateful 110
gaanjuei screwdriver AN -baa 52.29
gaanjyue to feel 280.56
gaankuay hurry up and 112
gaanmiengl by tomorrow, some day 178.42
gaanshieh to be grateful, to express gratitude (to) 296.33
gae to alter, to correct 210.1d
gae₀cherng change into 239²⁷
gaeliang improve 239²⁷
gai ought 24.7; right, as one should 265.54
ga.jy'uo armpit 110
gal liver (as food) 220.17
gan dry 58, 70, 264.12
gang just, just now 159¹¹
gangbii steel pen AN -jy, -goan 129³⁸
ganggang just, exactly 205¹⁰
gangtsair just now 159⁵², 205²⁰
gan.jinq clean 283¹¹
gannma what for, why? 189¹⁹
gann-wan.le finished doing (it) 92
Gan₀suh Kansu 231¹⁷
gan(tzanq) the liver 220.17
gao *dialectal word for* nonq, *q.v.* 278.20
gau high 159²⁸, 251¹⁴
gaushen abstruse, advanced 288.36
gaushinq happy, in good spirits 183⁵⁴; glad 263⁵⁰; glad to 34.3
gaw.sonq tell 52.29, 175²³
gaw.suh tell 271.26
gay cover 24.7
ge to put 228.19
ge ballad, song 279.43
ge elder brother B 97
ge.bey the arm AN -gen, -gel, -tyau 219³⁶
ge.bey-jooutz the elbow 219³⁶

geei give 193.45; ₒgeei for, for the benefit of, to the harm of 177.25, 193.44; by 193.45; .geei to (see rheng .geei)
ge.ge elder brother 175³⁶
-geh (abbrev. -g) general AN 122.4
gehchuh various places, everywhere 239²⁰
gehgeh(l) every one 136.3
geh-sheeng the various provinces 51.29, 231⁹
gel root 30.13(6)
ge'l song 30.13(6), 279.43
gelgel.de shiaw giggle 297
ge'l-lea the two chums 265.66
gen follow, with, and 49.26; non-use of 121.2; with 156.3h
-gen, -gel AN for string, sticks, pillars, etc. 160.12
gen...iyanq same as... 227³⁵
gen...iyanq— as — as... 53.30, 169.21
genbeen fundamentally 235.33
gendii foundation, background 280.55
geng seventh heaven's stem 201.40
genq still more, still...-er 45.21, 167²²
genq.jia all the more 272.46
gerₒkai to separate, interposed 225⁴
germinq revolution, to make a revolution 199⁴⁰
goa widow B 99
goai to turn (a corner) 243⁵
goan bother about 207⁴⁷; pay attention to 243⁷; pretransitive for jiaw 49.25, 168.5
ₒgoanₒbao I am sure, I bet 198.4
goang broad 98
goangboh to broadcast 168.7
goangboh dianntair broadcasting station 168.7
Goangₒdong Kwangtung 233²⁶
goanggaw advertisement 254.5
Goangₒjou Canton 181³¹
Goangₒshi Kwangsi 233²⁶
goantz pipe AN -gen, -gel 253²⁹
goei ghost 34.3, 256.45
goei tenth heaven's stem 201.40
goen to roll 39.10e
goen-tanq, goengoen-tanq boiling hot, very hot 264.38
gong public B 285³¹
gong work, labor 247⁴³
gongchaang factory 237¹⁰
gongcherngshy engineer 239³¹
gong.fu(l) leisure 191.10
gonggonq-chihche bus AN -lianq (the vehicle), -tanq (a trip) 255.35
Gongher Indusco 240.15

gongₒkeh lesson 225¹
Gonglih public chronology, Occidental chronology 199.15
gongran publicly, openly 285³¹
gong.ren worker 239²⁰
gongsy company, firm 37.8
gongwen official document, official letter AN -jiann 285⁴⁰
gongyeh industry 239¹⁵
gonqhergwo republic 227²⁶
gow enough, sufficient 50.28, 167⁴⁵; sufficiently 219⁴⁴
gua melon 103
gua to scrape, scratch 278.15
gua-dao.le blow down 43.19
gua-feng .le there is a wind 192.14
guah to hang, suspend 205²¹
guahhaw register 110
guai shrewd; good (of children) 286.4
ₒguai.guai darling, baby 286.4
gua-lean to shave 55.33
guan an official 103
guan behold 271.25
guang light n. 277⁴⁹; smooth 257⁴; guang, guang.sh only, merely 219³⁶, 248.1
guanhuah official speech, Mandarin 275¹⁹
guann used, habituated 100, 214.12
guanncheh persevere, carry through L 291⁵
Guanney inside the Pass, China proper 231⁹
guanq to have an outing 265.56; to do sight-seeing 281.1b
guan.shih relation 225⁴
guanyu concerning, about, relating to 49.25, 271.31, 273.1c
gua-tzeel melon seeds 42e
guay queer 183.35, 185.36; to blame 240.7; odd 257⁵, 263⁶⁵
guei... it is up to... to 36.6d
guei.jeu rule, manners 263.10
guei.jyh to put in order, to tidy up 262.4
guenn rod B 103
guey expensive 253³¹; Guey- your (honorific) 143.16
Gueyₒjou Kweichow 233²⁶
Gueyshinq? What is your (sur)name, please? 143.16
guh to hire, engage 278.23
guhshiang old homestead L 277⁴⁹
guh.shyh story 277.12
gulih to be isolated 229.34
guo pot 95

VOCABULARY AND INDEX 311

guoh to pass 70, 197⁹; -.guoh did or have . . . before 54.33, 138.33
guoh₀chiuh to pass 217⁴
. . . guohhow afterwards, after 191⁴⁶
guoh-nian to pass (or celebrate) the New Year 54.33, 199³⁷
guoh-yiin to satisfy a craving, satisfying 288.32
Gusu *old name for* Soochow 275⁴⁷
guu ancient 233¹⁸
guu- bone 215.25
guuday ancient times 234.21
guu-jaang to applaud L 294.14
guushy antique poem 279.47
gwo country, state, nation (*n. or quasi-AN*) 95, 136.1
gwodu capital of the country 235.24
gwofarng national defense 235.28
Gwofuh Father of the Republic 235.36
gwoge, gwoge'l national anthem 291⁴, 295
Gwoin Charngyonq Tzyhhuey 'Vocabulary of Common Characters in the National Pronunciation' 11.11
gwojia country, state, nation 225¹⁹
gwojih- international B 228.28
gwojih.de international 285⁴⁰
gwolih national calendar 199⁴¹
gwowang a king 261³⁶
gwowen, gwowel Chinese (as a school subject) 280.54
Gwoyeu National Language, Mandarin 10.8, 272.45
Gwoyeu Romatzyh National Romanization 11.11
gwu.tou bone AN -gen, -gel, -kuay 213²⁸

H

Haafor Harvard 293¹²
ha.chian a yawn 285⁵⁰
hae sea 159²³
haedao island (of the sea) AN -tzuoh 159²⁵
haemiall.shanq on the surface of the sea 241.1c
haeshianq walrus 262.1
haetal, haetan beach 264.23, .28
.Hah! *interjection of elation* 159²⁹; *of satisfaction* 195⁴
Ha ha ha! Ha ha ha! 293¹⁸
Hai! *interjection of disapproval* 209.47
hair child B 103
hair still, again 159³⁵; rather 214.20; interest in new aspects 254.3; *use of as afterthought* 256.48

hair . . . ig another, one more 52.29
Hair . . . .ne! You call that . . . ? 198.5
hair.sh after all 146.58
(₀hair.sh) . . . ₀hair.sh (whether) . . . or 58b, 145.47
hairtz child 199.11, 283²
hairtz.men children (*collec.*) 199.11
₀hann, ₀hay, her with, and 49.26
Hann.chaur the Han dynasty 233²⁴
Hann₀ren the Han people, Chinese 234.10
hao good 165²⁰; good, all right 146.54; in order (the better) to 56.34, 240.22; in order that 256.41; easy to 176.11; good to 176.11; *predicative use of* 184.18; Hao . . . ! How . . . !, What a . . . ! 254.12
hao₀bii such as, for instance 184.13, 245²⁵
hao.chuh advantage, benefit 186.42
haochy good to eat 176.11
haoduo a good many, a good deal 281.1g
haohaul(.de) well 56.35; properly 57.36, 170.40; good and sound 191³⁵
hao.i.deal (a little) better 169.27
Hao-jia.huoo! Goodness, gracious! My goodness! Dear me! 50.27, 193.40, 245²⁷
haojii-biann quite a few times 263⁵³
haojii-chuh quite a few spots 213²⁸
hao-jyi.le very good, fine 112, 143⁵⁸
haokann good-looking, beautiful 34.2, 161.25, 216.2a
hao-ren a good man 181⁶; a well man 237.2a
haorong.yih how easy!, i.e. after great difficulty 240.21
hao₀shianq seem, as if 160.13
haoshie, haurshie a good deal, a lot 177.29
haoshow feel good, comfortable 176.11, 195⁴
Haoshuo haoshuo! Thanks for the compliment! 219⁵⁰
hao₀tzay good thing that, fortunately 193.37
haotzuoh easy to do 176.11
haowal to be fun 161.29
haoyih.sy to have the nerve, to have the cheek 273.54
-harng line, profession 245¹⁸
harngkong-muujiann aircraft carrier AN -tyau, -jy 248.27
Harn Shan Syh Cold Hill Temple 275⁷⁵
harnshuu-beau (household) thermometer 111

haurshie (= haoshie)
haw courtesy name 144.20; -haw number... 142.4, 143.4; *in dates in the solar calendar* 200.21
hawtz rat, mouse AN -jy 190.1
hay twelfth earth's branch 201.40
he to drink 175[38]
.He! Gee! 195[6]; Dear me! 245[27]
he-char drink tea 27.10
heen very 53.30, 159[24]; *weak force of* 176.10; *predicative use of* 185.31
.Heh! Gosh! 219[39]
.He.he! *sound of chuckling* 154.22
hei black 154.30
.Hei! Hey! 159[42]
heibaan blackboard AN -kuay 153.13
hei.shiah night 152.2
hei-yun black cloud AN -kuay 205[20]
.he.je, .he.sh (either) or 56.35, 145.47
heng propitious L 63
heng, heng.heng to hum 279.46
henn hate 173[20]
Herbeei Hopeh 231[17]
herbih why must? 192.19
her.chih kindly, pleasant, charming 216.54
her.chii.lai put together 231[15]
Herjiang Hokiang 231[5]
Herlan, Heh.lan Holland 228.21
Her₀nan Honan 231[17]
herng.sh anyway 192.24
hershyh suitable 52.29
her.taur walnut 176.11
hertorng a contract 285[40]
hertzuoh cooperate, -ion 240.14
heryall riverside 253[42]
.he.sh, .he.je (either) or 56.35, 145.47
Hng! *sound of contempt:* Hm! 269[48]
hoei destroy 96
hong to bake, to heat 98
hong-tarng dah-shiaw the whole audience laughed 296.28
hoong to coax 99
horng red 205[16], 286.3
Horng Hae Red Sea 225[5]
horngliuh-deng traffic light 249.3b
Hornglou Menq 'Dream of the Red Chamber' 288.25
horngshau-row pork stewed with soy sauce 111
hour marquis B 70
how back, behind 152.1
howhoei to regret it 41.13
howl, how.tian day after tomorrow 160.1, 202
howlai afterwards 213[23]
how.nian year after next 202

how.tou back, behind 152.2
howyuall backyard 251[14]
huah to draw, to paint 160.14
huah speech, words AN -jiuh 136.1; -huah language, dialect 136.1
-huah -fy, -ize 228.31
huahshyatz chatterbox, phonograph 168.5
huahshyue chemistry 247.21
hualhalha! *crashing sound* 159[44]
huall picture, painting AN -fuh, -jang 160.14, 242.2j
huang₀huangjangjang.de helter-skelter 40.12
huang.jang flustered 40.12
huann change, exchange 100
huan'yng welcome 294.9
huasheng-tarng peanut candy AN -kuay 26.9
huay bad 165[20]; *predicative use of* 184.18
huay.i.deal (a little) worse 169.27
huay .le have spoiled 47.24; gone out of order 251[6]; Huay. le! Oh gosh! 291[1]
huei dust 96
huen muddled, obscure 98
huenn to mix up 209.38
huenn.janq *term of abuse* 209.38
huey meet 96; can, know how to 136.4, 148.51; know (as a language) 186.61; will likely 55.33; association 227[27]
huey-huah conversation (as a language exercise) 270.16
huey-keh to receive callers 38.10
hueyyih compound ideograph 60
huh protect B 212.2
huh.shu brief-case 27
huh₀shyh (hospital) nurse 216.56
huohjee perhaps 285[35]
₀huoh.jee, ₀huoh.sh, .he.je, .he.sh (either) or 56.35, 59b, 145.47, 285[34]
₀huoh.jee . . . ₀huoh.jee either . . . or 56.35, 59b, 145.47
₀huoh.sh . . . ₀huoh.sh either . . . or 56, 145.47
huoh₀wuh goods 239[33]
huoo fire 175[38]
huooche (railroad) train AN -jyel (car), -tyau (train), -tanq (trip) 167[22]
huooche-jann railroad station 112
huoochi sealing wax 261[36]
huoo.jih waiter 280.57
huool .le to get mad 40.13
huootoei ham AN -jy 289.57
huran(.de) suddenly 191[40]
hu.shi breath, breathe 220.20

VOCABULARY AND INDEX 313

hwa slippery 29.3, 103
hwa to row (a boat) 209.43
hwai chest, bosom 98
hwan *reading pron. of second* hair; to return (loans, etc.)
hwang yellow; brown 208.17
Hwangher the Yellow River 231[16]
hwangl yolk 40.13
Hwang Shan the Yellow Mountains (of Anhwei) 281.1g
hwangyou butter 265.57
Hwasha Warsaw 227[41]
Hwashenqduenn Washington 227[41]
Hwashyh Fahrenheit 214.14
hwa.suann think over 39.12
hwei return B 96
-hwei *AN for verbs:* number of times, a time 197[8]
hwei.chiuh to go back 179.4g; -.hwei-.chiuh *directional complement:* back 161.28
hweidar answer, reply 189[4], 269[32]
hweihwei, hweihwel every time 51.29
hwei.lai to come back, to return home 159[5]; ₀hwei.lai by and by 253[14]; -.hwei.lai *directional complement:* back 161.28
hweisheng echo 254.14
hweitour by and by 212.4
hwel soul, spirit 30.13(4)
hwu pot 283[13]
hwu lake 29.3
Hwubeei Hupeh 233[26]
hwu-huah nonsensical words 215.22
hwujiau (black) pepper 265.48
hwul (fruit) stone 30.13(4)
hwu.li fox AN -jy 51.28
hwu.lihwutwu(.de), hwu.lihwudu(.de) fuzzy-wuzzy 41.13
Hwu₀nan Hunan 233[26]
hwu-shuo talk nonsense 234.6
hwu.twu, hwu.du indistinct, muddled, confused 41.13, 214.21

I

i one B 142.4; *use of before* shyr 201.43; a 121[14]; *omission of* 154.25; *tone sandhi of* 107; the whole, all over the 46c, 129[26], 198.7; once 161.22
i...i....de one...after another 161.24
i...₀jiow once..., as soon as... 159[35], 168.14
ia to detain in custody 102
.ia *particle used for* .a *when following an open vowel sound* 122.10, 140.3g

ial, ian smoke (other than tobacco) 207.4
ian (tobacco) smoke 160.10
ianchiual a smoke ring 159[0]
iang beg; center B 98
ianjeual cigarette AN -gel 160.12
ian.syy to drown 159[33], 205[25]
iatz duck AN -jy 48f
iau the waist 98
iautz kidney 220.17
iball one-half 185.32, 239[33]
iban.de the average 285[27]
ibann one-half 219[37]
ibeytz all one's life 186.49
i-biann once through, once over 217[15]
i-dah-tzao since early morning 237[2]
-.i.deal -er, more ... 53.30, 169.21; ₀i₀deal some, a little 52.29, 72.2, 107
ideal ideal .de little by little 205[6]
ideal yee bu, ideal dou bu not at all ... 231.3c
i-dih a floorful 46c, 129[26]
idinq certainly 49.26
idinq bu ... certainly not ... 176.17
ie to choke 98
i-fangmiann on the one hand 239[27]
i.fwu clothes AN -jiann (piece), -taw (suit) 54.32, 93
ig one, a 51.28, 107, 122.4; *omission of* 123.12; *substitution of* g *for* ig 36.6d, 261[44]
ig-bann one and one-half 199[39]
igonq all together, in all 192.24
i-guoh.le ... jiow right after 199[37]
₀i₀hoel a moment 107, 160.19
i-jeu leang-der to kill two birds with one stone 241.25
ijyr straight ahead 161.36; straightway 291[1]
ikuall together 185.23
i-lai in the first place, firstly 186.48
i-luh all the way, on the way 213[37]
in the female principle, *yin* B 201.38
Ing English B 98
inggai ought 181[7], 265.54
Ing.gwo, Ingjyilih England; Great Britain; United Kingdom 137.12, 228.25
Ing.gwo-huah (spoken) English 137.13
Ing.gwo₀ren Englishman, Britisher 136.2
Inglii mile 249.3b
Ing'wen English (written or spoken) 135[14]
inlih lunar calendar 201.38
inpyng, inpyngsheng 1st Tone 25.7
in₀wey because 57.36, 151[32]

in₀wey ....de yuan.guh   (see sh ....de
    ₀yuan.guh)
iong ordinary, mediocre L 98
iou quiet B 96
iseel insistently 294.3
i.shang clothes AN -jiann (piece), -taw
    (suit) 237⁴
isheaul from childhood 278.17
i-shen all over someone 198.7
i.sheng physician 215.38
ishianq all along, hitherto 275¹⁹
ishyr for the moment 197²⁸
ishyue science of medicine 219⁴⁰
i-tian-daw-woan all day long 168.33
itourl . . . itourl (doing one thing) while
    (doing another) 170.45
iu literal-minded, to be a stickler 95
iuan wronged 95
iue to make an appointment 240.11
iuehuey engagement, appointment
    270.10
iun dizzy 95, 215.37
iun.guoh.chiuh to faint 215.37
i'wey *slurred form of* in₀wey 208.15,
    263.6
iyanq alike, same 107, 137.18, 174.3;
    equally 203.3a
i-yanq(l) one kind, a variety 174.3
iyanq .de same sort of thing 137.19
iyuann hospital 215.48
I.yueh January 197²⁹

J

-j (.jy, .je) *suffix for progressive action*
    41.13, 48
-jaan *AN for lamps* 122.4, 129³²
jaan.buh cloth (for wiping), rag AN
    -kuay 283¹¹
jaang grow 40.12; elder B 103, 199.11
-jang *AN for tables, beds, sheets of paper*
    130.5
Jang *very common surname* 121¹⁰
Jang Jih Chang Chi 275⁴⁶
Jang San Lii Syh John Smith and Tom
    Brown 121¹⁸
jann occupy 234.3
jann.bu-woen cannot stand steady 287.8
jannche (military) tank AN -lianq
    248.26
jann .de ... stand at ... 191⁴³
jann.de-juh can stand steady 223.2f
jannj to be standing 178.3e
jannjeng warfare 239¹⁸
janq account AN -bii 209.38
janq distend, swell 92
jao look for 93, 208.11
jao.bu-iaur cannot find 52.29

jao.daw find 219⁴⁸
jao₀jaur.le find 208.11
jau-jyi to get nervous 192.20
jau.pair signboard AN -kuay 247.12
-₀jaur *complement for* getting at, touching, realized 193.43
jaur-huoo .le there is a fire 192.14; catch
    fire 206.3
jau-tzu to let, for rent 254.1
jaw to shine 257²; according to 199⁴⁶
jaw-shianq to take photographs 54.33
jea false, unreal 99, 173⁷
jea first heaven's stem 201.40
jeajieh borrowed character 61
jeajuangl(.de) pretend to 288.46
jeandan simple, simplified 239¹⁵
jeandan-huah simplify 239³²
jeang talk about, explain 182.1; to lecture 231¹
jeang oar AN -baa 208.29
Jeang *common surname* 233²⁹
jeangshyue-jin scholarship, fellowship
    296.22
jeangtair lecture platform 294.7
jeangyean, yeanjeang lecture, to lecture
    294.1
jeanjyr downright, simply 167⁴⁵
jeantz scissors AN -baa 103
jearu if 49.26, 165²²
Jeatzyy the year 1924 ($\pm$ n $\times$ 60)
    201.40
jeau foot AN -jy 219³⁹
jeauwanntz ankle 219³⁹
jeeng whole 193.42
jeenggehl(.de) the whole thing 193.42
jeen.tour pillow 43.18
jeh this 45.22, 127¹
jeh.hoel this moment 163.2 I(4), 199⁴⁷
Jeh₀jiang Chekiang 27, 233²⁶
jeh ₀jiow right away 277⁵⁸
jeh.lii here 245²⁸; *comparison with* jell
    130.18, 296.29
jeh niantourl nowadays 251¹
jeh.sh this is, there are 129.2
jell this place, here 109, 130.18; -.jell
    general localizer for near reference: at
    the place of, *Fr. chez* 109, 131.2,
    152.2
jemm so, to this degree 221.42 (*see also*
    tzemm)
jen real, true; how ...! 160.16, 248.1
-jen syringe, hypodermic 220.9
jeng fight over; argue 240.8
jeng to steam (food) 96
jeng to open (one's eyes) 162.51
Jeng.yueh the first moon; January
    197²¹, 198.8, 202

jen hao   how nice!   95
jenq   right, upright   174.1; just ... -ing 55.33,   179.4; ... jenq   exactly ... 210.2c;   jenq-   (dong)   due   (east) 210.2c
jenqfaan-tzyh   (a pair of) antonyms 174.1
jenqfuu   a government   227[34]
jenqhaol   just right   46.23
jenq.jing   serious   283[13]
jenqjyh   government, politics   233[27]
jenq₀miall   right side (*opp. of* faanmiall) 173[4]
jenq-shyy   regular history   285[27]
jenq₀yaw   just going to   186.47
jeong   in narrow straits, embarrassed   99
jeou   nine B   142.4
jeou   long (time)   191[35]
jeou   wine, liquor, etc.   45.21, 247.22
jeou.chyan   wine-money,—tips   35.5a
jeoug   nine
jeoujing   alcohol   247.22
jeou₀shyr   ninety; jeou.shyr-   ninety- 142.4
Jeouyeang jeouyeang!   I have long wished to meet you!   247.15
jerl   nephew   51.28
jershyue   philosophy   288.40
jertz   folding notebook   256.39
jeu   to lift (from below)   99, 241.25
jeuan   to roll   29.5
jeu-shoou   to raise one's hand   233[36]
jey-   this, these   129.2
jey.bial   this side, over here   131.20
jeyg   this (one)   128.2; *as filler-in*   183.6, 293[16,25]
jey.hoel   this moment   163.2
jey₀hwei   this time   197[8]
jey₀leang-tian   these days, the next few days   146.50
jey.shieg   these, this lot   130.9
jey₀tzoong, jey₀joong   this kind of   191.7
ji   chicken AN -jy   35.4
ji   dustpan B (*forms of the script*)   67-68
jia   add, plus   197[30], 211[18]
jia   home   181[24]; -jia -ist, -er   288.40; *AN, see* -jial
jiachyan   pliers AN -baa, -fuh   43.17
jia-duo   increase   249.1d
jiah   holiday, leave, vacation   200.23
-jiah   *AN for machines, airplanes, etc.* 145.38
jiah.chyan   price   41.14c, 255.30
jiahshyy   to pilot   205[22]
jiahshyy-yuan   a pilot   205[22], 217.2c
jiahtz   framework, a front   216.55
jia.jiuann   family, wife and children   239[20]

Jiajou   California   294.11
-jial, -jia   *AN for stores, etc.*
jia.lii   at home, in the home   181[24], 242.2b
-jian   *AN for rooms*   46.22, 155.36; space between two columns   254.8
Jianadah   Canada   227[35]
jianbaangl   the shoulder   213[30]
jiang   river AN -tyau   93
Jiang-   Jeh-   short for Jiangsu and Jeh- jiang, *q.v.*   233[30]
jianglai   future, in the future   271.28
Jiang₀shi   Kiangsi   233[26]
Jiang₀su   Kiangsu   233[26]
jiann   see, interview, meet 40, 251[3]; -.jiann (*see* kann.jiann, ting.jiann)
jiann   build L   291[5]
-jiann   *AN for words meaning thing or affair*   130.6
Jiannchyau   Cambridge   294.12
jiann-goei   to see apparitions   251[3]
jiannjial.de,   jiannjiann.de   gradually 211[8]
jiann-miann   to see, to meet with   265.51
jiannsheh   establish, reconstruct   239[21]
jianq   descend, drop   67-68, 211[11]
jianqluoh-saan   parachute   208.21
jiashiang   homestead   278.24
jiau   teach   283[17]
jiau.aw   conceited, haughty   52.30(2)
jiauhuann   exchange   293[12]
jiau-shu   teach school   278.25
jiaw   call, is called, mean (by), is meant (by)   137.15; make, tell ... to   167[45]; to order (dishes, etc.)   287[57]
jiaw.bu-jaur   cannot get by ordering 281b
jiawshow   professor   267[14]
jiaw.yuh   educate, -ion   248.40
jibeen   basis, basic   239[27]
ji.chih   machine, engine AN -jiah   207[38], 239[20]
jidanngau   sponge cake   110
Jidujiaw   Christianity   53.30
jie   meet (arrival of); join   53.30
jie   street AN -tyau   112
jiee   from   49.25, 199.18
jiee   unfasten, untie   234.7
jiee.jiee   elder sister   177.37
jieejyue   solve (a problem)   239[22]
jieel   what day of the month?   199.19
jiee₀mey   sisters (*collec.*)   175[38]
jiee-shooul   to go to the toilet (to urinate) 221.18
jiee.shyh   to explain   234.7
jie-guu   to set bones   215.25
jieh   to lend, to borrow   53.30, 100
jieh₀shaw   to introduce   245[14]

jiej continuing 227[30]
jiel today 141[30], 202
jiell, jinn strength 209.44
jiel woan.shanq tonight 195[2]
jie.shanq in the street, in town 191.11
ji.gu to grumble 39.11, 235[36]
jih to tie 237[4]
jih to record, remember 100
-jih *quasi-AN:* season 122.4, 197[37]
jih.de remember 167[38]
jih-hao tie up 264.30
jih₀huah-jingjih planned economy 117
jihj remember 167[37]
jih₀niann commemorate 197[26]
jih₀niann-ryh anniversary 197[26]
jihran since, if, inasmuch as 49.26, 131.19, 185.37
jih.shiah.lai to note down 253[41]
jih.shinq memory 36.5
jihshy technician 239[20]
ji.huey chance, opportunity 235[36]
jii to crowd 264.36
jii self B 161.20; sixth heaven's stem 201.40
jii- several, a few 132.39
jii-dean (jong) what o'clock? 145.36
jiig how many?, a few 52.29
jii-haw what day of the month? 197[29]
jiin tight 99
jiing a well AN -koou 110
jiing warning B 99
jiinggaw warn(ing) 293[19]
jiin₀goan all you want 271.19
jiinyaw urgent and important 42.16
jii.shyr when, what day? 143[49]
jin gold B 113.411, 251[17]; jintz gold
jin- now, present B 33.1, 96
-jin catty (= 1⅓ lbs.) 46b
jingcherng capital (of a country) 229.39
jing₀guoh to pass through 220.11
jingjih economic(s) 233[28]
jinglii manager 245[12]
jing-shu the classics 283[13]
jing₀yann experience 239[20]
jinn promote advance L 291[5]; -jinn *AN for rows of rooms:* courtyard, compound 254.11
jinn near 205[19], 223.2g
jinn ... tzer(₀renn) to do (one's) duty 222.52
jinn₀buh progress, to advance 221.41
jinn.chiuh to go in 28.11, 179.4g, 219[52]; -.jinn.chiuh *directional complement:* in, Germ. *hinein-* 161.28
jinn.deal nearer 229.1b
jin.nian this year 202
jinn, jiell strength 209.44

jinnjyy prohibit 288.29
jinnlai recently 271.33
jinn.lai to come in 251[8], 271.33; -.jinn- .lai *directional complement:* in, Germ. *herein-* 161.28, 215.47
jinq mirror B 100
jinq purely, keep ... -ing 168.9, 211[21]
jinrow, jirow muscle 215.31
jin.tian, jiel today 160.1
jinyu goldfish AN -tyau 251[17]
jiow rescue 205⁰
jiow old (not new) 72.2, 93, 175.8
jiow namely, simply, just 137.16; then (*after* if) 49.26; soon, immediately, right away 146.48; even 213[32]
... jiow .... tzay— the ... lies in— 256.44, 256.1
jiow-hwo.le revive 209.1b
Jiow Jinshan, Jinshan San Francisco 131
jiow-jyi first aid, to give first aid 215.44
jiow.sh only thing is ... 113
jiowshang-che ambulance AN -lianq 215.46
jiowsheng-chiuan life-belt 209.45
.jiow.sh.le *final particle:* that's the only thing 137.24
jirow, jinrow muscle 215.31
jisel, jisy chicken shreds 289.57
jitzeel hen's egg 26.9
jiu live, dwell L 103
jiuann silk (for painting) 100
jiue-tzoei to pout 263.8
jiuh according to 100
-jiuh sentence, *AN for words for speech* 165[19]
jiuhtz a sentence 267[6]
jiuhua(l), jyuhua(l) chrysanthemum (as tea) 276.4
jiumin inhabitants 231[13]
jiun king, sovereign L 45.21, 103
jiunjuu monarch 228.30
jiunn mushroom; bacteria, germs 100
jiunyonq-piin military articles 245[24]
jiuran actually, indeed 220.10
-j .ne *lively intensive* 278.13
joa claw B 99
joan to turn 99, 208.30
joang fat. (dialectal) 99
joanjuh derivative characters 63.3
joen permit, allow 175[23]
joen accurate 99, 175[43], 192.23
joenchiueh accurate, exact 285[38]
jong (large) bell AN -koou 275[47]; clock AN -jiah 144.32; o'clock AN -dean 144.32
jong loyal L 291[5]
jong middle B 96

jongbuh middle part 233³⁰
Jong.gwo China 136.1
Jong.gwo-huah (spoken) Chinese 136.1
Jong.gwo₀ren a Chinese 136.2
Jonghwa- China, Chinese B 41.14b
Jonghwa Mingwo The Republic of China 200.25
jongiang central 165⁷
Jong₀iong 'Doctrine of the Mean' 278.33
jongjiall middle 152.1
jongjyy, jongguulou middle finger 221.38
Jongshan Chungshan 233³⁵
jongshin center 233²⁶; central 253³⁵
jongshyue high school 280.51
jongtour(l) an hour 247⁴⁶
Jongwen Chinese, written Chinese 135²⁵
jonq heavy; strongly 175²³; with emphasis 179.5; serious (injury) 219⁴⁷
jonq to plant 251¹⁷
jonqyaw important, weighty 227²⁴
joong swollen 219²⁰
-joong kind, sort; species 181³⁰
jou continent B 225⁴
jou congee 96
Jou.chaur the Chou dynasty 233²⁴
jow wrinkled 72.2, 93
ju pig AN -jy 92
Ju common surname 64
juan specially 245¹⁷
juang install 253²⁹
Juang Tzyy Chuang Tzŭ 287.17
juanmen specialty, technical fields 239³⁰; specially 245¹⁶
juann record, biography 40.12
juann to turn around, to (cause to) turn 100, 208.30
juanntzyh seal characters 67
juanq status B 100
juay to drag 100
juei chase 103
juey dangle 100
juh live, reside 54.31, 100; -₀juh firmly, fast 207⁴⁵
juhin fwuhaw, juhin tzyhmuu National Phonetic Letters 9.8
juhtz pillar, column AN -gen 191⁴⁵
-juo table B 46c
juol.shanq on the table (or desk) 152.2
juotz table, desk AN -jang 130.5
juotz.nall at the table, at the desk 131.22
jurow pork 37.7
jutz pearl, bead AN -ke 221.33
juu to boil, to cook (in water) 264.37
juushyi chairman, presiding officer 235.30
juuyih principle, -ism 248.34

jwutz bamboo AN -ke, -gel, -gen 251¹⁶
jwu.yih intention, decision 190.3
₀jy literary equivalent of .de 214.19
jy know B 97
-jy AN for pencils, cigarettes, etc. 130.10
-jy AN for one of a pair, animals, etc. 151¹⁴
Jyakeh Jack 57.36
jy-buh weave cloth 247.17
jyeguoo result, outcome 219⁴⁷
jyh heal, treat 94, 219⁴⁴
jyhfwu a uniform AN -jiann (piece), -taw (set) 245²³
jyhshao at least 189²⁴
jyh.tzaw manufacture 239²⁹
jyh₀yu as to, as for 49.25, 234.4, 273.1e
. . . jy i one of 229.33
jyi hurried 56.35; urgent 189²⁰; nervous 192.20
jyifarng jau-tzu vacant house for rent 254.1
. . .-jyi.le awfully . . . 53.30, 160.5
Jyi₀lin Kirin 231⁵
jy.jea, shooujy.jea, fingernail 221.38
jypiaw a cheque AN -jang 296.22
jy.shyh knowledge 239³⁰
jyue.de feel, find that, notice that 269³⁷
jyuedinq decide 189¹⁹, 253³⁵
jyueduann decision, decisiveness 191⁴⁶
jyueduey absolutely 186.57
jyuej feel, find that, notice that 161.23, 253³¹, 293²³
jyueshin determination 240.19
jyutz tangerine 47.24
jyy stop L 29
jyy only, merely 135²², 197²³
jyy paper AN -jang 131.27
jyy finger B; to point at 221.38
jyydao to guide 296.34
jyydean to guide 296.32, .34
jyy₀goan only care about 265.52
jyy hao the only thing to do is . . . 215.39
jyyshiu only need 222.45
jyyshyh simple ideograph 60
jyy-tonq relieve pain 213³⁹
jyy.wanq expect 237²
jyy yaw.sh if only, so long as 185.41

K

kaeshu model writing, regular writing (style of characters) 67
kai open, turn on 132.33, .35; operate 205²²; boil (of water) v.i. 237⁴; make out, write out, 253³⁷; -₀kai off, away 143⁵¹
kaibann start, set up 248.36

kai-che .le (they are) starting the train (bus, etc.) 273[7]
kai-dau to operate (surgically) 215.26
kai-gong start work 247[43]
kai-hual to blossom 56.35
kai-huey open a meeting; hold a meeting 291[1]
kaijian number of rooms in a row 251[9]
kai.kai just open; open up 132.33
kai-men open the door 133.5b
kai-meng to begin school (of a child) 278.21
kai-shoei boiling water 237[4]
kaishyy to commence 234.1, 239[16]
kai-tzwu.le open to the full 209.34
kai-wanshiaw to make fun 271.21
kan to watch 212.3, 253[23]
kanhuh, kannhuh (hospital) nurse 212.3
kann look, look at 129[29]; call on 144.28; to read (silently) 156.3a, 175[39]; think, believe 177.27
...kann just...and see 216.57
kann.bu-jiann cannot see 145.39
kann.chii.lai at first sight 177.31
kann.chu.lai make out (from looking) 157.5d
kann.de-jiann can see 145.39
kannj wal read for fun 285[27]
kann.jiann see 128.33
kann.kann just look 129[29], 131.30
kanqjann resist(ance) by war 240.16
kao examine, quiz 235[38]
kaw to lean 162.41, 205[28]
kaw-ann to dock 215.45
kaw.dejuh dependable 209.33
ke carve 95
-ke *AN for plants* 162.45
-ke *AN for small round things*
kebaantzyh printed characters 67
kee thirsty 167[37], 219[20]
₀kee (*parenthetical*) however 49.26, 161.27; whether 264.20; kee- -able 265.59
keeguan remarkable 271.25
keelian pitiable, pitiful 265.59
keen willing (to) 177.26, 186.43
₀kee.sh but, however 49.26, 203.3g
kee.shi too bad, it's a pity 288.42
kee.yii may, permitted 173[22]
keh guest, traveler 275[47]; an order (of a dish, etc.) 277.7, 287[57]
-keh *quasi-AN*: lesson 46e, 120.1
-keh (jong) quarter (hour) 201.46
keh.chih polite 28.11, 222.54
keh.ren guest, caller 51[29], 245[14]
kehtarng classroom AN -jian 155.37
kehting reception room AN -jian 251[9]

ker.shigall knee cap 219[39]
ker.sow to cough 277[56]
keshyue science 239[27], 277[52]
kong empty 146.51
konglonglong *rumbling sound* 191[40]
konq unoccupied, vacant 146.51
konql space, leisure 146.51
koongpah I am afraid that, perhaps 205[24], 285[37]
Koong Tzyy, Koong.futzyy Confucius 234.19
koou mouth, opening; -koou *AN for ability to speak a language* 272.49; kooul opening 193.39
koou.chih tone, expression 288.33
koou₀in local accent 235.32
koouyeu spoken language L 288.38
ku weep 259[16], 263[58]; cry 283[1]
kuay fast, quick 162.43, 165[22]; on the point of, about to 55.33, 189[27], 198.6; hurry up and 95.3, 189.30
-kuay *AN for boards, lumps, etc.* 153.13
-kuay chyan dollar 253[36]
kuay.deal... ...faster; hurry up and ... 209.43
kuay.hwo happy 183[54], 293[23]
kuay-mann speed 170.43
kuaytz chopstick AN -gel, -shuang 129[39]
kuay yaw soon, about to 179.4e
kuei.de thanks to 219[40]
kuenn sleepy 39.10, 285[52]
kuhtz trousers, pants AN -tyau 54.32
kuoh rich, wealthy 53.32
kuoh-dah enlarge 245[18], 248.1
kuu bitter; miserable 239[20]

L

-l *diminutive suffix* 30.13, 40.13
laan lazy; laanlhal.de lazily 192.31
lah to leave behind 193.44
lai come 136.8; *forms of the script* 67; bring (in ordering food) 264.44; *as pro-verb* 47.24; ₀lai (in order) to 55–56.34, 264.33; -.lai *directional complement:* here, Germ. *her-* 161.28; *separation of from* chu- 144.24; -.lai -odd, some odd 192.25
laibin (formal) visitor 248.46
lai.bujyi have no time for, too late to 207.7
lai.dejyi have time for, soon enough 207.7
lai.guoh did come 141[29]
.lai.je *particle for recent past* 208.14
lai-wan.le come late 148.5

VOCABULARY AND INDEX

lan blue, dark blue 205[18]
lang wolf AN -tyau 96
lanq.tou wave 257[3]
lao old (not young) 199.13; always, all the time 92, 112, 160.17; *prefix to surnames* 131.21; *prefix in names of animals* 40.13, 190.1
laobae.shinq the common people 241.30
lao bu never 160.17
lao .le grown old 199.13
laomhatz maid-servant 259[17]
lao.sh always 171.4e
laoshuu rat, mouse AN -jy 190.1
laoshy teacher 294.15
laotz father, 'the old man' 287.16
Lao Tzyy Lao Tzǔ 287.16
Laujiah! Much obliged! 222.53, 243[12]; Excuse me! May I trouble you? 239[33], 243[1]
lawbiing a large, coarse hot-cake 41.14a
.le *particle for new situation* 132.36, 138.31, 146.59, 177.28; *list of uses of* 193–4; *telescoping of two* .le *into one* 40–41; *in lively enumeration* 240.3; -.le *word suffix for completed action* 54.33, 194; *with quantified object* 160.3, 194
lea *fused form of* leangg 124.26
lean the face 54.32, 219[31]
leang- two, *used with AN* 142.4; ... .leang a couple, a few 254.6
leangg two 122.4
leangg leangg two and two; twice two 123.21
leang-san'g two or three 133.3i
leangyanq different 138.32; leang-yanq, leang-yanql two kinds, both kinds 138.32
leau finish 265.67
leau.bu.de wonderful 271.27
....le .dou *afterthought word:* even 240.1
leeng cold 175.9
leou willow B 103
leu to put in order 38.9
leugoan hotel 44.20
leukeh traveler 283[1]
leushyng travel 59d
ley tired 159[4]
-ley AN category, kind 213[42], 275[19]
lha to pull 207[45]
lha.juh hold fast 207[45]
lha-shyy to defecate 221.18
lhianj joining, connected 225[4]
li (distance) from 38.10c, 208.16
lian join; include 124.30; even 181[13]
lian ... day both ... and 207.5, 239[20]

lian ... yee (*or* dou) even 160.6
lianbang commonwealths, dominions, union 227[32]
liang cool 19, 40.12, 96, 175.9
lianghao excellent 219[49]
liang.kuay cool (of the weather) 251[15]
liang-shoei cold water 38.9
lianher unite 199[49]
Lianher Gwo the United Nations 199[49]
lianmang hurriedly 264.40
lianmeng league, alliance 227[28]
liann to refine (oil) 245[31]
liann₀shyi practice, exercise 267[3]
lianq bright 103, 192.32; it is light, (the day) breaks 203.1c
lianq to sun, to dry 40.12
-lianq *AN for vehicles* 213[45]
Liaubeei Liaopeh 231[5]
Liau₀ning Liaoning 231[5]
liau-tial to chat 271.20
liaw.daw to foresee 239[16]
li.ba fence, hedge 28.11, 40.13
lieh cracked 215.29
liengl (small) bell 143.7
lihchaang standpoint, point of view 285[46]
lihhay advantages and disadvantages 42.16
lih.hay powerful, fierce 42.16, 193.36; serious(ly), bad(ly) 219[32]
lih₀hwang oyster 259[21]
lihkeh immediately, at once 192.19
lih.lianq strength, power 239[27]
lihru e.g. 177.34
lihshiann constitutional 228.30
lihshu, lihtzyh scribe's writing (style of characters) 67
lihshyy history 239[15], 277[51]
lih.yonq make use of 56.35
lii reason 174.5
-lii *li* (= ⅓ mile) 46b, 237[10]
lii inside B 155.33; -.lii inside, 53.31; *comparison with* -l 130.18, 296.29
Lii *very common surname* 121[10]
liibay week 144.30, 200.27; Liibay Sunday 144.30
Liibay'i, -cll, ..., -liow Monday, Tuesday, ..., Saturday 144.30, 202
liibayjii what day of the week? 58a, 144.30
Liibayryh, Liibaytian, Liibay Sunday 144.30
Lii Bor Li Po 280.48
lii-fah dress-hair,—to give (or have) a haircut 37.6
Liijih 'Book of Rites' 279.39

320　VOCABULARY AND INDEX

liiliiwayway.de　inside and out　217[14]
liing　to lead　99, 251[8]
liingtz　collar　AN -tyau　54.32
liishyuejia　(Sung) philosophers　288.40
lii.tou　inside　151[31-33]; -.lii.tou inside, in 151[36]
lii-way　inside and outside　155.33
li.kai　to leave, to go away from　208.16
lin　woods B　7.6
ling　sill L　64
ling　zero　202.49, 211[19]
ling　efficacious　219[43]
ling　(small) bell B　235.37
linq₀way　separately, extra　228.18
linshyr　temporary, for the time being　215.43
liou　to flow　221.22
liou　to leave (behind), remain　253[36]
liouanjih　sulfanilimide　222.44
liou₀lih　fluent　267[17]
lioushengji　phonograph　AN -jiah　168.6
liou-shin　to notice, to pay attention to　272.39
lioushyuesheng　"returned student"　241.32
liouyuh　(river) basin　234.17
liow　six B　142.4; liowg　six
liow₀shyr　sixty; liow.shyr- sixty-　142.4
liu　donkey　AN -pi, -pii　237[9]
liueh　outline B　100
liuh　green　205[16]
liuhshy　metric poem　279.47
.lo　*particle for obviousness:* of course　184.11, 225[9]
long　deaf　263[53]
Longjiang　Lungkiang　231[5]
Longjiing　Dragon Well (brand of green tea)　276.3
lou　storied house, upstairs　185.38
luann　confused, disordered　70, 263.5
luel, luentz　wheel　30.13(6)
luenchwan　steamship　AN -jy, -tyau　165[22]
Luenduen　London　227[41]
Luen₀yeu　'(Confucian) Analects'　278.34
Lugou Chyau　Lukouchiao, Marco Polo Bridge　111
luh　road　AN -tyau　80, 213[37], 243[5]; -luh type, sort　278.19
luhbeei, -dong, etc.　north (east, etc.) side of the street　253[40]
luhdih　land (as opp. to water)　227.3
luhkooul　intersection, road junction　243[7]
luo.bo　radish; turnip　AN -gel, -ke　39.11, 251[18]
luoh　fall B　208.21; 275[46]
luojih　logic　39.11
luol　small mule　30.13(6)

Luomaa　Rome　227[41]
luoshyuan-jeang　screw propeller　208.29
luo.sy　screw　208.29
lutz　stove　111, 195[2]
Luu.gwo　the state of Lu　233[19]

M

.M.　M-hm., Yeah.　59d, 139.3
m—　*sound of hesitation:* um—　275[46], 283[13]; W-e-ll　285[33]
ma　hemp　29, 86
.ma　*(high pitch) interrogative particle*　59d, 137.22, 138.36, 139.3; *comparison with* .me　177.24
maa　horse　AN -pi, -pii　86
maafei　morphene　215.40
maalih　horsepower　207[33]
maan　full　285[52]; fill　275[46]
Maan₀jou　Manchuria　231[5]
maashanq　right away, at once　192.18
maatoong　commode　255.29
mae　buy　11.11, 41.14c, 253[32]
mae.may　trade　41.14c, 241.27
mah　abuse, scold　86, 267[11]
mai　bury　11.11
mang　busy　189[13]; be in a hurry to　251[20]
mann　slow, slowly　145.40; lose (of time pieces)　203.3h
mann.i.deal　a little more slowly　145.40; take it easy!　205[28]
mannmhal(.de)　slowly　231[6], 259[16]
mao　fourth earth's branch　201.40
Masheeng　Massachusetts　294.11
masherngl　cord (made of hemp)　AN -gel　43.17
matzuey-yaw　anesthetic　215.40
mau　fur hair (of the body); feather　AN -gel, -gen　130.15; -mau　*AN:* dime　35.4
maubii　writing brush　AN -jy, -goan　130.15
maufarng　the toilet　AN -jian　221.18
maw-ial　emit smoke　207.4
mawtz　hat　AN -diing　41.13, 240.4
may　to sell　11.11, 41.14c, 239[33]
may, moh　the pulse　220.6
.me　*particle of hesitation*　228.6
.me　*particle with impatient tone:* you see! don't you see?　177.24, 181[28], 191[35], 235[36]
-meau (jong)　second (of time)　199[47]
meei　beautiful　103, 277[47]
meei-　each　33.1, 51.29, 128.2
Meei　American B　109, 136.10
Meei.gwo　America, United States　136.10

VOCABULARY AND INDEX 321

Meei.gwo-huah American Language 135[13]
Meei.gwo₀ren an American 135[11]
Meei₀jou, yahmeeilihjia, Yea- America (the continent) 225[12]
Meeilihjian (Herjonqgwo) The United States of America 229.42
mei coal 195[4]
mei, mei₀yeou have not (*followed by substantive*) 47.25, 57.37, 131.25; have not, did not (*followed by verb*) 47.25, 58, 191[42]
mei — nemm ... (*see* mei.yeou — nemm ...)
mei ... -.toul not worth ... -ing 240.8
mei ... yiichyan before ... 209.49
mei bann.faa can't do anything about it 167[45]
mei fartz not to know what to do; can't help it 170.38
mei guan.shih it doesn't matter 239[30], 253[40]
mei guei.jeu without manners, rude 263.10
meiguey rose AN -duoo(l), -ke 56.35
meijoel no telling, perhaps 49.26, 192.23
mei konql not free, busy 146.51
mei.mau eyebrows 219[37]
mei-shyh nothing the matter with it, without incident 221.31
meiyeou (*see* mei)
mei.yeou — nemm ... not so ... as — 53.30, 169.21, 171.2
mei yih.sy uninteresting 173[22]
meiyou kerosene 248.32
men door AN -shann 130.8; doorway AN -g 143.11; -men AN for subjects of study 293[19]
-.men *suffix for collective nouns* 40.13, 197[11]
-.men, -m *plural suffix for pronouns* 40.13, 123.16
menfarngl gateman's room AN -jian 251[8]
menkooul doorway 193.39
menliengl doorbell 141[8]
menpair house number 256.40
menq a dream AN -charng 162.54
Menq ₀Tzyy 'Mencius' 278.35
mey.mey younger sister 175[37]
mha ma 86, 287[57]
mha.mha mamma 40.12, 287[57]
mho to feel with the hand 97
miall face, side 152.7
mian sleep L 275[47]
mian.hua cotton 26.9
miann flour 264.45

miannbau bread AN -g (loaf), -kuay, -piann (slice) 264.45
miann₀chyan forefront, front 265.64
miannshann the face is familiar 36.5
mianntz face, courtesy 287.12
miaw wonderful 219[28], 257.1h
miengl, ming.tian tomorrow 145.47, 160.3, 202
Miengl jiann! See you tomorrow! 143[59]
mii (uncooked) rice 46b
minchyuan people's (political) rights 248.35
ming.bair clear, to be clear about, understand 175.6
Ming.chaur the Ming dynasty 233[25]
ming.nian next year 200.20, 202
mingren celebrity 233[35]
ming.tian, miengl tomorrow 145.47, 160.3, 202
ming.tzyh (given) name (of persons) 144.20; name (of things) 225[9]
mingwo republic 41.14, 199.14
mingyueh the moon L 280.49
minjuu democratic 229.35
minjuugwo(jia) a democracy 229.35
minq life (opp. of death) AN -tyau 220.3
minsheng the people's livelihood 264.1
mintzwu race, nation 248.33
mishinn superstition, -ous 253[47]
mm (*exclusive*) we, us 47.24, 26[42], 263[55]
Mm! Oh, no! 50.27, 146.55
moh, may the pulse 220.6
mohbor pulse beat 220.6
moh-ming-chyi-miaw can't make head or tail out of it 272.47
Mohshige Mexico 227[30]
mohshoel, mohshoei ink 247.23
Mohsyke Moscow 227[40]
moo to smear 265.58
mooumoou-ren so-and-so 167[29]
moouren a certain person 169.28
mo-poh to abrade 221.30
motsa friction 221.30
muh wood B; tree L 64
-muh act (of plays) 267.3
muhdih objective, aim 293[23]
muh.jianq carpenter 262.2
mushyng (miniature) model 245[27]
muu.chin mother 175[35]
muu.dan peony AN -duoo(l), -ke 56.35

N

na hold, take 156.2c
na ... danq(₀tzuoh) take ... as 201.41

na — danq₀tzuoh ... yonq use — as ... 201.41
naa- which? 45.22, 128.2
naal where? 122.8; somewhere 52.29; *use of in telephoning* 143.14; *use of for denial* 229.37
naal dou, naal yee anywhere 52.29, 185.33
naal dou bu (*or* mei), naal yee bu (*or* mei) not anywhere, nowhere 52.29, 185.33
naa.lii where? 130.18, 286.7
naapah no matter if, be it 185.24
naa-shie which ones 235.29
nae.nae grandma (on father's side) 278.22
nah in that case 137³⁰, 194(6); nah-that 45.22 (*see also* ney-)
nah.lii there; *comparison with* nall 130.18
nah.sh that's, those are 129.2
nah.shyr.howl meanwhile, at that time 159³⁷
nahtsuey- nazi- 227³⁰
naj g ... being a (respectable) ... 256.47
nall that place, there 109, 127¹⁹, 129¹⁹; -.nall *general localizer:* at the place of, Fr. *chez* 109, 131.22, 152.2
nan hard, hard to; bad to, badly 176.11
Nan.bian, Nan.bial the South 205⁹, 233²⁶,³⁰
Nan.bian-huah southern dialect 278.18
Nan Bingyang Antarctic Ocean 228.17
nanbuh southern part 228.16
nan-chiang-beei-diaw mixed accent 185.35
nan.chuh difficulty 257.1b
nanchy to taste bad 176.11
nan₀daw ... .ma? do you mean to say that ... ? 169.32
Nanfang the South 233²⁹
Nanfang'in southern pronunciation 275²⁶
nan guay hardly odd, no wonder 265.65
Nanhwa Jing work by Chuang Tzŭ 287.17
Nan₀jing Nanking 187.3
Nanjyi North Pole 228.8
nankann ugly 176.11
nan-neu torng-shiaw co-education(al) 296.26
nan.ren man (as distinguished from woman) 47.24, 175³⁴
nansheng, nanshyue.sheng men students 294.25
nanshow feel bad, uncomfortable, miserable 43.17, 176.11, 183⁵⁵
nanting to sound ugly 176.11
nan tzuoh hard to do 176.11
nantzyy-hann manly man, he-man 256.47

nan₀weichyng embarrassed 272.53
Nanyang the South Seas 230.2c
naol brain (as food) 220.17
nao, naotz the brain 220.17
naw to be noisy 48c; to make noise, to disturb 168.8
naw-goei *impersonal verb-object compound for* ghosts' haunting 253.45
nawj yaw to clamor for 219²⁰
naw-shiing.le to wake 211⁵
.... ne is ... -ing 55.33; .... ne? and ...? how about ...? then ...? 122.9; .ne *particle for pause* 225¹, 228.6
neaul bird AN -jy 259¹⁴
neei- which? 128.2
neei.bial which side? 131.20, 156.2h
neeig which? 122.8
neeig dou bu ... none ... 52.29
neei-tian what day? 141²⁹
neem(.me) which way? how? 40.13
.ne.me well, in that case, then 121¹⁸, 138.30
nemm(.me) so, in that manner, to that degree, that ... 123.11, 138.30
nemmj, nemm₀yanql (do) that 47.24, 177.23
nemm₀shie so much, that (much) 156.3(1)
neng able, can 153.19
nenggow can 219⁴⁵
Neouiue New York 227⁴¹
neu.erl daughter 175³⁵
neuharl girl 187.4c
neukeh woman guest, woman traveler 283²
neu.ren woman 47.24, 175³⁴
neusheng, neushyue.sheng woman student 293⁵
ney- that, those 129.2; the other (of two) 52.29
ney.bial that side, over there 131.20; the other side (of two sides) 52.29, 207.10; -.ney.bial the side of 207.10
neybuh internal parts 220.14
neydih the interior (of a country) 281.1g
neyg that 127⁶; the other (of two) 52.29; *repetition of in long qualifying clauses* 208.22
ney₀hwei that time 197⁸
ney-i-ley that sort 275¹⁹
ney-i-luh that type 278.19
neyke internal medicine 215.51
Ney Mengguu Inner Mongolia 234.16
ney-shang internal injury 217¹⁶
ney-shieg those, that lot 127¹⁵, 131.19
ney₀tsyh that time 239¹⁶
nhie pinch 29.7

ni mud 103
-nian year 198.1, 202
nianching youthful 293[8]
Nian-chu'i New Year's Day 197[24]
niang mother 29.7
niann read (aloud) 184.8
niann-shu to study 53.31, 270.4
nih greasy, too rich 289.56
nii you (*singular*) 47.24, 121.1, 125; *use of in commands* 143.5; *non-use of in respectful language* 222.49
nii.de your(s) 131.26
nii.men, niim you (*plural*) 47.24, 121[23], 125
nii.men.de, niim.de your(s) 131.26
nii.nall where you are, with you, Fr. *chez vous* 131.22, .24
Nin you (*singular, polite form*) 143.14; *non-use of in respectful language* 222.49
..., .Nin .a! ..., sir! 239[33], 243[1]
Nin.de your(s)
Ningshiah Ninghsia 231[17]
niou cattle, bull, cow AN -tour; *surname* 213[49]
niourow beef 37.7
noan.hwo warm 175.9, 195[4]
nonq fix, arrange 251[20]; to tinker with 281.1e
nonq-huay.le spoil, ruin 283[5]
nonq.shanq.lai to carry up 215.35
nonq-tsuoh.le to be mistaken 227[25]
Nuennjiang Nunkiang 231[5]
nuo₀guoh.chiuh move over 267[9]
Nuouei Norway 227[25]

O

.Oh. Oh (I see). 130.7; I see 149[7]
oou lotus stem AN -gen, gel 21.2
.ou *particle of mild warning:* mind you! 193.33, 199[46], 237.8
Ou₀jou, Ouluoba Europe 227.4
ow macerate, soak 100

P

pah afraid, fear 175[28]
pai-shoou to clap hands 294.14
panq fat (of persons) 103, 261
pao to run 41.13, 90, 189[30]
pao .de gone to 205[12]
par crawl 72.2
parl board, tray 200.30
parng side, lateral B 70
parngbial (lateral) side 159[41]
parngting listen in, audit 270.2

parnnishilin, piannnisylin penicillin 222.44
paurtz (lined) robe AN -jiann 286.5
paw to steep, soak 289.51
pawl bubble 207.4
pay send, despatch 29.6, 56.34
peir to keep company with, accompany 248.45
penq collide 92, 205[28]
penq.jaur, penq.jiann meet with, happen upon 28.11, 219[47]
pern basin 28.12
perng.yeou friend 165[1], 189[29]
pey to fit 52.29
pey.fwu admire, respect 213[55]
-pi, -pii *AN for* maa, etc.
-pii *AN for cloth:* bolt
pian one-sided, biased 209.39
piann to fool 56.34
-piann slice, piece 228.7
pianntz calling card AN -jang 253[36]
pianpial.de (this) of all things, (now) of all times 209.39
piau to float 205[7]
piaw.lianq elegant, polished, smart 272.51
pih-ching light as wind 286.3
pin.faa spelling, orthography 43.17
pinminq with all one's strength 262.3
po spill, splash 97
poh broken; dilapidated 100, 192.27, 215.29
pohchwu abolish, eradicate 253[47]
Polan, Bolan Poland 229.41
pu to spread 70
pu-chwang to make the bed 47.24
puhtz store, shop AN -jial 253[32]
puutong general, ordinary 239[27], 248.28
puutong-huah Mandarin (in the wide sense) 272.44
pwu.sah bodhisattva 39.11
pyan.yi cheap 239[33]
pyi skin AN -kuay 219[29], 221.37
pyi.fu skin (of a person) 221.37
pyishye (leather) shoes AN -jy, -shuang 248.24
pyng level 176.22
pyng'an peaceful, safe 220.11
pyngcharng(l) ordinarily 176.22
pyngmin the common people 248.40
pyngpyng'an'an.de safe and sound 220.1
pyngsheng even tone 25.7

R

raan to dye 21.3
raang shout 151[39], 159[40]

ran to burn; thus, so L 61
ranhow and then, then only 239[32], 229.1 Example
ranq yield, let 49.25, 161.35, 189[22]
ranq... lai let... do it 47.24
-.ranq *slurred form of* -.shanq 153.11
rau spare (from punishment) 287.13
raw go around, to wind 208.32
rawyeuan make a detour 208.32
reh hot 175.9
rehchiell warmth; reh-chih hot air 198.3
rehduh (high) temperature 213.8, 214.16
rehduhbeau (clinical) thermometer 211[13]
Rehher, Rehher'l Jehol 231[15]
reh.naw bustling, full of life 271.34
rel person 259[23]
ren man, woman, person, human being, people 122.5; self, person, body 155.34, 161.20; (state of) mind 214.20
ren ninth heaven's stem 201.40
ren'ay benevolent 24.6
rengjiow still, continue to 285[41]
ren.jia people, others 168.4
renjial a family, household AN -jia(l) 168.4
renkoou population 231[2]
renmin people, inhabitants 231[3]
renn learn to recognize 275[27]
renn.de know, acquainted with 41.13; can recognize 211[23]
renn.shyh know, acquainted with 273[7]
renren every man 148.5h, 239[18]
rentsair personnel; talented person 241.31
rheng .geei throw to 207[45]
rheng.le throw away 47.24
roan soft 21.3, 112, 173[9]
rong.yih easy 176.11
row flesh; meat 93
Rueydean Sweden 227[29]
Rueyshyh Switzerland 227[25]
ru₀guoo if indeed, if 245[41]
ruher what like, how? L 222.48
ruh Guan enter the Pass 234.9
ruhkoou entrance (door) 93
-ruhmen 'Introduction to...' (*in titles of books*)
ruh-yuann enter hospital 221.23
Rulin Wayshyy 'Informal History of Literary Men' 288.26
ryh day B 94
Rhybeen Japan 229.36
ryhtz day; date 156.2k, 197[9]
ryhyonq daily use 239[24]

S

saa to spill 283[2]
saan umbrella AN -baa 208.21
saangtz voice 112; the throat 219[20]
san three B 142.4
san'g three 121[18]
Sangwo Jyh 'History of the Three Kingdoms' 288.27
Sangwo (Jyh) yeanyih, Sangwo 'Story of the Three Kingdoms' 288.27
sa-niaw to make water 221.18
sanjeaul-shyng triangular 247.11
sanluenche pedicab AN -lianq 253[35]
Sanmin Juuyih the Three Principles of the People 248.34
sann scatter 160.18
sann-buh to take a stroll 264.22
sann-huey meeting adjourned 296.37
sannian-jyi third-year class 110
sann₀kai scatter 160.18
sanshian-tang three-flavor soup 110
san₀shyr thirty; san.shyr- thirty- 142.4
Santzyh Jing (... *Jiengl*) 'Three Character Classic' 278.29
sanyeal-jiing, sanyean-jieengl well with three openings 110
sao-ching.le to sweep clear 259[19]
sa-shoou let go (of the hand) 207[45]
sh is, be, etc. 52–53.30, 122.7; *comparison with* yeou 153.9; have (temperature, etc.) 214.17; *use of before adjectives* 52–53.30, 155.30, 168.20; *loose use of in predication* 35.4; sh *in emphatic assertion:* do, is, etc. 52–53.30; .sh *unvoicing of after 4th Tone* 28.11
....sh... *concessive use of:* to be sure, all right 52–53.30, 184.12, 187.1, 288.45
sh — — .de... It was — that —... 55.33
— sh... .de ₀yih.sy — means... 145.45, 148.5, 149[6]
sh....de ₀yuan.guh, sh in₀wey....de ₀yuan.guh it is because, it is for the reason that 57.36, 221.21, 265.1
.sha *emphatic particle* 286.2
shaa foolish 48b
shaang.huo around noon time 170.37, 173.5h
shaangsheng, shanqsheng 3rd Tone 25
Shaan₀shi Shensi 231[17]
shaatz fool 35.5b
shae color 263[50]
sha.le kill (off) 44.19
shan mountain, hill AN -tzuoh 160.14
Shan₀dong Shantung 231[17]
shang injure, -y 215.28

Shang.chaur the Shang dynasty 233²⁴
shang.le feng .le have caught a cold 57.36
shangwuh commercial affairs 285⁴⁰
Shanhae Guan Shanhaikuan 234.9
shan.ja-gau hawthorn jelly 42.14e
-shann *AN for door* (as a thing) 130.8
shanq to go up, to go to 146.53; to apply (medicine) 213⁴⁰ -.shanq, -.shanq.tou *localizer:* top, on 53.31, 152.2; *see also* tzay ... -.shanq; *see also* shanqg
shanq ... .chiuh to go to 246.4
shanq.bann.tian forenoon 192.13
shanq.chiuh to go up; -.shanq.chiuh *directional complement:* up, Germ. *hinauf-* 161²⁸
shanq-danq to be tricked 265.55; to be fooled 289.48
shanq₀farng master's room(s) 254.10
shanq-farng to go up the housetop 264.39
shanqg, shanq last, *special meaning of* 200.31, 202
Shanq₀hae Shanghai 181³¹, 233³¹, 275¹⁹
shanq-jie to go to the street, to go shopping 255.32
shanq-keh to hold a class 155.43
shanq.lai to come up; -.shanq.lai directional complement: up, Germ. *herauf-* 207⁴⁵,⁴⁷
shanq.ren a parent 177.36
... shanqshiah ... or thereabouts 189²⁴, 211¹⁶
Shangshu, Shu.jing 'the Book of History' 279.37
shanq.tou top, above 149⁶, 152.2; -.shanq.tou *localizer:* top, on
shanq₀tsyh last time 225²
shanq.wuu forenoon 144.31
Shan₀shi Shansi 231¹⁷
shanshoei-huall, shanshoei landscape painting AN -fuh, -jang 160.14
shao little; few 11.11, 93, 165²²; *predicative use of* 169.30
shaoshuh small number, a minority 289.1h
shatz sand 259¹¹
shau to burn 11.11, 41.14b; a fever 213.6
shau.biing a hot biscuit with sesame seeds AN -kuay 41.14a
shau-hwu.le to scorch 219³⁸
shau-jaur.le kindle, catch fire 207.6
shaw youthful 11.11
shaw.ye "Master"; your son 192.22
₀sh .bu.sh? isn't that so? Fr. *n'est-ce pas?* 59d, 124.24

Sh .de. Yes. That is so. 59d, 124.28
sheang enjoy B 63
sheang to sound, to ring *v.i.* 143.6; loud 156.3d
sheang think, believe 127¹³; to want, to desire 112, 139.2b; eager 264.29
sheang.chu.lai to think up 56.34; recall 179.4f
sheang₀daw to think of, to recall 233³⁵
sheang fartz ... to try to ... 271.32
sheang-jia homesick 277⁵⁰
sheau small 53.30, 93
sheaubiann urine, urinate 220.18
sheauchwal small boat 207⁴⁶
sheauhairtz, sheauharl child 55.33, 177.35, 199.11
sheau.jiee Miss; your daughter 192.22
sheaujyr.tou, sheaujyy, sheaunhiounhiou the little finger 221.38
sheau sheauharl small child 177.35
sheau.shin careful; look out! 208.28
sheau-shooujiuall, shooujiuall handkerchief AN -kuay, -tyau 263⁶², 283⁴
sheaushuo(l), sheaushuol-shu a novel AN -buh 287.18
sheau.shyr.howl childhood 278.26
Sheau Yahshihyah, Sheau Yea- Asia Minor 230.2e
-sheeng province 231⁴, 234.15; state 294.11
sheh₀bey equipment 213³⁸
shehlih establish 249.2a
Shehshyh Celsius, Centigrade 214.13
sheir, shwei who, whom? 122.8
sheir dou jy.daw anybody knows 185.33
sheir dou neng anybody can 52.29
₀sheir ₀jy.daw who knows but that ... 162.52
shell (*see third* shyh)
shen ninth earth's branch 201.40
shen deep 207³¹, 289.1a
sheng to give birth to, to be born 55.33, 233¹⁹; unripe; uncooked; unfamiliar 185.21
-sheng sound 254.14; *AN for verbs* shuo, wenn, *etc.* 46d
shengchaan produce, production 239²⁷
shengren stranger 185.21
sheng.hwo life; livelihood 220.3, 239²²
sheng.in sound 143.6
shengjaang to be born and brought up 275¹⁷
shengminq life (opp. of death) 220.3
shenn extremely L 271.22
shenn, shenntzanq the kidney 220.17
shenn₀jyh(₀yu) in extreme cases, even 271.22, 273.1d

shenq.le there remains, left over 275³⁹
shen.tii the body 211¹⁵
shentz the body 159⁴⁴; fuselage 205⁴
sher broken, severed 215.29
sherm(.me) what? 123.11; what (kind of) 130.11; something 52.29
Sherm(.me) "..."?! What do you mean "..."?! 182.2; *in indirect question form* 234.12
....sherm.de and so forth, and what not 160.11, 253³⁵
sherm(.me) ₒdou... anything... 52.29, 169.23, 269¹⁸
sherm(.me) ₒdou bu (*or* mei, mei.yeou) not anything, nothing 52.29, 169.23, 185.33
— sherm....ne? What's the point in — -ing..., then? 184.16, 188.5
sherm sherm such and such 171.3e
sherm .shyr.howl what time, when? 137³⁰, 141³⁰
shermyanql what kind of 139.1b
sherm yee bu not anything, nothing 213³⁷
shern gods, spirit 103; energy, spirit B 38.9
sherngtz rope AN -tyau 207⁴⁵
sher.tou the tongue AN -tyau 219³³
sheu permit; may; perhaps 155.39, 173²²
sheuan to elect (a course) 293¹⁹
sheuanjeu to elect, election 55.33
sheuduo a great lot 162.40
sheue snow AN -chaang 195⁵
sheuejiang blood plasma 219²⁶
sheue, shiueh, shiee blood 221.23
Shg. *abbrev, for* .Shian.sheng 182.2
shi, shishao sparse 231⁴
shia shrimp AN -jy 20
shia blind 162.49; shia- at random 234.6
shiah scare, startle 192.30
shiah down B 152.1; *use of for weather phenomena* 192.14; next-, *special meaning of* 200.31; to lay down 240.19
shiah.bann.tian afternoon 192.13
shiah.chiuh to go down 251²; -.shiah-.chiuh *directional complement:* down, Germ. *hinab-* 159³⁴, 205⁶
shiah .de dou... so scared that... 265.50
shiahfarngl servants quarters AN -jian 251¹⁴
shiah, shiahg next 200.20, 200.31, 202
shiahₒhwei next time 225¹⁹
shiahₒiₒjann next station 251¹
shiah-i-tiau to be startled 57.36
shiahjyh summer solstice 200.33

shiah-keh to dismiss class 235.37
shiah.lai to come down 44.19; -.shiah.lai *directional complement:* down, Germ. *herab-* 191⁴²,⁴⁵, 253⁴¹
shiahₒnian next year, the following year 200.20
shiah-sheue .le it is snowing 195⁶
shiah.tian summer 201.37
shiah-wuh .le there is a fog 192.14
shiah.wuu afternoon 141³¹
shiah-yeu .le it is raining 192.14
shia-liau to chat at random 288.47
-shiall stroke, *AN for verbs* 254.6
shian first, ahead 193.34; shian- my (deceased) 279.42
shiang incense AN -jy, -gel (stick), -guu (bunch) 93
shiangdang correspond; shiangdang.de fairly 228.24
shiangduey relative, correlative 177.33
shiangduey-luenn relativity theory 177.33
shiangfaan contrary, opposite, opposed 177.33
shiangfarng wing (of a couryard) 254.10
shiang'ian cigarette AN -gel, -jy 160.12
shiangjiau banana AN -gel 43.17, 59d
shiang.shiah the country 240.13
shiangshinn believe 183⁴⁴
shiangyi suitable 285³⁵
shiann appear 40.12, 103
shianncherng(l).de ready (for use) 219²⁶
shiannday contemporary, modern 219⁴⁰
shianntzay now 46.23, 139.1j
shianq towards 243⁵
shianq elephant AN -pi, -pii 262.1
shianq like, similar 193.47
shianqlai have always been... 285⁴⁴
shianq sherm nemm ...... like anything 264.12
shianqshyng pictograph 60
shianren-jaang cactus AN -ke 110
shian.sheng gentleman, sir 144.19; teacher 227³⁷;....Shian.sheng Mr. ... 51.28, 144.19
shian tzoou to go first 49.26, 193.34
shia-shuo to talk nonsense 234.6
shiashuo-badaw stuff and nonsense 26.9
shiau-dwu to prevent infection, to sterilize 215.41, 223.3h
shiaumo to wear off, to kill (time) 289.49
shiauyeh midnight supper 289.53
shiaw laugh, smile 186.55
shiaw.huah joke; to laugh at 42.17, 272.41; ridiculous! 237⁰
shiawjaang president, principal 293⁸
Shibanya Spain 227²⁵
shibeei northwest 207.9

VOCABULARY AND INDEX 327

shi.bial the west 171.1k
shichyi strange, to find strange 42.16
shie to rest 95, 160.9
-₀shie some, lot, amount 130.9
shiee, sheue, shiueh blood 221.23
shiee to write 137³⁴, 149¹¹
shiee.chu.lai to write out 156.2f
shiee-tzyh to write (as a form of activity) 153.15
Shieh.shieh! Thank you! 95, 275¹⁶
shie.shie to rest a little 95, 160.9
shi.gua watermelon 112
shih department (in a college) 277⁵⁴
shih fine 220.15
shihorng-shyh tomato 110, 255.19
shihshi(el).de thoroughly 220.15
shihshin careful, meticulous 286.6
shii.huan to like 59d, 167.3
shii-lean to wash one's face 237²
shiing awake, wake up 165¹³
shiingj awake 173¹³
shii-tzao to take a bath 255.26
Shikang Sikang 233²⁶
Shi₀lah Greece 227⁴¹
Shilih Occidental chronology 201.42
shin heart 35.5c, 186.50; mind 209.36, 286.6
shin new 173⁷
shin eighth heaven's stem 201.40
shinan southwest 207.9
shing star B 40.12
Shin Gaang, Shin Jeang New Haven 297
Shing'an Hsingan 231⁵
shingch(y)i week 200.27
Shingch(y)i'i, Shingch(y)i'ell, ...
 Shingch(y)iliow Monday, Tuesday, ... Saturday 200.27
shingch(y)ijii what day of the week? 200.27
Shingch(y)iryh, Shingch(y)i Sunday 200.27
shing.shing star AN -ke 40.12
shingwanq flourish 234.22
shin hao to have a good heart, goodhearted 35.5c, 186.50
Shinhay the year 1911 ($\pm$ n $\times$ 60) 201.40
Shin₀jiang Sinkiang 231⁴
shinkoou the chest 221.36
shinlii psychology 42.17, 228.29
shin.lii in the mind 42.17, 228.29
shinn faithful, honest L 61, 291⁵; to believe 34.3; a letter AN -feng 38.10
shinnfengl envelope 111
shinn-for to believe in Buddha 48e
Shinnian New Year 199³⁸

shinq a surname 144.20; to have the surname of . . . 144.16
shinq₀chiuh interest 280.56
shinq.chyng temperament 186.53
shinqjyi quick-tempered 36.5
shinq.kuei fortunately 49.26, 191⁴², 205²³
shinq.minq life, life and death AN -tyau 220.3
shinshyh .de new style 253²⁵
shin.terng to grudge 42.15
shintzanq, shin the heart (organ) 220.7, .17
shinwen news AN -jiann 112, 132.31
Shin Wenshyue The New Literature 285³³
sh in₀wey . . . .de ₀yuan.guh (see sh . . . .de ₀yuan.guh)
shiong.dih brothers (collec.); a younger brother; I (polite form, in a speech) 177.38, 293¹⁸
shiongjair haunted house AN -suoo(l) 253⁴²
shiou shame 253⁴⁸
shishao, shi sparse 231⁴
shi-tian the western sky 170.48
Shitzanq Tibet 231⁴
shiu eleventh earth's branch 201.40
shiueh, sheue, shiee blood 221.23
shiueh-bair white as snow 286.3
shiun to smoke, to scent 98
shiunnliann train(ing) 239²⁰
shiwanq hope, to hope 167³¹
Shi.yangren an Occidental 271.36
shoei water 207.4
shoeiguoo fruit 52.30
Shoeihuu, Shoeihuu Juann 'Water's Strand (Chronicles)' 287.24
shoou hand AN -jy 151¹⁴
shoou to watch; to defend 198.1
-shoou AN for poems 279.45
shooudu capital (of a country) 229.40
shoou.jin towel AN -tyau, -kuay 245¹⁸
shooujiuall, sheau-shooukiuall handkerchief AN -kuay, -tyau 263⁶², 283⁴
shooujy.jea, jy.jea fingernail 221.38
shooujy(r).tou finger 221.38
shoou₀shuh (surgical) operation 215.26
shoou-suey to watch the year out 198.1
shooutawl gloves AN -jy, -shuang, -fuh 240.4
shoou-tyibau, tyibau suitcase 267⁷
shoouwanntz wrist 219³⁶
shoou.yih handicraft 239²⁷
shou to receive, to admit 296.24
shouinji (radio) receiver AN -jiah 248.31
shour ripe; cooked; familiar 185.21
shourren an acquaintance 185.21

shoutyaul a receipt AN -jang 43.17, 256.38
show thin, lean 34.3
show-shang to receive injury 215.32
show-tzuey to suffer misery 49.25, 239[20]
Sh, sh! Yes sir, yes sir! 287.10
shu book AN -been, -beel (the thing), -buh (the work) 152.5
shu to lose (opp. of win) 49.26; to transfer, to transfuse 221.25
shua to brush 261[29]
shuai to fall down; to smash 159[31]
shuang frost 275[46], 277[49]
shuang double B; -shuang a pair 129.39
shuang-guahhaw register with return receipt 110
shua-ya to brush the teeth 237[3]
shuey to sleep 189[30]
shuey-jaur.le to fall asleep 159[53], 173[13]
shuey-jiaw to sleep 137.20, 179e
shutarng the study, school 278.27
shu.fwu comfortable 198.5
shuh tree 159[45] AN -ke
shuh-koou to rinse the mouth 237[3]
shuhshyue mathematics 280.53
shuh tree 159[45] AN -ke
Shu.jing see Shangshu
shujuol desk AN -jang 283[22]
shuo to speak, to say 135[0], 141[38]; *introducing a quotation* 189[4]
shuo.bu-dinq one can't tell for sure, perhaps 189[24]
shuo.bu-guoh cannot surpass in speaking 296.35
shuo.bu-shanqlai cannot tell clearly, to be uncertain about 185.30
shuo.bu-shanq sherm . . . there is no point in saying . . . 184.17
shuo.de-joen can speak accurately 175[43]
shuo.de-lai congenial 110
shuo.faa way of saying, expression, term 239[15]
shuo-huah to talk 137.20, 165-167
shuo Jang San charng Lii Syh doan to gossip about Smith and Jones 169.26
shuo-lai shuo-chiuh after all that talk 270.13
shuo menqhuah to talk in one's sleep 165[12]
shuo-shinn to convince 52.29
shu-sheue transfuse blood 221.25
shuu rat, mouse B 190.1
shuu to count 219[29]
shy wet 259[11], 283[9]
shy poetry, poem AN -shoou 279.41
shyang detailed B 29.3
shyanshu novel, fiction AN -buh 287.20
shyatz a box 168.5

shye shoes AN -jy, -shuang 208.17, 248.24
shyedall shoelace AN -gel, -fuh 237[4], 261[29]
shyesheng, shyngsheng phonetic compound 62
shyh scholars, warriors L 291[5]
shyh to try 293[19]
shyh, shell, shyh.chyng thing, affair, event AN -jiann 94, 128.1, 176.16; work, job, employment 239[21], 241.2 Example
-shyh Mr. 214.13
shyhbiing dried persimmon 41.14b
shyhchaang market 253[33]
shyh.chyng (*see third* shyh)
. . . .shyh.de as if . . . 160.15
shyh.jieh the world 169.24
shyh.jieh.shanq in the world 169.24
shyhtz persimmon 41.14b
shyhwuh things and affairs L 176.16
shyjaang faculty member (in relation to student) AN -wey 296.31
Shy.jing 'the Book of Odes' 279.36
shyng to perform 176.12, 184.10; will do, okay 175[22], 184.10; *forms of the script* 67
shyng-i to practice medicine 219[52]
shyng.lii baggage AN -jiann 291[4]
shyngsheng, shyesheng phonetic compound 62
shyngshu running hand (characters) 67
shyr ten B 142.4
shyr time B 70; o'clock 213.11
shyrch(y)i stage 217[4]; time, period 239[18]
shyr.dou to tidy up 213[57]
shyrg ten
shyr.howl time 138.29
shyri, shyr'ell, . . ., shyrjeou eleven, twelve, . . ., nineteen 142.4
shyrjian time, interval, duration 289.50
shyrjii- ten-odd 149[5]
shyr.dou to tidy up 213[58]
shyr.tou stone, rock AN -kuay 261[32]
shyrtzay really, truly 283[5]
shyrtzyh a cross 228.27
shyryou petroleum 248.32
shyue learn, study 175[40]
shyue.bu-huey cannot learn 111
shyue-cherng.le to have mastered 178.48
shyuelii learned theory 288.37
shyue.sheng student 241.11
shyueshiaw, shyuetarng (modern) school 278.27
shyueshuh science, learning 271.23
shyue₀wenn learning, erudition 216.53
shyueyuann college 288.28
shyunyang-jiann cruiser 111

shyy to use 209.44; to make, to cause to 296.27
shyy to resolve L 291⁵
shyy-jong from beginning to end 291⁵
soen bamboo shoots 70
Songjiang Sungkiang 231⁵
songshuh pine tree AN -ke 251¹⁶
sonq to see (someone) off 53.30; to send 215.47
Sonq.chaur the Sung dynasty 233²⁵
sou to turn sour 28.11
Ss—! *interjection of hesitation* 190.6; *of feeling cold:* Brr! 198.2
suan sour 265.47
suann garlic AN -tour, -ke 52.29
suann reckon, regard 176.13; to be considered, to be regarded as 211¹³; considered settled 287.9
suannshuh arithmetic 280.53
suannshyue mathematics 280.53
Su Eh Lianbang U. S. S. R. 227⁴⁰
Suen *common surname* 235.36
-suey years old 198.1
suey broken to pieces 215.29
suhcherng-ke rapid course 296.21
suhsheh dormitory 294.4
suh-yeh from morn till night L 291⁵
Su.jou Soochow 275¹⁹
suoo lock AN -baa 52.29
-suoo(l) AN for houses 155.36; actually, do 184.20; *translation of by* which, whom, *etc.* 57.36, 184.20; all, all which 220.5
suoo tzay whereat 227²⁸
suoowey what you call; so-called 186.45
suoo yeou .de ... dou all the ... (that there is) 51.29
suoo₀yii therefore 49.26, 57.36, 121²³; that's why 245²⁸
Suweiai Soviet 228.20
Suyishyh Suez 225⁴
sweibiann as you please, no matter 168.18; 174.3; freely 217.2g
sweiran although 167³⁴; *use of after subject* 181¹²
sweishyr any time 221.27
Sweiyeuan Suiyuan 231¹⁵
swo.shinq might as well 49.26
swuyeu proverb AN -jiuh 293¹⁵
sy though L 277⁴⁸
sy private; selfish 102
syh sixth earth's branch 201.40
syh four B 142.4
Syh₀chuan Szechwan 233²⁶
syhg four 122.4
syh.hu apparently, seem to 285³³
syh-jih the four seasons 197³⁷

syhmiann all around 161.22
Syh Shu the Four Books 275³⁵
syh₀shyr forty; syh.shyr- forty- 142.4
sy-poh.le tear apart 54.32
syshwu family school 278.27
syy die, dead 159³¹, 191⁴²

T

ta he, she, it, him, her 47.24, 122.3; *use of for a plurality of things* 287.19
ta to collapse 192.28
taang to lie down 87
taangj lying down 45.21
taang₀ruoh₀sh if 222.47
taankehche (military) tank AN -lianq 248.26
taantz rug, blanket AN -tyau, -kuay 245¹⁸
ta.de his, her(s), its 131.26
Tairfuu your courtesy name (*honorific*) 144.20
Tair₀uan Taiwan, Formosa 233²⁶
ta.men, tam they, them 47.24, 123.16; *non-use of* 131.19
ta.men.de, tam.de their(s) 131.26
tan he, etc. (*honorific*) 235.34
ta.nall where he is, Fr. *chez lui* 131.22
tang soup 87
tang-miann soup-noodles 287⁵⁶
tann probe, inquire about; inquire after 212.1
tann-binq to inquire about sickness L 212.1
tanq hot 87; to iron 54.32; to scald, to burn 283²
taoluenn discuss 269²², 285⁴¹
taoyann to loathe 223.3c; to be a nuisance, what a nuisance! 209.35; Pshaw! 211.2k
tarn to talk, to chat; to discuss 166.1, 261³⁶
tarng sugar 62, 87; candy AN -kuay 26.9
Tarng.chaur the T'ang dynasty 233²⁵
ta.shiah.lai to collapse 191⁴²
tau.chu.lai to fish out 265.61
taur to escape 36 ftnt 5, 103, 205⁶
tay too (excessively) 34.3
Tay₀pyng Yang Pacific Ocean 228.12
tay.tay Mrs., wife 35.5b, 181²⁴, 251¹
tay.yang the sun 170.48, 207.10; the temples (of the head) 221.32
tehbye special(ly) 181³⁰
terng painful, ache, it hurts 36.5, 159⁴⁷, 283¹³; to love, to be fond of 36.6b

tial the weather 170.49, 191.7; day, daytime 197[34]
tian sky; heaven 160.1; -tian day 160.1
tian to add, to replenish 247.20
tian.chih the weather 189[4]
tian-dii.shiah under heaven 174.2
tiangan heaven's stem 201.40
tianhua-baan ceiling (*dialectal*) AN -kuay 77.11
tian lianq .le it is light, the day breaks; tianlianq daybreak, dawn 192.32, 273[5], 285[41]
tianshiah the world 174.2
tiau to choose 207[39]; to pick out 265.49
tiaw to jump 90; to beat (of the pulse) 220.6
tiee iron 262.2
tiee.jianq blacksmith 262.2
tiee-yinq hard as iron 286.3
tih to substitute 39.10e
tii₀lianq to be considerate (to) 264.43
tiing pretty, quite, rather 53.31, 170.42, 251[2]
ting listen, listen to 138.33
ting.bu-doong cannot understand (from listening) 145.39
ting.chu.lai to make out (by listening) 144.23
ting.de-doong can understand (from listening) 145.39
ting-huah to listen to speaking; to listen, obey 270.5
ting.jiann to hear 138.33
tingshiee writing from dictation, dictation exercise 267[6]
ting shuo hear (it said) 239[20]
toei leg AN -tyau 213[28]
tong to go through 221.19; logical, grammatical, rational 229.38
tong-horng red through and through 286.3
toong pail 122.4
torng same; with, and 288.41
torng brass, copper, bronze 262.2
tornghuah assimilate 234.11
torng.jianq coppersmith 262.2
torng-juh to live together (with) 189[28]
torng-shyh to work together (with); torngshyh a colleague 185.26
torngshyr at the same time, simultaneously 156.3c, 240.23
torng-shyue to study at the same school (with); torngshyue schoolmate, fellow student 294.10
tou to steal 287.22
-.tou *noun suffix* 40.13, 152.3
tour the head 36.5; *AN for cattle*

tour.fah hair (of the head) AN -gen, -gel 38.9, 219[37]
tour-guu skull 219[30]
touri- the (very) first 221.24
tour-pyi scalp 219[29]
toutoul.de stealthily, secretly 287.22
tsa to wipe 58, 283[4]; to abrade 219[32]
tsaan tragic, *hyperbolic use of* 221.40
tsai to guess 189[24], 259[19]
₀tsair for the first time, only then, Germ. erst 124.30, 138.35
— ₀tsair . . . — before . . . 186.51, 243.3j, 248.43, 249.3e
— ₀tsair . . . .ne it is only — that . . . 203.3b
tsair.ferng tailor 42.16
tsair.liaw material 239[32]
tsanguan to visit, to make a tour of inspection 240.12
tsann.tou coward(ly) 36 ftnt 5
tsao grass AN -gel, -ke 70
tsaoshu, tsaotzyh cursive characters 67
tsarng to hide 283[22]
tsay vegetable AN -ke 251[17], 253[20]; provisions 56.34, 253[32]; dishes (of food) 46c
tsaydantz, tsaydal menu 289.54
tsayyuan vegetable garden 251[17]
tsehsuoo the toilet 221.18
-tserng layer, tier 185.38
tserng₀jing did once before 227[30,40]
tsong.ming clever 56.35
tsorng from 49.25, 136.8; by way of 143.10
tsorngchyan formerly, once upon a time 190.1
tsornglai bu never before, have never . . . 211[11]
tsornglai mei(.yeou) never have 190.4; never before, have never . . . 273[7], 281.1 Example
tsorngsheaul from childhood 293[18]
tsorng tsyy (yiihow) henceforward, from that time on 193.46
tsu coarse, coarse-grained 286.6
-tsuenn (Chinese) inch 42.16
tsuey brittle 92
tsuh vinegar 265.47
tsuoh wrong 227[25], 239[33]
tsushin careless 286.6
tswen to store 219[26]
tswenkoan funds deposited, deposit; tswen-koan to deposit funds 43.18
tsy deviation L 94
tsyh prickle AN -gel 94
-tsyh *AN for verbs:* number of times, a time 225[2], 239[16]

tsyr word, syntactic word 33.1; type of poetry (with lines of unequal length) AN -shoou 279.43
tsyr porcelain 94
tsyrtiee enameled ware 255.28
tsyr, tsy female L 97
tsyy this L 99, 193.46
tu bald 94
tuei to push 208.30
tueijinn-chih propeller 208.30
tuey retreat, withdraw; subside 92, 215.24
tuh to vomit 94
tuu soil, earth 94
Tuueelchyi Turkey 227⁴¹
twu diagram 94
-tyau *AN for rope, tongue, rivers, etc.* 207⁴⁵
tyauiue treaty 285⁴⁰
tyaul a strip, a slip 43.17, 256.38
tyauwen text, statute (of law, etc.) 285⁴⁰
tyi to cry 275⁴⁶
tyi to lift (from above); raise (the subject of), mention 184.15, 269³⁹
tyibau, shoou-tyibau suitcase 267⁷
tyichanq promote 245³⁹, 253⁴⁷
tyi-gau raise (*fig.*) 241.29
tyi.muh topic, subject 269¹⁸, 285⁴⁸
tyng to stop 166.1, 203.3f
tyngtz pavilion 166.1
-tz *noun suffix* 40.13; *unvoicing of after 4th Tone* 28.11
Tz! *sound of admiration, etc.* 221.28
Tz! tz! Tsk! Tsk! 221.28
tza to smack 98
tzang dirty 283⁹
tzanncherng to be in favor of 285⁴⁴
tzao early 165²²
Tzao .a! Good morning! 220.1
tzao.chin, tzao.chern morning 168.13
tzao-dean(.shin) breakfast 192.17
tzaofann morning meal 192.17
tzaopern bathtub 253²⁸
tzar smash 39.10g
tzar-duann.le crushed, cut off 191⁴⁵
tzar₀huoh-pull general store AN -jial 255.34
tzarjyh magazine AN -fell 51.29, 285⁴⁰
tzar.men, tzarm (*inclusive*) we, us 47.24, 123.17, 125, 148.5b
tzar.men.de, tzarm.de our(s) 131.26
tzau dregs, mess (*lit. or fig.*) 162.46
Tzaugau! What a mess! 162.46; Gosh! 205⁴; Pshaw! 237⁰
Tzau .le! Too bad! 203.3h
tzaw build 57.36; manufacture 240.24
tzay once more, again 145.43; *difference of from* yow 161.37; ₀tzay for the first time, only then 146.49, 147.4i (*cf.* tsair)
tzay to be at, in, on 53.31, 130.17, 155.35; right there, . . . -ing 55.33, 264.15
tzay . . . -.deal still . . . -er 179.5
tzay — (gen) . . . .de jongjiall between — and . . . 154.27
tzay . . . ig another, one more 52.29
tzay . . . -.shanq in regard to, -ically 235.27
tzay guoh . . . in (after) another . . . 202
tzay.hu to care for 287.14
tzay.jell to be present here, to *be* here 109, 131.23
tzay jell to be *here* 109, 130.18, 131.23
₀Tzay₀jiann!, .Tzay.jiann.tzay.jiann! Goodbye! 146.61
tzay.nall to be present there, to *be* there 109, 131.23
tzay nall to be *there* 109, 131.23
₀tzay.nall . . . (.ne) right there, . . . -ing 55.33, 155.41
tzeem.me, tzeem how? 123.11; somehow 197¹⁰; how is it that . . . ? why? 144.25; do what? 145.46
tzeem(.me) . . . dou any old way 52.29
tzeem(.me) yee bu . . . in no way, by no means 52.29
tzeemyanql .de ig what sort of a 208.13
tzel, tzel, . . . squeak, squeak, . . . 191⁴²
tzemm(.me), jemm(.me) so, in this manner, to this degree, this . . . 123.11, 137.14, 138.30
tzemm₀shie such a lot 144.26
tzemm₀yanql like this 137³⁴; (do) this 176.23
tzemm₀yanql .de ig such a 208.13
tzengjia increase, augment 239²⁷
Tzeyanzeyan! 'bye! 146.61
tzoei mouth AN -jang 175³⁸, 167³⁷
tzoeibahtz cheek 219³²
tzoeichwen, -chwel lip 221.34
-tzong *AN* lot, group 191.7; aim L 291⁵
tzongseh palm-colored, brown 208.17
tzoong always, all the time 160.17; surely 184.19; in any case 219²⁹
-tzoong (*see* jey-tzoong)
tzoong bu never 160.17
Tzoongjyu Main (telephone exchange) 142.3
tzoongtoong president (of a republic) 55.33
tzoou walk, go on foot 237¹⁰; leave, go away 47.24, 191³³,³⁴; go, move, travel (along) 163.1g, 165²²

tzoou.bu-kai cannot get away 143[51]
tzoou-dawl to walk 144.34
tzoou-guoh.le to go past 243[5]
tzoou-guoh.chiuh to go further on 243[7]
tzu rent 251[0]
tzu.chyan rent (money) 253[30]
tzuey drunk, intoxicated 92
tzuey most, -est 53.30, 167.3
tzueyjinn very recently 219[42]
tzuoh sit 34.3, 195[5]; ride (vehicle, ship, etc.) 113, 144.35
-tzuoh AN for mountains, squatting objects, etc. 247.10
tzuoh-daw.le to carry out, accomplish 181[12]
tzuoh-dong to be host 287[57]
tzuoh-menq to have a dream 162.54
tzuoh-ren to behave (as a person) 184.9
tzuoh-shyh to work 171.4c
tzuoh-wan.le to finish doing 160.2
tzuoo left (side) B 152.1
tzuoo.bial left side, the left 205[20]
Tzuoo₀juann 'Tso's Chronicles' 279.38
tzuoo₀shoou the left hand 153.17
... tzuooyow ... or thereabouts 197[33]
tzuufuh (paternal) grandfather 278.22
tzuumuu (paternal) grandmother 278.22
tzwol, tzwo.tian yesterday 141[30], 160.1, 202
tzwo.liaw seasoning 265.46
tzwutzwu fully 199[44]
tzy consult L 291[5]
tzy herewith L 97
tzybeen capital (in trade) 239[25]
tzyh word; character; writing 33.1, 153.10, 184.14
tzyhdean dictionary AN -buh 34.3
tzyhgeel, tzyhjii oneself 161.20, 215.23
tzyhjyh to practice self-government 248.42
tzyhjyy-looul waste-paper basket 113
tzyhlai-shoei water from a pipe system 255.24
tzyh₀ran natural; naturally, of course 49.26, 215.34
tzyhran-keshyue natural science AN -men 277[52], 281.1e
tzyhshyng-che'l bicycle AN -lianq, -jiah 113
tzyhtsorng... (yiihow) ever since ... 199[39]
tzyhyou free, freedom 248.33
tzyy purple, violet 205[18]
tzyy son B 45.21; first earth's branch 201.40
tzyydann cartridges AN -lih, -ke, -fa 245[30]

tzyy-neu sons and daughters, offspring 175[36]
tzyy.mey sisters; brothers and sisters 279.44

U

u house, room B 155.36, 159.22
u raven L 94, 275[46]
ua frog L 98
uai crooked, not upright, oblique 98
.Uai! Hello! 143.13; Hey! 159[40]; Yoohoo! 251[14]
uan bend 28.12
uang to ooze; *surname* 98
uang.chu.lai to ooze 265.60
uei prestige B 98
uen lukewarm B 98; to warm over B (*see* uen₀lii)
uenduh temperature 214.16
uen₀lii, uen₀shyi to review (as lesson) 225[2,19]
u.lii in the room 159[22], 242.2c
uo nest 98
utz room AN -jian 155.36
utz.lii in the room 152.2

V

vx *the two preceding syllables repeated* 146.61

W

wahtz sock, stocking AN -jy, -shuang 40.13, 237[4]
wal to play 40.13, 161.29
wal.wal to have a good time 52.29
wan finish 160.2
wanbih is at an end 235.38
wanchyuan complete(ly) 95, 137.21, 213[38]
Wang *very common surname* 121[8]
wann towards (*see* wanq, wann)
-wann ten-thousand 46b, 201.49
wann-shiah downwards 159[35]
... wannsuey! Long live ... ! 201.49
wanq, wanq.jih, wanq.le forget 170.44
wanq hope 100; gaze 277[49]
wanq, wann towards 159[35], 231[16], 154.23
wanqyeuan-jinq telescope AN -jiah 113
wanyell toy, trifle 248.25; trick 56.34
wa.wa doll 40.12
way outside B 34.2, 155.33
way.gwo foreign country 136.6
way.gwo-huah foreign language 136.6
way.gwo₀ren foreigner 136.6, 269[40]

wayke surgery 215.51
way₀luh-koou.in foreign accent 271.35
way.tou outside 34.2, 151³⁵, 191⁴², 195⁶
wei surround 102
wei be, act as L 291⁵; *forms of the script* 67
weiborl muffler AN -tyau 44.20
weiji crisis 220.12
weishean danger(ous) 53, 175²⁸
wen line, streak; writing, literature, culture 62; -wen language, -ese 135¹⁴,²⁵
wenhuah culture 233¹⁸, 293¹⁹
wen.jang article, essay AN -pian 285⁴⁰
wenlii literary quality or structure of a composition 8 ftnt 4
wenn i-jiuh huah to ask a question 168.19
wenntyi problem 113, 186.58
wenn.wenn just ask 239³³
wen₀shyue literature 285³³
wenyan literary language, *wenli* 8 ftnt 4, 95, 286.1
wey for 48, 263⁵⁸
wey have not (yet) L 64; eighth earth's branch 201.40
wey stomach 220.17
-wey *polite form of AN for persons* 143.15
wey.le on account of 237⁴
weysherm(.me) why? 138.27
weytz seat 293⁸
woa tile AN -kuay 99, 262.2
woai to scoop 99
woa.jianq mason 262.2
woan bowl, deep dish AN -jy 160.7
woan.bann.tial late afternoon 191.9
woanfann evening meal 192.17
woang have not L 62; a net 62
woangwoang frequently 231¹¹
woan.shanq evening; night 168.11
woei to delegate B 99
woei.ba, yii.ba tail AN -tyau 190 1, 205⁵
woei₀yuan member of a committee or commission 235.30
woen stable, steady 99, 287.8
woh to lie down B 100
woo I, me 47.24, 121²; *neutral tone of after verbs* 27.10, 144.29
woo.de my, mine 131.26; *non-use of* 153.16
woo.jell where I am, Fr. *chez moi* 131.22
woo.men, woom, mm (*exclusive*) we, us 47.24, 123.17, 124.29, 125, 148.5c; *use of in inclusive sense* 226.2, 293⁸
woo.men.de, woom.de, mm.de our(s) 131.26
woo shuo as I was saying 137.17
wu have not L 29, 67–68, 94; wu- without, -less 29, 190.1, 111.213, 111.244

wuh fifth heaven's stem 201.40
wuh fog 30.12, 94
wuh thing, object L 176.16
wuh-dean to miss the hour, — to be behind schedule 143⁴⁴
wuhlii physics 280.52
wuhpiin articles, goods (*collec.*) 239²⁴
Wuhtzyy the year 1948 (± n × 60) 201.40, 203.2a
wuhua-guool fig 111
wuluenn no matter (what), irrespective of 174.4
wumingjyy, syhjyy, huhgwosyh ring finger 221.38, .39
wushiann-diann wireless; radio 111, 248.31
wusuoowey there is no point in speaking of 228.9
wuu dance B 67–68
wuu five B 142.4
wuu military 61
wuu noon B 144.31; seventh earth's branch 201.40
wuuchih military weapons 245³³
wuufann noon meal 192.17
wuug five
Wuu Jing the Five Classics 275³⁵
wuu.juh to cover up (physically) 167⁴⁶
wuushiang- allspice 280.50
wuu₀shyr fifty; wuu.shyr- fifty- 142.4
wuwoei-shuu tailless rat 190.1
wu-yuan wu-guh .de without cause or reason 270.12

X

x *preceding syllable repeated* 131.30

Y

ya tooth 219³³
yah to crush 191⁴²; to put one's weight on 207⁴⁷
yahgel to start with, in the first place 235.35, 261³⁰, 285⁵¹
yah-jaur (actually) crush 193.43
Yah₀jou, Yahshihyah, Yeashihyea Asia 227.4
yan salt 46.23
yang the male principle, *yang* B 201.39
yangche ricksha AN -lianq 240.9
yangcheudengl, cheudengl matches AN -gel 111, 278.16
yang-farng(tz) foreign-style house AN -suoo(l), -tzuoh 113, 243¹⁰
yanggoeitz foreign devil 293¹⁵
yanghuoo matches AN -gel 278.16

Yang.jou Yangchow 275[18]
yanglih solar calendar 201.39
yang lutz foreign-style stove 111
yangpyng, yangpyngsheng 2nd Tone 25
yangren, yangrel foreigner, an Occidental 294.8
yangrow mutton, lamb 37.7
Yangtzyy Jiang Yangtze River, *infrequent use of* 235.26
yan₀jiow study, research *v. or n.* 239[32]
yanluenn opinion (as expressed) 248.41
yann loathe B 100
yanql, yanqtz appearance, look 95, 205[14]; *see also* . . . .de yanqtz
yanq₀yanql every kind 178.2a; everything 181[12]
yan.seh, yan.shae color 205[14], 208.19
yau to shake 5.3, 191[37], 259[26]
yaw to want, to want to 34.2(3), 89, 219[20]; will 55.33, 162.42; must 176.18; if 162.48; if, *omission of* 131.19
yaw medicine, drug 34.2(3), 220.9
yawburan or else, otherwise 205[24]
yaw.de desirable 41.13; okay 248.47
yawjiin important 42.16, 159[3]
yawminq (*see* . . . .de yawminq)
yaw.sh if 49.26, 165[20], 173[22]; *use of after subject* 170.47
yaw.shyr key AN -baa 28.11, 52.29
ye sire B 98
yea dumb, hoarse 99, 280.59
yea elegant, artistic 103
Yeadean Athens 227[41]
yeang rear, keep, cultivate 99, 255.17
yeanjienql eye-glasses AN -fuh 240.4
yean.jing eye AN -jy, -shuang 162.49
yeanjutz eyeball 221.33
yeanlell, yeanley tears AN -di 264.21, 265.60
yeanley-uang'uangl.de tearfully 265.60
yeanshuo to make a speech, a speech 294.1
yeau 99, 219[34]
yee also, too 123.14; even 144.27
Yee? *interjection of surprise* 208.12
yee . . . yee both . . . and 56.35
yee bu nor 129[38]
yee.sh also 123.14
yeh night 197[34]
yehbann midnight L 275[47]
yeh.lii night, in the night 168.11, 197[33]
Yeluu Yale 297
yeong permanent B 99
yeong brave B 291[5]
yeou tenth earth's branch 201.40
yeou have 131.24; there is, there are, etc. 131.29, 152.5; *comparison with sh* 153.9; *in indefinite reference* 206.1; with, -ed, -ful 239[20,33]; is as much as 201.47
yeou — (nemm) . . . as . . . as — 53.30, 169.21
yeou . . . -.toul worth . . . -ing 240.8
yeou chiuell interesting, fun 270.15
yeou daw.lii right, cf. Fr. *avoir raison* 208.26
yeou .de some 52.29
yeou₀deal a little, somewhat 211[7]
yeou ₀shyr.howl sometimes 138.29
yeou-shyh busy 171.3j
yeouyih intentionally 42f
yeou yih.sy interesting, fun 161.30
yeou yonq useful 239[33]
yeu rain AN -chaang 192.14
yeu with, and L 270.1
yeuan far 38.10c, 95, 205
yeuan.chull a distance 249.3d
yeuan'iual(.de) at a good distance 49.26
yeuluh records of lectures (on Buddhism) 288.39
yeun promise, permit B 95
yeuyan language, speech 296.20
ye.ye grandpa (on father's side) 278.22
yi soap B 86
yi suspect L 277[49]
yih meaning, idea B 86
-yih *name of number equal to* wannwann, i.e. 10^8 202.49
yihcharng unusual(ly) 186.54
Yihdahlih, Yih.gwo Italy 228.26
yih.jiann opinion, view 213[26]
Yih.jing 'the Book of Changes' 279.40
yih.luenn discuss(ion) 167[24], 271[54]
yih.sy meaning 145.45, 148.5, 149[6], 259[27]
yii *particle similar to final* .le L 40 ftnt 9
yii chair B 86
yii to the . . . of 228.16; take, with L 49.25, 99; thereby L 291[5]
yii . . . wei juu take . . . as the main thing 285[41]
yii second heaven's stem 201.40
yii.ba, woei.ba tail AN -tyau 190.1, 205[5]
Yiichoou the year 1925 ($\pm$ n $\times$ 60) 201.40
. . . yiichyan ago 179.4b; 202; before 225[1]; as terminal marker 209.49
. . . yiihow after . . . 168.15, 179.4f
yii.jing, yiijinq already 176.15
yiijinq . . . yiihow after . . . 209.49
. . . yiilai ever since . . . 231[9]
yiin draw, attract 99

VOCABULARY AND INDEX 335

yiing shadow B 99
yiitz chair AN -baa 40.13, 112, 152.2
yiiwei take for, take it (wrongly) that 162.44; regard as 183⁴⁵
yinn print 30.12(9)
Yinn.duh India 225¹⁹
Yinn.duh Yang Indian Ocean 225¹⁵
yinnshua printing 248.37
yinnshua-suoo printing establishment, press 248.37
yinq hard, stiff 30.12(9), 173⁹
yinq.sh the hard fact is ... 240.10
yitz soap AN -kuay 245²²
yn silver B 98, 262.2; yntz silver
yn third earth's branch 201.40
yng to win 49.26
yn.jianq silversmith 262.2
yonq to use 151¹⁷, 173¹⁶
yonq.bu-guann cannot get used to using 214.12
yonqpiin useful articles 245²⁸
yonq.ren servant 185²⁵
yonq-shin careful(ly), to be attentive 39.10d
yonq-tzyh use words, diction 173¹⁶, 269¹⁷
you oil 96, 248.32
youchyi(.sh) especially 219⁴², 283¹⁷
youjenqjyu post office 111
yow again; moreover 96, 181¹; *difference of from* tzay 161.37
yow ... yow both ... and 56.35; *non-use of before substantives* 138.28
yow right (opp. of left) B 152.1
yow.bial righthand side, the right 152.2, 205¹⁰
yow.sh ig ... another ..., a different ... 181⁶
yow.sh i-joong another kind again 277⁴⁷
yow₀shoou the right hand 153.16
yu at, in, on, to 49.25, 70; -₀yu 273.1
yu elm B 62
yu fish AN -tyau 95, 112, 255.17
yu fisherman L 275⁴⁷
yuan round 95, 205¹⁴

yuan- primary, original 201.44
-yuan member (of personnel) 205²²
Yuan.chaur the Yuan dynasty 233²⁵
yuan.guh reason, ground 57.36, 183³⁷, 221.21, 265.1
yuanjyi place of origin 277.8
yuanlai so the explanation is ... 256.43
yuan.lianq to pardon, to excuse 283⁴, 293¹⁷
yuann institution, hospital 221.23
yuann willing B 95
yuann complain 103
yuan-nian first year (of an era), year 1 201.44
yuanntz courtyard 251⁹
yuann.yih willing, glad to 186.43; to wish 263⁵³
yuanshian originally 277.9
yuantzyy atom 117
yuan.yi to make a sound, to say a word 264.26
yueh month 200.20; -.yueh month (*in names of the months*) 198.8, 202
yueh ... yueh the more ... the more, the ... -er ... the ... -er 167⁴⁵,⁴⁶; more and more, ..-er and ... -er 161.38, 191³⁵, 269³³
yueh.fenn-parl (hanging) calendar 200.30
yueh.lianq the moon 198.8, 280.49
yuh jade AN -kuay 95
yuh ... yuh (= yueh ... yueh) 169.31, 173.5f
yuh.bey to prepare 235³⁸
yuhliaw predict 219⁴⁸
yun even, uniform 219²⁰
yun cloud B 95
yunn rhyme 95
yunn to transport, to ship 103
Yun₀nan Yunnan 233²⁶
yunn.chih luck, lucky 220.13
yunn₀donq (social, literary, etc.) movement 239¹⁵, 285³³
yunnher canal AN -tyau 228.5
yun.tsae cloud AN -kuay, -piann 205¹⁰

ABBREVIATIONS AND SYMBOLS

AN   auxiliary noun, classifier, measure word
B   bound, not used as a free word
F   free
L   literary
g   short for –.*geh* 'piece, individual,' general AN
j   short for –.*jy* or –.*je*, progressive suffix, '–ing'
sh   short for *shyh* 'is'
tz   short for .*tzy*, noun suffix
'a   primary stress on *a*
ˌa   secondary stress on *a*
ˌˌa   tertiary stress on *a*
.a   neutral tone, i.e. no numbered tone, on *a*
₀a   optional neutral tone on *a*
*x   The form *x* does not exist.
, —   The form before shows the structure, the form after shows the actual meaning, as *guh.shyh* 'old-story, — story.'

Synopsis of Tonal Spelling

(2)¹	1st Tone:	叉cha	喝he	喫chy	偷tou	方fang
	2nd Tone:	茶char	河her	遲chyr	頭tour	房farng
(3)	1st Tone:	千chian	汪uang	清ching	呼hu	西shi
	2nd Tone:	前chyan	王wang	情chyng	胡hwu	席shyi
(4)	1st Tone:	思sy	山shan	清ching	接jie	兜dou
	3rd Tone:	死syy	陝shaan	請chiing	姐jiee	斗doou
(5)	1st Tone:	江jiang	乖guai	宣shiuan	該gai	蒿hau
	3rd Tone:	講jeang	枴goai	選sheuan	改gae	好hao
(6)	1st Tone:	夫fu	該gai	收shou	翻fan	湯tang	分ㄦfel
	4th Tone:	婦fuh	蓋gay	受show	飯fann	燙tanq	份ㄦfell
(7)	1st Tone:	貓mhau	蔫nhian	溜lhiou	扔rheng		
	2nd Tone:	毛mau	年nian	流liou	仍reng		
(8)	3rd Tone with initial:	九jeou	古guu	火huoo	寫shiee
	3rd Tone without initial:	有yeou	五wuu	我woo	也yee
(9)	4th Tone with initial:	會huey	叫jiaw	地dih	路luh
	4th Tone without initial:	位wey	要yaw	意yih	物wuh

¹ Figures refer to rules of tonal spelling, p. 28.

HARVARD-YE

This book must be